Laurence Sterne's

A Sentimental Journey

TRANSITS:
LITERATURE, THOUGHT & CULTURE, 1650–1850

A long running and landmark series in long eighteenth-century studies, *Transits* includes monographs and edited volumes that are timely, transformative in their approach, and global in their engagement with arts, literature, culture, and history. Books in the series have engaged with visual arts, environment, politics, material culture, travel, theater and performance, embodiment, writing and book history, sexuality, gender, disability, race, and colonialism from Britain and Europe to the Americas, the Far East, and the Middle East. Proposals should offer critical examination of artifacts and events, modes of being and forms of knowledge, material culture, or cultural practices. Works that make provocative connections across time, space, geography, or intellectual history or that develop new modes of critical imagining are particularly welcome.

Recent titles in the *Transits* series:

Laurence Sterne's "A Sentimental Journey": A Legacy to the World
W. B. Gerard and M-C. Newbould, eds.

Transatlantic Women Travelers, 1688–1843
Misty Krueger, ed.

Hemispheres and Stratospheres: The Idea and Experience of Distance in the International Enlightenment
Kevin L. Cope, ed.

Rewriting Crusoe: The Robinsonade across Languages, Cultures, and Media
Jakub Lipski, ed.

Narrative Mourning: Death and Its Relics in the Eighteenth-Century British Novel
Kathleen M. Oliver

Lothario's Corpse: Libertine Drama and the Long-Running Restoration, 1700–1832
Daniel Gustafson

Romantic Automata: Exhibitions, Figures, Organisms
Michael Demson and Christopher R. Clason, eds.

Beside the Bard: Scottish Lowland Poetry in the Age of Burns
George S. Christian

The Novel Stage: Narrative Form from the Restoration to Jane Austen
Marcie Frank

The Imprisoned Traveler: Joseph Forsyth and Napoleon's Italy
Keith Crook

Fire on the Water: Sailors, Slaves, and Insurrection in Early American Literature, 1789–1886
Lenora Warren

Community and Solitude: New Essays on Johnson's Circle
Anthony W. Lee, ed.

The Global Wordsworth: Romanticism Out of Place
Katherine Bergren

For a full list of *Transits* titles, please visit our website: www.bucknelluniversitypress.org.

Frontispiece "The Case of Delicacy" by Maurice Leloir, from *A Sentimental Journey through France and Italy* by Laurence Sterne (London: George Routledge & Sons, 1885).

Laurence Sterne's *A Sentimental Journey*

A LEGACY TO THE WORLD

Edited by
W. B. GERARD AND
M-C. NEWBOULD

Bucknell University | University Press
LEWISBURG, PENNSYLVANIA

Library of Congress Cataloging-in-Publication Data

Names: Gerard, William Blake, editor. | Newbould, Mary-Céline, editor. | New, Melvyn, editor.
Title: Laurence Sterne's A sentimental journey : a legacy to the world / edited by W.B. Gerard and M-C. Newbould, with Melvyn New.
Description: Lewisburg, Pennsylvania : Bucknell University Press, [2021] | Includes bibliographical references and index.
Identifiers: LCCN 2020025610 | ISBN 9781684482764 (paperback ; alk. paper) | ISBN 9781684482771 (hardcover ; alk. paper) | ISBN 9781684482788 (epub) | ISBN 9781684482795 (mobi) | ISBN 9781684482801 (pdf)
Subjects: LCSH: Sterne, Laurence, 1713–1768. Sentimental journey through France and Italy.
Classification: LCC PR3714.S43 L38 2021 | DDC 823/.6—dc23
LC record available at https://lccn.loc.gov/2020025610

A British Cataloging-in-Publication record for this book is available from the British Library.

∞ The paper used in this publication meets the requirements of the American National Standard for Information Sciences—Permanence of Paper for Printed Library Materials, ANSI Z39.48-1992.

www.bucknelluniversitypress.org

Distributed worldwide by Rutgers University Press

Manufactured in the United States of America

For Blake

CONTENTS

Abbreviations and Conventions xi

Introduction: *A Sentimental Journey*'s Critical Legacies 1
W. B. Gerard and M-C. Newbould

PART ONE: Men, Women, and Other Animals

1 Refining Masculinity in Yorick's *Journey*: Courtesy, Chivalry, Gallantry 23
Shaun Regan

2 Yorick's War: Patriot Politics, Military Men, and Willing Women in *A Sentimental Journey* 42
Julia Banister

3 Sterne's Journey into Animal Affect 58
Glynis Ridley

PART TWO: Words, Structures, Things

4 Spatial Digression and the Borders of Knowledge in *A Sentimental Journey* 79
Chris Ewers

5 (O)economy and Order: Laurence Sterne's Chaptering 98
Alexander Hardie-Forsyth

6 Yorick's Speech and the Starling's Song: The Limits of Elocution in *A Sentimental Journey* 121
FRASER EASTON

7 Things of the Spirit: Vibrant Matter in *A Sentimental Journey* 150
JENNIFER PRESTON WILSON

PART THREE: Historical Contexts, Rewritten Texts

8 Boswell and Sterne in 1768 171
MELVYN NEW

9 The Shadow of Eliza: Sterne's Underplot in *A Sentimental Journey* 194
PETER BUDRIN

10 Debt, Death, and Literary Inheritance: The Ends of Sterne and *A Sentimental Journey* 213
PAUL GORING

Afterword 234
PAT ROGERS

Acknowledgments 243

Bibliography 245

Notes on Contributors 261

Index 265

ABBREVIATIONS AND CONVENTIONS

STERNE'S WORKS

All quotations are taken from the Florida edition of Sterne's works, full citation of which is given in the Bibliography. The format of in-text citations is as follows:

The Life and Opinions of Tristram Shandy, Gentleman: *TS*, volume.chapter.page

The Life and Opinions of Tristram Shandy, Gentleman: *The Notes: TS Notes*, page

A Sentimental Journey through France and Italy: *ASJ*, page

Bramine's Journal: *BJ*, page

The Sermons of Laurence Sterne: *Sermons*, page; and *Sermons: Notes*, page

The Letters: *Letters*, page

OTHER

Alan B. Howes, ed., *Sterne: The Critical Heritage* (London: Routledge and Kegan Paul, 1974): *CH*, page

Arthur H. Cash, *Laurence Sterne: The Early & Middle Years* (London: Methuen, 1975): *EMY*, page

Arthur H. Cash, *Laurence Sterne: The Later Years* (London: Methuen, 1986): *LY*, page

Note on spellings: French place names are given in their modern spelling rather than Sterne's. The "Seven Years' War" includes the apostrophe.

Laurence Sterne's *A Sentimental Journey*

INTRODUCTION

A Sentimental Journey's Critical Legacies

W. B. Gerard and M-C. Newbould

Horace Walpole places Sterne's second fictional work in direct conversation—or, rather, disagreement—with its famous predecessor: "Sterne has published two little volumes, called, *Sentimental Travels*. They are very pleasing, though too much dilated, and infinitely preferable to his tiresome *Tristram Shandy*, of which I never could get through three volumes. In these there is great good nature and delicacy."[1] Whereas Walpole, like several early readers, finds *Tristram Shandy* to be crude, bawdy, and frustratingly protracted, *A Sentimental Journey through France and Italy* (though its mere "two little volumes" were apparently too "dilated" for Walpole's taste) presents something rather different. It is more "delicate," being both "good-natured and picturesque" (as Walpole commented elsewhere),[2] and appeals to the "heart of sensibility" in a more touching, and more morally instructive, way.

Opinion about *Tristram Shandy*, and its variously admired and derided author, could never entirely be divorced from appreciation of Sterne's second work; indeed, he wove together the actual and fictional identities of himself, Tristram, and Yorick throughout his works and in his personal life. His several sojourns abroad between 1762 and 1766 (*ASJ*, xi–xii, xvii–xviii) provided the background for both volumes 7 and 9 of *Tristram Shandy* and his last work, a biographical element that further complicates these connections. *A Sentimental Journey*'s very title aligned it with Sterne; "By Mr. Yorick" is often dropped from the title page of modern-day publications, but for early readers it undoubtedly recalled the parson whose death is marked by the much-discussed black page in volume 1 of *Tristram Shandy*. The name also aligned *A Sentimental Journey* with the nominal author of the four volumes of sermons Sterne published in his lifetime (in addition to three published posthumously), the first installment of which—initially advertised as the "Dramatick Sermons of Mr. Yorick"—famously included a frontispiece engraving of Reynolds's 1760 portrait of Sterne. The complete collection of *Tristram Shandy*'s volumes and of the *Sermons of Mr. Yorick* were frequently listed in the first newspaper advertisements for *A Sentimental Journey*.[3] Entangled by this web of identities, early and subsequent reactions to the text alike reflected the initial mixed response to *Tristram Shandy*. Many readers found that *A Sentimental Journey* spoke to its purported theme of sensibility with touching, and morally edifying, pathos; these qualities, however, were held in suspicion as often as they were admired, and the ironic ambiguities of the work tended to leave readers either pleasurably bemused or frustrated.

Sterne reportedly told Richard Griffith that *A Sentimental Journey* was his "*Work of Redemption*" (*ASJ*, lxii–lxiii), and he wrote to Anne James that his design was "to teach us to love the world and our fellow creatures better than we do" (*Letters*, 629). While such claims intrigue, *A Sentimental Journey* remains for us largely enigmatic. It continues both to please and to puzzle modern readers and critics who examine from fresh perspectives what Jakub Lipski has recently termed its "paradoxes of sentiment," alongside an array of other mysteries.[4] It raises numerous perplexing questions: Does it promote sentimentalism or satirize its superficiality? Is the text a mediation of Sterne's spiritual concerns during the last year of his life? What kind of text is it (a novel, travel narrative, memoir, or something else)? And what are we to make of the parallels and the slippages between the real-life Sterne and his fictional creations, including the inclusion of his not-so-secret inamorata Eliza Draper (1744–1778)? While some readers may simply appreciate the charming, whimsical account of a parson's travels through mid-eighteenth-century France, for others these questions have driven critical inquiry of *A Sentimental Journey*, generating divergent and challenging responses.

INITIAL REACTIONS

Horace Walpole's muted praise of *A Sentimental Journey* mirrors the initial mixed reactions to Sterne's final fiction. Ralph Griffiths writes in the *Monthly Review* that "the highest excellence of this genuine, this legitimate son of humour, lies not in his humorous but his pathetic vein." The "original vein of humour" characterizing Sterne's writing is enriched by "the moral and the pathetic," states the *Political Register*. *A Sentimental Journey*'s "humour," however, was rarely seen to be unmixed, and one reviewer could admire *A Sentimental Journey*'s pathos while another could critique its "thoughtless insipidity," its "lewdness," and its "dissipation," all in the same month of March 1768.[5] From the outset, it seems, this text provoked curiosity, admiration, and critique, often simultaneously, both for its inherent characteristics and for the broader contexts from which it emerged.

New editions of *A Sentimental Journey* appeared as stand-alone volumes, as part of Sterne's *Works* that began to appear from the 1780s onward (suggesting an almost-immediate parity with established, "classic" writers granted similar collections),[6] and in excerpted form in magazines and in increasingly popular anthologies featuring extracts from favorite authors' works: George Kearsley's highly successful anthology *The Beauties of Sterne* had run to thirteen editions by 1800. Editions of *A Sentimental Journey* began to include critical investment in the form of annotations, introductory essays, and other explanatory apparatus: one "critical" edition of 1782 included a glossary of French terms; a version was published in Paris in 1800 with explanatory notes; an annotated edition appeared in London in 1803 with an introduction and extensive footnotes aimed at a contemporary readership.[7] In addition, new editions, imitations, and critical responses appeared across Europe and in America in the latter decades of the eighteenth century, while translations in Danish, Dutch, French, German, Italian, Polish, and Russian all demonstrated the text's international reach and its engagement in a broader cultural conversation.[8]

Critical apparatus inevitably blurred into interpretation, as these commentators—like the anthology editors whose subjective selections were apparently representative of Sterne's work—helped to influence readers' perception of his writing according to the tenor of the times. Like the correspondence published posthumously by Sterne's daughter, Lydia Medalle (*Letters of The late Rev. Mr. Laurence Sterne, To his most intimate Friends* [1775]; *Letters*, 7.xlix), the late-century tendency was to diminish the impression of the bawdy, Shandean Sterne and to promote "Yorick," the didactic sentimentalist. One interlocutor in Clara Reeves's *The Progress of Romance* (1785) echoes Ralph Griffiths, claiming *A Sentimental Journey* to be "indisputably a work of merit.—Where *Sterne* attempts the Pathos, he is irresistible; the Reviewers have well observed, that though he affected humour and foolery, yet he was greatest in the pathetic style."[9] The promotion of affective sympathy as morally beneficial, as well as individually pleasurable, helped ensure *A Sentimental Journey*'s lasting appeal. Writing in 1783, Robert Burns boldly (and perhaps ironically) called it one of the "glorious models after which I endeavour to form my conduct."[10] Sterne's (often conveniently pocket-sized) work accompanied many readers on their own travels, figurative and real, to become a companion offering both pleasure and guidance.

Sterne's British and international readers alike engaged with the work's immersive qualities by producing their own creative versions of *A Sentimental Journey*. Literary adaptation and an interest in the "afterlives" of fiction were a widespread phenomenon in this period but notably characterized Sterne's reception. Few eighteenth-century authors' works were adapted, parodied, and illustrated as creatively and as widely as were Sterne's. Thomas Keymer's observation that the creative responses generated throughout *Tristram Shandy*'s serialization provide a "cultural barometer" for gauging how Sterne was being read, by whom, and when might be said of Sterneana in general.[11] The salacious, Shandean Sterne is foregrounded in some eroticized imitations of *A Sentimental Journey*, such as *A Sentimental Journey, Continued . . . by Eugenius* of 1769, which exploit both the opportunity of the work's incompleteness and its seeming ambiguity toward sexual adventure. Others promote a more unproblematically sentimental Sterne. Adaptations such as *The Letters of Maria* (1790) and *Sterne's Maria: A Pathetic Story* (1800?) continue the character's story line beyond the pages of the original text, displaying the prevalent appeal of sentimental novels, female heroines as icons of sensibility, the Gothic novel, and Continental travel in this period.[12]

A Sentimental Journey was not universally admired, however, partly on account of its lingering negative associations with *Tristram Shandy*, partly because of its problematic sensibility, which increasingly met with skepticism regarding how it was practiced and its sincerity.[13] Sterne as author also remained problematic; as Elizabeth Carter wrote to Elizabeth Vesey in 1768 of the "Sentimental Traveller," "I have neither read [it] nor probably never shall; for indeed there is something shocking in whatever I have heard either of the author, or of his writings."[14] Sterne's originality as a writer came under scrutiny, too. As early as 1768, the *Critical Review* claims that "Mr. Yorick has barbarously cut out and unskilfully put together [material] from other novels."[15] By 1798, John Ferriar, whose *Illustrations of Sterne* provided the first extended study of the author's borrowings, is dismissive of *A Sentimental Journey* on similar grounds, noting only that it "seems to have been taken from the little French pieces, which have had such celebrity."[16]

Ferriar's appraisal indicates a notable feature of *A Sentimental Journey*'s critical reception. Is it just another sentimental fiction? And once the "puzzle" of sentiment is taken out of the equation, is this so very perplexing a text to understand? Differing attitudes toward sensibility continued to shape the text's reception in the subsequent century; but once the relevance of this fashion began to lessen, *A Sentimental Journey* increasingly began to be viewed as the simple sibling to the complex *Tristram Shandy*.

THE NINETEENTH CENTURY

Johann Wolfgang von Goethe declared in 1792 of his *Sorrows of Young Werther* (1774) that "one must not fail to recognize the influence of Yorick-Sterne," and that by reading Sterne "the 19th century may also learn what we owe him and realize what we can still borrow from him."[17] Goethe's British contemporaries seemed less convinced of *A Sentimental Journey*'s merits, or indeed of Sterne's "beautiful spirit"; while the author continued to enjoy a buoyant readership abroad his reputation and popularity began to dwindle on home soil.[18] Fewer new, illustrated, or critical editions of *A Sentimental Journey* appeared during the nineteenth century than in its initial heyday and compared with a resurgence of interest in the early twentieth century. It generated fewer critical responses, perhaps unsurprisingly; the first flurry of reviews had dissipated, and English literary criticism as a discipline was still embryonic. As that institution began to take shape through the decades of the nineteenth century and critical analyses of native texts were increasingly published, it is notable how far *A Sentimental Journey* tended to recede in critical discussions of Sterne while *Tristram Shandy* dominated. Walter Scott makes no mention of the later fiction in his essay on Sterne prefacing Ballantyne's 1823 series of classic novels.[19] Samuel Taylor Coleridge remarked that while he admired "the first part of *Tristram Shandy*," he found *A Sentimental Journey* to be "poor sickly stuff"—a growing distaste for sensibility that particularly afflicted an author who had previously been heralded as one of the mode's most noteworthy proponents.[20]

Paralleling this dwindling appreciation of Sterne's fiction was a declining opinion of the author fostered largely by renewed attention directed at the perceived disjuncture between his bawdy writing and his clerical profession, as well as disapproval of his private life. Initial criticism of the *Sermons* often pointed to Sterne's abuse of his "sacerdotal" character as an "aggravation of the indecency" of the author of *Tristram Shandy* publishing sermons, especially under the fictional pseudonym of "Yorick."[21] Yet negative appraisal of Sterne's work, based on condemnation of his personal life, found ample accommodation in an increasingly conservative society, while the encroaching perception of Sterne as plagiarist colored the latent assumption that the author (and his work) was somehow dishonest. By 1810, the American publisher Matthew Carey credits *A Sentimental Journey*'s decline, in sales and in reputation alike, to accusations of plagiarism that push Ferriar's commentary several stages further: "Few works, if any, were ever received with more unbounded applause, than the *Sentimental Journey*. Its circulation was immense. It produced a revolution in public taste. . . . But alas! . . . it has been hurled down, and [Sterne] has now sunk, in the public estimation, into the disgraceful character of a petty thief."[22] While figures such as Byron, writing in his journal in 1813, seemed to relish just such a reputational slur on man and work ("Ah, I am as bad as that dog Sterne, who preferred whining over 'a dead ass to relieving a living mother'—villain—hypocrite—slave—sycophant! But *I* am no better"),[23] Sterne's supposedly questionable authorial character increasingly tinted views of his apparently suspect fiction. *A Sentimental Journey* entered the Vatican's *Index Librorum Prohibitorum* of banned books in 1819.

Compared to the profusion of several dozen editions of the book during the first fifty years following its publication (with more than half of them illustrated), the number of new editions of *A Sentimental Journey* fell to fewer than twenty during the subsequent decades of the nineteenth century. General enthusiasm for Sterne also diminished: few editions appeared of *Tristram Shandy* (despite attention from figures such as Scott) or of Sterne's collected works. Uncle Toby, however, remained perennially popular. In a period that also saw fewer adaptations of any of Sterne's works, Toby acquired new creative afterlives; besides his appearance in some dramatic pieces, C. R. Leslie's 1830s paintings depicting Toby and the widow Wadman in the sentry box were particularly popular; the image was reproduced on a range of material objects (including mass-produced Prattware pot lids), parodied in satirical prints, and even deployed in tobacco advertisements.[24] Similarly, *A Sentimental Journey*'s afterlife was at least partially defined by the enduring popularity of an individual character: Staffordshire statuettes of Maria and her Sylvio (rather than her goat from *Tristram Shandy*) adorned Victorian homes, just as many designs of Wedgwood stoneware had featured her image during the late eighteenth century.[25] Despite this visual heritage—which included two heavily illustrated editions published in 1841 and 1885[26]—fewer new editions of *A Sentimental Journey* appeared than of *Tristram Shandy*, and it seemed the less popular, perhaps because (in Coleridge's terms) the more "sickly" of the two texts. Thus the backlash against sentimentalism seemed even more pronounced than that against Sterne's bawdry, although the two merged in Victorian eyes: it was suggested that the personal indecency of the author inevitably shaped the insinuating prurience of the pernicious (libertine, voyeuristic) sensibility of his work.

William Makepeace Thackeray was the most forceful mid-nineteenth-century voice against Sterne, even if he was more impassioned with moralistic outrage than critically acute. His public lectures of 1852, published as *The English Humorists of the Eighteenth Century* the following year, painted a despicable caricature of the author, formed in part from the perceived hypocrisies of a lewd married clergyman (*EMY*, xii), which extended to his texts: "There is not a page of Sterne's writing but has something that were better away, a latent corruption—a hint as of an impure presence."[27] Fortunately for Sterne, at this nadir of his reputation, Percy Fitzgerald offered an important corrective to Thackeray's "biographical distortions" (*CH*, 28) in the first modern scholarly biography of the author, *The Life of Laurence Sterne* (1864), which began the reversal of negative opinion on Sterne's writings by adopting a more factual and aesthetically considerate approach to his work, although one not free from implicitly judging Sterne's "indiscretions."[28]

In reviewing Fitzgerald's work, Walter Bagehot was also somewhat more sympathetic toward the "queer parson," although he diminishes Sterne's achievement with the condescending affection characteristic of some nineteenth-century critics regarding earlier writers (such as Jane Austen); while conceding that Sterne "is a great author . . . this is certainly not because of great thoughts, for there is scarcely a sentence in his writings which can be called a thought; nor from sublime conceptions which enlarge the limits of our imagination, for he never leaves the sensuous."[29] Similarly, Sidney Lee (in his entry on Sterne for the *Dictionary of National Biography*), Leslie Stephen (in his essay on the author in *Hours in a Library*), and George Saintsbury (in the introduction to his edited *Works* of 1894) all mollify Thackeray's unforgiving appraisal while retaining the tone of demeaning judgment. Stephen, for instance, accuses Sterne of "a want of principle" in his personal life but claims that these faults should not prohibit appreciation of his work: "It is impossible for any one with the remotest taste for literary excellence to read 'Tristram Shandy' or the 'Sentimental Journey' without a sense of wondering admiration."[30] Echoing Thackeray's approach, however, Saintsbury considers Sterne's humor to be of a more puerile than sublime order: "Sterne, with the rarest exceptions, is always sniggering when he is naughty. Now the snigger is a very unlovely thing. . . . Sterne, on the worse side of him, is compact of sniggers: the Journey itself of course dealing largely in them."[31] Despite such conditional appreciation of the author and his work, these dispersed positive opinions collectively helped to pave the way toward a more sympathetic appraisal of Sterne's work in the twentieth century. Then, as previously, critical appraisal of *A Sentimental Journey* was inextricably bound up with shifting approaches to its sentimentalism but also with the text's aesthetic appeal, its invitation to adaptation, its perceived morality, and its literary value. Attitudes toward Sterne's other work, and an expanding appreciation of his literary (textual) genius in the modern (and subsequently postmodern) senses of the term, also came to shape appreciation of *A Sentimental Journey* in significant ways.

EARLY TWENTIETH CENTURY

Wilbur L. Cross, Sterne's great champion, built on the biographical redemption suggested by Fitzgerald to produce the first modern collected edition of Sterne, *The Complete Works and Life of Laurence Sterne* (1904). Cross included the first publication of *Bramine's Journal* under the title *Journal to Eliza*. This work had been discovered in 1878 and gifted to the British Museum in 1894, although it was available earlier to Thackeray as he composed his lectures (*ASJ*, xxvi);[32] as the Florida editors emphasize and as Pat Rogers notes in the afterword to the present volume, its public appearance in 1904 had a decided impact on opinion and understanding of *A Sentimental Journey*. Addressed to Eliza Draper after her departure to India during the last year of Sterne's life, *Bramine's Journal* recorded his emotional state about their relationship as well as fantasies about the future. The sentimental expression of the *Journal* is less restrained and more self-revelatory than that of its more overtly fictional companion, and it provides valuable clues regarding the composition of *A Sentimental Journey* as well as to the author's physical and mental state at the time. The *Life* that Cross initially included in his *Works* was Fitzgerald's—its revised and expanded third edition of 1906 presented an even more favorable assessment of its subject—but five years later Cross published his own biography, *The Life and Times of Laurence Sterne*. Cross's *Life* was less inclined toward old gossip, adopting a more realistic perspective on the author's supposedly flawed moral behavior. Equally crucial, though, was the careful critical scrutiny brought to the *Works*, which finally elevated Sterne's texts for genuine aesthetic and scholarly consideration.

As Victorian social conservatism ebbed in the early twentieth century, cultural attitudes shifted toward positive evaluation of Sterne, abetted by the biographical work of Fitzgerald and Cross. This, in conjunction with a reawakened appreciation for sentimentalism (and perhaps in an accompanying eroticism) created a fertile popular environment for *A Sentimental Journey*. The 1920s saw the title's renaissance—and perhaps its popular peak—with more than a dozen new editions, including further translations into French, Italian, and now Serbo-Croatian (a Czech-language edition in 1903 was ahead of the trend) and four English-language editions in 1926 alone. Significantly, this period also saw the greatest number of illustrated editions of *A Sentimental Journey* since the late eighteenth century, indicating not only a renewed interest in the text but also its appeal to visualization; some of these illustrations—such as those of J. E. Laboureur (1928) and Polia Chentoff (1929)—revel in lascivious interpretations of Yorick's story, a counterpart to the sentimental bias of depictions from the late eighteenth century (although some bawdy illustrations appeared in the earlier period, too).[33]

Many of these illustrated editions seemed intended primarily for visual enjoyment, but Sterne was also emerging as a writer of both philosophical and aesthetic import, most notably in the praise heaped on him by Friedrich Nietzsche.[34] *A Sentimental Journey* was also significant to Viktor Shklovsky—perhaps best known in Sterne studies for his 1921 essay on *Tristram Shandy*—as suggested by the title of his *Sentimental Journey: Memoirs, 1917–1922*, which describes his experiences during the Russian Revolution.[35] It might nevertheless be suggested that, for all that Sterne as a writer was gaining new admirers, in particular for his supposedly avant-garde creation of so-called modernist narrative tactics, his remarkable style was more frequently appreciated in *Tristram Shandy* than in *A Sentimental Journey*, which criticism of this period often tended to regard as the less complex (hence more accessible) of Sterne's major fictions.

Virginia Woolf's perceptive introduction to the 1928 Oxford World Classics edition of *A Sentimental Journey* provides a benchmark in Sterne criticism. Woolf reappraises Sterne's style more broadly, finding ballast equally in both fictions to support an appreciation that is less distracted by sentiment on the one hand or bawdry on the other; she also reevaluates broad-brush Victorian approaches to Sterne's life and work to emphasize instead his texts' aesthetic value.[36] Unlike earlier readers who were ready to align his idiosyncratic technique with what was perceived to be the whimsical character of a self-styled "original," Woolf recognizes the artistry of Sterne's seemingly spontaneous method, as he "achieved this illusion only by the use of extreme art and extraordinary pains." She also identifies an intellectual substance that earlier critics had sometimes ignored, noting that the text, "for all its levity and wit, is based on something fundamentally philosophic." Woolf finds in Sterne a kindred spirit, whose "disconnected" style with its "suddenness and irrelevancy" of ideas creates prose that feels "more true to life than to literature." As such, he anticipates the modernist proclivity toward stream-of-consciousness: "in this preference for the windings of his own mind to the guidebook and its hammered high road, Sterne is singularly of our own age."[37]

Herbert Read stresses the text's potential simultaneously to uphold the sentimental and the comic in his introduction to the Scholartis Press edition of *A Sentimental Journey*, published a year later (1929). He refutes Saintsbury's earlier identification of the Sternean "snigger," which is "bitter and cynical." Instead, he finds "Sterne is tender and generous"; the author's successful husbandry of humor and pathos creates "a positive harmony which is one of the great charms of Sterne's writing. . . . The sentimental is relieved by the humourous, the humourous is redeemed by the sentimental—two contrary principles that together give perfect equilibrium."[38] Read's understanding of the delicacy as well as the ambiguity of Sterne's balance between humor and sentiment grounds future discussion of *A Sentimental Journey* as poised between ethical precept and all-too-human impulse.

Read observes both the humane and the human in the "mutual toleration" that the work's characters exercise in pursuit of sentimental sociability, with Yorick as an exemplar of valuable, ethical interactions throughout his travels.[39] Read gestures toward this ideal of sociable harmony as a reason for the widespread enthusiasm *A Sentimental Journey* has consistently excited across the Continent, presciently suggesting that it "has done more for the creation of a tolerant European consciousness than all of the peace treaties of a century and a half."[40] He also weaves biography into his critical commentary more subtly than had his predecessors; he recognizes, for example, the fundamental textual influence of Sterne's illness, pointing out that "it is the book of a sick and harassed man."[41] Finally, he brings fresh attention to the crucial opportunity that Sterne's letters, and especially *Bramine's Journal*, offer for an understanding of the author's state of mind during 1767–1768, providing "a complete revelation of Sterne's spiritual state."[42] Read's use of this material prompted another milestone in Sterne studies, Lewis Perry Curtis's authoritative *Letters* (Clarendon, 1935), which provides abundant annotations to further illuminate Sterne's life and work, while also valuably shedding the Sterne canon of problematic attributions dating back to Lydia Medalle's 1775 edition of her father's correspondence.

Perhaps the first monograph to exercise a deep, methodical, and extended critical view of *A Sentimental Journey*, W. B. C. Watkins's *Perilous Balance* (Princeton University Press, 1939) addresses biographical and philosophical issues as well as prose technique in the text. For Watkins, Sterne is worthy of consideration by possessing "genuine intellectual seriousness."[43] He praises Sterne in "his portrayal of individual consciousness, in the extraordinary acuteness of his psychology, and in his complexity in the presentation of time," asserting his anticipation of Proust[44] and (following Cross and proleptic of future commentary) reinforcing Sterne's interest in Locke, in whom he found "the intellectual basis for his own beliefs."[45] Watkins reiterates and extends discussion of the relevance of Sterne's health initiated by Read for a better understanding of Sterne's writings.[46] His operative metaphor, "perilous balance," productively addresses *A Sentimental Journey*'s sentimental humor: "The lightness of tone in that work may cause us to overlook the genuinely serious purpose underlying it."[47]

Other critics of this period are less generous in evaluating the text, in particular regarding Sterne's use of sentiment: Rufus Putney, for instance, writing in 1940, sees this quality to be essentially empty, an interpretation echoed by Ernest Dilworth in 1948.[48] Accusations of insincerity, or indeed vacuousness, have continued to affect some recent appraisals of the ambiguity of Sterne's sensibility. However, Watkins's perception of "elements of real tragedy and an underlying seriousness which explain the profundity of his greatest comedy, so light in texture, so brilliant on the surface" has nevertheless informed subsequent attempts to elevate *A Sentimental Journey* from the merely amusing or aesthetically pleasurable.[49] If the technical brilliance of *Tristram Shandy* was held to be easier to admire by some because more obvious to detect, it is the deft style of *A Sentimental Journey*, which by its sustained tone of interrogative irony unpacks the very quality it purportedly promotes, that gains particular traction in later critical appraisals of the work. Many of these respond to and sustain ongoing reassessments of sensibility itself, while also seeking alternative critical avenues for evaluating Sterne's text.

MID-TWENTIETH CENTURY

Supported by the biographical and editorial work of Fitzgerald, Cross, and Curtis, as well as the critical discussions of Woolf, Read, Watkins, and others, the focus on Sterne blossomed midcentury, although the critical bias toward his earlier work persisted. The 1950s saw important criticism on *Tristram Shandy* from D. W. Jefferson, Wayne C. Booth, and John Traugott, but it was in the later 1960s that *A Sentimental Journey* began to receive more extensive critical attention. Like Read and Watkins, the Sterne biographer Arthur Hill Cash asserts *A Sentimental Journey*'s philosophical significance over its potential to be seen as superficial. His monograph, *Sterne's Comedy of Moral Sentiments: The Ethical Dimension of the "Journey,"* examines the text's relation to Sterne's spiritual writings, succinctly positing that "[he] took a moral stand in his fictions which differed hardly at all from that of his sermons."[50] Given the distance between the reasoned benevolence of the sermons and Yorick's sometimes-impetuous sensibility, Cash argues that the construct of Yorick is used to poke fun at unconsidered expressions of emotion, albeit affectionately rather than derisively, in his influential reevaluation of Sterne's ambiguous sentimentalism as positive rather than subversively sexual or satirical. Emancipating Sterne from two centuries of accusations of both excess and hypocrisy, Cash's in-depth study advances instead a valuable discussion of the author's ethics and humor, both informed by Sterne's eighteenth-century Christian beliefs and his age's literary practice.

Gardner D. Stout's extensively annotated critical edition of *A Sentimental Journey* (University of California Press, 1967) proved foundational to future critical discussion; his careful establishment of a copytext, sensitivity to the factual historical context of both the author and his work, and inclusion of rarely seen early illustrations stimulated future analysis. Stout further justifies the substance of *A Sentimental Journey*, asserting that it "demonstrates that a comic sense of life is a 'gift of God' enabling us to read the shandean parable of existence aright—as a revelation of its infinitely charitable Author."[51]

Monographs addressing Sterne's work in the later 1960s include *A Sentimental Journey* in their purview. Henri Fluchère's *Laurence Sterne: From Tristram to Yorick* usefully surveys the broad scope of recent and contemporaneous scholarship.[52] John Stedmond's *The Comic Art of Laurence Sterne: Convention and Innovation in*

"Tristram Shandy" and "A Sentimental Journey" adopts a formalistic approach to the style, structure, and generic form of Sterne's works, with a particular interest in Sterne's humor.[53] Focusing on the Scriblerian satiric inheritance evident in the earlier work, Melvyn New's *Laurence Sterne as Satirist: A Reading of "Tristram Shandy"* also contends that serious consideration to Sterne's sermons is necessary to any meaningful engagement with his later fictions.

The late 1960s also saw the coalescence of a scholarly community interested in Sterne's life and works. As Rogers notes in his discussion of "anniversaries" and Sterne studies in the afterword to this book, the 1967 formation of the Laurence Sterne Trust (first chaired by Herbert Read), followed by the rehabilitation of Shandy Hall in Coxwold by Kenneth Monkman, set the stage for an international bicentenary conference of Sterne scholars, preserved in part in an eclectic but significant proceedings volume published in 1971, *The Winged Skull.* Monkman also arranged for the reinterment of Sterne's remains from an ignominious London location to the churchyard of St. Michael's Church, Coxwold, where Sterne spent his last years as nominal vicar of the parish.

In the early 1970s, R. F. Brissenden's *Virtue in Distress* discusses Sterne's approach to sentiment across his writings and within the broader contexts of the period. He voices, but modulates, important questions surrounding the ambiguous sincerity and "moral status of Yorick's sensibility."[54] Brissenden views Yorick favorably, however, by developing the strand of human/humane qualities that Read had detected in *A Sentimental Journey*: he is both "a sexual and a social being," "in which the sacred and the secular, spiritual love and carnal, are suddenly and comically, but somehow not inappropriately linked together."[55] This approach reflects the religious impulse behind Sterne's sentiment and promotes *A Sentimental Journey* as presenting one of "the most positive, spontaneous and sophisticated" products of "the sentimentalism of the age."[56]

Cash's masterful two-volume scholarly achievement, *Laurence Sterne: The Early & Middle Years* (1975) and *Laurence Sterne: The Later Years* (1986), enriches the informed relationship between biography and criticism that subsequent scholarship would enjoy. Cash provides the first extensive revisitation of the author's life since Cross and helps ground Sterne and his texts as targets of serious literary consideration. The first volume traces the details of Sterne's clerical career and the creative turn that led to the incipience of *Tristram Shandy*, while the second traces his rise to fame and fortune and continuing literary activity from 1760 until his death, with a brief glance toward Sterne's posthumous reputation. Cash carefully examines contemporary printing and bookselling practices in both York and London, the reception history of *Tristram Shandy* and *A Sentimental Journey*, and Sterne's domestic life and foreign travel, all invaluable to understanding his creative genius.

Cash's biography was followed by the first full scholarly edition of Sterne's entire canon published by the University Press of Florida between 1976 and 2014. Volume 6, *"A Sentimental Journey" and "Continuation of the Bramine's Journal,"* edited by Melvyn New and W. G. Day, appeared in 2002. Building on the work of Curtis (who includes a version of *Bramine's Journal* in his edition of the letters), Cash, and Stout, the juxtaposition of both works underlines the editors' emphasis on the understanding of one text as essential to that of the other, a crucial thread running through both the volume's introduction and its annotations.

RECENT CRITICISM

The *MLA Bibliography* lists more than 1,800 essays and notes on Sterne since the 1970s, with more than 250 on *A Sentimental Journey* alone. Salient critical trends emerge in the approach to Sterne in general and *A Sentimental Journey* in particular, which continue, expand, or refute many earlier strands of criticism. They also increasingly seek to map the text's reception across the remarkably reshaping contours of eighteenth-century scholarship and literary criticism more broadly, to embrace feminism, travel literature, reception, animal studies, visual culture, and affect theory, among many other fields. It is perhaps significant that the majority of recent critical discussions of *A Sentimental Journey* have appeared in essay-length studies rather than monographs, which are more often dedicated to *Tristram Shandy* or Sterne in general. Now, as before, Sterne's final published work is often considered in the context of (and perhaps overshadowed by) current attitudes toward the broader complexities of his persona and literary output.

The notable emergence of critical interest in sensibility, sentimentalism, and the culture of affective sympathy has seen many later eighteenth-century works reevaluated in attempts to untangle what can typically appear to be a contested, ambiguous, and conflicted terrain: how "feeling" and "reason" might be negotiated in tandem; the relation between performance and "the natural," sincerity and affectation, and irony and "pure" emotion. It is little surprise that Sterne's complex journey narrative should frequently feature as a key text for examining such interlocking concerns. And, as such, much recent critical work on *A Sentimental Journey* returns to the initial contexts in which it was first evaluated: reading Sterne's text through the lens of sensibility might be inevitable, but as many critics reveal, that need not restrict it to polarized or reductive responses.

Among scholarship discussing *A Sentimental Journey* in the context of sensibility, Robert Markley's 1987 assessment is influential: it addresses how sentiment both "valorizes masculine sensitivity as a virtue" and "explicitly promotes narrowly conservative and essentialist views of class relations, implicitly identifying the victims of social inequality . . . with 'feminine' powerlessness." Perhaps restricted by his lack of attention to textual detail, Markley sees Yorick as engaged in a self-satisfying, empty "performance" of feeling that can "never transcend limited and limiting acts of isolated, individual charity," a secular appraisal that cynically overlooks the ethical (not to mention spiritual) impulse Yorick brings to many of his encounters.[57]

The notion of sentimental "performance" has led several critics beside Markley to suspect Yorick of insincere, self-interested feeling, or at least more broadly to question Sterne's approach to sentiment, albeit with greater nuance than critics such as Putney and Dilworth; many follow Brissenden's position instead. John Dussinger's 1987 discussion of Yorick as "man of feeling" rather than dispassionate cynic offers one such positive assessment.[58] John Mullan's important critical study of eighteenth-century sentimentalism, *Sentiment and Sociability* (1988), provides an engaged and sensitive appraisal of Sterne's career against the backdrop of this contemporary phenomenon, which sees *A Sentimental Journey* as subtly critiquing but not debunking sentimentalism.[59] Tim Parnell (1997) adopts a similarly more appreciative route, arguing that the religious dimension of Yorick's journey underscores his claims to what might appear to be merely surface-level, demonstrative expressions of emotion.[60]

An increased interest in affect theory as psychosomatic, evinced in the extensive and varied uses of body language by Sterne's characters, has produced further readings of *A Sentimental Journey*'s supple handling of sensibility that are less critical than Markley's. Ann Jessie Van Sant (1993), for instance, recalls Dussinger—and Jonathan Lamb's 1980 investigation of Sterne's relation to Hartleian associationism—by addressing contemporary physical and optic theories to reassess Yorick's identity as a "man of feeling."[61] A comparable interest in the body, drawing attention to Sterne's interest in oratory as a preacher as well as a writer of sentimental fiction, emerges in Paul Goring's important 2005 study *The Rhetoric of Sensibility*.[62]

Thomas Keymer offers a different angle to Sterne's ambiguous handling of sentiment in his 1993 discussion of the possible parodic allusion to Marvell belonging to the portrait of Maria.[63] The popularity of this character, and her prolific afterlife in text and image, indicates another significant aspect of *A Sentimental Journey*'s reception: adaptation and visual culture. Indeed, the Florida editors describe the work as "one of the most frequently illustrated of all eighteenth-century fictions" (*ASJ*, lxx). Building on the research of Catherine Gordon, among others, several studies seek to highlight these illustrations as visual interpretations of the text and their originating culture.[64] These have become a strong feature of the annual *The Shandean*, the journal founded in 1989 and carefully edited since by Peter de Voogd. W. B. Gerard and Brigitte Friant-Kessler's multi-installment catalogue of Sterne illustrations, published in *The Shandean* (2005–2011), provides an important scholarly resource for examining *A Sentimental Journey*'s numerous visualizations and how they might instigate fresh interpretations of the text itself. Gerard's 2004 article on how changing depictions of Maria reflect shifting approaches toward sentiment indicates how far creative adaptations can prompt potential rereadings of Sterne's text, an important interpretation complemented by his 2006 *Laurence Sterne and the Visual Imagination*.[65]

Adaptation studies has generated significant interest in the wider context of Sterne's reception, from scholars including Anne Bandry-Scubbi, René Bosch, Warren Oakley, and M-C. Newbould; *A Sentimental Journey* has duly encountered attention on account of the numerous continuations, sequels, and alternative versions it inspired, particularly in the early phase of its reception.[66] Following Keymer's concept of a "cultural barometer," these often suggest prevalent popular responses to the text at any given time and the predominance of certain themes, including sensibility, the politics of travel and its practicalities, gender, and sexuality. Recent work on Sternean adaptations has revealed the chronological and geographical reach of *A Sentimental Journey*'s creative afterlives, often within the wider context of responses to *Tristram Shandy* and to Sterne's reputation. *The Reception of Laurence Sterne in Europe*, edited by Peter de Voogd and John Neubauer in 2004, for instance, indicates the breadth of European interest in Sterne and the role that divergent creative reactions played in his reception.[67] It also demonstrates how *A Sentimental Journey* was typically the more popular text among Sterne's European readership and the most frequently adapted into new forms, despite the focus given to *Tristram Shandy* in some critical accounts of Sterne's reception.[68]

The growing impulse across Sterne studies is to reassess how *A Sentimental Journey* has been read (when, where, and in which cultural contexts), in a manner that takes full account of its relation to Sterne himself and to his other works, and to dominant contemporary phenomena such as sensibility. Recent criticism nevertheless seeks to nuance both how sentimentalism is understood in itself, and in Sterne's writing, but also to avoid limiting readings of *A Sentimental Journey* solely to this well-worn route. Just as initial reactions to the text reflected contrasting interpretations and surprising interpretive possibilities, so new work promises to expand ever-evolving critical approaches toward it, which parallel its ongoing appeal to a wide readership.

A Sentimental Journey continues to be reprinted in trade and scholarly editions alike. The popular Penguin Classics series issued a fresh *Sentimental Journey* edited by Paul Goring (2001) noteworthy for its introduction. Goring revitalizes questions surrounding the inherent ambiguities and ironies of Sterne's text, stressing their contextual significance, as well as the pleasure in allowing some of those mysteries to remain unraveled.[69] The 2006 Hackett edition of *"A Sentimental Journey" and "Continuation of the Bramine's Journal"* is based on the Florida edition, making the richness of Melvyn New and W. G. Day's annotations available to a wider audience, with appendices designed to illuminate understanding of the text and its contexts.[70] The Broadview Press text, edited by Katherine Turner (2010), provides a serviceable *Sentimental Journey* with an appendix of contextualizing material designed to assist students in pedagogic environments.[71]

While *A Sentimental Journey* continues to be widely read and studied, has been the subject of many essays, and has often featured in surveys of Sterne and of English literature, it has not always encountered the dedicated critical attention it deserves, instead playing a sometimes more muted role in discussions of *Tristram Shandy* or Sterne at large. This collection aims to redress the imbalance by bringing *A Sentimental Journey* center stage, fueled by the redemptive impetus of the past fifty years of Sterne criticism that has pursued fresh readings in new textual, cultural, historical, and theoretical contexts. The essays in the present collection reflect many of the innovative avenues of exploration touched on here and open up yet further lines of inquiry that enrich *A Sentimental Journey*'s critical and creative legacy.

NOTES

We are very grateful to Melvyn New for his input into and revisions of this introduction.

1. Horace Walpole to George Montagu, March 12, 1768, in *CH*, 202. For the purposes of this introduction, we have largely restricted our sampling of contemporary commentary to the survey readily available in Howes's *Critical Heritage* volume.
2. Horace Walpole to Thomas Gray, March 8, 1768, in *CH*, 202.
3. Siv Gøril Brandtzæg, M-C. Newbould, and Helen Williams, "Advertising Sterne's Novels in Eighteenth-Century Newspapers," *Shandean* 27 (2016): 45.
4. Jakub Lipski, "The Masquerade Metaphor and the Paradoxes of Sentiment in *A Sentimental Journey*," in *Sterne, Tristram, Yorick: Tercentenary Essays on Laurence Sterne*, ed. Melvyn New, Peter de Voogd, and Judith Hawley (Newark: University of Delaware Press, 2016), 187–199.
5. Horace Walpole to George Montagu, March 12, 1768, in *CH*, 202; [Ralph Griffiths], *Monthly Review* 38 (March–April 1768), in *CH*, 200; *Political Register* 2 (May 1768), in *CH*, 201.
6. For further discussion of *A Sentimental Journey*'s status as a "classic" text, see Susan Pickford, "Les notes éditoriales comme élément constitutif du statut d'un ouvrage classique:

L'exemple de *A Sentimental Journey* de Laurence Sterne," in *L'espace de la note*, ed. Jacques Dürrenmatt and Andréas Pfersmann (Rennes: La Licorne, 2004), 213–215.

7. See M-C. Newbould, "'Illustrating' *A Sentimental Journey*: The 'First Annotated Edition' of 1803?" *Shandean*, 24 (2013): 103–124.
8. For a useful bibliography of editions of *A Sentimental Journey*, see W. G. Day, *Laurence Sterne: "A Sentimental Journey": A Bibliographical Catalogue of Editions Spanning Nearly Two and a Half Centuries* (York, UK: Spelman, 2005).
9. Clara Reeve, *The Progress of Romance, through Times, Countries and Manners*, 2 vols. (Colchester, UK: W. Keymer; London: G.G.J. and J. Robinson, 1785), 2:31. Also quoted in *CH*, 263.
10. Robert Burns to John Murdoch, January 15, 1783, in *The Letters of Robert Burns*, ed. J. DeLancey Ferguson and G. Ross Roy (Oxford: Oxford University Press, 1985), 17. See also Carol McGuirk, "Sentimental Encounter in Sterne, Mackenzie, and Burns," *Studies in English Literature, 1500–1900* 20, no. 3 (1980): 505–515.
11. Thomas Keymer, *Sterne, the Moderns, and the Novel* (Oxford: Oxford University Press, 2002), 86.
12. Miss Street, *The Letters of Maria; To which is Added, An Account of her Death* (London: Kearsley, 1790); Anonymous, *Sterne's Maria: A Pathetic Story; With an Account of her Death, at the Castle of Valerine* (London: Rusted, [1800?]).
13. See Stephen Ahern, *Affected Sensibilities: Romantic Excess and the Genealogy of the Novel, 1680–1810* (New York: AMS, 2007), 11–13.
14. Elizabeth Carter to Mrs. Elizabeth Vesey, April 19, 1768, in *CH*, 203.
15. *Critical Review* 25 (March 1768), in *CH*, 198.
16. John Ferriar, *Illustrations of Sterne: With Other Essays and Verses* (London: Cadell and Davies, 1798), 178. On Ferriar's *Illustrations* and accusations of plagiarism in Sterne, see Melvyn New, *Laurence Sterne as Satirist: A Reading of "Tristram Shandy"* (Gainesville: University Press of Florida, 1969), 60–62; Richard Terry, *The Plagiarism Allegation in English Literature from Butler to Sterne* (London: Palgrave, 2000), 194.
17. Johann Wolfgang von Goethe, *Campagne in Frankreich 1792* (1820–1822), in *CH*, 432; Goethe, *Aus Makariens Archiv* (ca. 1828), in *CH*, 433.
18. For a discussion of differences between Sterne's British and Continental reception, see Peter de Voogd and John Neubauer, "Introduction: Sterne Crosses the Channel," in *The Reception of Laurence Sterne in Europe*, ed. Peter de Voogd and John Neubauer (London: Thoemmes Continuum, 2004), 1–9.
19. Laurence Sterne, *The Novels of Sterne, Goldsmith, Dr. Johnson [and others] . . . To which are prefixed memoirs of the lives of the authors [by Sir Walter Scott]*, Ballantyne's Novelist's Library 5 (London: Hurst, Robinson, 1823).
20. Samuel Taylor Coleridge, *Table Talk*, August 18, 1833, in *CH*, 357–358.
21. "An Account of the Rev. Mr. ST****, and his Writings," *Grand Magazine* 3 (June 1760), in *CH*, 98.
22. Matthew Carey, "Remarks on the Charge of Plagiarism Alleged Against Sterne," *Port Folio* (October 1810), in *CH*, 334.
23. Lord Byron, *Journal*, December 1, 1813, in *CH*, 346; cf. *CH*, 305. The journal was not published until 1830.
24. See W. G. Day, "Charles Robert Leslie's 'My Uncle Toby and the Widow Wadman': The Nineteenth-Century Icon of Sterne's Work," *Shandean* 9 (1997): 83–108.
25. W. G. Day, "Sternean Material Culture: Lorenzo's Snuff-Box and His Graves," in *The Reception of Laurence Sterne in Europe*, ed. Peter de Voogd and John Neubauer (London: Thoemmes Continuum, 2004), 248.

26. The 1841 edition (London: Joseph Thomas) is illustrated by Charles Jacque and Joseph Fussell (82 illustrations), and the 1885 edition (Philadelphia: J. B. Lippincott) is illustrated by Maurice Leloir (11 full-page and 220 partial-page illustrations).
27. W[illiam] M[akepeace] Thackeray, "Sterne and Goldsmith," in *The English Humorists of the Eighteenth Century: A Series of Lectures* (London: Grey Walls, 1949), 190.
28. Percy Fitzgerald, *The Life of Laurence Sterne*, 2 vols. (London: Chapman and Hall, 1864), 2:24.
29. Walter Bagehot, *The Works and Life of Walter Bagehot*, vol. 4 (London, 1915), 229, 236.
30. Leslie Stephen, "Sterne," in *Hours in a Library*, vol. 3 (London: Smith, Elder, 1909), 133–134, 132.
31. George Saintsbury, introduction to *A Sentimental Journey through France and Italy* and *The Journal to Eliza*, by Laurence Sterne, vol. 4 of *The Works of Laurence Sterne*, edited by George Saintsbury (London: Dent, 1894), xiii.
32. The Florida editors note (as does Rogers in the afterword) that Thomas Washbourne Gibbs, who had discovered *Bramine's Journal*, had shown it to Thackeray, "whose lecture on Sterne in 1851 (published in *English Humourists* [1853]) was almost certainly colored by having perused it" (*ASJ*, xxvi).
33. There is at least one notable late eighteenth-century erotic illustrated edition of *A Sentimental Journey*, published in New York in 1795. See W. B. Gerard, "The First 'Temptation' of Yorick, or, a Pirate Tale," *Shandean* 15 (2004): 107–116.
34. See Melvyn New, *"Tristram Shandy": A Book for Free Spirits* (New York: Twayne, 1994), 68–70; and Duncan Large, "'The Freest Writer': Nietzsche on Sterne," *Shandean* 7 (1995): 9–29.
35. Shklovsky's "A Parodying Novel: Sterne's *Tristram Shandy*" exists in multiple translations; for instance, a partial translation by W. George Isaak is reprinted in *Laurence Sterne: A Collection of Critical Essays*, ed. John Traugott (Englewood Cliffs, NJ: Prentice Hall, 1968), 66–89. See Anastasia Eccles, "Formalism and Sentimentalism: Viktor Shklovsky and Laurence Sterne," *New Literary History* 47, no. 4 (2016): 525–545. On Shklovsky's *Sentimental Journey*, see Melvyn New, "Three Sentimental Journeys: Sterne, Shklovsky, Svevo," *Shandean* 11 (1999–2000): 125–134.
36. Woolf's essay appears in several different forms; it first appeared in the *New York Herald Tribune* on September 23, 1928. Woolf revised the essay for her introduction to the Oxford World's Classics edition of *A Sentimental Journey*, published in 1928 and reprinted six times in the following decades; it was further revised for *The Second Common Reader*. Woolf, "The 'Sentimental Journey,'" in *Collected Essays by Virginia Woolf*, ed. Stuart N. Clarke, vol. 5 (London: Hogarth, 2009), 401–410. Citations here are taken from the Oxford World's Classics edition.
37. Woolf, introduction, xv, vii, viii.
38. Herbert Read, introduction to *A Sentimental Journey*, by Laurence Sterne (London: Scholartis, 1929), xxx, xxix.
39. Read, xxii.
40. Read, xii.
41. Read, ix.
42. Read, xi.
43. W.B.C. Watkins, *Perilous Balance: The Tragic Genius of Swift, Johnson and Sterne* (Princeton, NJ: Princeton University Press, 1939), 130.
44. Watkins, 132. On Sterne and Proust, see in particular Melvyn New, "Proust's Influence on Sterne: Remembrance of Things to Come," *Modern Language Notes* 103, no. 5 (1988): 1031–1055. An indication of Sterne's ethical relevance to modernist and postmodernist

thought can be found in New's expansion of this essay, "Reading Sterne through Proust and Levinas," in *In Proximity: Emmanuel Levinas and the Eighteenth Century*, ed. Melvyn New with Robert Bernasconi and Richard A. Cohen (Lubbock: Texas Tech University Press, 2001), 111–140; and, in the same volume, Donald R. Wehrs's brilliant reading of *A Sentimental Journey*: "Levinas and Sterne: From the Ethics of the Face to the Aesthetics of Unrepresentability," 141–165.

45. Watkins, *Perilous Balance*, 117.
46. Watkins, 101.
47. Watkins, 119.
48. Rufus Putney, "The Evolution of *A Sentimental Journey*," *Philological Quarterly* 19 (1940): 349–369; Ernest Dilworth, *The Unsentimental Journey of Laurence Sterne* (New York: King's Crown, 1948).
49. Watkins, *Perilous Balance*, 155–156.
50. Arthur Hill Cash, *Sterne's Comedy of Moral Sentiments: The Ethical Dimension of the "Journey"* (Pittsburgh: Duquesne University Press, 1966), 126.
51. Gardner D. Stout, introduction to *A Sentimental Journey through France and Italy by Mr. Yorick*, by Laurence Sterne (Berkeley: University of California Press, 1967), 47. An earlier version of this discussion appears in Stout, "Yorick's *Sentimental Journey*: A Comic 'Pilgrim's Progress' for the Man of Feeling," *ELH* 30, no. 4 (December 1963): 395–412.
52. Henri Fluchère, *Laurence Sterne: From Tristram to Yorick: An Interpretation of "Tristram Shandy,"* trans. Barbara Bray (London: Oxford University Press, 1965).
53. John M. Stedmond, *The Comic Art of Laurence Sterne: Convention and Innovation in "Tristram Shandy" and "A Sentimental Journey"* (Toronto: University of Toronto Press, 1967).
54. R. F. Brissenden, *Virtue in Distress: Studies in the Novel of Sentiment from Richardson to Sade* (London: Macmillan, 1974), 218.
55. Brissenden, 234, 240.
56. Brissenden, 242.
57. Robert Markley, "Sentiment as Performance: Shaftesbury, Sterne, and the Theatrics of Virtue," in *The New Eighteenth-Century*, ed. Felicity Nussbaum and Laura Brown (New York: Methuen, 1987), 225.
58. John A. Dussinger, "Yorick and the 'Eternal Fountain of Our Feelings,'" in *Psychology and Literature in the Eighteenth Century*, ed. Christopher Fox (New York: AMS, 1987), 259–276.
59. John Mullan, "Laurence Sterne and the 'Sociality' of the Novel," in *Sentiment and Sociability: The Language of Feeling in the Eighteenth Century* (Oxford: Clarendon, 1988), 147–200.
60. Tim Parnell, "A Story Painted to the Heart? *Tristram Shandy* and Sentimentalism Reconsidered," *Shandean* 9 (1997): 122–135.
61. Ann Jessie Van Sant, "Locating Experience in the Body: The Man of Feeling," in *Eighteenth-Century Sensibility and the Novel: The Senses in Social Context* (Cambridge: Cambridge University Press, 1993), 98–115; Jonathan Lamb, "Language and Hartleian Associationism in *A Sentimental Journey*," *Eighteenth-Century Studies* 13, no. 3 (1980): 285–312.
62. See especially Paul Goring, "Epilogue: Politeness, Performance, and Aposiopesises," in *The Rhetoric of Sensibility in Eighteenth-Century Culture* (Cambridge: Cambridge University Press, 2005), 182–201.
63. Thomas Keymer, "Marvell, Thomas Hollis, and Sterne's Maria: Parody in *A Sentimental Journey*," *Shandean* 5 (1993): 9–31. See also W. B. Gerard, "Poor Maria as Model of Empathic Response," in *The Palgrave Handbook of Affect Studies and Textual Criticism*, ed. Donald W. Wehrs and Thomas Blake (London: Palgrave Macmillan, 2017), 481–512.

64. Catherine Gordon, "'More than one handle': The Development of Sterne Illustration 1760–1820," *Words: Wai-te-Ata Studies in Literature* 4 (1974): 47–58; Gordon, *British Paintings of Subjects from the English Novel, 1740–1870* (New York: Garland, 1988).
65. W. B. Gerard, "'All that the heart wishes': Changing Views toward Sentimentality Reflected in Visualizations of Sterne's Maria, 1773–1888," *Studies in Eighteenth-Century Culture* 34 (2004): 197–269; Gerard, *Laurence Sterne and the Visual Imagination* (Aldershot, UK: Ashgate, 2006).
66. Anne Bandry, "Imitations of *Tristram Shandy*," in *Critical Essays on Laurence Sterne*, ed. Melvyn New (New York: G. K. Hall, 1998), 39–52; René Bosch, *Labyrinth of Digressions: "Tristram Shandy" as Perceived and Influenced by Sterne's Early Imitators*, trans. Piet Verhoeff (Amsterdam: Rodopi, 2007); Warren L. Oakley, *A Culture of Mimicry: Laurence Sterne, His Readers and the Art of Bodysnatching* (London: Maney, 2010); M-C. Newbould, *Adaptations of Laurence Sterne's Fiction: Sterneana, 1760–1840* (Farnham, UK: Ashgate, 2013).
67. See de Voogd and Neubauer, "Introduction."
68. See for instance Lana Asfour, *Laurence Sterne in France* (London: Continuum, 2008).
69. Laurence Sterne, *A Sentimental Journey through France and Italy by Mr. Yorick*, ed. Paul Goring (London: Penguin, 2001).
70. *"A Sentimental Journey" and "Continuation of the Bramine's Journal," with Related Texts*, ed. Melvyn New and W. G. Day (Indianapolis: Hackett, 2006).
71. *A Sentimental Journey through France and Italy*, ed. Katherine Turner (Peterborough, Ont.: Broadview, 2010).

Part One

MEN, WOMEN, AND OTHER ANIMALS

1

REFINING MASCULINITY IN YORICK'S *JOURNEY*

Courtesy, Chivalry, Gallantry

SHAUN REGAN

FOR A NOVEL THAT IS SO OFTEN ASSESSED in terms of its narrator's relationships with women, it is perhaps surprising to realize that the everyday world of *A Sentimental Journey* is populated primarily by men. Alongside the oft-noted *filles de chambre* and *grissets*, the dramatis personae of the work include a commercial cast of male figures: landlords, waiters, porters, errand boys, barbers, coachmen, and assorted other servants and serviceable employees. In the narrator's own thinking, traveling is itself conceived as a masculine activity. Yorick's sense that travel presumes maleness is embedded in the very language of the work's preface ("my dear countrymen"; "my reader, if he has been a traveler himself")—even as he also counsels prospective tourists against embarking at all (for "a man would act as wisely" by staying at home). While writing the preface, Yorick is addressed in his *desobligeant* by fellow—English, male—travelers. Although, as he insists, he does not travel to France to see "*English men*," his interactions with men are nevertheless crucial to Yorick's peripatetic endeavor to fashion himself as a gentleman (*ASJ*, 15–17). In *A Sentimental Journey*'s opening lines, Yorick is overset by the worldly knowledge of his servant, the "civil triumph" with which this "gentleman" employee counters his pronouncement regarding (unspecified) matters in France. To a significant degree, it is a desire to rectify this deficiency in his own claims to civility that propels Yorick to France in the first place (*ASJ*, 3).

This chapter explores a number of historical frameworks for interpreting masculinity in *A Sentimental Journey*, focusing particularly on modes of manly behavior that are encountered, practiced, and desired by Yorick himself. While his masculine identity might be multifaceted and eccentric, Yorick nevertheless exhibits attachments to particular behavioral ideals and preferred self-images that appeal to his sense of self and animate his imagination. Foremost among these is a model of polite masculinity and the social forms that expressed it, variously categorized under the rubric of "courtesy" or "civility"—terms that, along with their cognates ("courteous," "civil"), are used largely interchangeably in the text. The idea of politeness in the eighteenth century was informed by particular conceptions of masculine conduct. To its contemporary proponents, as Philip Carter observes, politeness was "the means to acquire a suitably refined, yet virtuous, personality that proved superior to many existing forms of manly virtue which, on account of their association with elitism, violence or boorishness, were judged detrimental to truly polite sociability." This was a form of "gentle*manliness*" that, in principle, could be cultivated by a broader stratum of men than those who, by dint of elite status, had traditionally been regarded as "gentlemen." Importantly, polite masculinity was not just a "social" but a "sociable category," which inhered in "men's capacity for gentlemanly social performance." During the course of the period, as Sterne's writing itself exemplifies, this conception of masculine refinement was recast in accordance with the priorities of sensibility. Whereas critical discussions of Sterne and sensibility have tended to efface politeness, Carter situates sensibility itself as a "significant reworking of existing definitions of male refinement."[1] As Hester Chapone stated in the essay "On Conversation" (1775), it was the "boast" of the age to have "discovered, that true politeness consists, not in modes and ceremonies, but in entering with delicacy into the feelings of our companions."[2]

Polite masculinity, with its precise (if increasingly delicate) social forms, is not the only manly mode with which Sterne engages in *A Sentimental Journey*. At various points, Yorick also evinces an interest in models of masculinity founded on notions of chivalry and aristocratic "honour." While seemingly antiquated, or increasingly outmoded, these codes were of renewed interest during the middle decades of the eighteenth century. Michèle Cohen, for instance, has traced a shift at this time "from the hegemonic ideal of politeness to a new ideal of gentlemanliness incorporating elements of a revived chivalry."[3] Although Yorick himself might have "flourish'd . . . in no court" (*ASJ*, 112), his apprehension of the world is informed by chivalric ideals and idioms that had emerged within courtly settings. The narrator's characterization of himself as a "gentle traveller" (*ASJ*, 47) can itself be said to conflate the idea of the "gentleman" traveler with visions of "gentle" knights-errant. In *A Sentimental Journey*, chivalry and honor are invoked as alternative or adapted models of polite manliness—if not necessarily ones that Yorick himself can easily access.

In relation to women, modern chivalry shaded into gallantry. While Yorick extols the virtues of his "gallant" servant, La Fleur, his own interactions with women threaten to unsettle his refined self-fashioning and more exalted notions of manly integrity and sophistication. Specifically, the central terms and concepts examined here—courtesy, chivalry, gallantry—tended to bleed into one another regarding women. Such indeterminacy testifies to both the fitful process of historical change and the intersection of value systems. Anna Bryson observes in her study of the movement away from medieval and chivalric ideals that "courtesy" continued to be used as the subject term even in later works that sought to distinguish "civility" as a new and emerging concept. Bryson also notes that "courtesy was one of the defining marks of chivalry," lending Yorick's intermittent use of "courtesy" instead of "civility" chivalric overtones.[4] Cohen indicates, moreover, that in relation to women, politeness and chivalry "share[d] a courtly language of gallantry and courtesy"; overlapping terminology thus blurred the edges between otherwise distinct historical models and modes of masculine conduct.[5] At particular moments, the terms themselves could also be conceived and evaluated in very different ways. Samuel Johnson's *Dictionary* (1755), for instance, defines "gallantry" with remarkable variety: as "splendour of appearance; show; magnificence; glittering grandeur; ostentatious finery"; "bravery; nobleness; generosity"; "courtship; refined address to women"; and "vicious love; lewdness; debauchery."[6] A further level of complexity derives from the fact that courtesy, chivalry, and gallantry all possessed French roots and resonances that also inform Yorick's encounter with France. Not least, as Marcus Tomalin outlines, in France as in England, "the lexicon of gallantry was inherently polysemous," so that "different kinds of gallantry began to emerge," with distinctions between Gallic forms of virtuous and vicious gallantry: "la belle galanterie" and "la galanterie licencieuse."[7]

At one level, this ambiguous and overlapping language contributes to the arch, ironic mode with which Sterne narrates Yorick's progress through France. The French derivations and overtones of these key terms for masculine identity and gendered interaction form an important reminder that the location of Yorick's journey is a foreign country, where they do things differently. In the eyes of many eighteenth-century Britons, certainly, France was not the locus of polite sophistication and finesse but a realm of affected mannerisms and uncertain virtue, of modes of social behavior that were merely ceremonial, if not downright vicious.[8] In the novel's wry account of Yorick's social interactions, *A Sentimental Journey* raises questions about the commensurability of English/British and French notions of politeness and masculine conduct. At the same time, it is also necessary to account for the marked difference in tone between *A Sentimental Journey* and other contemporary travel narratives concerning France, most notably Smollett's *Travels through France and Italy* (1766) but also volumes 7 and 9 of *Tristram Shandy*. For all *A Sentimental Journey*'s verbal playfulness, its entwined exploration of masculinity and social refinement also discloses the work's cosmopolitan impulses—even as Yorick's attempts at refining himself in France are shown to fray at the edges of international tolerance and cross-cultural understanding.[9]

* * *

The predominance of men in Yorick's travelogue is partly a function of the day-to-day reality of Continental tourism, supported as it was by a human infrastructure of service-industry operatives and employees.[10] *A Sentimental Journey* shows that this industry was facilitated by the interpersonal forms of civility, so that Yorick is continually engaged in small gestural interactions: low-level courtesies such as bows, compliments, and verbal pleasantries. In Bryson's historical study of the early modern period, she terms such rituals the "stereotyped gestures of deference and respect." She contends more broadly, though, that such social signifiers are not merely gestural (in the weak sense of that term): manners are not "peripheral or trivial" but rather "all pervasive." Early modern "civility" involved both a standard of conduct, in terms of control over and presentation of the self, and a "flexible" social code of submissiveness and assertion.[11] From the moment Yorick steps foot on French soil, it is this code of social behavior—the everyday rituals of this foreign environment—that he endeavors to master.

As the French setting suggests, then, this social code needs to be read in terms of nationality as well as gender. In Yorick's interactions with men, his attempts at refinement involve mimicking the civility of the French themselves. In volume 2, for instance, the Count de B**** acts with "courtesy" to Yorick, saying many "civil things" to him before asking his name "politely" (*ASJ*, 118, 111). Notably, Yorick's involvement in this polite verbal exchange is not quite as deferential as the Count's own. The register of polished *politesse* is partly undercut, for instance, when Yorick proceeds to speak "frankly" about the "excess," or "*excesse*," of French politeness (*ASJ*, 118).[12] Yorick's parting remark also complicates the civil code of assertion and submission, blurring the distinction between the conferral and the receipt of honor involved in invitations to dine: "I promised the Count I would do myself the honour of dining with him" (*ASJ*, 120). Appropriating an "honour" that, if offered, would be done *to* him, Yorick archly reveals how polite submission could itself constitute a form of social assertion. Even as he finally articulates his reservations about the French, though, Yorick still casts his hosts as "loyal," "gallant," and "generous" (*ASJ*, 118–119), and the meeting between the men remains cordial and civilized, despite their disagreement over the "*excesse*" of Gallic *politesse*. For all the episode's local ironies, it highlights the important difference between national constructions and prejudices (the larger narrative of English-French rivalry) and smaller-scale, interpersonal relationships: the possibility for (relative) concord at the level of everyday speech and conduct.

In recent decades, criticism on *A Sentimental Journey* has tended to focus more on feelings than on manners: on tactility and proximity, movements of the blood and nerves.[13] Yet it would be a mistake to overlook the prevalence, and to underestimate the significance, of this behavioral register of small-scale rituals, Yorick's "small sweet courtesies of life" (*ASJ*, 69). Such polite (in)formalities and exchanges represent the social face of commercial interaction, the granularity of existence within a civilized society. *A Sentimental Journey* is suffused with such moments of ritual courtesy, often during encounters between men. At the opening of volume 2, for instance, the bookseller informs Yorick, "civilly," that the Count de B**** is an Anglophile; Yorick proposes to reward this *politesse* through a purchase, upon which the bookseller bows (*ASJ*, 87).[14] Exceptions to this polished sociability tend to prove the rule. Despite the *grisset*'s husband being, as Yorick terms him, a "rough son of Nature," even he bows, declaring that Yorick does him "too much honour" in feeling his wife's pulse (*ASJ*, 72).[15] As elsewhere in the narrative, the excessive liberality of this sentiment suggests the limits of Gallic civility. *Politesse* here can be viewed as constraining behavior, or restraining speech, as much as facilitating polite communication: What would Yorick actually have to do, we might wonder, for the husband's polite—commercial—mask to drop? As such moments attest, Sterne's representation of French manners is to some degree an ironic distillation of British travelers' less sympathetic observations on the French and their conduct—even as Yorick hesitates to voice these same prejudices directly.

The routine civilities on display in such scenes, at once serviceable and sociable, are simultaneously a public show, a commercial lubricant, and a means of smoothing over differences. Early in Yorick's travels, for instance, Monsieur Dessein "most complaisantly" follows him: "to put me in mind of my wants." Dessein's conduct during this episode indicates that the French are both more adept at and freer with polite social forms and punctilios. A scenario of amicable contention follows, a dance of compliments and bows, which is precisely not the scene of violence that Yorick imagines as an alternative, a sword duel in Hyde Park (*ASJ*, 18–20). Inevitably, such "polite" interactions and exchanges are not always entirely smooth or successful. Nor does *A Sentimental Journey* fail to evaluate and to ironize this hyperbolized code of civil conduct: Yorick's remark about Dessein's commercialized "complaisance" is itself indicative of Sterne's arch approach to such instrumental civility. The degree to which such exchanges recur in *A Sentimental Journey* might make us suspect parody, in which such social forms are cast as a mere mystification of the commercial greasing of palms. For all the ironic subversion, though, in volume 1 especially, Sterne's "sentimental" traveler enters willingly into the polite (and commercial) spirit of things, such that this arena of low-level courtesy constitutes the social landscape through which Yorick moves: the sociable texture of *A Sentimental Journey* itself.

Above all, it is this register of polite polish to which Yorick seeks to accommodate himself—to "learn better manners" in a fuller sense than simply improving future treatment of Franciscan monks—so as to claim the gentlemanly "rights" that Continental travel could convey (*ASJ*, 11, 3). The notion of France as a finishing school for British gentlemen was in fact coming under increasing pressure at this time: as Cohen observes, by the 1760s there was a backlash in Britain against "the very notion of travel as a means of fashioning the gentleman."[16] Nor was the process ever as straightforward as simply absorbing easily interpretable modes of French conduct. Writing in 1770, John Andrews contended that Englishmen were "perfectly bewildered" by the continual "round of compliments" heard in France.[17] Nevertheless, for the most part, Yorick is a willing participant in the process of polite self-fashioning, open to the register of French sociable exchange to a degree that many contemporary travelers (and travel writers) were not. In his own social interactions, we might say, Yorick acts the gentleman, practicing and aspiring to sophisticated polish in the refining environment of France.

Although partly ironized, then, mastery of this polite social register is indispensable to Yorick as a tourist-traveler and would-be gentleman seeking to confirm his status through his conduct and largesse. Particularly pertinent to this self-presentation as a generous gentleman traveler is his "first publick act" (or social performance) of charity before the beggars at Montreuil. This scene, one of the most remarkable in the text, encapsulates both the focus on men and the polished filter through which Yorick perceives France. Remarking on the mixture of "beggary" and "urbanity" with which he is confronted as he leaves his hotel, Yorick situates the episode as only the most surprising attestation to French politeness. What we are presented with here is, of course, a highly refined view of philanthropy in action. Yorick contributes to this civilized atmosphere through ethical interpretations of his own, as with the dubious assertion that the polite "honour" he does the "dwarfish" fellow, by taking snuff from him, is more valuable than the material "charity" of giving him money. Notably, Yorick also informs us that the group of beggars is gender balanced, consisting of eight men and eight women. Yet in (narrative) practice, only one of the beggars whom Yorick actually describes is specified as female—and that, for a sly clarification regarding possible lewdness. While the chapter overall confirms the extravagant preoccupation with "urbanity" throughout French society, then, this focus on *male* conduct, even among mendicants, also reflects the fact that politeness was a code of behavior that, in public at least, was more easily displayed by men and that one of the ways of doing so was precisely through marked deference to women. "*Place aux dames*," one of the beggars exclaims, for which he is suitably rewarded by the self-styled "gentle traveller," Yorick (*ASJ*, 47–48).[18]

"Honour" is one of the key terms in the idiom of politeness in *A Sentimental Journey*, as indicated during the scenes with the Count, the *grisset*'s husband, and the beggars. Like other such terms—"courtesy," "civility," "gallantry"—"honour" possessed multiple, and potentially contradictory, connotations and resonances. Here, we can begin to distinguish between the codes of conduct to which Yorick attempts to adhere and alternative modes of masculinity that he holds in high esteem. Not least among these are forms of honor associated with military men and nobility. Yorick relates the piteous tales of a number of men formerly of service and status, most notably in "Le Patisser" and "The Sword." The former concerns a Chevalier de St. Louis reduced to selling pastries in order to earn a crust. Yorick relates that the Chevalier had been "a gallant officer"—a man of "honour and integrity." The Chevalier feels no "dishonour" in making his living through this commercial trade, illustrating his essentially honorable nature (*ASJ*, 106). In the second of these vignettes, in Brittany the Marquis d'E**** reclaims his "nobility," emblematized by his sword, by means of two decades' successful (if pointedly unspecified) commerce in Martinique. In Yorick's relation of the requisition ceremony, the sword becomes not just a hereditary manifestation of noble status but also, in its redundant potency, an affective object—a sentimental symbol that, Yorick tells us, the Marquis looks upon as a long-separated "friend." The scenario proves irresistible to emulative sympathy and masculine identification: "how I envied him his feelings," the admiring Yorick emotes (*ASJ*, 108).

Together, these tales foreground an interest in varieties of masculine "honour": of service, status, and conduct. Significantly, the figures portrayed here are as much civil as sentimental, in the affective sense of that term. The Chevalier, like the considerate beggar at Montreuil, eschews soliciting favor to forward his own interests, and the Marquis is shown making a ceremonial bow to the guardians of his sword.[19] Nor are these men the only such figures in the narrative. Yorick is also much taken with the "kindly old French officer" he encounters at the *opera comique*, whom he compares to Uncle Toby. Observing, "I honour the man whose manners are softened by a profession which makes bad men worse," Yorick conveys honor to this refined man of arms. As he also remarks here, it is for the sake of Uncle Toby that he has "a predilection for the whole corps of veterans" (*ASJ*, 76). Even the mendicant Franciscan monk, in the narrative's opening pages, has a martial backstory: following "some military services ill requited," Yorick relates, he had "abandon'd the sword and the sex together" (*ASJ*, 27). While Yorick's weeping at his graveside constitutes one of *A Sentimental Journey*'s sentimental apogees, it should not go unnoticed that, as he relates their initial contention and snuffbox-centered reconciliation, Yorick also recalls the appearance of "courtesy," and the "courteous spirit," of Father Lorenzo (*ASJ*, 7, 27).

Besides Yorick's esteem for Uncle Toby, how should we account for *A Sentimental Journey*'s combined concern with former military men and genteel conduct, swords and codes of "honour"? A partial answer is provided by Karen Lacey, who asks, "Why does fictional narrative in the eighteenth century frequently include military characters?" Lacey argues that, rather than simply being replaced by polite notions of "refinement," the code of "honour" was still active within idealizing conceptions of masculinity at this time. More particularly, even though "the demise of the sword on the battlefield was nearly complete" by the eighteenth century, the sword itself—the "fetish object" of this "honour culture"—still retained a symbolic allure.[20] As the various veterans and swordsmen catalogued in the text attest, Yorick is attracted to this venerable model of military masculinity. As with *Tristram Shandy*'s bowling-green reenactments, this narrative interest involves a displacement of actual combat. Significantly, the military men Yorick encounters have not seen recent service: these are not the casualties of the Seven Years' War (1756–1763) but veterans of earlier campaigns, such as the War of the Austrian Succession (1740–1748). By contrast to the reality of modern battlefields, with their rifles and cannons, Yorick entertains a nostalgic and symbolic vision of nobility restored and gentlemen formerly of arms.[21] The Marquis's sword is ceremonial—related to status and honor, rather than to battle—and Yorick is drawn to a model of masculine honor symbolically associated with swordsmanship but not involved in interpersonal violence, with the sword purely as the "symbol of an ancient, idealised masculinity," as Lacey puts it.[22]

This is, in some ways, a peculiar focus. Even in a denuded or deracinated form, detached from actual violence, this is a model of masculinity to which Yorick has no real, personal access, being himself neither a military man nor a nobleman. Back in the civil sphere, the code of honor and the use of swords were most associated with the practice of dueling.[23] As noted earlier, Yorick instinctively thinks in these terms, if only to disavow them, in his dance of complaisance with Monsieur Dessein (*ASJ*, 20). Although the scenario of the duel that Yorick imagines is rejected as overly antagonistic, he fails to remark that it is not altogether applicable to either man: even though the term "honour" is used of both Yorick and Dessein in these pages, neither is clearly a "man of honour" in status terms. In effect, Yorick is caught here between two distinct codes that shared the common vocabulary of "honour": honor as an ethical constituent of polite conduct, and a separate set of rules that was traditionally applicable to aristocratic men and that was embodied in an institution—dueling—that was increasingly regarded as disreputable within a broader vision of civil, and civilized, society.[24]

While this "honour" code clearly inhabits Yorick's imagination, then, the manly regions of noble honor and honorable service are not easily applicable to Yorick himself. The same might also be assumed of Yorick's interest in chivalry. Early during his time in Paris, Yorick perceives the capital in chivalric terms, watching the old and the young together "all tilting at it like fascinated knights in tournaments of yore for fame and love" (*ASJ*, 65). As with dueling, so with jousting: we are privy here to Yorick's mental landscape, again occupied with remote forms of masculine combat. The Rabelaisian innuendoes can be interpreted as Sterne casting a satiric glance at Richard Hurd's contemporaneous *Letters on Chivalry and Romance* (1762), which had positively reappraised the literature and ideals of medieval chivalry.[25] This lewd register features again in volume 2, as Yorick expresses fascination with the Marquis de B****'s personal history of amorous "tilts and tournaments": "in days of yore," Yorick relates, "he had signaliz'd himself by some small feats of chivalry in the *Cour d'amour*" (*ASJ*, 145).

Although the suggestive diction of these passages appears to undercut "chivalric" discourse, the idea of chivalry also informs *A Sentimental Journey* in broader ways. The clearest expression of Yorick's own chivalric modus operandi comes with his subsequent casting of himself as a sentimentalized Don Quixote—Yorick being, he says, "like the Knight of the Woeful Countenance, in quest of melancholy adventures" (*ASJ*, 149). It would be possible to refer this analogy to Sterne's own definition of "Cervantic humour": "describing silly & trifling Events, with the Circumstantial Pomp of great Ones" (*Letters*, 95).[26] Yet these parodic, mock-heroic overtones seem far less apparent in Yorick's travelogue than in *Don Quixote* itself. Like Tristram Shandy, Yorick voices no overt criticism of "the peerless knight of *La Mancha*" and his "honest refinements" (*TS*, 1.10.23). Addressing Yorick's comparison of himself to Don Quixote, Ann Jessie Van Sant observes a pertinent contrast between Yorick's interiorization of external events and Quixote's exteriorization of a private vision.[27] There is also another aspect to the comparison, which concerns Yorick's imaginative projections and self-fashionings: his investment in a modern form of chivalric masculinity that represented a refinement on the idea of the polite gentleman.

The cultural context for this broader invocation of chivalry, beyond the mock heroic or satirically Cervantic, was the renewed interest in chivalry in mid-eighteenth-century Britain. Cohen has argued that this rediscovered chivalry had "plural meanings" but that it possessed particular resonances for constructions of masculinity at this time.[28] In 1767, for instance, what Adam Ferguson praised in chivalry was not the martial prowess of knights but their "refined courtesy" and "scrupulous honour."[29] Hurd's own contribution to the chivalric revival is itself pertinent here. Discussing the ethical qualities of chivalric knights, he highlighted their "romantic ideas of justice; their passion for adventures; their eagerness to run to the succour of the distressed; and the pride they took in redressing wrongs, and removing grievances." For Hurd, the "courtesy, affability, and gallantry" of these adventures corresponded to the "generosity, hospitality, and courtesy" of the heroic age.[30] Although Hurd's text is more often viewed as a formative influence on the Gothic novel, we can see here correspondences with Yorick's own mode of sentimental chivalry.[31] Like these knights of yore, Sterne's "gentle" traveler is himself animated not by feats of arms but by gallant "adventures" and by offering succor to virtuous distress—even if Yorick himself cannot quite be credited with "redressing wrongs, and removing grievances."[32]

More broadly, the chivalric ideals pinpointed by Hurd, Ferguson, and others were increasingly positioned not just as consonant with but as formative influences on modern manners.[33] The chivalric "revival" was itself part rediscovery, part recognition of certain continuities between chivalry and modern ideals of politeness and masculinity. One further emphasis in contemporary discussions that is particularly significant to the chivalric cast of *A Sentimental Journey* concerns what Yorick terms the knightly focus on "love" as well as "fame" (*ASJ*, 65). Even though the code itself elaborated the required characteristics of a knight, women (at least, noblewomen) were accorded particular significance within medieval chivalry as figures of reverence, loci of meaning, and the motivating forces behind heroic adventures. "Love," as Cohen notes, was "central to the chivalric system."[34] Discussing the "respect and veneration" for women in the feudal age in *Observations Concerning the Distinction of Ranks in Society* (1771), for instance, John Millar argued that "to be in love was looked upon as one of the necessary qualifications of a knight; and he was no less ambitious of showing his constancy and fidelity to his mistress, than of displaying his military virtues."[35] In this light, the half-dozen references to the emblematized "Eliza" can be seen to play a more significant role in *A Sentimental Journey* than merely advertising Sterne's own flirtation with Eliza Draper. It is Eliza whom Yorick thinks of, for instance, when resisting the temptation to travel to Brussels on the trail of Madame de L***, having sworn "eternal fidelity" to her. This commitment has its own ironies: even as Yorick salves his conscience through reaffirming his fidelity to Eliza, he admits that she is not the first lady to whom he has devoted himself (*ASJ*, 58). This positive portrayal also obscures the status of Sterne's own liaison with Eliza Draper for the extramarital dalliance it actually was. Nevertheless, here Yorick presents his "fidelity" as a kind of chivalric troth, so that Eliza becomes the "dulcinea" that he ever has in his head, animating his better self (*Letters*, 449–450).[36] However whimsically and incongruously, Sterne's narrator thus endeavors to position Eliza as the subject of his questing devotion, as the source, symbol, and measure of his chivalric loyalty and honor.

To a significant extent, Yorick's chivalric self-fashioning—as a sentimental knight-errant, devoted to his mistress, nobly seeking out distresses—is a creaky and unsustainable fantasy. As with more recent modes of military and titled masculinity, though, the imaginative attraction of chivalry lay in its association with manly action and honor. A related term for modern chivalric behavior was "gallantry." This, again, was a word of varied import, as *A Sentimental Journey* demonstrates. As Yorick seeks to ensure his continued residence in France, for instance, he employs the term to suggest a sense of generosity and fairness that, he hopes, will secure him a passport. Intending to ask the Duc de Choiseul for his "protection," Yorick appeals to the idea of the "man of gallantry" who treats the interests of others in the same way (i.e., of equal significance) as his own (*ASJ*, 101–102). In his subsequent interview with the Count de B****, Yorick uses the term "gallantry" to describe the French national character, particularly where "invalids," such as Yorick casts himself, are concerned (*ASJ*, 109). Both of these appeals are again supported by Yorick with civil, supplicating, bows. The "gallantry" invoked here is, in combination, an ethical principle, a masculine code, and a national trait. In this regard, it is noteworthy that Tobias Smollett was also willing to praise the French military officers for their "gallantry and valour," in particular, for "that generous humanity which they exercise towards their enemies, even amidst the horrors of war." This "liberal spirit" was, Smollett averred, a laudable vestige of "antient chivalry."[37]

If gallantry, like chivalry, could relate to masculine ethics and the principles of war, both terms also possessed more everyday social resonances. The more common usage of "gallantry" concerned masculine self-presentation and relations between the sexes. As Johnson's *Dictionary* implies, "gallantry" might ambiguously conflate, or simply confuse, the chivalric ideal of love with a less exalted practice of lovemaking. John Cleland's narrower *Dictionary of Love* (first published in 1753 and republished in the 1770s with the subtitle *The Language of Gallantry Explained*) described the "professed gallant" as "one who is master of the whole academy of Love; who is perfectly versed in the languages and practice of that art. He abounds in *sentimental* expressions, without having one grain of sentiment."[38] Despite Yorick's own criticism of the idea of "making love by *sentiments*" (*ASJ*, 33), the amorous gallantry the entry describes is an art that Sterne's traveler wishes to acquire. In *A Sentimental Journey*, it is the affable servant, La Fleur, who becomes the focus of Yorick's interest in gallantry of this hue. La Fleur is another former military figure, albeit one whose service had only involved beating a drum (*ASJ*, 41). In contrast to the professional multitasking of Corporal Trim, who served Uncle Toby in the field as "valet, groom, barber, cook, sempster, and nurse," La Fleur possesses few useful skills (*TS*, 2.5.109). However, La Fleur perfectly suits Yorick's chivalric self-fashioning and his emphasis on loyalty, whether of servant to master or of suitor to mistress. Although La Fleur has few "talents" in the way of conventional service, what he does importantly offer is "fidelity"—Yorick requiring only that his "dispositions" are as soundly generous and loyal as had been initially advertised (*ASJ*, 40–42, 92).

Above all, La Fleur is described in terms of gallantry; having set out in life "gallantly" in military service, he has now become a gallant servant (*ASJ*, 41). Although critics sometimes characterize him as a Sancho Panza to Yorick's Quixote, he does not register in the narrative as a lower, plebeian presence.[39] Rather, Yorick represents La Fleur to us in terms that might be characterized as gallantry naturalized. To La Fleur's English employer, this French servant exhibits only "nature," not "art" (*ASJ*, 43). Yet this invocation of the natural itself reflects Yorick's own penchant for pastoralizing. His seeming "eternally the same" (*ASJ*, 43) aligns La Fleur with the realm of manners—in the form of unruffled self-possession—as much as with an innocent absence of cultivation. At the very least, La Fleur is a *smooth* son of nature. Later in the narrative, following the interview with the Count, La Fleur appears "so gallantly array'd" in his Sunday best. Unlike Yorick himself, his servant here exhibits a mastery of easy, fetching self-presentation. Even in Yorick's own account, then, La Fleur can be seen to improve artificially on the gifts of "nature" in order (as he puts it) to "*faire le galant*," practically achieving what Yorick himself can only verbally profess (*ASJ*, 131–132).

This interest in amorous gallantry resonates with certain strands in contemporary thinking about masculine sociability. As Ryu Susato observes, the contribution of Scottish Enlightenment writers to the midcentury debate surrounding chivalry "lies in their emphasis upon gallantry as the basis of modern manners."[40] In Hume's view, as outlined in "Of the Rise and Progress of the Arts and Sciences" (1742), gallantry was both "*generous*" and "*natural*."[41] Yet in making this case, Hume was not thinking about servants: despite his talk about "natural" behavior, the debate about gallantry concerned the conduct appropriate to gentlemen. This is a distinction that Yorick, in his descriptions of La Fleur, fails to observe. Conflating chivalry with gallantry, for instance, Yorick notes that La Fleur is as yet "unsuccessful in his feats of chivalry," without also noting the oddity of viewing a servant as a potentially chivalric figure (*ASJ*, 59). Later, the master regards his servant as a comrade in dignity: like Yorick's own, La Fleur's "honour" is apparently at stake over the sending of a return letter to Madame de L*** (*ASJ*, 64). As elsewhere, the reader is invited to read this invocation of "honour" skeptically: in ethical terms, at least, there is little that is honorable about the platitudinous adaptation, for the purposes of formal courtesy, of a drummer's letter arranging an illicit liaison (*ASJ*, 63–64). Equally significant, for my purposes here, is Yorick's sense of La Fleur's own stake in the discourses of chivalry and gallantry. From the Humean perspective, certainly, part of Yorick's eccentricity in *A Sentimental Journey* lies in viewing his servant, if not quite as a "flower" of chivalry, then as a candidate for refined masculine conduct and a touchstone for his own gallant self-fashioning.

This apparent misprision of a servant for a gallant can be read as a deflection of other, less positive thinking about gallantry at this time. In Britain, the negative assessment of gallantry was especially prominent in writings about France. In a sequel to *An Account of the Character and Manners of the French*, for instance, John Andrews focused specifically on the "notorious and scandalous Infidelity prevailing in France": if "France is a country where Gallantry is in the highest Vogue," this was because gallantry was both a means of and a mask for adultery.[42] Smollett was even more acerbic about the supposed amorous gallantry of Frenchmen. By contrast to his admiration of the honorable gallantry of French officers, Smollett argued that "that kind of address, which is here distinguished by the name of gallantry . . . is no more than his [a Frenchman's] making love to every woman who will give him the hearing." In Smollett's account, such gallantry was both indissociable from French politeness and a mode of outrageous debauchery. Gallantry might be "considered in France as an indispensable duty on every man who pretended to good breeding," but it was also the rationale given for treacherous sexual conquests: the French gallant, Smollett contested, "will even affirm, that his endeavors to corrupt your wife, or deflower your daughter, were the most genuine proofs he could give of his particular regard for your family."[43]

As a member of the servant class, La Fleur stands largely outside of this critique of the libidinous gallantry, or libertinism, of French (gentle)men. Yorick, however, as part of his apprenticeship in manners, can be viewed practicing the same mode of amorous gallantry that had outraged Smollett.[44] Even before he employs La Fleur, Yorick tries "making love" to one particular woman who will give him the hearing—as Madame de L***, the lady in question, points out (*ASJ*, 34). Here, Yorick determines on the "civil" rationale for offering Madame de L*** space in his coach despite the risk, or perhaps appeal, of the "mighty mischief" this might provoke (*ASJ*, 28–29). Yorick's amorous endeavors during this episode are not entirely successful: his attempt to be "gallant" is forestalled at one point by the "hundred little delicacies" of courteous politeness (*ASJ*, 29–30). Doubling down on his efforts in the confines of the coach, though, he partly retrieves the situation by incorporating wry observations about "the gallantry of a Frenchman" into his own, fledgling art of amorous gallantry (*ASJ*, 33).

Carol Kay has argued in her analysis of *A Sentimental Journey* in relation to Hume that Yorick's conduct toward women, such as Madame de L***, is entirely justifiable on the model of "gallantry" outlined in "Of the Rise and Progress of the Arts and Sciences." This positioning of Yorick as a satisfactorily Humean "gallant" might easily be regarded as undercritical of the gendered politics at work within contemporary conceptions of masculine sociability. Even as Hume argued that a refined form of male gallantry might "alleviate" the imbalance between the genders, he conceived of gallantry itself as (in Kay's own words) a "civilised form of authority exercised by a modern male over a modern female."[45] As Barbara Taylor observes, this "enlightened gallantry" was a way of shoring up the sexual distinction between (delicate) women and newly feminized, polite men, a "nonviolent expression of male ascendancy."[46] Later in the century, Mary Wollstonecraft produced a wholesale critique of such patronizing male conduct. Distinguishing "the modest respect of humanity, and fellow-feeling" from the "libidinous mockery of gallantry," Wollstonecraft disparaged gallantry as a "heartless attention to the sex," which was "reckoned so manly, so polite" but which was, in her view, a pernicious "vestige of gothic manners."[47] As Taylor also indicates, though, during the middle decades of the century, more subtle attempts were being made in Britain to discriminate between "vicious" and "virtuous" gallantry, for instance, in David Fordyce's *Dialogues Concerning Education* (1745).[48]

Yorick's interactions with women walk a fine line between these two ways to "*faire le galant*." By paying more sympathetic attentions to women than did the libertine conduct and sexualized impositions associated with the elite, Yorick strives to fashion a newly sentimentalized form of gallantry that is expunged of overt sexual conquest. Accordingly, in recounting his dealings with the *fille de chambre* of Madame de R***, Yorick defends his sexual rectitude, distinguishing between his amorous/sexual impulses and his chaste/decorous actions (*ASJ*, 121–124). For all the innuendoes that saturate this defense, and despite the incredulity of La Fleur (who regards it as "*deroger à noblesse*"), Yorick is thus able to claim that he will leave Paris with his "virtue" intact (at least, as secure as when he entered the city; *ASJ*, 129). Yet this is not to argue that Sterne's "gentle" traveler is entirely consistent or that his "gallantry" is always securely virtuous. A case in point appears during *A Sentimental Journey*'s sole Italian episode, in which Yorick stands in for the "*Chichesbeo*" to the Marquesina di F*** (*ASJ*, 78). That Yorick makes no comment on the situation of a *cicisbeo* marks once again his difference from the traveling Smollett. Turning his sights on Italian "gallantry," Smollett had proclaimed,

"I would rather be condemned for life to the gallies, than exercise the office of a cicisbeo, exposed to the intolerable caprices and dangerous resentment of an Italian virago."[49] In contrast to Smollett, Yorick appears to embrace his role, if not necessarily the lady herself. However we interpret his pleasurable "connection" with the Marquesina, this flirtatious scenario of Italianate gallantry undoubtedly risks undercutting Yorick's aspirations to "virtuous" gallantry and the chivalric "fidelity" he had earlier pledged to his beloved Eliza (*ASJ*, 78).

Masculine "gallantry," Yorick's amorous adventures suggest, could connote chivalric conduct, decorous flirtation, or sexual accomplishment. The ambiguity created by complexities of language, behavioral mode, and national location also complicates Yorick's claims to "honour" as a social and ethical quality. At the milliner's, for instance, the *grisset*'s "courtesy" is, conjecturally at least, related to her "beauty." While the scene proceeds largely through the language and gestures of politeness (the *grisset* curtsies, requests Yorick's "complaisance" in stepping into the shop, and finally praises Yorick for the "politeness" and the "honour" he shows her), the encounter itself is more erotically charged than (British) standards of politeness or sensibility would allow (*ASJ*, 70, 75).[50] Later, at the Parisian salons, Yorick engages in a three-week campaign of courtesy that involves being obsequiously "of every man's opinion" he meets in order to advance socially; the effect is only briefly satisfying. Pointedly, "every sentiment of honour" finally revolts against this "*beggarly system*" of ingratiation, which becomes a "most vile prostitution" of Yorick's—masculine—self (*ASJ*, 147–148).[51] For a time in the Bourbonnais, Sterne's "sentimental" traveler is able temporarily to revitalize his soul through an equal but opposite reaction against "Art" in search of "Nature" (*ASJ*, 148). Like La Fleur, the region's peasants are "simple" souls, characterized by a natural "festivity" of "temper" that appeals to Yorick yet that he himself does not fully possess (*ASJ*, 43). This pastoral retrieval of his salon-tainted honor can, then, only ever be partial. Having done the "honours" of the bedchamber, the final chapter sees Yorick playing up his cough, so as not to have to relinquish one of the two beds in the main room of the inn. Disingenuously, he claims that his verbal "ejaculation"—"O my God!"—is part of his "prayers" and thus covered under article 3 of the evening's "treaty of peace." Yorick's conduct here is, we might say, simultaneously discourteous and ungallant, while his defense of his "word and honour" represents the final corrosion of a discourse of "honour" that has come under considerable strain during the course of his Continental peregrinations (*ASJ*, 161–165).

Yorick's varied and imperfect adaptation to French society, his uneven success in his attempt to "learn better manners," constitutes much of the comic appeal of *A Sentimental Journey*. The verbal richness and indeterminacy of his travelogue also reflects the complex nature of masculinity at this time, not least in the French context of the *Journey*. As Yorick's travels demonstrate, masculinity is at once a lived reality, an identity construction, and an imaginative projection. In this regard, Yorick can usefully be situated in relation to the distinction Anthony Fletcher makes between "manhood" and "masculinity." In broad terms, Fletcher posits a shift during the eighteenth century from "manhood"—a public, performed role (or set of roles)—to "masculinity," a more interiorized experience. As an "internalized identity—an interiority of the mind and emotions"—masculinity is thus opposed to "any sense of role-playing" of the kind that would be exposed in the 1770s by the publication of Chesterfield's *Letters to His Son* (1774).[52] *A Sentimental Journey* shows, though, that even an "internalized" masculinity had to exist, and to adopt roles, within a contemporary social context. Just as masculinity in the text concerns men other than Yorick, the Continental excursion it portrays is played out in more public arenas of sociability than the solitary self. At the same time, the construction of masculinity in *A Sentimental Journey* partly inheres in the imaginative appeal to Yorick of masculine modes or styles to which he is emotionally attached but that he is unable personally to inhabit. Such interior imaginings are not merely fanciful: they possess a performative force, influencing behavior and values, meaning and memory. In the novel's multilayered investigation of these verbal registers and scenes of manhood, the interior landscape as well as the social, *A Sentimental Journey* fascinatingly documents the shifting formation of masculinity during the third quarter of the eighteenth century.

NOTES

1. Philip Carter, *Men and the Emergence of Polite Society, Britain, 1660–1800* (Harlow, UK: Pearson, 2001), 1, 6, 209, 93.
2. Hester Chapone, *Miscellanies in Verse and Prose* (London, 1775), 29. Chapone's essay is concerned with transgressions of polite and moral principles, especially within fashionable conversation.
3. Michèle Cohen, "'Manners' Make the Man: Politeness, Chivalry and the Construction of Masculinity, 1750–1830," *Journal of British Studies* 44, no. 2 (April 2005): 325.
4. Anna Bryson, *From Courtesy to Civility: Changing Codes of Conduct in Early Modern England* (Oxford: Clarendon, 1998), 47, 35. On the shifting vocabulary of manners up to the nineteenth century, see also Keith Thomas, *In Pursuit of Civility: Manners and Civilization in Early Modern England* (New Haven, CT: Yale University Press, 2018), especially chapter 1.
5. Cohen, "'Manners' Make the Man," 319, 325.
6. Samuel Johnson, *A Dictionary of the English Language in which the Words are Deduced from Their Originals and Illustrated in Their Different Significations by Examples from the Best Writers*, 2 vols. (London, 1755), vol. 1, n.p.
7. Marcus Tomalin, "Coquettes and Gallants: (Re-)Assessing Eighteenth-Century English Translations of French Memoirs," *Journal for Eighteenth-Century Studies* 36, no. 1 (March 2013): 90.

8. For the range of viewpoints, see for instance Gerald Newman, *The Rise of English Nationalism: A Cultural History, 1740–1830* (London: Weidenfeld and Nicolson, 1987); Robin Eagles, *Francophilia in English Society, 1748–1815* (Basingstoke, UK: Macmillan, 2000); John Richard Moores, *Representations of France in English Satirical Prints, 1740–1832* (Basingstoke, UK: Palgrave Macmillan, 2015).
9. The broader relationship at this time between English masculinity, politeness, and France is discussed in Michèle Cohen, *Fashioning Masculinity: National Identity and Language in the Eighteenth Century* (London: Routledge, 1996), especially chapter 3. I explore the cosmopolitan impulses of *A Sentimental Journey* more fully in "Peripatetic Philosophy: Sterne and Cosmopolitanism," *Textual Practice* 31, no. 2 (2017): 265–282.
10. For an overview of the personnel and practicalities, see Jeremy Black, *The British Abroad: The Grand Tour in the Eighteenth Century* (Stroud, UK: Sutton, 1992).
11. Bryson, *From Courtesy to Civility*, 208, 2, 96.
12. Jakub Lipski also remarks the apparent subversion of the Count's "politeness and human interest in the other's plight" in this scene. Lipski, "The Masquerade Metaphor and the Paradoxes of Sentiment in *A Sentimental Journey*," in *Sterne, Tristram, Yorick: Tercentenary Essays on Laurence Sterne*, ed. Melvyn New, Peter de Voogd, and Judith Hawley (Newark: University of Delaware Press, 2016), 193.
13. See especially John Mullan, *Sentiment and Sociability: The Language of Feeling in the Eighteenth Century* (Oxford: Clarendon, 1988); Ann Jessie Van Sant, *Eighteenth-Century Sensibility and the Novel: The Senses in Social Context* (Cambridge: Cambridge University Press, 1993).
14. If anyone is at fault here, it is again Yorick. Despite stating that the bookseller's politeness obliges him to make a purchase, Yorick does not actually do so. Instead, he simply leaves with the *fille de chambre*: "As I had nothing more to stay me in the shop" (*ASJ*, 87).
15. In *The British Abroad*, Black quotes from a number of contemporary sources that cast light on the husband's behavior. In 1729, for instance, an anonymous tourist noted that women dominated business in France (a tradeswoman's husband being "but a cypher"), while in 1734 a contributor to the *General Evening Post* commented pertinently on the "freedoms" that Frenchmen allowed to their wives: "a Frenchman will almost suffer you to court his wife before his face" (27, 194).
16. Cohen, *Fashioning Masculinity*, 60.
17. John Andrews, *An Account of the Character and Manners of the French; with Occasional Observations on the English*, 2 vols. (London, 1770), 1:138.
18. It is worth noting that it is not only the lower orders who practice these polite flatteries in *A Sentimental Journey*. Revealing in this regard is the artful flatterer, with whom Yorick is so intrigued in Paris. Despite his lowered condition as a "beggar," Yorick notes that he "bow'd" during his supplication and has an air of "frugal *propretè*" about him (*ASJ*, 125). In effect, the flatterer reverses the poles of this earlier scene at Montreuil: rather than an urbane beggar, the flatterer more closely resembles a begging gentleman.
19. In this emphasis on civility and status as much as sensibility and soldiery, these tales depart from the more pathos-laden narratives discussed by Simon Parkes in "Wooden Legs and Tales of Sorrow Done: The Literary Broken Soldier of the Late Eighteenth Century," *Journal for Eighteenth-Century Studies* 36, no. 2 (June 2013): 190–207.
20. Karen Lacey, *A Class Apart: The Military Man in French and British Fiction, 1740–1789* (Bern: Peter Lang, 2016), 2–3, 35, 26.
21. Notably, in Toby's "apologetical oration" for his hobbyhorse in *Tristram Shandy*, he himself asks, "What is war, but the getting together of quiet and harmless people, with their swords in their hands" (*TS*, 6.32.557).
22. Lacey, *Class Apart*, 37.

23. On the honor code and its relationship to dueling, see Markku Peltonen, *The Duel in Early Modern England: Civility, Politeness and Honour* (Cambridge: Cambridge University Press, 2003); and Donna Andrew, *Aristocratic Vice: The Attack on Duelling, Suicide, Gambling, and Adultery in Eighteenth-Century England* (New Haven, CT: Yale University Press, 2013), chapters 1 and 2.
24. On the ambiguity of the "man of honour" in this context, see Andrew, *Aristocratic Vice*, 22–23.
25. On the Rabelaisian innuendoes here, see for instance Melvyn New, "Proust's Influence on Sterne: Remembrance of Things to Come," *Modern Language Notes* 103, no. 5 (1988): 1031–1032; and Paul Goring, introduction to *A Sentimental Journey through France and Italy*, by Laurence Sterne (London: Penguin, 2001), xxix.
26. The letter, whose addressee is unknown, is dated roughly to summer 1759.
27. Van Sant, *Eighteenth-Century Sensibility*, 99.
28. Cohen, "'Manners' Make the Man," 315. Also relevant here is Lacey's argument that "it is necessary to separate the *idea* of chivalry from the chivalric romance—the latter *might* have been discredited by Cervantes, but the former lingered on in the *imaginaire* of the ancient nobility and in contemporary assessments of masculinity" (*Class Apart*, 14).
29. Adam Ferguson, *An Essay on the History of Civil Society* (Edinburgh, 1767), 308.
30. Richard Hurd, *Letters on Chivalry and Romance* (London, 1762), 13, 15, 35–36.
31. On Hurd and Gothic, see for instance Markman Ellis, *The History of Gothic Fiction* (Edinburgh: Edinburgh University Press, 2000). As Ellis notes, Hurd associated the Gothic with "highly-valued medieval characteristics like gallantry, loyalty, heroism and chivalry" (23).
32. Noting the "decline of bearing arms as a core attribute of masculinity" during this period, John Tosh observes acutely that "the vogue for medieval chivalry . . . far from socialising men to military ways, displaced valour and danger into a safe haven of agreeable fantasy." Tosh, "The Old Adam and the New Man: Emerging Themes in the History of English Masculinities, 1750–1850," in *English Masculinities, 1660–1800*, ed. Tim Hitchcock and Michèle Cohen (London: Longman, 1999), 222.
33. This recognition is particularly significant within Hume's thinking about contemporary commercial society. As Ryu Susato notes, for instance, "Hume consistently sought the origins of some of the more positive aspects of modern civilization in chivalry, while simultaneously criticizing its extravagant and violent attributes." Susato, "The Idea of Chivalry in the Scottish Enlightenment: The Case of David Hume," *Hume Studies* 33, no. 1 (April 2007): 171n1.
34. Cohen, "'Manners' Make the Man," 320.
35. John Millar, *Observations Concerning the Distinction of Ranks in Society* (London, 1771), 56–57. On the role of women in eighteenth-century discussions of chivalry, see also Karen O'Brien, *Women and Enlightenment in Eighteenth-Century Britain* (Cambridge: Cambridge University Press, 2009), 136–151.
36. Sterne to John Wodehouse, August 23, 1765.
37. Tobias Smollett, *Travels Through France and Italy*, ed. Frank Felsenstein (Oxford: Oxford University Press, 1979), 135.
38. John Cleland, *The Dictionary of Love* (London, 1753), n.p. *The Dictionary* was a partial translation of Jean-François Dreux du Radier's *Dictionnaire d'amour* (1741); Cleland here adapts Radier's description of the "Galant." As Hal Gladfelder indicates, Cleland's "forensic" translation was geared toward "unmasking the essentially criminal aims underlying the cant of professed lovers." Gladfelder, *Fanny Hill in Bombay: The Making and Unmaking of John Cleland* (Baltimore: Johns Hopkins University Press, 2012), 170.
39. For the comparison between La Fleur and Sancho, see for instance Lipski, "Masquerade Metaphor," 195.

40. Susato, "Idea of Chivalry," 160.
41. David Hume, "Of the Rise and Progress of the Arts and Sciences," in *Essays Moral, Political and Literary*, ed. Eugene F. Miller (Indianapolis: Liberty Classics, 1987), 132.
42. John Andrews, preface to *Reflections on the Too Prevailing Spirit of Dissipation and Gallantry; Shewing its Dreadful Consequences to Publick Freedom* (London, 1771), 50.
43. Smollett, *Travels*, 57, 59–60.
44. The phrase "apprenticeship in manners" is adapted from Elizabeth Davidson, "*A Sentimental Journey*, Volume I: Yorick's Apprenticeship of Manners," *College Language Association Journal* 37, no. 4 (June 1994): 453–466.
45. Hume, "Of the Rise and Progress," 133; Carol Kay, *Political Constructions: Defoe, Richardson, and Sterne in Relation to Hobbes, Hume, and Burke* (Ithaca, NY: Cornell University Press, 1988), 253–254.
46. Barbara Taylor, "Feminists versus Gallants: Manners and Morals in Enlightenment Britain," *Representations* 87 (Summer 2004): 135. See also Jenny Davidson, *Hypocrisy and the Politics of Politeness: Manners and Morals from Locke to Austen* (Cambridge: Cambridge University Press, 2004), chapter 3.
47. Mary Wollstonecraft, *"A Vindication of the Rights of Men" and "A Vindication of the Rights of Woman,"* ed. Sylvana Tomaselli (Cambridge: Cambridge University Press, 1995), 211, 179. On Wollstonecraft's critique of chivalry and gallantry, see also Claudia L. Johnson, *Equivocal Beings: Politics, Gender and Sentimentality in the 1790s: Wollstonecraft, Radcliffe, Burney, Austen* (Chicago: University of Chicago Press, 1995), chapter 1.
48. Taylor, "Feminists versus Gallants," 133. Taylor misdates the work to 1760.
49. Smollett, *Travels*, 230–231.
50. Pertinently, John Scott, Earl of Clonmell (1739–1798), observed in the marginal annotations to his copy of *A Sentimental Journey* that the portrayal of Yorick's encounter with the *grisset* involved "describing French Manners by an Incident of Gallantry." See Paul Franssen, "'Great Lessons of Political Instruction': The Earl of Clonmell Reads Sterne," *Shandean* 2 (1990): 158.
51. Yorick's reaction against this system of flattery interestingly echoes Shaftesbury's private concerns, as expressed in his notebooks, about seeking the approval of others: "Must not I (if this familiarity be aim'd at) prostitute myself in the strongest manner, & be a Hippocrite in the horridest degree?" Quoted in Lawrence E. Klein, *Shaftesbury and the Culture of Politeness: Moral Discourse and Cultural Politics in Early Eighteenth-Century England* (Cambridge: Cambridge University Press, 1994), 94n14.
52. Anthony Fletcher, *Gender, Sex and Subordination in England, 1500–1800* (New Haven, CT: Yale University Press, 1995), 322–323. See also Tosh, "Old Adam," 230–233.

2

YORICK'S WAR

Patriot Politics, Military Men, and Willing Women in *A Sentimental Journey*

JULIA BANISTER

> In the union of the sexes, both pursue one common object, but not in the same manner. . . . The one should be active and strong, the other passive and weak. . . . The violence of his desires depends on her charms; it is by means of these she should urge him to the exertion of those powers which nature hath given him. . . . Hence arise the various modes of attack and defence between the sexes, the boldness of one sex and the timidity of the other; and, in a word, that bashfulness and modesty with which nature hath armed the weak, in order to subdue the strong.[1]

STERNE'S RISE FROM COUNTRY CLERGYMAN to London literary celebrity occurred in a decade shaped by the Seven Years' War (1756–1763). Literary critics have long been interested in, and in disagreement about, Sterne's writing on war. The debate about the significance of Sterne's dedication of the London edition of the first volumes of *Tristram Shandy* to William Pitt, the "patriot" politician and architect of Britain's Seven Years' War victories, is a case in point. For Thomas Keymer, Sterne's address to Pitt "pulls markedly away from the aggressive expansionism that was the dominant Whig posture of the day," and this is one of several indications that the self-consciously contemporary *Tristram Shandy* pulls back, albeit it in "its own characteristically ludic and elliptical way," from celebrating British success in the Seven Years' War.[2] In contrast, Carol Kay reads the dedication to Pitt as one of several indications that "Sterne likes war" or, as Madeleine Descargues argues, albeit more cautiously, that Sterne "shares probably in the national pride of his compatriots over the British successes in the Seven Years War."[3] Both Kay and Descargues acknowledge the danger of trying to decode the serious playfulness of *Tristram Shandy* but agree that it is, as Descargues puts it, a text in which "bellicose aspirations" are not countered by "corrective discourse."[4]

This chapter suspends the question of whether Sterne's writing critiques or supports nationalistic militarism. Kathleen Wilson argues that during the 1750s public opinion was dominated by "imperial anxieties and widespread francophobia" but also pervasive "fears of the emasculation and degeneracy of the British body politic." These fears, Wilson suggests, led to "efforts to eradicate behaviors and practices (sexual and consumer as well as political) that blurred gender lines," notably male behaviors that were deemed to be effeminate.[5] Philip Carter and Robert Jones have shown that these concerns persisted into the 1760s and 1770s.[6] Given this, the aim here is to place *A Sentimental Journey* in relation to not the nationalism of the war years but the gender politics—captured in Rousseau's binary equation of activity and strength, violence and boldness, with manliness—that had equal currency in this period.[7] Sterne scholars have focused their discussion of war and militarism on *Tristram Shandy*, the first installments of which were written during the Seven Years' War but which avoids addressing that war directly: it is the Siege of Namur by the Allies (1695), part of the Nine Years' War (1688–1697), and the battles of the War of the Spanish Succession (1701–1714) that are re-enacted on the bowling green at Shandy Hall, contained by the garden wall as a form of recreation.[8] In contrast, though *A Sentimental Journey* was written after the Seven Years' War, it is set during that war, and Yorick's journey brings him into direct contact with his nation's enemy. Tristram may have a military uncle, but Yorick is confronted by a number of French military men. However, rather than treat these men as foes, *A Sentimental Journey* calls on their services. Young and old, serving and retired, the French military men show Yorick, through negative and positive example, how best to combine sentimentality with the violence of desires that, as the sentimentalist Rousseau has it, equip a man for the heterosexual game of "attack and defence."

* * *

In the period between the publication of the first volumes of *Tristram Shandy*, in December 1759, and the first volumes of *A Sentimental Journey*, in February 1768, Britain was shaped by military successes orchestrated by a politician who, a decade earlier, had been out of high office. In the early 1750s, William Pitt had sought to further his career by drawing together disparate opposition politicians under the banner of "patriotism."[9] The term "patriotism" had been claimed in the 1730s by a previous generation of opposition politicians, but as Matthew McCormack has argued, the patriot politicians of the midcentury employed a new kind of "antigallican, Protestant and imperial rhetoric" in the service of "bellicose nationalism."[10]

This form of patriotism courted public opinion by criticizing the modern morals and manners of the social elite: Pitt and his fellow patriots "identified themselves with the nation at large and its manly ancient virtues, against the effeminate vice of the court and the newly moneyed."[11] As this suggests, though, Pittite patriotism was equally a populist political agenda and a partisan intervention in gender politics. The patriots "promoted a model of manliness that embodied the supposedly national traits of sincerity, straightforwardness, courage and independence," and the close relationship between the midcentury patriots' politics and their binary notions of masculinity contributed, McCormack concludes, to a shift in the concept of citizenship in the early nineteenth century "from a paradigm of rank to one of gender," thereby "hardening the boundaries between (independent) men and (dependent) women."[12]

Although Sterne referred in his correspondence to the Seven Years' War as one of "the greatest Concerns that ever affected the Interest of this kingdome" (*Letters*, 249), he seems to have had little interest in the battles with which Pitt was, initially, most concerned: those fought for trade and empire in America and India.[13] Indeed, Sterne opposed a hike in land tax (1758), proposed by Pitt as a means to fund the nation's military commitments.[14] However, in several letters written to Stephen Croft, squire of the parish of Stillington, Yorkshire, and the father of an army officer, Sterne mentions the war in Europe. In a letter of December 1760, one month after King Frederick of Prussia's attack on the Austrians at Torgau, Sterne provides grimly sensational reportage on what had been a hard-fought and marginal victory for Britain's ally: "'Tis fear'd the war is quite over in Germany; never was known such havock amongst troops—I was told yesterday by a Colonel, from Germany, that out of two battalions of nine hundred men, to which he belong'd, but seventy-one left!" (*Letters*, 178).[15] That said, Sterne's interest in the political debate about the war in Europe brought him into closer contact with patriot politics. At the start of the war, Pitt had argued against committing men and money to the hostilities between Prussia and Austria, hostilities that affected the British monarch's ancestral lands in Germany. By 1760, Pitt had come around to the view that Britain should continue to support the war on the Continent, and with it the king's interests, despite the rapidly escalating cost.[16] In a letter dated February 1761, Sterne writes at length about watching a "pitched battle" in the Commons, one that the "great combattant [*sic*]," William Pitt, was obliged to miss on account of being seized by a "political fit of the gout," leaving Pitt's beleaguered allies to defend the patriot position (*Letters*, 183–184).[17]

Sterne's correspondence only confirms his interest in, not enthusiasm for, patriot politics, but it is possible to read *Tristram Shandy*'s central military man as a model for the manliness of "sincerity, straightforwardness, courage and independence" that the patriots promoted in the midcentury. Uncle Toby's "*apologetical oration*" defends the manly virtues of men engaged in the profession of arms on the basis that their desire for war is as much a desire to serve others as it is to satisfy their own ambitions.[18] Toby asserts, "when a man, whose profession is arms, wishes, as I have done, for war," he is motivated by both "public spirit and a thirst of glory" (*TS*, 6.32.554, 556). In response to Yorick's assertion that "*so soft and gentle a creature, born to love, to mercy, and kindness, as man is, was not shaped for [war]*" (*TS*, 6.32.557), Toby further assures his audience that men who choose the life of a soldier do so from a sincere desire to protect others: "For what is war? what is it, *Yorick*, when fought as ours has been, upon principles of *liberty*, and upon principles of *honour*—what is it, but the getting together of quiet and harmless people, with their swords in their hands, to keep the ambitious and the turbulent within bounds?" (*TS*, 6.32.557). For Toby, the sincerity of the soldier's desire to help others is underpinned by his capacity for sentimental feeling. The man whose heart inclines him in "leap first down into the trench, where he is sure to be cut in pieces," is equally able, Toby claims, to "ache for the distresses of war" (*TS*, 6.32.556).

For all Toby's efforts to defend his connection between sentimentality and militarism, though, his seeming harmlessness is also made manifest in his dealings with widow Wadman. Susan Staves argues that *Tristram Shandy* "share[s] in the common patriotism and pride of the English over their successes in the Seven Years' War" but that Sterne "presents his version of the new masculine character—the man of feeling purged of traditional heroic violence, aggression, and sexuality—in the guise of the most stereotypical old hero, the soldier."[19] Certainly, the text endorses Trim for his "honest heart" when he refutes the idea that the profession of soldering is such that violence and aggression will always "trample" on the "cries of the unfortunate": "I never refused quarter in my life to any man who cried out for it;—but to a woman or a child, . . . before I would level my musket at them, I would lose my life a thousand times" (*TS*, 2.17.160–161). Yet as Keymer writes, the "imaginative pleasures" Toby derives from his bowling-green war games seem to be "personally debilitating" when he is offered the possibility of sexual activity.[20] Carol Watts observes that Sterne was, on the page as he was in life, "a child of military barracks" and that, much though *Tristram Shandy* endorses Toby's position on the soldier as "benevolent patriot," Toby's failings with widow Wadman contribute to the text's "fear of impotency."[21] Indeed, for Kay, Sterne's own military enthusiasm extends in *Tristram Shandy* to a "yearn[ing] for the vigorous militarism of a more sexually segregated society," which "should probably be called something like 'remasculinization.'"[22]

It is possible to argue, as Frank Brady has done, that *Tristram Shandy* makes a serious case for the "joys of the senses," that is, for the physiological similarity between sentimental and sexual feeling; but if so, the text does not route this through its central military man.[23] Of course, Toby's inability to secure widow Wadman is presented with kindness as well as comedy: "so naked and defenceless did [Toby] sit upon the same sopha with widow Wadman," Sterne writes, "that a generous heart would have wept to have won the game of him" (*TS*, 9.23.778). But for all Sterne's sympathy for Toby, the wounded soldier is, as Melvyn New argues, too sensitive to be sexual.[24] In turning to Sterne's "other" engagement with war and militarism, *A Sentimental Journey*, I want to suggest that he returns to the figure of the military man in order to (re)write that man as a model for a kind of masculinity that elaborates upon the masculinism that the patriots had promoted in the midcentury by joining sentimentality to a Rousseauian understanding of sexuality. *A Sentimental Journey*—a text in which, as Eve Kosofsky Sedgwick suggests, "every touch, every relationship, every exchange, seems to beg to be translated into sexual language"—is, for Elizabeth W. Harries, less affected by the "strange mix of misogyny and male anxiety" evident in *Tristram Shandy*.[25] Following Sedgwick and Harries, I suggest that *A Sentimental Journey* drafts into its pages a series of military men who, unlike the quiet and harmless Toby, show that sensibility can be used to legitimize the "strong and active" masculinity required for the sexual battle of "attack and defence."

* * *

During the Seven Years' War, Britain acted with multiple allies and against multiple enemies, but, as Stephen Conway observes, in the popular imagination the conflict was "unambiguously . . . an Anglo-French struggle," and France the "principal enemy."[26] British hostility to France endured after the peace of 1763: although the "extraordinary succession of victories brought an unprecedented accession of power and prestige" to Britain in the 1760s, that power had a "brittle quality," and by the end of the decade, pamphleteers were debating furiously about the strength of Britain's and France's military establishments.[27] The cultural entrepreneurs of the later eighteenth century were quick to identify the propaganda potential both of the militaristic patriot in *Tristram Shandy* on the one hand and of Sterne's tales of an Englishman's travels in France on the other. As Warren Oakley has documented, one eighteenth-century dramatist, Leonard MacNally, found in *Tristram Shandy* material enough to fashion a "positive patriotic image of British nationhood" for the 1780s.[28] Likewise, M-C. Newbould has observed that *A Sentimental Journey* was adapted in ways that rehearsed the "negative nationalism [that] clearly continued to exert a lasting hold on the popular imagination."[29] And yet the Yorick of *A Sentimental Journey* seems not to be attuned to national enmities and insecurities, as he claims to have forgotten that England and France are at war and that the conflict might have ramifications for traveling civilians: "I had left London with so much precipitation, that it never enter'd my mind that we were at war with France; and . . . that there was no getting there without a passport" (*ASJ*, 91).

Yorick, "being but a poor sword's-man," finds his mettle tested when dueling, figuratively, with Monsieur Dessein for a carriage, but it is only when faced with possible imprisonment in Paris for forgetting his passport that he characterizes a Frenchman as his enemy, for he imagines the aristocrat to whom he must appeal for help as a hostile opponent: "I should not like to have my enemy take a view of my mind, when I am going to ask protection of any man: for which reason I generally endeavour to protect myself" (*ASJ*, 101). Yorick appeals successfully to Monsieur Le Count de B**** on the basis of their shared love of Shakespeare, but their conversation is not without tension. Yorick bristles at having to inhabit the role of a jester as his means to the ends of a passport. He makes it known to the count that the English court no longer needs a fool: "our manners have been so gradually refining, that our court at present is so full of patriots, who wish for *nothing* but the honours and wealth of their country—and our ladies are all so chaste, so spotless, so good, so devout—that there is nothing for a jester to make a jest of" (*ASJ*, 115). The hyperbole works against Yorick here, for this jest turns him into a jester, and with this Sterne punctures the pomposity of his uncharacteristic prudishness and patriotic boasting.

While the text does not endorse Yorick's sudden and uncharacteristic effusion of nationalistic and patriotic pride, it does accommodate his frequent surges of sexual passion. For Susan Lamb, the interest in *A Sentimental Journey* lies not in Yorick's social interactions with French men but in his encounters with French women; in her view, the text follows "the usual . . . contemporary British [travel writer's] interest in monks, beggars, military men, peasants, and the Paris elite" but adds to this something that the serious male traveler writing for a "polite" readership could not: women as objects of "erotic knowledge."[30] This can be developed further to indicate how far Yorick combines his sentimental journey with sexual adventuring and in so doing combines sentimentality and "strong and active" sexuality.[31] On arrival in Calais, Yorick sees an unaccompanied woman and experiences what he initially identifies as pure sentiment: "When the heart flies out before the understanding," he opines, "it saves the judgment a world of pains." However, the briefest of observations are enough for Yorick to identify a "pleasurable ductility about her," and this leads to two, somewhat premature, exclamations: "—Good God! how a man might lead such a creature as this round the world with him!—" (*ASJ*, 22). To be "ductile" is to be impressible and malleable, and the text establishes a connection between what Yorick terms "pleasurable ductility" and his enthusiastically imagining that the lady might be "led," as both terms idealize gender relations in which women give way willingly to the force of a man's sexual desire. The lady at Calais is the first of the ductile women in the text: the *grisset* encourages Yorick to press down on her pulse; the *fille de chambre* allows Yorick to place her newly heavy purse back in her hand.

Yorick's encounter with the lady at Calais indicates how, in the text, sentimental feeling is employed to legitimize a specific kind of sexual desire. In Elizabeth Kraft's view, *A Sentimental Journey* accommodates with ethical sincerity women as desiring subjects: "the ebb and flow of aggression and passivity in erotic relationships is not gendered behavior but the rhythm of mutual longing."[32] True enough, Yorick is not a Mr. B or a Lovelace, but by gendering and eroticizing "ductility," the text indulges in a Rousseauian fantasy of the genders as "pursu[ing] one common object, but not in the same manner": women may be actively willingly and willingly active, but their willingness must include the specific willingness to, at some stage in the seduction process, capitulate. Rousseau's Sophie may have the power to "subdue the strong," but she, like Yorick's women, can conquer only by being conquered. As the binary counterpart to the willingly "ductile" woman, the man of feeling is allowed to exercise the "violence" of his desires with a kind of rigidity and force that the woman does not share. This difference helps to explain why Yorick finds himself most exercised about his masculinity when he is taken up by Paris's beau monde. Having briefly accepted the jester's identity in return for a passport, Yorick finds that he must once again perform a role required of him by others in order to be accepted into French high society. Yorick eventually deplores what he sees as a "dishonest *reckoning*": "it was the gain of a slave—every sentiment of honour revolted against it" (*ASJ*, 148). The "gain" seems implicitly dishonorable and effectively demands a ductility that exposes Yorick to a *"beggarly system"* founded on a "vile prostitution," terms that suggest the loss of a masculine identity founded on having the liberty to exercise one's own will rather than capitulate to others' desires.

Like *Tristram Shandy*, *A Sentimental Journey* responds to the development in the eighteenth century of a culture of sensibility that permitted and encouraged the feminization of masculinity but in so doing destabilized notions of manliness. G. J. Barker-Benfield has argued that, while many men valued this culture for, among other things, creating opportunities for heterosociality, others were anxious about losing old privileges and distinctions.[33] Yorick's sentimental journey is less an education in the benefits of sensibility for the feminization of masculinity than an attempt to resolve the incongruity between sentimental behavior and the "violence" of desires that are necessary for the Rousseauian heterosexual game of "attack and defence." To achieve this resolution, Sterne drafts into the text a number of military men, beginning, obliquely, with Lorenzo the monk.

Scholars have noted the similarity between William Hogarth's patriotic rendering of *O the Roast Beef of Old England (The Gate of Calais)* (1748) and Yorick's encounter with a French Catholic monk at Calais but also that Sterne dispenses with Hogarth's Francophobic iconography. Rather than Hogarth's bloated friar, Yorick meets with a figure that "Guido has often painted": a "thin, spare form" and a head "free from all common-place ideas of fat contented ignorance" (*ASJ*, 8). In David Salter's words, "this episode represents an important milestone in the moral development of Yorick as a traveller, marking, on the one hand, his chauvinism and cultural insularity, but signalling at the same time his desire to cultivate a more cosmopolitan and ecumenical outlook."[34] There is, however, a wider significance in the fact that Yorick's less-than-charitable impulses are checked by the monk's courtesy and generosity, for in warming to one who is "foreign" to him, he is also warming to one who has been in military service. This is foreshadowed when Yorick takes a pinch of the monk's snuff as a sign of peace: the monk blushes "as red as scarlet" (*ASJ*, 26), that is, the color of a French Catholic cardinal's vestments but also of the military man's aggression. Like Uncle Toby, whose enthusiasm for military campaigning on the bowling green produces a blush of joy "as red as scarlet" (*TS*, 2.5.111), this blush is a trace of past militarism. Yorick later learns that the monk turned to the cloisters as a result of "disappointments" in both military service and the "tenderest of passions" (*ASJ*, 27). Although the supplicant monk has given up on both the military life and the pursuit of women, his presence in the text establishes that the successful devotee of "the sword and the sex" is an ideal (military) man of feeling.

Sterne employs Lorenzo the monk to indicate that the man of feeling can, and should, actively pursue his passions. However, Sterne also includes the military-man-turned-monk in an episode that shows Yorick that he must use sentiment to manage, or rather disguise, the force of his desires. The monk interrupts Yorick and the lady in close conversation, and Yorick's desire to command the lady's interest leads him to pretend compassion for the monk. At this moment, Yorick's sentimentality is too obviously instrumental, too much a means to the end of securing the lady's attention, and so he does not achieve his objective. Yorick secures a small victory over the monk, but his triumph does not last, for although he feels "something within him" as the lady prepares to leave, he concludes that "a hundred little delicacies" forbid him from doing so much as asking the lady her name: "there was no such thing as a man's asking her directly—the thing was impossible" (*ASJ*, 30). The arrival of another military man—"a little French *debonaire* captain"—gives

Yorick the opportunity to witness a rival make the same mistake, that is, fail to sufficiently disguise the force of his desire.

Keymer has argued that throughout the novel, Sterne aligns Yorick's interpretation of sensibility—too often directed toward "sickly concupiscence," "too self-absorbed, too fickle in his attentions," too frequently producing "self-gratification"—with an inability to take practical action.[35] Certainly, in hesitating to ask the lady's name, Yorick had been on the verge of failing, like Uncle Toby with widow Wadman, but the little officer's interruption shows him that a man might go on the attack. On the one hand, then, the little captain serves Yorick and the text as a model for (sexually) "active and strong" manliness. He proves that a (military) man can do what he wishes, as he sets about displacing Yorick and attempting to secure the lady. Although, or rather because, he is humiliated by the French captain's potency, Yorick finds that he admires his opponent. After the captain has departed, Yorick reflects, somewhat ruefully, "had I served seven years apprenticeship to good breeding, I could not have done as much" (*ASJ*, 31). However, the captain's behavior also provides Yorick with a lesson in the importance of ensuring that the "violence" of virile desires is concealed from the objects of those desires by sentimentality, for although Yorick is too timid, the little captain is too forward in his approach. The little captain leaves Yorick and the lady in no doubt about his military prowess by referring to his contribution to the "bombardment of [Brussels] last war" (*ASJ*, 31). During the eighteenth century, the phrase "bombardment of Brussels" was usually used to describe a French campaign against the allied British, Dutch, and Austrians that was intended to break the Siege of Namur during the Nine Years' War.[36] The little captain must mean the siege of Brussels (1746), a French maneuver against the Austrians in the War of the Austrian Succession. Sterne's slippage of terminology invokes two aggressive actions—one an attack on Yorick's nation and both attacks on the lady's country of origin—but the combination exposes the little captain's desire both to vanquish Yorick and to win the lady.

The little captain is, then, both a model and a warning: the text does not condemn his pursuit of sexual success, but it does suggest that his desires are too nakedly bellicose without the drapery of sentimentality. The absence of feeling is most acute when, having crudely manipulated Yorick in order to secure an introduction to the lady, the little captain presses her for information about herself in what becomes an uncomfortable and awkward because prolonged guessing game. Although the little captain initially dominates the conversation between himself, Yorick, and the lady, he finds that she is unwilling to be "ductile," and he departs without discovering her identity, something Yorick later manages to do. Put simply, the little captain's feelings are shown to be too direct, too combative, and too brazen to solicit her cooperation in the game of "attack and defence." Instead, the text introduces other military men, notably La Fleur, to illustrate ways to combine sentimentality and sexuality more effectively.

Having dispatched the little captain, who seems to be in active military service, Sterne turns back to the military figure who is less obviously a man of violence: the veteran. With this, Sterne returns to the world of *Tristram Shandy*. In that novel, Uncle Toby is tutored in how to achieve the right relationship between "the sword and the sex" by his fellow veteran and faithful corporal, Trim. Trim explains to Toby that romance is a matter of "attack and defence": "Love . . . is exactly like war, in this; that a soldier, though he has escaped three weeks compleat o'Saturday-night,—may nevertheless be shot through his heart on Sunday morning" (*TS*, 8.21.700). Toby has to be guided in matters of passion by Trim, literally, in the sense that Trim engineers their assault on mistress and maid: "we'll march up boldly, as if 'twas to the face of a bastion; and whilst your honour engages Mrs. Wadman in the parlour, to the right—I'll attack Mrs. Bridget in the kitchen, to the left; and having seiz'd that pass, I'll answer for it, . . . that the day is our own" (*TS*, 8.30.715). In *Tristram Shandy*, the man who should be looking to "lead" women has to be led himself.

Although the first veteran to appear in *A Sentimental Journey* is the monk, the next is La Fleur, who is to Yorick as Trim is to Toby. Like the monk, La Fleur has not had a glittering military career. Having served for a few years, and thereby "satisfied the sentiment," La Fleur "found . . . that the honour of beating a drum was likely to be its own reward, as it open'd no further track of glory to him" (*ASJ*, 41). The text implies that La Fleur left the army without an official discharge, but it also gives no reason for the reader to doubt Yorick's view that he will make a faithful subordinate: "the genuine look and air of the fellow determined the matter [of employment] at once in his favour" (*ASJ*, 41). Although Yorick claims, when he looks back on his travels, that he had no need of a foot soldier—that La Fleur's "talents of drum-beating and spatterdash-making, . . . tho' very good in themselves, happen'd to be of no great service" to him (*ASJ*, 43)—by hiring an ex-soldier for a servant, Yorick becomes a replacement officer as well as a new master. Sterne further likens Yorick and La Fleur to Toby and Trim by borrowing directly from *Tristram Shandy*. Just as Trim takes advantage of his officer's courtship of widow Wadman to seduce her maid, Bridget, so La Fleur takes advantage of his master petitioning the count for a passport in order to woo one of the count's servants.

Of course, unlike Toby, Yorick is not himself a veteran, nor is he quite so unsure of himself when it comes to romantic activity; but like Trim, La Fleur is a role model with regard to "active" sexuality. Yorick's education at the hands of the military man may begin with the little captain, but he is replaced by the figure of La Fleur. The little captain is characterized by his propensity to treat the street as a ball: he arrives "dancing down the street" (*ASJ*, 30) and departs in the same manner. In contrast, Yorick and La Fleur form a band together: when La Fleur states that he can play the fiddle, Yorick responds by implying that they might accompany each other: "Bravo! said Wisdome—Why, I play a bass myself, said I—we shall do very well" (*ASJ*, 42). As La Fleur is not a rival, unlike the little captain, Yorick can learn from his success with women. The little captain tries his hand, unsuccessfully, with the lady at Calais; La Fleur kisses the hands of "half a dozen wenches" on his departure from Montreuil. La Fleur's years of beating the drum seem to have prepared him for arduous activity of quite a different kind, judging by his promise to "bring them all pardons from Rome" (*ASJ*, 44). It is important to note that the women at Montreuil seem to desire La Fleur as much as he desires them, but the six women seem only to have as much desire in total as one man, and the rhythm of their relationships with him is dictated by his decision to leave, not by mutual consent.

By rewriting Toby and Trim as Yorick and La Fleur, Sterne offers a less ambiguous account of the ideal relationship between sentiment and sexuality for men. Yorick does not share Toby's extreme modesty, nor does La Fleur explicitly describe courtship in terms of marching and attacking (as Trim does in a doomed attempt to rouse his master's amorous passions); but Yorick benefits from the example set by the military man. La Fleur is unlike the little captain, who resorts to all-too-naked stratagems to impress the lady, as he deals with the six women at Montreuil with apparently sincere sentimentality. As La Fleur makes his good-byes to all the women at once, "thrice he wiped his eyes" (*ASJ*, 44). His sentimental tears gesture back to, rather than undermine, the virility of his sexual desires, for in only wiping his eyes three times, he effectively batches the six women into three pairs. As much as the women desire him, they are as "ductile" as the lady, the *grisset*, and the *fille de chambre*: they receive La Fleur's kisses impressed on their hands and are "led" by his leaving them. Here, then, is a model for Yorick in how best to use sentiment to win the war with willing women.

Oakley argues in his reading of *A Sentimental Journey* that Sterne sought in earnest to join the "pulsations" of the sentimental heart and those of the sexual organs and thereby to allow his "alter ego to enjoy the physiological reactions to desire with a clean conscience."[37] Certainly, the contrast between the little captain and the ex-soldier La Fleur indicates the importance to the text of ensuring that the "violence" of sexual desire is dressed in sentimentality rather than being nakedly aggressive. However, the union of sentimentality and "attack and defence" heterosexuality is not fully secured in the latter episode. This vignette offers a

Rousseauian fantasy of a multitude of women willingly giving way: La Fleur's six women bid him good-bye without jealousy about the other women's part share in his affections or complaint about his departure. The introduction of three more "military" men to the text goes some way toward combating this obvious descent into masculinist fantasy, as in each case the military man makes a serious case for the decency of his sentimentality.

The difficulty of combining sentimentality and the masculine "violence" of "attack and defence" heterosexuality is addressed in the episode in the theater in Paris, in which Yorick meets a "kindly old French officer" (*ASJ*, 76). Yorick decides to approach him, explaining, "I love the character, not only because I honour the man whose manners are softened by a profession which makes bad men worse; but that I once knew one—for he is no more—and why should I not rescue one page from violation by writing his name in it, and telling the world it was Captain Tobias Shandy, the dearest of my flock and friends, whose philanthropy I never think of at this long distance from his death—but my eyes gush out with tears. For his sake, I have a predilection for the whole corps of veterans" (*ASJ*, 76).

The Yorick who questioned Toby about war in *Tristram Shandy* is visible in this Yorick's reflection on soldiering as a profession that "makes bad men worse." That said, the Yorick of *A Sentimental Journey* seems to have come round to Toby's argument about the social virtue and sentimental capacity of soldiering, as he recalls Toby as a philanthropist. The kindly officer in the theater indicates that he is a military man of feeling by holding forth on the topic of sentiment. The officer delivers an oration on national character, during which he asserts that "there is a balance . . . of good and bad every where; and nothing but the knowing it is so can emancipate one half of the world from the prepossessions which it holds against the other" (*ASJ*, 83–84). Travel, the kindly officer concludes, "[teaches] us mutual toleration; and mutual toleration, . . . [teaches] us mutual love." Yorick concurs with the officer's thesis, albeit in a way that directs appreciation toward himself: "I thought I loved the man; but I fear I mistook the object—'twas my own way of thinking—the difference was, I could not have expressed it half so well" (*ASJ*, 84).

In this episode, the kindly officer makes a serious argument for "sentiment" as the means to develop "mutual love" rather than sexual relations. However, the text's interest in sexual desire is only temporarily displaced, for Yorick interrupts his account of the meeting with the kindly officer in order to reminisce about his affair with an Italian noblewoman. The one does segue to the other to some extent: Yorick indicates that he and the benevolent officer communicated with gestures, the one by removing his spectacles, the other by bowing. This prompts Yorick to recall the encounter with the Marquesina di F***, which, thanks to his and her fluency in reading bodily language, resulted in a "connection" that, he says, "gave me more pleasure than any one I had the honour to make in Italy" (*ASJ*, 78). Like the lady at Calais, this woman is a ductile participant in their sexual relationship. Yorick and the Marquesina meet in a doorway and so begin their affair by matching each other's bodily movements, the one trying to let the other pass such that neither succeeds: he makes an effort to "let [her] go out," she to "let [him] enter." However, their contributions in the subsequent back-and-forth of attack and defense at the door of her carriage are not the same: Yorick succeeds by her "making room" for him (*ASJ*, 78). Here, as elsewhere in the text, women are, fortuitously for Yorick, equally eager but not equally forceful: ultimately she must give way to Yorick's desire to impress himself upon her. Having begun with a military man's account of mutual love, Yorick ends by boasting about sexual conquest.

The juxtaposition of the kindly officer's high-minded oration and Yorick's titillating tale is comic, but it also undermines the attempt to shore up the combination of sentimental feeling and the violent passions of sexuality. The old officer's homily to "mutual love" moves him too far from the military man's function as exemplary devotee of "the sword and the sex," and the text slides back toward the eroticized idealization of female ductility and masculine virility. The task of securing the union of sentimentality and the sexuality of "attack and defence" falls to the two "military" men who bring up the rear of the text's parade of old soldiers: the *patès* seller and the Marquis at Rennes. Both are former military men, the one by actual service and the other by membership of the traditionally armigerous class. Yorick's attention is attracted to the *patès* seller's basket of cakes, but his "pity" and "esteem" are engaged by the man's medal of the Order of St. Louis (*ASJ*, 105). The veteran is a casualty of the "last peace," on which his regiment had been disbanded, but he is content with his new life as a *patisser*: "He had a little wife, he said, whom he loved, . . . and . . . he felt no dishonour in defending her and himself from want in this way" (*ASJ*, 106). Like the tale of the *patès* seller, the story of the Marquis at Rennes is one in which the "military" man has lost his military status and taken up commercial activity. Unable to purchase his way into the army, the down-at-heel Marquis had to surrender his sword and turn to commerce to provide for his family.

Whereas Yorick undermines the narrative of his meeting with the kindly officer with a digression on sexual conquest, he explicitly joins the tale of the *patès* seller to that of the Marquis at Rennes. As Yorick explains, "the two stories reflect light upon each other,—and 'tis a pity they should be parted" (*ASJ*, 106). The kindly officer's lecture on sentiment is interrupted by Yorick's comic erotic reveries, and the same pattern threatens to appear in the account of the Marquis at Rennes. Yorick is, inexplicably, present when the Marquis reclaims his sword in a formal ceremony. Yorick thinks he sees the Marquis shed a tear for and on his long-sheathed and rusted sword. "O! how I envied him those feelings!" (*ASJ*, 108), Yorick exclaims, in a manner that seems to be heartfelt. The depth of both men's feelings about the too-long sheathed and obviously phallic sword threatens to destabilize the earnestness of the sentiment, but the connection between the tales of the *patès* seller and the Marquis at Rennes keeps the comedy in check. In both stories, sentiment is presented as fully compatible with the binary of female ductility and male "violence." The man who once courageously defended his nation has been reduced to selling cakes, but in doing so, he chivalrously defends his wife from poverty. Likewise, the Marquis resigned his sword in order to be able to fight commercial battles for the benefit of his wife and children, who watch him regain his ancestral weapon.

* * *

As a text set during the Seven Years' War and written in its aftermath, *A Sentimental Journey* might have satirized the French soldier in ways that would have been consistent with the nationalism of midcentury Pittite patriotism. Rather than treat these military men as enemies, however, Sterne enlists them to assist Yorick in his pursuit of ductile women, women who willingly succumb to his advances. The veterans in the text, principally La Fleur, but also the *patès* seller and the Marquis, show Yorick how to deploy sentimentality to advance Rousseauian binary gender roles that—while allowing each gender to be equally committed to the same ends—permit, and encourage, an understanding of heterosexual relations as a game of "attack and defence."

NOTES

1. Jean-Jacques Rousseau, *Emilius and Sophia; or, A New System of Education*, vol. 4 (London: T. Becket and P. A. de Hondt, 1763), 3–4.
2. Thomas Keymer, *Sterne, the Moderns, and the Novel* (Oxford: Oxford University Press, 2002), 212, 190. See also Keymer, "Paper Wars: Literature and/as Conflict during the Seven Years' War," in *The Culture of the Seven Years' War: Empire, Identity, and the Arts in the Eighteenth-Century Atlantic World*, ed. Frans De Bruyn and Shaun Regan (Toronto: Toronto University Press, 2014), 134–135.
3. Carol Kay, *Political Constructions: Defoe, Richardson, and Sterne in Relation to Hobbes, Hume, and Burke* (Ithaca, NY: Cornell University Press, 1988), 236; Madeleine Descargues, "*Tristram Shandy* and the Appositeness of War," *Laurence Sterne's "Tristram Shandy": A Casebook*, ed. Thomas Keymer (Oxford: Oxford University Press, 2006), 243.
4. Descargues, "*Tristram Shandy* and the Appositeness of War," 243, 255. For Sterne and "national pride," see also Andrea Speltz, "War and Sentimentalism: Irony in Voltaire's *Candide*, Sterne's *Tristram Shandy*, and Lessing's *Minna von Barhelm*," *Canadian Review of Comparative Literature* 44, no. 2 (2017): 288.
5. Kathleen Wilson, *The Sense of the People: Politics, Culture and Imperialism in England, 1715–1785* (Cambridge: Cambridge University Press, 1995), 178, 185, 187.

6. Philip Carter, *Men and the Emergence of Polite Society, Britain, 1660–1800* (Harlow, UK: Pearson, 2001); Robert W. Jones, *Literature, Gender and Politics in Britain during the War for America, 1770–1785* (Cambridge: Cambridge University Press, 2011).
7. For the reception of *Émile*, see James H. Warner, "*Émile* in Eighteenth-Century England," *PMLA* 59, no. 3 (1944): 773–791. As Warner indicates, in England protofeminist criticism of *Émile* grew during the 1780s (778–779). See, for example, Claudia L. Johnson, *Equivocal Beings: Politics, Gender and Sentimentality in the 1790s: Wollstonecraft, Radcliffe, Burney, Austen* (Chicago: University of Chicago Press, 1995).
8. For war as a game, see Richard A. Lanham, "Pastoral War," in *"Tristram Shandy": The Games of Pleasure* (Berkley: University of California Press, 1973), 78–91. Later scholars have identified Toby's garden campaigns as a serious engagement with military architecture, as an extreme version of contemporary gardening fashions, and as an exercise that has psychological benefits. See Stephen Soud, "'Weavers, Gardeners, and Gladiators': Labyrinths in *Tristram Shandy*," *Eighteenth-Century Studies* 28, no. 4 (1995): 397–411; Jonathan Lamb, "Sterne, Sebald and Siege Architecture," *Eighteenth-Century Fiction* 19, no. 1 (2006): 21–41; Anders Engberg-Pedersen, "The Refraction of Geometry: *Tristram Shandy* and the Poetics of War, 1700–1800," *Representations* 123, no. 1 (2013): 23–52. For Sterne's contribution to a culture invested in "miniaturizing war" in the bowling green models, see Melinda Alliker Rabb, *Miniature and the English Imagination: Literature, Cognition, and Small-Scale Culture, 1650–1765* (Cambridge: Cambridge University Press, 2019), 134.
9. For Pitt's career and patriotism, see M. John Cardwell, *Arts and Arms: Literature, Politics, and Patriotism during the Seven Years War* (Manchester: Manchester University Press, 2004), esp. 17–42. See also Fred Anderson, *Crucible of War: The Seven Years' War and the Fate of Empire in British North America, 1754–1766* (London: Faber and Faber, 2000).
10. Matthew McCormack, *The Independent Man: Citizenship and Gender Politics in Georgian England* (Manchester: Manchester University Press, 2005), 72.
11. Matthew McCormack, "Citizenship, Nationhood and Masculinity in the Affair of the Hanoverian Soldier," *Historical Journal* 49, no. 4 (2006): 977.
12. McCormack, *Independent Man*, 72, 77, 208.
13. Laurence Sterne to Thomas Belasyse, Lord Fauconberg, April 10, 1762.
14. For Sterne's opposition to land tax, see Laurence Sterne to John Blake, July 5, 1758, in *Letters*, 51–52.
15. Laurence Sterne to Stephen Croft, December 25, 1760. Frank A. J. Szabo concludes that the Prussians gained little from the outcome of the battle and notes that the high number of Prussian causalities at the Battle of Torgau remained a state secret until the nineteenth century. Szabo, *The Seven Years War in Europe, 1756–1763* (New York: Pearson Longman, 2008), 322–323.
16. Stephen Conway, *War, State, and Society in Mid-Eighteenth-Century Britain and Ireland* (Oxford: Oxford University Press, 2006), 159–163. See also F. Anderson, *Crucible of War*; Daniel Baugh, *The Global Seven Years War, 1754–1763* (New York: Pearson Longman, 2011).
17. Laurence Sterne to Stephen Croft, February 17, 1761.
18. Some critical accounts problematize Toby as a character, for instance, Melvyn New, *"Tristram Shandy": A Book for Free Spirits* (New York: Twayne, 1994), 76–77. Robert C. Gordon summarizes these approaches and offers a corrective in *Arms and the Imagination: Essays on War, Politics, and Anglophone Culture* (Lanham, MD: Rowman and Littlefield, 2009), 231, 246. For a discussion of the apologetical oration, see Paddy Bullard, "*Tristram Shandy*, Lord George Sackville, and Uncle Toby's Apologetical Oration," *Shandean* 14 (2003): 94–103.
19. Susan Staves, "Toby Shandy: Sentiment and the Soldier," in *Approaches to Teaching Sterne's "Tristram Shandy,"* ed. Melvyn New (New York: Modern Language Association of America, 1989), 84.

20. Keymer, *Sterne, the Moderns, and the Novel*, 211, 214.
21. Carol Watts, *The Cultural Work of Empire: The Seven Years' War and the Imagining of the Shandean State* (Edinburgh: Edinburgh University Press, 2007), 17, 84, 97.
22. Kay, *Political Constructions*, 17, 232.
23. Frank Brady, "*Tristram Shandy*: Sexuality, Morality, Sensibility," *Eighteenth-Century Studies* 4, no. 1 (1970): 49. For Juliet McMaster, *Tristram Shandy* is both "*about* misogyny and against it." McMaster, "Walter Shandy, Sterne and Gender: A Feminist Foray," in *Critical Essays on Laurence Sterne*, ed. Melvyn New (New York: G. K. Hall, 1998), 213.
24. New, *Book for Free Spirits*, 73–76.
25. Eve Kosofsky Sedgwick, *Between Men: English Literature and Male Homosocial Desire* (New York: Columbia University Press, 1985), 74; Elizabeth W. Harris, "Words, Sex and Gender in Sterne's Novels," in *The Cambridge Companion to Laurence Sterne*, ed. Thomas Keymer (Cambridge: Cambridge University Press, 2009), 119.
26. Conway, *War, State, and Society*, 6.
27. Paul Langford, *A Polite and Commercial People: England, 1727–1783* (Oxford: Clarendon, 1989), 617, 620.
28. Warren L. Oakley, *A Culture of Mimicry: Laurence Sterne, His Readers and the Art of Bodysnatching* (London: Maney, 2010), 65.
29. M-C. Newbould, *Adaptations of Laurence Sterne's Fiction: Sterneana, 1760–1840* (Farnham, UK: Ashgate, 2013), 60.
30. Susan Lamb, *Bringing Travel Home to England: Tourism, Gender and Imaginative Literature* (Cranbury, NJ: Associated University Press, 2009), 156, 151.
31. The combination of sentiment and sexuality is a recurrent feature of discussions of Sterne and sensibility, which see a more "embodied" approach toward it in his work. For instance, see R. F. Brissenden, *Virtue in Distress: Studies in the Novel of Sentiment from Richardson to Sade* (London: Macmillan, 1974), 221–222; John Mullan, *Sentiment and Sociability: The Language of Feeling in the Eighteenth Century* (Oxford: Clarendon, 1988), 199; Paul Goring, *The Rhetoric of Sensibility in Eighteenth-Century Culture* (Cambridge: Cambridge University Press, 2005), 183–184, 199.
32. Elizabeth Kraft, "Laurence Sterne and the Ethics of Sexual Difference: Chiasmic Narration and Double Desire," *Christianity and Literature* 51, no. 3 (2002): 378.
33. G. J. Barker-Benfield, *The Culture of Sensibility: Sex and Society in Eighteenth-Century Britain* (Chicago: University of Chicago Press, 1992).
34. David Salter, "Remembering the Catholic Middle Ages: The Franciscans, English National Identity, and William Hogarth's *The Roast Beef of Old England*," *Logos: A Journal of Catholic Thought and Culture* 16, no. 4 (2013): 102.
35. Thomas Keymer, "*A Sentimental Journey* and the Failure of Feeling," in *The Cambridge Companion to Laurence Sterne*, ed. Thomas Keymer (Cambridge: Cambridge University Press, 2009), 90, 88.
36. For accounts of the "bombardment of Brussels," see Nicholas Tindal, *The History of England*, 3 vols. (London: John and Paul Knapton, 1744), 3:296; Tobias Smollett, *A Complete History of England*, 3rd ed., 9 vols. (London: James Rivington and James Fletcher, 1759), 9:66–72. See also John Childs, *The Nine Years' War and the British Army, 1688– 1697* (Manchester: Manchester University Press, 1991), 289–290.
37. Oakley, *Culture of Mimicry*, 81, 86.

3

STERNE'S JOURNEY INTO ANIMAL AFFECT

Glynis Ridley

In July 2012, an international group of neuroanatomists, cognitive neuroscientists, computational neuroscientists, and neuropharmacologists put their names to the Cambridge Declaration on Consciousness, affirming their belief that a range of nonhuman animals experience affective states: "The absence of a neocortex does not appear to preclude an organism from experiencing affective states. Convergent evidence indicates that non-human animals have the neuroanatomical, neurochemical, and neurophysiological substrates of conscious states along with the capacity to exhibit intentional behaviors. Consequently, the weight of evidence indicates that humans are not unique in possessing the neurological substrates that generate consciousness. Nonhuman animals, including all mammals and birds, and many other creatures, including octopuses, also possess these neurological substrates."[1]

For many animal behaviorists and ethologists, the declaration simply confirmed and gave scientific legitimacy to what they felt they already knew. As Marc Bekoff succinctly puts it, "To live with a dog is to know firsthand that animals have feelings. It's a no-brainer."[2] The disciplines represented by signatories to the declaration are distinct from Bekoff's field of ecology and evolutionary biology, and they all may seem a world away from English studies, where a text's animal actors are often read as symbolic and rarely considered in and of themselves. Yet the proclamation of the declaration has coincided with the appearance of a small but growing body of texts coming from outside the sciences that have begun to use the insights offered by animal studies and affect theory to explore the possibility that a range of nonhuman animals can be credited with recognizably human emotions.[3] The implications for reconsidering the art and literature of sentimentality have rarely been considered. For example, critical readings of *A Sentimental Journey* have typically viewed its dead ass and caged starling as both pathetic tableaux and as vehicles allowing Yorick to display his own acute sensibility, where "the background typically loses significance . . . to focus all attention on the foreground portrayal of the victim and his or her sympathizer."[4] However, read in light of animal studies and affect theory, the text's nonhuman actors prove to have their own agency and purpose. They are not simply mirrors for human emotions or catalysts for displays of human sensibility: rather, Sterne describes the ass and starling as evincing recognizable human feelings and awareness, raising ethical questions. With *A Sentimental Journey* as the central focus, this chapter situates Sterne's work amid eighteenth- and twenty-first-century explorations of animal affect.

The most extended exploration of human-animal interaction in *A Sentimental Journey* occurs across a triptych of chapters centered on "Nampont: The Dead Ass." While these can be read as a self-contained unit that functions as "a displacement of the Balaam story," the chapters can also be seen as simply one expression of Sterne's repeated engagement with the question of whether nonhuman animals experience recognizably human feelings.[5] Both within *A Sentimental Journey* and elsewhere in Sterne's canon, the Old Testament story of Balaam's ass seems to have provided Sterne with a cornerstone for his explorations of animal affect.

From Aesop to Charles Perrault and the brothers Grimm, the talking animal is a quintessential character in fables, fairy stories, and folk tales. It is certainly not an invention of, or particular to, the eighteenth century, although Perrault's *Histoires ou contes du temps passé* (1697) brought together some of the best-known talking animals in the popular imagination, including those found in "Little Red Riding Hood" and "Puss in Boots." Earlier in Western history, in myths dealing with humans transfigured into nonhuman animals, such as those in Ovid's *Metamorphoses*, the facility of human speech is typically lost in the transfiguration process, and the feelings of those who are transfigured can be inferred only from wordless noises. In stories that treat talking animals as routine (such as fables and fairy tales), no animal speaker ever pauses in a moment of existential reflection on the state of his or her being. (Seemingly not until Frankenstein's monster formulated the agonizing question of what sort of creature he was and how he came to be did an other-than-human speaker consider such questions.) For Sterne's first readers, two talking animals belied their ability to confine animal speakers to the world of pagan myths, moralizing fables, and low art: the Serpent of the Book of Genesis, and Balaam's ass from Numbers.

As Anne Cline Kelly has shown, the amount of biblical exegesis devoted to the Serpent and Balaam's ass across the centuries has been immense.[6] These tales generate apprehension, according to Kelly: "The Serpent and Balaam's ass create anxieties because not only species boundaries but also generic boundaries are transgressed. Talking animals are associated with fables and myth, so they seem anomalous in a text claimed to contain Divine Truth."[7] The story of the Serpent of Genesis is surely better known today than that of Balaam's ass, and since it is the latter that Sterne reworked, it is worth considering the unique features of the original. Offered money by the Moabite king to denounce Israelites camped across the River Jordan, Balaam initially declines but then changes his mind and sets out with the Moabite chiefs. To demonstrate to him the error of his ways, God sends an angel to block his path. Seeing the angel, the ass that Balaam is riding veers off the road, only to be beaten by Balaam. The journey continues, and at a narrow point on the road, the ass again sees the angel. When the ass presses against a wall and crushes Balaam's foot, she receives a second beating. When the journey resumes and the ass sees the angel for a third time, she lies down under Balaam, who beats her savagely with a stick: "The Lord then made the ass speak, and she said to Balaam, 'What have I done? This is the third time you have beaten me. . . . Am I not still the ass which you have ridden all your life? Have I ever taken such a liberty with you before?'"[8] When the angel enables Balaam to see what the ass has seen, he prostrates himself in contrition. What is remarkable about the story is that, given the facility of speech, the ass comments on her daily, lived reality, reminding Balaam that she has been the tireless executor of his commands. In other words, the ass comments on the experience of being an ass, and if one were asked to characterize her retort to Balaam, it appears to indicate that the physical pain he has inflicted on his beast has a counterpart in her hurt feelings. Balaam's ass is a feeling animal, in every sense of the term.

On the road to Nampont, the refusal of La Fleur's post horse to pass by a dead ass that is blocking the travelers' route engages with the story of Balaam's ass in multiple ways. One might read Sterne's substitution of a visibly dead (and possibly pungent) ass for an invisible angel as inappropriate, or one could view this first mention of the dead ass as a realistic portrayal of the visceral encounters to be had on an eighteenth-century road. The apparent gusto with which La Fleur "got up and came to the charge again astride his bidet, beating him up to it as he would have beat his drum" (*ASJ*, 50) certainly seems a sadly realistic description of the sort of casual brutality meted out by coachmen to their horses, as William Hogarth illustrated in the second plate of *The Four Stages of Cruelty* (1751), where Tom Nero mercilessly flogs a downed horse. (That La Fleur has been separated from his jackboots by a kick from the ass gives his exposed feet greater similarity to those of Balaam.) La Fleur's insistence that his bidet is, as Yorick translates it, "a conceited beast" (*ASJ*, 50) projects a human affect onto a nonhuman animal and is offered as the only explanation of the bidet's behavior. But given that the story of Balaam's ass would certainly be known to the first readers of *A Sentimental Journey*, Sterne's substitution of a dead ass for an angel surely gestures simultaneously toward sacrilege and profundity in equal measure: What if the bidet will not pass the dead ass because it experiences something that the human actors in the scene do not?

As Richard Bulliet notes in relation to the story of Balaam's ass and its living counterparts, these animals occupy a rich traditional role "as mediators with the unseen world on behalf of a seer."[9] While an ass is admittedly a different animal, literally and figuratively, the small, stocky bidet was an all-purpose beast of burden in eighteenth-century France and interchangeable with asses and donkeys for the purpose of carrying loads—or bearing double entendres. As Christopher Plumb says of eighteenth-century English, "'Ass' and 'arse' were sometimes homophones, . . . and other connotations often coalesced."[10] Sterne's mention of either "ass" or "bidet" (or here both) may provide a scatological undercurrent to his reworking of the story of Balaam's ass. In addition, Melvyn New and W. G. Day point out that Le Roux's *Dictionnaire* gives one interpretation of "bidet" as "le membre viril" (*ASJ*, 286n50.1). But perhaps Sterne also found the bidet a suitable vehicle for shouldering a symbolic burden or bearing the weight of unanswerable questions: Given that both La Fleur and Yorick will allow the possibility of the bidet being "conceited," what if they have simply attributed the wrong affect to the bidet and it is really an animal of sensibility, unwilling to pass the dead ass because of some fellow feeling it experiences?

The idea that Sterne may be asking us to entertain the possibility of sensibility in the bidet might seem laughable, were it not for the fact that the succeeding chapter ("Nampont: The Dead Ass") explicitly engages with claims that the ass had evinced recognizably human emotions. Offering a stark contrast to La Fleur's utilitarian view of his bidet, the owner of the deceased ass is initially mistaken by Yorick for a man mourning a child (*ASJ*, 53). The mourner handles "the remains of a crust" he would have "shared" with the ass, "who had been a patient partner of his journey. . . . it had eat the same bread with him all the way, and was unto him as a friend" (*ASJ*, 53–54). Reflecting the "vexed and uncertain" process of Le Fleur offering a gift, the mourner rejects monetary compensation for the loss of the ass.[11] He explains that his bond with the animal was not only forged in the shared physical experience of undertaking a pilgrimage to St. Iago (i.e., Santiago de Compostela) but also in a shared emotional bond: "The ass, he said, he was assured loved him—and upon this told them a long story of a mischance upon their passage over the Pyrenean mountains which had separated them from each other three days; during which time the ass had sought him as much as he had sought the ass, and that they had neither scarce eat or drank till they met" (*ASJ*, 54).

Whatever the truth of their three days' separation, the mourner is firm in his conviction that the ass loved him and neglected to care for himself as he searched for his master in the Pyrenees. Love, longing, and the hope to see one's dearest friend again: these are sentiments that the chapter suggests might exist in both man and beast and sentiments that might frame the relationship of one to another. Yet the ass who loved his poor master could only ever show his devotion and never tell it, for unlike Balaam's ass, he is never given the gift of speech. Only after the death of the ass can his grieving owner present its narrative and articulate what his ass never could.

Commenting on "The Dead Ass," New and Day see the episode as "a challenge [Sterne] set for himself: could he wax sentimental about an ass, while simultaneously keeping alert to the ludicrousness of doing so?" (*ASJ*, 288n53.2). But the grief of the ass's master is surely genuine, even if ludicrous to others. Furthermore, the episode is not the only instance of Sterne's exploration of what asses other than Balaam's ass might say if, like her, they were able to verbalize their physical and emotional feelings. In *Tristram Shandy*, Tristram is moved by the plight of an ass standing at the door threshold of an inn at Lyon. Tristram surmises that the ass lives in fear of a beating and that the only reason it repeatedly attempts to eat an artichoke is that it is desperately hungry and has been offered nothing else. As Tristram admits to offering the ass a macaroon more out of amused curiosity than benevolence, the chapter allows two possibilities for his following reflections: either Tristram projects feelings onto the ass or he attributes recognizably human emotions to the ass, insisting that any feeling person can understand what the ass is feeling:

> there is a patient endurance of sufferings, wrote so unaffectedly in his looks and carriage, which pleads so mightily for him, that it always disarms me; . . . I generally fall into conversation with him; and surely never is my imagination so busy as in framing his responses from the etchings of his countenance—and where those carry me not deep enough——in flying from my own heart into his, and seeing what is natural for an ass to think—as well as a man, upon the occasion. In truth, it is the only creature of all the classes of being below me, with whom I can do this: for parrots, jackdaws, *&c.*——I never exchange a word with them . . . —But with an ass, I can commune for ever. (*TS*, 7.32.630–631)

Here, to be a man of feeling is to be able to enter imaginatively into the inner life of an ass ("seeing what is natural for an ass to think"): both unspoken and assumed here is that asses have inner lives that we could access if we would. Affect is attributed to the ass that, among other things, is described as "thoughtful" and is said to have "looked wistfully" and "pensive" (*TS*, 7.32.631–632). Divorced from the insights afforded by the field of animal studies and the affirmations of the Cambridge Declaration on Consciousness, it is possible to read these descriptions as the "sentimental scenarios" that Markman Ellis suggests, "personalized, unique and discrete, so as to place the maximum pressure on the relation between the subject and the viewer."[12] Yet such a reading suggests that the scene is simply an example of anthropomorphism on Tristram's part, and, in doing so, it overlooks the imaginative effort that Tristram makes to enter into the experience of the ass. In puzzling over why the ass persists with the artichoke that it finds distasteful, Tristram reviews options from the point of view of the ass, caught "in the little peevish contentions of nature betwixt hunger and unsavoriness," and Tristram is at pains to get to the heart of what the ass feels, both physically and emotionally: "And now thy mouth, if one knew the truth of it, is as bitter, I dare say, as soot" (*TS*, 7.32.631). It is noticeable that when Tristram insists that he can fly from his own heart to that of the ass and see what the ass is thinking, Sterne's sentence construction is a movement from Tristram's feelings to those of the ass to those of any "man, upon the occasion" (*TS*, 7.32.630). A fundamental assumption of sensibility—that one's own emotional and physical responses are a good barometer by which to gauge the responses of others—is of course one of its fundamental problems. Acknowledging the impossibility of ever truly knowing another's feelings, whether a human's or nonhuman animal's, the sentence nevertheless argues for Tristram's awareness of his own affective response, his belief that the same passions are present in the ass, and from this he infers what any other (feeling) man will experience on the occasion. This can only be possible if Tristram assumes that the same feelings animate both man and ass and might be considered interchangeable between the two species. Given that the feeling asses of both *Tristram Shandy* and *A Sentimental Journey* need a human speaker to bear witness to their experiences, it is little wonder that Sterne appeared intrigued by the ability of Balaam's ass to narrate its own story.

Such a reading of this episode in *Tristram Shandy* is in sharp contrast to those analyses that cannot see beyond "asinine" comedy in their insistence that "the encounter with the ass of Lyons tends to invite two different types of reading—ironical and humorous."[13] To see Tristram's sympathetic encounter with the ass of Lyon as largely or even wholly comedic is surely to hold a utilitarian view of the ass (as a vehicle for comedy) and therefore to see it with its master's eyes rather than with Tristram's heart. When Tristram says that he communes with the ass "from the etchings of [its] countenance" (*TS*, 7.32.630), he asserts that the ability we all claim (to a greater or lesser degree) to know what another person is thinking by looking at his or her face is something that can be extended across species boundaries. In the growing field of human-animal interaction, visual contact between the human and nonhuman animal is neither ironical nor humorous but rather the prelude to a series of questions about what we might see, if we could see ourselves through other species' eyes.[14]

By Tristram's own admission, then, he experiences an imaginative engagement with asses that he does not enjoy with any other animal. Unlike Tristram, Yorick is moved not by a live ass but by the human mourner of a dead one. Even as the mourner expresses his own regrets over his treatment of the ass, Yorick fails to make any explicit connection between the beating of asses, La Fleur's cruel beating of his bidet, and the postilion's meting out of "an unfeeling lash to each of his beasts" (*ASJ*, 55) on the road to Amiens. Travel delays occasioned by the dead ass of *A Sentimental Journey* are therefore the cause of two separate sets of beatings of other equids. Given how large the story of Balaam's ass looms over these chapters, an implicit question hangs in the air in these scenes: What would La Fleur's bidet or the postilion's horses say if they too were given the gift of speech?

Leaving Nampont, Yorick wants the pace to match his mood and then reflects that the benefit of finding himself worked "into a foolish passion" is that the postilion will then "go slower," that he "may enjoy the sweets of it" (*ASJ*, 55). There is an irony in Yorick thinking about the link between mental and emotional engagement and the speed of travel, but in doing so, he admits that he has lost his way in thinking "of the poor German and his ass" (*ASJ*, 56). Despite Yorick's thoughts wandering from this topic, the dead ass of *A Sentimental Journey*, the live ass of *Tristram Shandy*, and the specter of Balaam's ass lingering over both make it seem unremarkable that Sterne might return to discussion of Balaam's ass elsewhere, including in his letters. Of thirty-nine letters collected by William Combe in his *Original Letters of the Late Reverend Mr. Laurence Sterne* (1788), all but three are now believed to be Combe's own forgeries.[15] Yet among Combe's attempts to capture Sterne's style and sentiments, it is striking that Combe thought the story of Balaam's ass to be a quintessential narrative vehicle for the writer he was trying to imitate:

> When I mounted my Hobby Horse, I never thought, or pretended to think, where I was going. . . . I let him take his own course; and amble, or curvet, or trot, or go a sober, sorrowful, Lackadaysical pace, as it pleased him best. It was all one to me. . . . I never pricked him with a spur, or struck him with a whip; but let the rein lay loosely on his neck, and he was wont to take his way without doing injury to any one. . . . Thus have we travelled together—but my poor *Rosinante* did not, like *Balaam's Ass*, stand still if he saw an *Angel* in the way, but directly pushed up to her:—and if it were but a damsel, sitting by the fountain, who would let me take a refreshing draught from her cup, she was, surely, an Angel to me. . . . Truth lies before us; it is in the high way path; and the Ploughman treads on it with his clouted Shoon. . . . Nature has her own Laws, which Art cannot always comprehend, and Criticism can never reach.[16]

Successful forgery relies on the appearance of authenticity, and Combe clearly believed that the reflections in this letter would not look out of place to a keen reader of Sterne. Whatever else can be asserted about this letter, it is undeniable that—here at least—the story of a horse and Balaam's ass functions as a metaphoric vehicle by which "Sterne" can supposedly best explain his own understanding of how he thinks and feels. And given Tristram's claims for his ability to communicate with the ass of Lyon and his certainty that he understands what it is to be an ass, it is perhaps not surprising that Combe constructed this forged letter to show man and beast sharing the same experiences and feelings. Inauthentic texts are, of course, not the same as inauthentic sentiments. In an astute and wide-ranging exploration of the place of nonhuman animals in sentimental literature and the difficulties of determining authenticity of feeling on the part of sentimental narrators, Tobias Menely notes that, in the "genealogy of unseemly sentimentality . . . Laurence Sterne's reputation has been closely linked with his fictional animals, perhaps to a greater degree than any other British writer of the eighteenth century."[17] It is little wonder, then, that for Combe, the authentic voice of Sterne was clearly one that extended notions of personhood.

While Yorick is affected by his encounter with the mourner of the dead ass, he himself has no direct engagement with it, and all the emotion he feels is for his fellow man. Narration regarding the dead ass may therefore be seen as a prelude to Yorick's later encounter with a caged starling. While the pathetic tableau of a man mourning his ass speaks to Yorick's heart and prompts him to feel, the caged starling speaks directly to Yorick and prompts him to act. The word "speaks" is chosen deliberately in the preceding sentence, and for more than the simple rhetorical effect of parallelism between its two halves: to assert that the starling "speaks" implies something other than mere mimicry and takes us to the heart of current research—and controversy—regarding consciousness in the nonhuman animal. As will be seen, Sterne unwittingly prefigures twenty-first-century researchers in his exploration of animal consciousness, precisely because the European context in which Yorick moves was one in which caged songbirds were plentiful, and today's leading avian researchers are, in some respects, simply rediscovering aspects of animal behavior that were observed, if not fully understood, by earlier generations. Yorick's encounter with the caged starling has been the subject of so considerable a body of analysis that it is worth returning to Sterne's text before exploring the sociohistorical context in which the episode's extraordinary exploration of animal feeling can be appreciated.

Yorick's first encounter with the starling occurs immediately following a conversation with the master of the Parisian inn where he is staying. An inquiry by the "Lieutenant de Police" has prompted the latter to ask if Yorick has a passport, and as Yorick insouciantly declares that he does not, the hotel proprietor predicts that such a lack of documentation will lead to detention in the Bastille (*ASJ*, 92). Yorick convinces himself that an innocent man will ultimately emerge unscathed from such a fate, reasoning that "albeit a man can't get out, he may do very well within, . . . and he comes out a better and wiser man than he went in" (*ASJ*, 94). Descending the stairs while wrapped up "in the hey-day of this soliloquy," Yorick is "interrupted" "with a voice which [he] took to be of a child, which complained 'it could not get out'" (*ASJ*, 95). Unable to locate any human speaker, two more repetitions of the same words let Yorick finally locate their origin in "a starling hung in a little cage.—'I can't get out—I can't get out,' said the starling" (*ASJ*, 95). Failing to open the cage door "twisted and double twisted so fast with wire," Yorick applies "both hands" to the task: "The bird flew to the place where I was attempting his deliverance, and thrusting his head through the trellis, press'd his breast against it, as if impatient—I fear, poor creature! said I, I cannot set thee at liberty—'No,' said the starling—'I can't get out—I can't get out,' said the starling" (*ASJ*, 95).

Yorick's immediate characterization of "the notes" as "mechanical" warrants consideration, for Alex Wetmore has suggested that "the sentimental novels of Mackenzie and Smollett, along with those of Sterne, consistently align men of feeling with mechanistic behaviors strikingly similar to those of automata."[18] Wetmore further reminds us that Yorick takes pride in "his ability to translate the emotional signifiers of the body into words. . . . Yorick claims that through custom or 'habitude,' he now performs the act [of translation] 'so mechanically' that as he walks the streets, 'I go translating all the way.'"[19] Against this background, it would be possible to argue that Yorick is merely "translating"—mechanically—what he believes to be the starling's sentiments, though Wetmore does not foreclose the possibility that the bird itself vocalizes the words that Yorick attributes to it, claiming that "Yorick is also aware that the bird repeats the phrase automatically, without any sense of the meaning of what it says."[20] In this, Wetmore is echoing Judith Frank's characterization of "the mechanical or imitated emotion of the caged starling."[21] The Cambridge Declaration on Consciousness, on the other hand, would assert that a range of nonhuman animals experience "affective states . . . along with the capacity to exhibit intentional behaviors"; I would suggest, in turn, that simply because Yorick prides himself on how automatic his "translating" of others' body language has become, the starling may not be in need of translation, if we allow that it is capable of speaking for itself.

So evident is the caged starling's power as a tangible symbol of captivity that the passage has spawned a host of explanations as to how it should be read. To rehearse even a fraction of the many interpretations of the scene is to be struck by how a range of different readings all share one thing: the starling is never considered in and of itself but is always a cipher for a human way of being or seeing. For example, Helene Moglen believes that "the plight of the caged bird is a rich metaphor for the condition of the man shut up in the prison of his own subjectivity," while Jim Owen thinks that "the bird becomes emblematic of the problem of self-enclosure: a person who becomes totally self-enclosed cannot 'get out' through the ministry of others."[22] The starling has also been identified as "a "literary descendant" of the "Man of Despair" from Bunyan's *Pilgrim's Progress*: "shut up [in despair], as in this Iron Cage. I cannot get out; O *now* I cannot."[23] These interpretations bring into sharp focus something that cannot be overemphasized about the representation of the nonhuman animal in art and literature: historically, the appearance of a nonhuman animal in visual or written media has typically been read as a symbol or a metaphor for the human condition; rarely is the representation of the animal considered as a successful or unsuccessful depiction of a living, breathing reality. This is not to say that an animal cannot function on both the literal and the symbolic levels; in the case of the starling of *A Sentimental Journey*, however, critics seem unable to allow the bird any function beyond the symbolic. To my mind, this is unfortunate, since it removes the starling from a historical moment in which it might be possible to find Sterne more in tune with modern thinking on animal consciousness than we have heretofore suspected.

A twenty-first-century reader's ability to understand how an eighteenth-century audience might have viewed Yorick's interaction with the caged starling as wholly realistic is enhanced by current research into starlings' vocal and cognitive abilities. Writing about Sterne, one is always acutely conscious (and wary) of the appearance of digression and the possible pursuit of a hobbyhorse, but in this instance the risk seems essential to the point I wish to make. In 2017, the journalist Lyanda Lynn Haupt published *Mozart's Starling*, a summation of her quest to understand a well-attested but scarcely researched fact of Mozart's life, namely, that on May 27, 1784, Mozart purchased a starling from a Viennese bird vendor, charmed and intrigued that the bird "sang the theme from the allegretto to Mozart's new concerto completed just one month earlier and never yet performed in public. Well, he almost sang the tune. The starling made a minor rhythmic modification (a dramatic fermata at the top of the phrase) and raised the last two Gs in the fragment to G-sharps, but the basic motif was unmistakable."[24] Mozart's own notebook shows him subsequently juxtaposing his version of his own composition with that of his newly acquired starling, distinguishing its variant on his motif with the words "Vogel Stahrl," that is, the name of the species.[25] The starling would become a fixture of the Mozart household. Haupt acquired her own starling chick and raised it in her home to aid her research, an experiment facilitated by U.S. law that regards starlings as invasive, nonnative, and therefore not subject to the protections that native American avifauna enjoy.[26] (The website starlingtalk.com shows a number of U.S. citizens taking similar advantage of this fact and chronicling the manner in which they share their domestic space with one or more starlings.)

The presence of the European starling in North America—and its status as a nonnative, invasive species—is entirely due to the fact that a nineteenth-century Shakespeare-loving resident of the Bronx, Eugene Schieffelin, made it his life's work to bring to North America all birds mentioned by the Bard. The checklist was ready made in James Edmund Harting's 1871 *Ornithology of Shakespeare*, and Schieffelin released a shipment of starlings into Central Park in homage to the passage in *1 Henry IV* where Hotspur dreams of being revenged on the king who will not ransom Hotspur's brother-in-law, Mortimer: "I'll have a starling shall be taught to speak / Nothing but 'Mortimer,' and give it him / To keep his anger still in motion" (1.3.224–226). Haupt notes that these lines would have made little sense to the groundlings had they not understood starlings to be extraordinary mimics of the aural landscape around them, capable of spontaneously imitating a range of naturally occurring sounds as well as human language. Outside aristocratic circles, starlings were common pet birds in early modern Europe: the breeding success that caused them to be viewed as a pest in North America made them a popular bird for the early European songbird trade.

Against this background, Yorick's explanation of the caged starling's insistence that "I can't get out" takes the reader of both the eighteenth and twenty-first centuries down a provocative train of thought. Yorick relates the caged starling's backstory that an English groom, whose master was visiting France, had come into possession of a fledgling: "he taught it in his mother's tongue the four simple words—(and no more)—to which I own'd myself so much it's debtor" (*ASJ*, 99). Perhaps in writing this passage, Sterne misremembered that the starling makes perfectly appropriate grammatical use of *five* words, not four, and the word it introduces—"no"—seems to capture the frustration of both man and bird and is syntactically correctly deployed: "'No,' said the starling—'I can't get out—I can't get out,' said the starling" (*ASJ*, 95). It is possible that Sterne misremembered how many words Yorick had originally attributed to the starling, to be sure, and it is also possible that the passage is meant to indicate Yorick's inattention to external detail in his solipsistic reverie. But given all that is currently known about starlings' vocal abilities, a more intriguing possibility exists than that Sterne simply made an error in ascribing to the starling a lexical world limited to four words rather than five.

Even had the English groom only *taught* the caged starling four words, its vocabulary would be greater simply by virtue of attending to the surrounding sonic landscape. There is surely a difference, however, in mimicking sounds seemingly at random and in producing sounds at appropriate times. And the ability of Haupt's pet starling Carmen to imitate a variety of regularly occurring household sounds was far from random; rather, Haupt consistently experienced Carmen's production of these sounds in their appropriate context. For example, Carmen imitated the sound of a creaking floorboard as Haupt was walking about; Carmen imitated the sound of the wine bottle's vacuum sealer when Haupt had the bottle in Carmen's view; Carmen mewed like the cat when the cat was within sight of her aviary within the house. Haupt's experience of context-appropriate sound production is common among those who live with starlings.

The leading starling researcher Meredith West, author of a seminal 1990 *Scientific American* paper on starling-human interaction, found that one of her seven resident starlings would wait until perched on her shoulder before offering a passable impersonation of West, where the bird would say, "Basic research, it's true. I guess that's right."[27] The entry of another human into the room would, however, elicit the phrase, "I have a question." To characterize this as simple verbal mimicry is inadequate to account for the specific context in which particular phrases are used; rather, it seems that certain visual cues prompt related verbal responses.[28] Against this background, Sterne would seem to have been a perceptive observer of the context-specific behaviors and vocalizations of the species. Yorick notes, "The bird flew to the place where I was attempting his deliverance, and thrusting his head through the trellis, press'd his breast against it, as if impatient" (*ASJ*, 95). What may initially seem merely poetic license on Sterne's part is, in fact, an accurate depiction of starling behavior; as Haupt notes, "when you talk to a tame starling, it jumps as close to you as it can get, tilts its head, and listens."[29] The bird therefore associates the appearance of a human at its cage door with release and has learned to vocalize a context-specific phrase on such an occasion. While it is possible that Yorick is imagining a verbal response from the bird, and thus convincing himself of his sympathetic engagement with others, such an argument resists engaging with the proven ability of starlings to interact, often vocally, with the people around them. Put another way, no reader of either Haupt's or West's work can be in any doubt that they intend their claims in respect of interacting with their birds to be taken literally, and not as evidence of their own imaginative flights of fancy. In composing this scene, then, Sterne depicts a starling behavior that eighteenth-century readers familiar with the species would have recognized—its context-specific vocalization—which is a characteristic that modern researchers continue to explore and speculate on.

Yorick's interaction with a caged starling shows that the bird offers more than simply a context-specific regurgitation of the *four* words it was taught by an English groom, however, since the bird seems to *engage* with Yorick when it responds to his declaration that he cannot set it free by prefacing its stock phrase with the word "No." The linguistic phenomenon that Sterne accurately depicts in this exchange is recursion: the ability to recognize a pattern, the rules that govern formation of that pattern, followed by the capacity to recognize and form variants on that pattern. In the influential paper "The Faculty of Language: What Is It, Who Has It, and How Did It Evolve?," Noam Chomsky and several colleagues assert recursion as the property that defines human language; they thereby ignited a heated debate, as the neurophysiologist Timothy Gentner countered that his starling research subjects could recognize recursive patterns in an artificially constructed language more than 90 percent of the time.[30] (An artificially constructed language designed to test hearers' pattern recognition is not, of course, a vehicle designed to convey emotion or test affective responses, and Gentner makes no claim about his starling test subjects' abilities beyond their facility with his tests.) As Gentner says of his study of recursion in starling vocalization, "Our research is a refutation of the canonical position that what makes human language unique is a singular ability to comprehend these kinds of patterns. . . . If birds can learn these patterning rules, then their use does not explain the uniqueness of human language." Eighteenth-century Europeans who kept caged starlings did not, obviously, have the concept of recursion to explain their birds' facility for taking sounds learned in one context and combining them—in ways that seemed to make sense to human auditors—with sounds learned in a different context. Yet they would, we must assume, have observed the same phenomenon on a regular basis as do modern scientists.

Yorick's experience of appearing to have a conversational exchange with a caged starling can therefore be read as realistic, even before one speculates on the bird's ability to function also as a symbol (of captivity, solipsism, or isolation, for instance). The English groom who believed he had taught the starling only four words could no more limit one of its species to such a narrow range of vocalizations than Hotspur could have restricted a starling to "nothing but 'Mortimer.'" Rather, the caged starling's ability to combine a word evidently not taught to it by the groom (that is, "No") with its stock phrase of "I can't get out" and to combine these elements into a grammatically accurate whole is now understood as a well-attested capability of a handful of avian species, most notably mynahs, parrots, and starlings. The question of where mimicry and an understanding of context-specific use might shade into understanding or consciousness of the meaning of such words is, of course, both fiercely contested and not presently capable of resolution; certainly, it is beyond the scope of this discussion. It is worth emphasizing, however, that *A Sentimental Journey* appeared in the decade following the publication of Rousseau's Second Discourse, *On the Origin and the Foundations of Inequality among Men* (1754), in which Rousseau states his views on sentience in the nonhuman animal: "Every animal has ideas, because it has senses. It even combines its ideas up to a certain point, and man is no different from a beast in this respect, except in degree."[31] Rousseau arrives at this conclusion in the middle of a century that saw fierce ongoing debates about the subject of consciousness in the nonhuman animal.[32] Like those previously-alluded-to discussions surrounding avian mimicry in contrast to understanding, it is not the purpose to provide extensive coverage of this issue here; suffice to say that no man or woman of letters during the period (including Sterne) could have been unaware of this philosophical and scientific debate about what nonhuman animals felt, knew, and understood.

For those readers of *A Sentimental Journey* for whom the starling is foremost (and perhaps only) a symbol, its eventual purchase by La Fleur and subsequent regifting among the English aristocracy necessitates arguing that its symbolism changes from one chapter to another. Initially an embodiment of various aspects of the human condition, the bird that is passed from "Lord A" to "Lord B" (*ASJ*, 100) has been read by one critic at least "as a cipher for pirated copies of Sterne's own works; in this reading, Sterne's 'bird' is one over which he asserts his rights of ownership, rejecting attempts to pass off a 'vile copy' as his own."[33] Such a reading overlooks the structure of the miniature "it-narrative" into which the starling has fallen and also elides the fact that the bird in question is, of course, Yorick's starling, not Sterne's. Since any starling could (in theory) be taught the same words as the caged starling encountered in Paris, all captive starlings could be passed off as copies of this individual. In Yorick's assertion of his ownership of the original, rather than any bird set up to copy it, he surely signals that he—or any reader—ought to know his bird because of its singularity. To him, the caged starling is an individual among a multitude, worth commemorating on his heraldic crest. Interpretations of Yorick's parting shot, "let the heralds officers twist his neck about if they dare" (*ASJ*, 100), could serve as a concentrated illustration of the problem with reading Sterne's nonhuman actors as symbols rather than flesh-and-blood creatures. In a detailed account of heraldic arms in Sterne's work, New and Day show the multiplicity of readings (and misunderstandings) that the comment has spawned, including the suggestion that, should heralds of the College of Arms twist the bird's neck (that is, so that it would appear to be looking over its shoulder), the Sterne family crest would then signify illegitimacy (*ASJ*, 332–333n100.13). But no such meaning for any animal regardant (looking backward) can be found in the annals of heraldry; and indeed, the College of Arms maintains that illegitimate family lines were not allowed to claim family crests, so illegitimacy is never indicated on any recognized crest.[34]

The dead ass and caged starling of *A Sentimental Journey* are, of course, by no means the only animals on whose emotions Yorick reflects. While it is beyond the constraints of this essay, a full account of the text's nonhuman actors would include the fact that, at Amiens, La Fleur leads the Count's servants "and all the household, dogs and cats, besides an old monkey, a-dancing" (*ASJ*, 59), while at Moulins, Maria has swapped a goat "as faithless as her lover" for "a little dog," tethered to her by a string (*ASJ*, 150).[35] Both scenes have proved popular with illustrators, with Maria and her dog also the subject of oil paintings by Angelica Kauffman and Joseph Wright of Derby, among others.

The affective power that the nonhuman animal can exercise over the human animal has never been in doubt. This discussion views emotional affect as an experience that may not be limited to the human animal alone and Sterne as a sympathetic inquirer into this possibility. Writing of Derrida's 1997 lecture series delivered under the title "The Autobiographical Animal," Heather Keenleyside sees Sterne as one of the early explorers of the supposed boundaries that separate humans from other living things: "As Tristram proceeds from watching the ass eat to imagining his feelings, his life history, and his first-person speech, Sterne suggests that sympathy or sentiment may be . . . a form of movement that cuts across even the bounds of species to establish a shared first-person form of life. In doing so, he signals a counter tradition of literary and philosophical thought to the one Derrida labels Cartesian, a tradition we might call upon as we endeavor to conceive animal life anew."[36]

Kathryn Shevelow shows the eighteenth century to be a period when two starkly opposing views of the nonhuman animal vied for public attention.[37] While many of Sterne's first readers believed the Cartesian view that animals were mere automata and their cries of pain simply a mechanical response like the sounds made by a musical instrument, Shevelow details the contrasting opinions of those whose concern for nonhuman animals led to the passage of the first animal-rights legislation in the world in Martin's Act of 1822.[38] These early campaigners insisted on the primacy of the question famously posed by Jeremy Bentham regarding the full spectrum of nonhuman animals: "The question is not, Can they reason? Nor, Can they talk but, Can they suffer?"[39] Thirty years after the publication *of A Sentimental Journey*, Edward Augustus Kendall's *Keeper's Travels in Search of his Master* (1798) utilized the narrative technique subsequently termed "free indirect style" to take readers inside the experience of a dog, attributing to Keeper a range of sensations, including fear, joy, longing, regret—and hope for the future.[40] Against this background, it is surely time for sentimental literature's men and women of feeling to be joined by consideration of a range of nonhuman others, with the capacity, equal to their human counterparts, consciously to feel.

NOTES

1. Philip Low, The Cambridge Declaration on Consciousness, ed. Jaak Panksepp, Diana Reiss, David Edelman, Bruno Van Swinderen, Philip Low, and Christof Koch, presented at the Francis Crick Memorial Conference on Consciousness in Human and Non-Human Animals, at Churchill College, University of Cambridge, UK, July 7, 2012. Further details may be found at http://www.animal-ethics.org/the-cambridge-declaration-on-consciousness/.
2. Marc Bekoff, *The Emotional Lives of Animals* (Novato, CA: New World Library, 2007), xx.
3. See, for example, Donovan Schaefer, *Religious Affects: Animality, Evolution, and Power* (Durham, NC: Duke University Press, 2015); Cynthia Willett, *Interspecies Ethics* (New York: Columbia University Press, 2014).
4. W. B. Gerard, *Laurence Sterne and the Visual Imagination* (Aldershot, UK: Ashgate, 2006), 119.
5. James Chandler, *An Archaeology of Sympathy. The Sentimental Mode in Literature and Cinema* (Chicago: University of Chicago Press, 2013), 268.
6. Ann Cline Kelly, "Talking Animals in the Bible: Paratexts as Symptoms of Cultural Anxiety in Restoration and Early Eighteenth-Century England," *Journal for Eighteenth-Century Studies* 33, no. 4 (2010): 438.
7. Kelly, 438.
8. Numbers 22:28–30. *The New English Bible* (Oxford: Oxford University Press, 1970).
9. Richard W. Bulliet, *Hunters, Herders, and Hamburgers: The Past and Future of Human-Animal Relationships* (New York: Columbia University Press, 2005), 155.
10. Christopher Plumb, "'The Queen's Ass': The Cultural Life of Queen Charlotte's Zebra in Georgian Britain," *The Afterlives of Animals*, ed. Samuel J.M.M. Alberti (Charlottesville: University of Virginia Press, 2011), 24.
11. Linda Zionkowski and Cynthia Klekar, introduction to *The Culture of the Gift in Eighteenth-Century England*, ed. Linda Zionkowski and Cynthia Klekar (New York: Palgrave Macmillan, 2009), 12.
12. Markman Ellis, *The Politics of Sensibility* (Cambridge: Cambridge University Press, 1996), 71, 72.
13. Marc Martinez, "Asses, Artichokes and Macaroons: The Joco-Serious Humour of *Tristram Shandy*," in *Hilarion's Asse: Laurence Sterne and Humour*, ed. Anne Bandry-Scubbi and Peter de Voogd (Newcastle, UK: Cambridge Scholars, 2013), 54.
14. As a founding text in this field, see John Berger, "Why Look at Animals?," *About Looking* (New York: Pantheon Books, 1980), 3–28. Interspecies eye contact has more recently been given memorable form in Bill Viola's digital video *I Do Not Know What It Is I Am Like* (1986); the excerpt "Owl" can be found online, inviting the viewer to stare into the eyes of a great horned owl, which reflect back the artist himself.
15. For a discussion of Combe's forgeries, see *Letters*, xlviii–li.
16. Laurence Sterne, *Original Letters of the Late Reverend Mr. Laurence Sterne; Never Before Published* (London, 1788), letter 16, 86–88.
17. Tobias Menely, "Zoöphilpsychosis: Why Animals Are What's Wrong with Sentimentality," *symploke* 15, nos. 1–2 (2007): 258.
18. Alex Wetmore, "Sympathy Machines: Men of Feeling and the Automaton," *Eighteenth-Century Studies* 43, no. 1 (Fall 2009): 46.
19. Wetmore, 47.
20. Wetmore, 47.

21. Judith Frank, *Common Ground: Eighteenth-Century English Satiric Fiction and the Poor* (Stanford, CA: Stanford University Press, 2002), 78.
22. Helene Moglen, *The Philosophical Irony of Laurence Sterne* (Gainesville: University Press of Florida, 1975), 102; Jim Owen, "Laurence Sterne and the Caged Starling of *A Sentimental Journey*," *CEA Critic* 64, nos. 2–3 (Winter–Spring/Summer 2002): 26.
23. Stephen Derry, "*Mansfield Park*, Sterne's Starling, and Bunyan's Man of Despair," *Notes and Queries* 44, no. 3 (1997): 322. Derry's interpretation is discussed by the editors of the Florida edition of *A Sentimental Journey*, 324–325, 95n10–11.
24. Lyanda Lynn Haupt, *Mozart's Starling* (New York: Little, Brown, 2017), 29.
25. Haupt, 30.
26. The first U.S. legislation enacting protections for avifauna was the Migratory Bird Treaty Act (MBTA) of 1918, codified at 16 U.S.C. §§703–712 (§709 omitted).
27. Meredith J. West and Andrew P. King, "Mozart's Starling," *American Scientist* 78 (1990): 106–114, quoted in Haupt, *Mozart's Starling*, 81–82. See also Meredith J. West, Neil Stroud, and Andrew P. King, "Mimicry of the Human Voice by European Starlings: The Role of Social Interaction," *Wilson Bulletin* 95, no. 4 (1983): 635–640.
28. On the possibility that starlings understand the relationship between cause and effect and vocalize specifically to achieve certain desired goals, see Haupt, *Mozart's Starling*, 94–95.
29. Haupt, 140.
30. Marc D. Hauser, Noam Chomsky, and W. Tecumseh Fitch, "The Faculty of Language: What Is It, Who Has It, and How Did It Evolve?," *Science* 298, no. 5598 (2002): 1569–1579; Timothy Q. Gentner, Kimberly M. Fenn, Daniel Margoliash, and Howard C. Nusbaum, "Recursive Syntactic Pattern Learning by Songbirds," *Nature* 440, no. 7088 (2006): 1204–1207, quoted in Haupt, *Mozart's Starling*, 157.
31. Jean-Jacques Rousseau, *Jean-Jacques Rousseau: Fundamental Political Writings*, ed. Matthew W. Maguire and David Lay Williams, trans. Ian Johnston (Peterborough, ON: Broadview, 2018), 116.
32. For an examination of prevailing eighteenth-century theories about animal consciousness and challenges to those theories, see Kathryn Shevelow, *For the Love of Animals: The Rise of the Animal Protection Movement* (New York: Henry Holt, 2008). A summary of philosophers' views before Darwin regarding animal capacities may be found in Pierre Le Neindre, Emilie Bernard, Alain Boissy, et al., "Animal Consciousness" (European Food Safety Authority, April 24, 2017), 26–27, doi: 10.2903/sp.efsa.2017.EN-1196.
33. For a summation of theories of what might be meant by "vile copy," see Owen, "Laurence Sterne and the Caged Starling," 27–30.
34. "The arms of a man pass equally to all his legitimate children, irrespective of their order of birth." College of Arms, "The Law of Arms," accessed August 25, 2020, https://www.college-of-arms.gov.uk/resources/the-law-of-arms.
35. The goat's symbolic history includes associations of lechery and disloyalty, so, like the ass, its polysemous meaning must have appealed to Sterne. Marc Martinez believes that Maria's goat "hybridizes the humorous and the sentimental" ("Asses, Artichokes and Macaroons," 64).
36. Heather Keenleyside, "The First-Person Form of Life: Locke, Sterne, and the Autobiographical Animal," *Critical Inquiry* 39 (Autumn 2012): 139–140. Keenleyside provides a more extended version of the thesis in this paper in her later book, *Animals and Other People: Literary Forms and Living Beings in the Eighteenth Century* (Philadelphia: University of Pennsylvania Press, 2016).
37. See Shevelow, *For the Love of Animals*.
38. In detailing how Martin's Act came to be passed, Shevelow shows that those who fought for consideration of the rights of nonhuman animals were also typically abolitionists and

early advocates for the rights of women: slaves, women, and animals being equally voiceless under the law. See Shevelow, 245–284.

39. Jeremy Bentham, *An Introduction to the Principles of Morals and Legislation*, ed. J. H. Burns and H.L.A. Hart (London: Athlone; Oxford: Clarendon 1970), 282nb.
40. Jane Spencer, "Creating Animal Experience in Late Eighteenth-Century Narrative," "Animals in the Eighteenth Century," *Journal for Eighteenth-Century Studies* 33, no. 4 (2010): 469–486.

Part Two

WORDS, STRUCTURES, THINGS

4

SPATIAL DIGRESSION AND THE BORDERS OF KNOWLEDGE IN *A SENTIMENTAL JOURNEY*

Chris Ewers

A SENTIMENTAL JOURNEY BEGINS at a remarkable pace. Yorick, having been told that his opinion that "they order" a certain matter much better across the Channel counts for little because he has never been there, goes "straight" to his lodgings, throws some clothes into a valise, books a place in the Dover stage, and by three the following afternoon is sitting down to his dinner "incontestably in France" (*ASJ*, 3–4). The inventor who boasted a decade earlier that his new wheel design would lead to "FRICTION ANNIHILATED" could have asked for nothing more.[1] If ease of communication was meant to usher in a new cosmopolitan outlook—that one could be at home anywhere—Yorick's account at first promises to dissolve distance, making light of the "one and twenty miles sailing" (*ASJ*, 3) between Dover and Calais. He refuses to be parochial (not everyone would allow that the French could outdo the British in anything), and the chapter seems as if it will efface national difference.

As Peter Budrin has observed, the first section is the only one without a title that serves to locate the action, perhaps because it spans two countries but possibly because it promises a viewpoint that transcends being framed in terms of place.[2] It is not long, however, before the world of nations and borders reasserts itself and the resulting friction slows the journey. In fact, it takes barely a dozen lines, as Yorick has to engage with French cuisine (always dangerous) and rails against Gallic law, picking an argument with Louis XV over the practice of impounding the goods of foreigners who die in French territory. It is a rapid *volta*, but there is still time for another change of direction when Yorick realizes he is being overhasty in his censure of the French king, admitting, "I have scarce set foot in your dominions—" (*ASJ*, 4). In one short introductory passage, the generalized "they" of France becomes a more concrete sense of its "dominions," and the speed of sailing and posting is juxtaposed with the importance of setting *foot* in a new land. If the work begins by glossing over the difference between Britain and France as "absolutely no further" than twenty-one miles of rapid travel, Yorick is quickly made aware of the very real distance between the two nations.

Much recent critical interest in *A Sentimental Journey* has focused on the way Sterne represents Yorick's attempt to gain a "passport" into a foreign land, with Charles L. Batten Jr., Chloe Chard, Melvyn New, James Chandler, Stephanie DeGooyer, Danielle Bobker, Shaun Regan, and Jesper Gulddal (to name but a few) considering the way "boundaries and fences" (*ASJ*, 13) prevent people from communicating beyond their own sphere.[3] The division between the self and the "other" is not only an obvious concern at the heart of the sentimental mode but also ties in with questions concerning the ethos of the Citizen of the World and the possibility of creating an identity that moves beyond national limitations. Regan is right to state that "while [Sterne's narrative] is not a 'cosmopolitan text' in any straightforward or idealistic sense," it "can be read as a comic exploration of the idea, which tests the viability, and uncovers some of the ironies, of the attempt to adopt and inhabit a cosmopolitan identity."[4] Building on this idea, I suggest that borders not only function as a leitmotif but pattern the text at a fundamental level. The concentration of chapters in Calais—Yorick's point of entry into France—and the gradual thinning out of noteworthy scenes as he becomes acclimated (especially once he gains a passport and starts to move quickly) follow the usual trajectory of "mastering" a foreign culture. However, this mastery is also problematic. Yorick wonders at the outset whether the "knowledge and improvements . . . to be got by sailing and posting" are "useful," "real," or "all a lottery" (*ASJ*, 16), and his own journey, with its diminishing returns, suggests that easy circulation and smooth progress might aid a more abstract, universal vantage point but also act against generating "useful" knowledge.

For Yorick, heightened experience is rarely the product of "sailing and posting" but of difficulty and digression when forward movement is frustrated. To use the passport metaphor, it is not simply a question of gaining access to a culture, accumulating knowledge, and moving on but instead of whether travel is a threshold to new understanding. Rather than Mary Louise Pratt's concept of the contact zone, of two cultures meeting and clashing, often in "asymmetrical relations of power," Sterne is much closer to the idea of the border formulated by Milan Kundera, in which it is less a line to be crossed than a liminal zone that "is constantly with us."[5] You never know, says Kundera, when you are about to cross a border. Staying in proximity with this frontier territory allows an intensity of experience that is not matched by the universal or generalized judgments arrived at once the border has been left behind. In a riposte to the often self-satisfied and pat Enlightenment ideas about how knowledge is "to be got" (*ASJ*, 16), like a commodity, Yorick's journey is punctuated by a series of jolts and blockages. By an inverse logic, moving forward is often antithetical to progress; it is the turnings that continually allow something new to happen.

The fundamental pattern of the text is a type of spatial digression, a journey of sidesteps, in which staying *within* the border allows fresh connections and ideas. At cultural checkpoints, Yorick constantly vacillates between subject positions. This is often regarded as a sign of indeterminacy, with one contemporary critic lambasting "doubly jumbled meanings" where the author "not only has failed to convey a meaning to his readers but probably did not understand the meaning himself," creating a sense of ambivalence at the heart of the text.[6] It is not that generalizations, such as Yorick's attempt to delineate the "distinguishing marks of national characters" (*ASJ*, 68), do not have validity but that complications arise with the realization that each generalization is only a partial truth and contingent on the circumstances that produce it. Yorick's general comments on cultures and people, rather than the crowning moments of his account, are instead conceived as a reduction of the experiences that gave rise to them.

This perspective is important for two reasons. First it enables a reading of *A Sentimental Journey* that moves beyond the binary possibility that Sterne is either celebrating or satirizing the sentimental mode. Second, it suggests that the text, often described as a watershed moment in travel literature, is indeed a turning point but perhaps not for the reasons usually ascribed to it. Batten, for instance, in his influential survey of travel writing in the period, points to Yorick's journey as the moment when accounts shift dramatically from an objective survey of "men and manners" to a much greater interest in the subjective and the personal.[7] Batten's thesis has been questioned by succeeding critics, with Anne Thell pointing out that much of the travel writing before Sterne was unavoidably involved in negotiating the boundaries between travel facts and personal accounts.[8] However, Sterne's plan to "write something new, quite out of the beaten track," still feels different from earlier accounts, particularly in its fascination with affect and the way these liminal spaces entangle and conflict with the traveler's sense of self. It would be interesting to consider whether the travel writers who followed Sterne, usually heading beyond the limits of the Grand Tour, were influenced less by subjectivity than by intersubjectivity, where the places they moved through forced the self constantly to renegotiate its own boundaries.

The chapter structure of *A Sentimental Journey* seems to hint at exactly this mapping of affect, in which the threshold is privileged over making "progress." The journey traces a straight line south of Calais as if Yorick had borrowed the ruler used to plan the Shandys' Grand Tour in *The Life and Opinions of Tristram Shandy, Gentleman* (fig. 4.1). The bird's-eye map view, as Pierre Bourdieu and

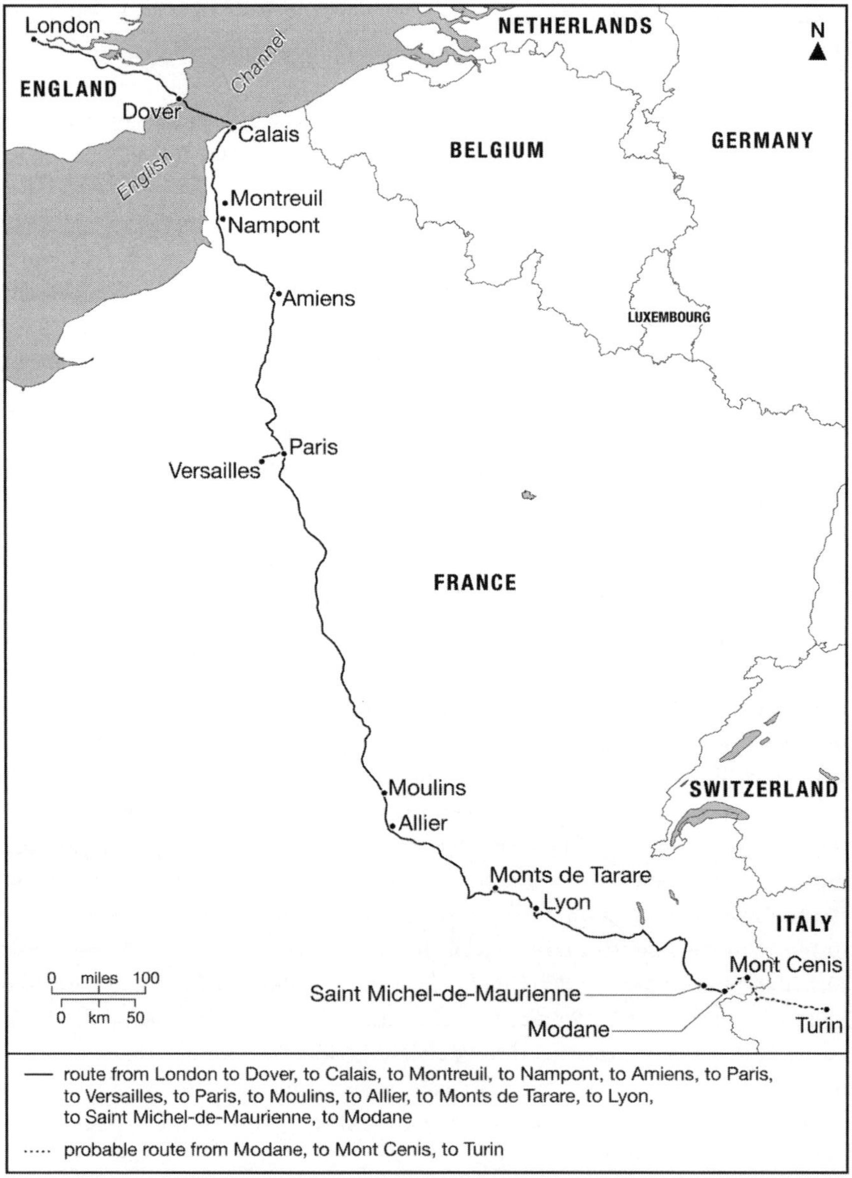

Figure 4.1 The route of Yorick's journey through France (design by Cath D'Alton)

J. B. Harley have warned, is suspect, and this can rarely have been truer than in Yorick's case.[9] Calais—rarely written about by travelers and rushed through by Sterne's previous stab at a Grand Tourist, namely, Tristram—now takes up one-fifth of the two volumes. The road to Paris takes one-seventh, the city itself one-half, the longest "stage" in the journey, from Paris to Lyon, just one-sixteenth. The claim that distance covered equals greater knowledge (specifically that traveling twenty-one miles confers authority) is undercut by Yorick's itinerary, which shows how "a large volume of adventures" can be packed into a "little span of life" (*ASJ*, 36). There is an inverse relationship between Yorick's miles and epiphanies per hour: at the border moments, time and experience thicken, while other location-times barely leave a trace. The encounter with Maria at Moulins, one of the few adventures Yorick deems worthy of relating in the 289 miles between Paris and Lyon, takes up two chapters. When he leaves Maria, he says, "The string I had touch'd ceased to vibrate" (*ASJ*, 153), and the journey goes back to tracing the thinnest of lines.[10] To be able to race past borders (like a VIP at an airport) may be relaxing and allow a feeling of harmony, but it also ensures a minimum of productive friction.

In one of Sterne's many reversals of expectation about travel, it is only after Yorick procures a passport that he starts to see less. The immediate effect is that it allows him to gain access to Parisian society, where his new "patron," Monsieur Le Count de B****, does him the favor of making him "known to a few people of rank": "they were to present me to others, and so on" (*ASJ*, 145). The phrase "and so on" indicates the beginning of Yorick's brief transformation into a Citizen of the Whirled, and within a few pages, he tells us of his meetings with the Marquis de B****, Monsieur P****, Madame de Q***, Madame de V***, Monsieur D***, the Abbe M***, and the Count de Faineant. The phrase is also used to describe how another minor celebrity, the caged starling, passes quickly through the hands of the English elite: "Lord A begg'd the bird of me—in a week Lord A gave him to Lord B—Lord B made a present of him to Lord C—and Lord C's gentleman sold him to Lord D for a shilling—Lord D gave him to Lord E—*and so on*—" (*ASJ*, 100; emphasis added). Sociability, either French or English, reduces characters to alphabet soup, suggesting that circulation glosses over identity, just as the listing foregrounds equivalence, rather than difference. Yorick admits that he gets on only in a "*beggarly*" way as he adjusts his identity to the Parisian coteries (*ASJ*, 148), pandering to his hosts with a series of bon mots. His words no longer produce difference but merely confirm his listeners' hobby-horsical opinions.

Paul Fussell, dividing those who travel abroad into tourists, travelers, and explorers, observes the linguistic element of each of these modes of mobility; while explorers may be confronted by objects for which they have no words, tourists move at speed through pure cliché, just as Yorick swaps Monsieur P for D and the starling goes from A, B, C, D, and E, never getting beyond the building blocks of language.[11] Franco Moretti, in his work on borders, notes that at threshold moments "figurality rises" (he discusses this while looking at Sir Walter Scott's Edward Waverley, a hero whose name seems to suggest the oscillations of border country).[12] Once past the border, distance and fixed vantage points can return. Similarly, Yorick becomes something of a national type (self-identified as one of "Les Messrs. Anglois" [*ASJ*, 145]) once he is part of the cosmopolitan "in" crowd, where the urbanity of the conversation is as frictionless as his own passage from one worthy to another. As Yorick admits, a traveler should be thankful for "ye small sweet courtesies of life, for smooth do ye make the road of it!" (*ASJ*, 69), while he explains about the thoughtfulness of the polite old French officer he meets at the *opera comique*, "[he] would have set me at unity with myself, in case I had been at variance" (*ASJ*, 82). Feelings of unity and smoothness are not to be underestimated, but in terms of gaining knowledge, they may make the road too easy; and a "passport" can paradoxically have the effect of increasing circulation while reducing the value of encounters.

The moment Yorick obtains a passport, Sterne introduces a debate about the effect of social exchange on identity. He explains to the Count de B**** that the French, like a coin moving quickly from pocket to pocket, end up so "polished" that they lose their individuality and "become so much alike" (*ASJ*, 119). Yorick's individual stamp also fades as he moves in polite circles; as he admits, "for three weeks together, I was of every man's opinion I met" (*ASJ*, 147). In contrast, Yorick claims that the English "like antient medals, kept more apart, and passing but few peoples hands preserve" their individual "sharpnesses" (*ASJ*, 119), foregrounding the connection between accelerated, borderless travel and identity that is as translatable and uniform as a unit of currency. Not only does the passport enable circulation, but it also indicates a degree of accommodation with the French state (Yorick now has no reason to argue with Louis XV) and allows him to "travel quietly along" (*ASJ*, 116). Yorick is moved to apply for a passport after attempting to imagine life in the Bastille and wondering whether he would have the inner strength to cope with being locked away. This incarceration, where the self is taken out of circulation, is oddly similar to being a "slave" (*ASJ*, 148) in the Parisian salons, where there is too much circulation. In both cases—the walls of the Bastille and the openness of the salon—the removal of borders is regarded by Yorick as a challenge to fashioning identity.

After Yorick suddenly recoils from Parisian society and decides to set out for Italy, his supposedly holistic journey through France feels suspiciously like the rapid circulation of the "posting" he mocks in the preface, where again ease of movement works against the value of experience. Yorick tells the reader how he traveled through the Bourbonnais: "with my affections flying out, and kindling at every group before me—and every one of 'em was pregnant with adventures" (*ASJ*, 149). However, he does not relate these adventures or report whether this "pregnant" state comes to any fruition, which is strange in a travel account that prides itself on its ability to pursue any digression it wants. Instead we are told, "Just heaven!—it would fill up twenty volumes—and alas! I have but a few small pages left of this to croud it into—and half of these must be taken up with . . . poor Maria" (*ASJ*, 149). The peripatetic philosopher Yorick, who previously boasts that he "walked forth without any determination where to go" (*ASJ*, 68), no longer appears so free; instead, he is constrained by time and space, both as traveler and as author. Although early on he informs readers of his determination to write his "journey" (*ASJ*, 12), it is something of a shock to find that the subject matter is being planned in advance, and not just as a narrative but in terms of pagination and the exigencies of production. It is also disquieting that Yorick moves from singular, recounted events to a landscape now encouraging plural "adventures," where he feels connected to "every group" rather than the individual meetings of the early chapters. Circulation continually encourages a move to a less precise register, to events so similar that they do not require relation.

It is true that Yorick's encounter with Maria became a remarkably popular sentimental scene, frequently celebrated by contemporary artists and lovers of "the beauties of Sterne." However, as a prearranged detour, it is quite different from earlier accidental encounters. Yorick makes his customary sidestep—he travels "half a league out of the road" (*ASJ*, 149) to see Maria and later sends his coach on ahead so that he can walk alongside her—but he also seeks her out, asking for directions. It is an attempt to stage what had earlier functioned as serendipity, going against the creed of one who is proud to announce, "I seldom go to the place I set out for" (*ASJ*, 103). It is not surprising that this passage has provoked so many questions about the sentimental mode, with Thomas Keymer noting Yorick's "smug self-approval," while in a letter to Wordsworth of 1801, Charles Lamb complained, "An intelligent reader finds a sort of insult in being told, I will teach you how to think upon this subject. This fault, if I am right, is in a ten thousandth worse degree to be found in Sterne, . . . who continually put a sign post up to shew where you are to feel."[13]

The meeting with Maria carries an undeniable charge, but it can also project Yorick as a sentimental tourist rather than a sentimental traveler. The scene gives rise to one of his bolder universal claims, that his ability to connect with Maria makes him conscious "of the existence of a soul" within him, and helps to affirm his Christian beliefs (*ASJ*, 149). There is no reason to doubt Yorick's sincerity, but again the way this feels "signposted" by the Maria scene associates it with a directed way of thinking that is closer to the axiomatic. It has a tagged-on quality and, just like his salon days and the Bourbonnais adventures, is written in summary form. These interpolations also use the past tense rather than the illusion of a continuous present, and this heightens their filtered, secondhand status, as if they are unmoored from a specific sense of place. Jonathan Lamb argues that such set pieces are removed from any "situational framework" and feel disingenuous because the "fancy can cheat as much as it pleases when given the scope of a 'general idea.'"[14] In fact, one of the issues that seems to fascinate Sterne is the way universals are situated by their very attempt to stand above more specific and more grounded moments of experience, especially the liminal territory that so much of the text inhabits.

Unlike the French *passeport*, which as DeGooyer observes translates as "to pass through the door," Yorick is continually placed amid borders or barriers.[15] Gaston Bachelard argues that the "threshold moment" dramatizes potential pathways, wondering "how many daydreams we should have to analyze under the simple heading Doors! For the door is an entire cosmos of the Half-open."[16] At these liminal moments, Yorick traces not a straight line but a form of sidestep (both physical and cognitive). He is constantly turning, oscillating from one idea or feeling to another, like a knight's move that disrupts the linear patterns of chess.[17] The Calais chapter titles, moving back and forth from the *remise* yard, the *remise* door, and the street, insist on a constant lateral move, just as at these moments Yorick exhibits a remarkably mobile mind. For instance, he accuses himself of a paltriness of spirit in preparing to barter with Monsieur Dessein but responds by turning himself about, "as a man naturally does upon a sudden reverse of sentiment" (*ASJ*, 20), later observing that his affections are subject to "the sudden turn of a corner" (*ASJ*, 58). When he decides to offer Madame de L*** a place in his coach and to ignore the "cabals" that "serve no purpose" that he knows of "but to encompass the heart with adamant," he "turn'd instantly about to the lady" (*ASJ*, 29)—although again the outcome is left hanging. Like the chapter titles, Yorick's actions are a pattern of variation, repetition, and retracing, rather than a directed move from one vantage point to another.

Forward movement is continually thwarted. Yorick barely moves beyond the coach yard in Calais for sixteen chapters, the dead ass in the road to Nampont puts "a sudden stop" to his journey (*ASJ*, 50), and the directions the *grisset* gives him to the *opera comique* include a bewildering set of left and right turns (which he cannot follow). One of the few incidents from the Italian part of the travels proleptically introduced (and perhaps carrying a freight of significance as a result) is the story of his meeting with the Marquesina di F*** at a Milan concert hall, where they keep blocking each other's way as they try to step aside: "We both flew together to the other side, and then back—and so on—" (*ASJ*, 77). Yorick is constantly involved in various forms of spatial digression, in which the sidestep ensures that doorways are rarely crossed, that the "entire cosmos of the Half-open" is continually left ajar. These lateral moves, instead of being frustrating, tend to be the moments to which Yorick ascribes value. He first gets close to Madame de L*** when Monsieur Dessein brings the wrong key to the *remise*, leaving the two strangers "attentive to the obstacle" of the locked door, which proves more propitious than standing with "faces turned towards the street" (*ASJ*, 21). The obstruction caused by the dead ass results in Yorick taking La Fleur inside his chaise, further cementing their mutual respect, while the ridiculous two-step with the Marquesina initiates a relationship he regards as the highlight of his time in Italy.

This spatial patterning is very different from the way borders and movement are conceived in *Tristram Shandy*, especially volume 7, which depicts a parallel journey through France. In this case Tristram, traveling as quickly as he can, avoids anything that slows his forward progress, choosing the fastest route from Calais to Paris via Beauvais, pointedly rejecting "the road by Lisle and Arras, which is the most about—but most interesting, and instructing" (*TS*, 7.3.579). The places he moves through have little more than a skeletal presence (he tries to sleep through the stages), and the material for his travel account is prompted by words or memories, anecdotes and remembered stories. The towns he visits become jumping-off points for his imaginative life, leading to ideas "volving and revolving in [his] fancy some time" (*TS*, 7.20.605). This also results in a series of temporal disjunctions; his account skips directly from Lyon to Avignon because, as he admits, "I have described this voyage down the Rhône, before I made it" (*TS*, 7.41.644). At one point Tristram describes himself as "entering Lyons," while remembering walking with his father and Uncle Toby in Auxerre many years previously, while adding that he is writing this on the banks of the Garonne (*TS*, 7.28.621–622). The digressions function on a temporal plane, where space is left in the background compared to the colorings of his associations and the layerings of his memory.

In Tristram's rapid journey, the anchoring of identity in terms of location hangs by a thread. In *A Sentimental Journey*, the continual proximity to borders encourages a series of cognitive shifts and a constant repositioning of the self. Judith Butler, critiquing biographies that produce linear narratives based on seamless cause and effect, posits that, paradoxically, the "truth of the person . . . might well become more clear in moments of interruption, stoppage, open-endedness."[18] Similarly, the frictionless information circuits that feed Enlightenment knowledge (such as salon conversations or a speeding coach) can frustrate and thwart "new" thinking. When Yorick wants to mull over the story of the dead ass, his postilion sets off at "a full gallop," ruining the moment for contemplation (*ASJ*, 55). If too much circulation is damaging, too little circulation is just as bad. When Yorick, writing a belated preface, boasts about his open, sentimental approach to travel while shut inside a stationary *desobligeant*, he ironically reduces his fellow travelers to "heads" and turns them into a list of epithets: "Idle," "Inquisitive," "Lying," "Proud," "Vain," "Splenetic," or even "Simple" (*ASJ*, 15). Bobker observes that the *desobligeant* functions as a walled-in space and points to a pervasive eighteenth-century association with "closet learning and theoretical knowledge . . . as though spatial boundaries necessarily condensed thought."[19] Yorick's shift to a general perspective is oddly generated by his physical situation: a boxed-off space leads to boxed-off thinking.

Yorick refuses to engage with the elite English tourists he subsequently meets, shutting himself away in his room, just as he later abandons the society of the salons, where the Marquis de B**** and Monsieur P**** are similarly reduced to "heads" (rather worryingly, the balance of sentimental travel rarely seems to work for Yorick with anyone in a socially superior position). It is no accident that Yorick's foray into a general essay is disturbed by the suggestive "see-saw" (*ASJ*, 13) of the coach, which brings him back to a more grounded realization of the place that he is inhabiting. The *desobligeant* also functions as an exemplary warning of how not to travel. We are told that it "had not profited much by its adventures" on the Grand Tour or from being marooned in the *remise* yard of Monsieur Dessein (*ASJ*, 17), again suggesting that, like the Bastille and the salons, stasis and circulation are equally unhelpful; it is the wavering on the threshold, the "see-saw," that provides the necessary impetus.

The *desobligeant* thus foregrounds the complex relationship between how people move and how they think, just as the text see-saws between binary opposites (the parochial and the cosmopolitan, the sentimental and the erotic); this fluctuating debate, often functioning at the level of language, is the central reading experience.[20] If circulation leads to a type of aphoristic shorthand, in which people are reduced to Lords A, B, and C, the border encourages figurative language, ambiguity, the dash, and the oxymoron. For instance, Yorick's journey is prompted by his gentleman's "*civil* triumph" (*ASJ*, 3; emphasis added), suggesting the strangely competitive element of *politesse*, and we are later told that there is often "as much *sour* as *sweet* in a compliment" (*ASJ*, 19). Oxymorons are the opposite of a universal language; they indicate that single words cannot adequately express a feeling or experience and suggest that moments of intensity defy categorization. Similarly, Sterne's unparalleled use of the dash to change sense or shift thought is a typographical rendering of the process of changing direction, of turning a corner and refusing to move forward by neatly structured sentences and full stops.

Samuel Johnson's *A Journey to the Western Islands of Scotland* (1775) provides a useful comparison. Johnson had more than a few borders to negotiate; between England and Scotland, between his *Dictionary* lexicon and the Gaelic of the Highlanders, and between his genteel ideas of landscape and the Scottish mountains. Throughout the account, there is also a tension between his determination to produce a scientific text and his attraction to the romance and grandeur of the Highlands. This border, though, is kept separate, with any sense of attachment immediately closed off by a full stop and a shift toward a more rational, distanced vantage point. For instance, when describing a peculiar rock formation, the Buller of Buchan, Johnson states, "We entered the arch, which the water had made, and found ourselves in a place, which, though we could not think ourselves in danger, we could scarcely survey without some recoil of the mind. The bason in which we floated was nearly circular, perhaps thirty yards in diameter."[21] The "recoil of the mind," as so often happens in this narrative, is immediately followed by a new sentence reasserting rational supremacy, here taking the form of an exact measurement. Johnson's chorographic format rarely includes descriptions of himself on the move, allowing a more distanced, map-like view, which helps him to keep different modes of cognition separate. In Yorick's essay-like and axiomatic preface, his rhetorical question "Where then, my dear countrymen, are you going—" is instead overheard by two English tourists and taken for a genuine inquiry: "—We are only looking at this chaise, said they—" (*ASJ*, 17). The dash allows abstraction to merge with a real encounter, monologue to turn into dialogue, and writing suddenly to come, alarmingly, face-to-face with its subject.

The way the dash encourages a bleeding between different ontological registers is similar to Brian Massumi's insight that such complex juxtapositions "could be seen not as binary oppositions or contradictions, but as resonating levels."[22] This "resonance"—like the vibration of a string or the see-saw of a coach—is often noted by critics and saturates the language they use to describe the effect of the book, with Chandler insisting on the "ambivalence and reflexivity" of the sentimental mode.[23] M-C. Newbould, in observing that Yorick's "encounters with women might possess an erotic rather than innocent dimension," allowing "several possible readings to be upheld simultaneously," outlines the way the text is felt as "trembling" and "hovering" between layers of signification.[24]

This oscillation is often set into overdrive because the sentimental mode, in John Mullan's neat phrase, "lives at the edges of speech."[25] As Newbould observes, this silent communication is not simple; the touch becomes a charged space where the altruistic and sentimental merge with the erotic. Newbould argues that for Yorick and for Tristram, when talking about their sexual activities, "saying less actually says more": "non-verbal indicators (such as a dash or an asterisk) can hint towards a possible meaning."[26] This is very close to Massumi's understanding of how affect functions, which he formulates as the moment of the event that is anterior to any cognitive structuring (though not to "thought") and that is enacted even before an emotion can be "filtered" into a word or an abstract summation. Massumi argues that affect inhabits a borderland of intensity where feelings, cognition, and volition are all characterized by an essential "two-sidedness"—the sense that, as Yorick himself admits, "there is nothing unmixt in this world" (*ASJ*, 116). In comparison, any "anchored perspective" may be able to "capture" part of the event, but something will always "escape."[27]

A classic example of this filtering process occurs when Yorick considers offering to share a chaise with Madame de L***. The desire to do her a service is also mixed with other, less generous possible motives, and this "two-sidedness" leads him to debate the course of action he should take. Yorick states,

> Every dirty passion, and bad propensity in my nature, took the alarm, as I stated the proposition—It will oblige you to have a third horse, said AVARICE, which will put twenty livres out of your pocket.—You know not who she is, said CAUTION—or what scrapes the affair may draw you into, whisper'd COWARDICE—
>
> Depend upon it, Yorick! said DISCRETION, 'twill be said you went off with a mistress, and came by assignation to Calais for that purpose—
>
> —You can never after, cried HYPOCRISY aloud, shew your face in the world—or rise, quoth MEANNESS, in the church—or be any thing in it, said PRIDE, but a lousy prebendary. (*ASJ*, 28–29)

In each case, ramifications conceived in precise circumstances (needing a third horse) are reduced to abstract constructions (avarice), all of which are constellated around an exterior, imposed, value-based framework (two are deadly sins). They are rationalizations that reduce complex motives to a single word, possessing an ironic, dictum-like quality, and Yorick decides to dismiss them because, he says, "I generally act from the first impulse" (*ASJ*, 29).

The "two-sidedness" of the scene accords with Massumi's claim that "the entire vibratory event is unconscious, out of mind," and its "anomaly is smoothed over retrospectively to fit conscious requirements of continuity and linear causality."[28] His ideas have an obvious application to *A Sentimental Journey*, in which Yorick admits, "there is no regular reasoning upon the ebbs and flows of our humours" (*ASJ*, 7), and the text continually undercuts fixed positions. Yorick speaks of universal generosity but then refuses to give the monk a single sou. His bravura peroration, using "systematic reasonings" (*ASJ*, 96) to make light of the Bastille, is suddenly overthrown by the starling-inspired notion of what imprisonment would really be like. As Yorick admits, "I heavily walk'd up stairs, unsaying every word I had said in going down them" (*ASJ*, 96). Massumi argues that moments of intensity allow the "new" to form and that the event brings "a tinge of the unexpected, *the lateral*, the unmotivated, to lines of action and reaction."[29] The rather conventional appeal to the "liberty of the mind" as a counter to the Bastille is now a subject of debate as Yorick repositions the angle from which he approaches the question, helping him to turn back in on himself, to renegotiate the boundaries of received ideas. Like Yorick's tracing and retracing of his steps on the stairs, the text also performs a continual mental sidestep, characterized by a lateral mobility that is closer to the vibratory than it is to the linear.

This narrative strategy forces the reader to make the same sort of journey Yorick undergoes, with Donald R. Wehrs arguing that Sterne's continual use of "redirection" and the "disruption" of his "anarchic sense" means that "we find ourselves converted, or turned around, despite ourselves."[30] The sexual double entendres carry an obvious comic payload, but they also force the reader to hold two possibilities at once and thus share the same cognitive experience as Yorick, wherein, as Melvyn New observes, "sexual enjoyment is always on the other side of the door or window or curtain."[31] These lateral shifts slow readers down, forcing them to make their own knight's move as they progress, to think in a see-saw, zigzag fashion. Peter de Voogd has argued that for Sterne "blanks are as meaningful as text," and the first edition is full of white space, creating borders of varying length between one chapter and the next, as if encouraging the reader to wander.[32] Certainly, the text makes it difficult for the reader to impose definitive meanings; it cannot simply be identified as ironic, sentimental, or erotic, cannot be reduced to a label or a single word.

Paradoxically, the passport has the opposite effect on Yorick, "smoothing over" anomaly and allowing him to move in a linear fashion. The passport creates an abstracted, fixed self, a reduction of all that is Yorick into the smallest of categories: a name and a rather unfortunate occupation (king's jester). Yorick admits, "there is not a more perplexing affair in life to me, than to set about telling anyone who I am . . . and I have often wish'd I could do it in a single word" (*ASJ*, 112). His solution, to point to his name in *Hamlet*, manages just such a contraction but also shoehorns him into a far-from-ideal persona. Sterne, who also had to make friends in order to acquire a passport while in France, had a similarly ambivalent reaction to being welcomed into the society of Baron d'Holbach and philosophes such as Diderot.[33] Gulddal argues that the passport enables "a type of cross-border travel that allows travelers to reap the benefits of communicating beyond their narrow circle of life while at the same time immunizing them against potential threats."[34] This is very true, except that the immunizing effect of the passport, while bringing comfort and security, also works against the process of "communicating." Yorick ends the first volume with this reflection, again connecting mobility to thought: "It is alike troublesome to both the rider and his beast—if the latter goes pricking up his ears, and starting all the way at every object which he never saw before—I have as little torment of this kind as any creature alive; and yet I honestly confess, that many a thing gave me pain, and that I blush'd at many a word the first month—which I found inconsequent and perfectly innocent the second" (*ASJ*, 84). His assimilation protects him from pain, torment, and embarrassment, but at the same time a creature "pricking up his ears" has an intensity of experience missing in one who learns to find difference "inconsequent." We hear little of his second month in Paris compared to the pages covering just his first few hours in France.

Yorick's sense of "fitting in" attains its pinnacle in "The Supper" and "The Grace," when he is welcomed into the home of a peasant family, after a peroration on the "great SENSORIUM of the world" (*ASJ*, 155), in which he argues that everything is connected on a planetary scale. Some critics have wondered whether this is the text's engineered high point, with the journey charting a gradual perfecting of the sentimental or the cosmopolitan mode. Martin Battestin and Regan see Yorick attaining his own type of Citizen of the World apotheosis as he delivers a paean to the "natural cosmopolitanism" of the peasant family.[35] Battestin suggests that the two chapters produce a "climax" where Yorick (and Sterne) manage to "find a place for the soul in the body, to some extent synthesizing or trying to accommodate the conflicting Latitudinarian and materialist positions."[36] This epiphanic moment is one in which Yorick admits, "my heart was sat down the moment I enter'd the room" (*ASJ*, 158), and it is tempting to think he has achieved something approaching "borderless" communion with his hosts. However, given the care with which Sterne questions and places Yorick's universal statements, "The Supper" and "The Grace" need to be read as partial truths rather than as a key to the text.

Yorick only meets the peasant family because, on the climb toward Mount Taurira, one of his horses loses not one but two shoes (as if the narrative god of contingency is determined to make a point about the importance of accidents and lateral events). Yorick's grand overview is also partly produced by the vista caused by an ascent and the fact that upland territory has a tradition of effacing boundary markers.[37] Paradoxically, the text insists on the situatedness of universals: Mount Taurira signals the start of a move to higher ground, and after reaching Lyon, Yorick then has to negotiate the Alps, as if elevated thoughts are the product of an elevated position. As Chloe Chard observes, the borderland world of treaties and negotiations then quickly returns on the road to Turin, promoting a "view of travel as transgressive and destabilizing," with the text ending not with closure but "at the point where the greatest possible curiosity has been aroused as to what is to happen next."[38] It is similar to the idealized description of Paradise Hall in *Tom Jones*, where Henry Fielding admits his vision of Mr. Allworthy's eminence is overdone: "Reader, take care, I have unadvisedly led thee to the top of as high a hill as Mr. Allworthy's, and how to get thee down without breaking thy neck, I do not well know. However, let us e'en venture to slide down together."[39] Yorick's slide is equally quick and painful, and the journey toward Turin is full of jolts: "Let the way-worn traveller vent his complaints upon the sudden turns and dangers of your roads—your rocks—your precipices—the difficulties of getting up—the horrors of getting down—mountains impracticable—and cataracts, which roll down great stones from their summits, and block his road up" (*ASJ*, 160).

In the urban milieu, dashes usually represent sudden shifts of direction and thought, like turning around a city corner, but here they function as a retardation, like blocks laid in the road to prevent forward movement. It is far from the hundred-miles-per-hour of the opening chapter, and just such a rockfall leads to another spatial digression. Yorick is forced to spend the night at a small wayside inn where he is obliged to share his bedroom with a female stranger, rather than the expected stop at the end of the stage. A "sufficient barrier" (*ASJ*, 163) has to be constructed to maintain decorum between the two stranded travelers, but after a comical list of treaty negotiations, including a promise to be silent, Yorick is deemed to have caused an infraction because, unable to sleep, he "turn'd and turn'd again" before crying out, "O my God!" (*ASJ*, 164). Even then the words of the treaty are open to debate; Yorick argues that by exclaiming "O my God!" he is covered by the fact that he is permitted to say his prayers (how far this "ejaculation" lies from his earlier apostrophe to heaven and the sensorium of the world again suggests the difficulty of taking "Grace" as the final word).

Lamb argues suggestively that just as "the ascent toward the spiritual realm is named by language that frees itself from any real ambiguity," so the "corresponding descent" then takes us back "toward the body."[40] Once again, the higher strain of abstraction can only function by leaving something out. This is not to say that Yorick does not make generalizations but that they are limited and are just as "situated" as his more particular experiences. It is also not to deny that Yorick makes "progress." He hopes to "learn better manners" as he gets along (*ASJ*, 11), and as Bobker argues, his decision to reject the one-person *desobligeant* signals a move to a more human form of travel. However, this progress is not the simple accretion of knowledge associated with Enlightenment rationality and empiricism.[41]

A Sentimental Journey has been credited with changing the way people thought about travel and travel writing, with Batten suggesting that it provided a turning point, encouraging a move toward more subjective accounts after a period in which objective fact-finding held sway.[42] This is an obvious simplification, but few would deny that there is a shift in the direction of the personal and the particular in this period. *A Sentimental Journey* seems to suggest that, rather than a move toward greater subjectivity or some concept of the Romantic traveler, what is really happening is that the spaces through which travelers started to move possessed greater affect, that the continual engagement with borders is something that moves *through* the traveler, rather than a landscape that is being looked at from a secure vantage point. In this, *A Sentimental Journey* may provide a turning point in travel discourse, not so much in promoting subjectivity but because it signals a move toward a realm where even subjective, emotional responses become destabilized. Equally, any attempt to attain the high ground of universalism, or to ascend to some elevated cosmopolitan ethos, collapses not just because of social, racial, gender, technological, or economic inequalities but because space is not created equal. The shift in travel narratives after 1760 is perhaps less a process of opening new territories, or a move to a more personal type of narrative, than of embracing borders, of being continually on the threshold.

Sterne's text begins with a grand gesture about how the French order things across the Channel, the first chapter confidently straddling two countries, and ends with two strangers, like two nations, negotiating a peace treaty with each other. Yorick's final act is to stretch out his arm across the "narrow passage" (*ASJ*, 165) separating their beds, in an almost human approximation of the dash. A travel account that started by promising clear demarcations finishes with a reassertion of the liminality of borders as Yorick is left groping in the dark, grabbing a deeply ambiguous part of the *fille de chambre*. Fittingly, the volume ends with a dash, not just as a sign of indeterminacy but because the dash so often functions as a border in this text, existing in the liminal space between two moments that are not linearly connected. At the same time, especially in Sterne's often extravagant typography, the dash suggests movement between two rival states, allowing what is different to be connected.

Much of eighteenth-century fiction, when it presents complex moments of experience, usually does so in order to make a concrete statement on meaning, on what an event signifies. Sterne is very different, continually complicating ideas about self-narrativization and questioning the validity of abstracted rules. Yorick's belief in the open, free, connected "Sensorium of the world" may work on Mount Taurira but proves of little use when he makes his descent from the Alps, just as the treaty made at the end starts to come unpinned as Yorick and the lady argue, their combat strangely weakening the barrier between them. This could be the final border at which Yorick is suspended—between the newness of the moment and the inadequate (but almost unavoidable) need to structure it, to reduce it to shorthand. The ending also suggests that the final problem Yorick struggles to reconcile is how an individual can get "useful knowledge" in a journey where the experience of the threshold is so much richer than the passport that unlocks doors.

NOTES

I would like to thank the editors, M-C. Newbould and W. B. Gerard, and Andrew Rudd at Exeter University for their insightful advice and suggestions, many of which are incorporated here.

1. Cited in Ralph Straus, *Carriages and Coaches: Their History and Their Evolution* (London: Martin Secker, 1912), 190.
2. Peter Budrin, "The Shadow of Eliza in *A Sentimental Journey*" (paper presented at "Alas, Poor Yorick!": A Sterne 250-Year Anniversary Conference, Cambridge, UK, March 18–21, 2018).
3. Rather than list them here, I discuss many of their ideas and insights later in the chapter.
4. Shaun Regan, "Peripatetic Philosophy: Sterne and Cosmopolitanism," *Textual Practice* 31, no. 2 (2017): 266.
5. Mary Louise Pratt, "Arts of the Contact Zone," *Profession* 91 (1991): 34; Milan Kundera, *The Book of Laughter and Forgetting*, trans. Michael Henry Haim (Harmondsworth, UK: Penguin, 1984), 217.
6. Richard Griffith, excerpt from *A Series of Genuine Letters*, cited in *CH*, 186.
7. Charles L. Batten Jr., *Pleasurable Instruction: Form and Convention in Eighteenth-Century Travel Literature* (Berkeley: University of California Press, 1978), 77–81. A feted contemporary account, Thomas Pennant's chorographic *A Tour in Scotland, and Voyage to the Hebrides: Part 1*, 2nd ed. (London, 1776), still reads like a map: "The length of *Ilay*, from the point of *Ruval* to the *Mull* of *Kinoth*, is twenty-eight miles; is divided into the parishes of *Kildalton*, *Kilarow*, *Kilchoman*, and *Kilmenie*. The latitude of Freeport, 55° 52" 29". The face of the island is hilly, but not high" (260–261).
8. See Anne Thell, *Minds in Motion: Imagining Empiricism in Eighteenth-Century Travel Writing* (Lewisburg, PA: Bucknell University Press, 2017); and also Jason H. Pearl, "Woodes Rogers and the Boundary of Travel Facts," *Eighteenth-Century Life* 30, no. 3 (Fall 2007): 60–75.
9. See Pierre Bourdieu, *Outline of a Theory of Practice*, trans. Richard Nice (Cambridge: Cambridge University Press, 1977); and J. B. Harley, "Deconstructing the Map," *Cartographica* 26, no. 2 (Spring 1989): 1–20.
10. It is worth noting the importance of vibrations to theories of the sentimental, in particular, the work of David Hartley. See Jonathan Lamb, "Language and Hartleian Associationism in *A Sentimental Journey*," *Eighteenth-Century Studies* 13, no. 3 (Spring 1980): 285–312.
11. Paul Fussell, *Abroad: British Literary Traveling between the Wars* (Oxford: Oxford University Press, 1980), 39.
12. Franco Moretti, *Atlas of the European Novel, 1800–1900* (London: Verso, 1999), 43.
13. Thomas Keymer, "*A Sentimental Journey* and the Failure of Feeling," in *The Cambridge Companion to Laurence Sterne*, ed. Thomas Keymer (Cambridge: Cambridge University Press, 2009), 91. The letter, dated January 30, 1801, is cited by Warren Oakley in "Physical Encounters as a Point of Contact between Sterne's *Journey* and De Quincey's *Confessions*," *Romanticism* 18, no. 2 (2012): 189.

14. Lamb, "Language and Hartleian Associationism," 291.
15. Stephanie DeGooyer, "The Poetics of the Passport in *A Sentimental Journey*," in *Sterne, Tristram, Yorick: Tercentenary Essays on Laurence Sterne*, ed. Melvyn New, Peter de Voogd, and Judith Hawley (Newark: University of Delaware Press, 2016), 202.
16. Gaston Bachelard, *The Poetics of Space*, trans. Maria Jolas (Boston: Beacon, 1994), 222.
17. Chandler observes the importance of "reversal" to the progress of the narrative and suggests that Yorick's volition often describes "a full rotation" enabling the reader to "feel all of the 'movements' to which the situation is incident." Chandler, *An Archaeology of Sympathy: The Sentimental Mode in Literature and Cinema* (Chicago: University of Chicago Press, 2013), 211.
18. Judith Butler, *Giving An Account of Oneself* (New York: Fordham University Press, 2005), 64.
19. Danielle Bobker, "Carriages, Conversation and *A Sentimental Journey*," *Studies in Eighteenth-Century Culture* 35 (2006): 252.
20. Mary Helen McMurran argues that the Citizen of the World ethos was involved "in an unresolved assessment of the complex relation of local attachment—consistently understood as both natural and the cause of narrow prejudices—and universal allegiance, which may be unnatural. The cosmopolite thus circulated in the eighteenth century as a flashpoint for these tensions." McMurran, "The New Cosmopolitanism and the Eighteenth Century," *Eighteenth-Century Studies* 47, no. 1 (Fall 2013): 32.
21. Samuel Johnson, *A Journey to the Western Islands of Scotland*, ed. Peter Levi (Harmondsworth, UK: Penguin, 1984), 46.
22. Brian Massumi, "The Autonomy of Affect," *Cultural Critique* 31 (Fall 1995): 94.
23. Chandler, *Archaeology of Sympathy*, 11.
24. M-C. Newbould, "Sex, Death and the Aposiopesis: Two Early Attempts to Fill the Gaps of Laurence Sterne's *A Sentimental Journey*," *Postgraduate English* 17 (March 2008): 14–15, 2.
25. John Mullan, "Sentimental Novels," in *The Cambridge Companion to the Eighteenth-Century Novel*, ed. John Richetti (Cambridge: Cambridge University Press, 1996), 241.
26. Newbould, "Sex, Death and the Aposiopesis," 2–3.
27. Massumi, "Autonomy of Affect," 96. Massumi insists that affect should not be confused with emotion, because the words used to describe emotions are an attempt to make the intensity of the event "narrativizable."
28. Massumi, 89.
29. Massumi, 87 (emphasis added).
30. Donald R. Wehrs, "Anarchic Signification and Motions of Grace in Sterne's Novelistic Satire," in New, de Voogd, and Hawley, *Sterne, Tristram, Yorick*, 93.
31. Melvyn New, "Proust's Influence on Sterne: Remembrance of Things to Come," *Modern Language Notes*, 103, no. 5 (1988): 1033.
32. Peter J. de Voogd, "*Tristram Shandy* as Aesthetic Object," *Word & Image* 4, no. 1 (1988): 387.
33. See the discussion in the notes to the Florida edition, *ASJ*, 345, 348–350.
34. Jesper Gulddal, "Porous Borders: The Passport as an Access Metaphor in Laurence Sterne's *A Sentimental Journey*," *symploke* 25, nos. 1–2 (2017): 49.
35. Regan, "Peripatetic Philosophy," 277.
36. Martin C. Battestin, "Sterne among the Philosophes: Body and Soul in *A Sentimental Journey*," *Eighteenth-Century Fiction* 7, no. 1 (October 1994): 35–36.
37. See James C. Scott, *The Art of Not Being Governed*: *An Anarchist History of Upland Southeast Asia* (New Haven, CT: Yale University Press, 2009).
38. Chloe Chard, "Crossing Boundaries and Exceeding Limits: Destabilization, Tourism, and the Sublime," in *Transports: Travel, Pleasure, and Imaginative Geography, 1600–1800*, ed. Chloe Chard and Helen Langdon (New Haven, CT: Yale University Press, 1996), 126, 117.

39. Henry Fielding, *Tom Jones*, ed. John Bender and Simon Stern (Oxford: Oxford University Press, 1998), 37.
40. Lamb, "Language and Hartleian Associationism," 309.
41. Judith Butler has argued that "universality has been used to extend certain colonialist and racist understandings of civilized 'man'" and that it is complicit in the exclusion of historically marginalized groups. Butler, "Restaging the Universal," in *Contingency, Hegemony, Universality: Contemporary Dialogues on the Left* (London: Verso, 2000), 38.
42. Batten credits *A Sentimental Journey* with being "one of the most significant influences" as travel writing starts to read like a memoir or a novel, rather than a sober display of important facts (*Pleasurable Instruction*, 79).

5

(O)ECONOMY AND ORDER

Laurence Sterne's Chaptering

ALEXANDER HARDIE-FORSYTH

COMMENTARY ON THE PAUCITY of Sterne's volumes dates to *Tristram Shandy*'s earliest reception, when reviewers evoked parallels between their size and their author's slender frame. The unidentified contributor of "Animadversions on Tristram Shandy" to the *Grand Magazine* (April 1760) asks, "Did you ever see *Shandy*? . . . If he does but twist his nose on one side, there's humor in the distortion . . . I only wish he was fatter—He looks as meagre as if he had pored over the metaphysical lamp."[1] Owen Ruffhead, writing for the *Monthly Review* (February 1761), dismisses Tristram's debut as "two pigmy octavos, which scarce contained the substance of a twelve-penny pamphlet."[2] Both reviewers iterate a prevalent eighteenth-century complaint: writers valued primarily for their novelty stoked an unnatural appetite in the reading public for books contributing little actual substance.

Tristram's slenderness and narrative diffuseness, however, could also be cast in a more favorable light. William Kenrick's early appraisal for the *Monthly Review* posits Sterne as a frugal author who "husbands his adventures with great oeconomy" such that they may provide for him for "as long as he lives."[3] To borrow Marc Shell's definition, "oeconomy" refers etymologically to "the conventions (*nomoi*) of and distribution (*nemesis*) within the household (*oikos*)."[4] As Karen Harvey states, while the term came to encompass new modes of production and distribution during the late eighteenth century's nascent industrialization, it continued to denote the wise distribution of household resources well into the early nineteenth.[5] Kenrick likens Sterne's narrative and publishing practices to good household management, exemplifying how the language of domestic "oeconomy" was often oriented to legitimize the middling sort within the public sphere.[6] Adept at literary husbandry, Sterne distributes his narratives across the divisions of his works using a seemingly erratic but nevertheless considered method of chaptering that bears the most profitable return when his books enter the marketplace.

Although "oeconomy" as a discursive term is predicated on principles of domestic management, the public-facing aspect of Sterne's practice as an author who wrote "not to be *fed*, but to be *famous*" (*Letters*, 116) situates him at a terminological fault line, one where the economic comes also to describe wider, abstract forms of market equivalence. As we shall see in *A Sentimental Journey*, the market's abstract exchange value and its circulation of commodities could be presented as a totalizing form of "commerce" that threatens to encroach on older notions of a "simple œconomy" (*ASJ*, 107) as the more discrete, often aristocratic, domain of estate management. Sterne's chaptering often presents itself within an analogous model of equivalence, albeit not at Adam Smith's level of abstraction in which the economy becomes, in Charles Taylor's terms, a "single objectified reality" based on a principle of mutual benefit.[7] *Tristram Shandy* cannot operate according to such abstraction, for the narrative turns and gaps staged by Sterne often arise from Tristram's intrusive attempts to micromanage every aspect of textual transmission. (O)economy provides, therefore, a useful dual approach to examine Sterne's use of chapters; it marks the precise point where material considerations of how to "husband" or distribute one's narrative resources meet the question of how that distribution might affect a work's value.

A Sentimental Journey's chaptering provides continuity with *Tristram Shandy* but also a refinement of technique; while Tristram functions as a self-conscious textual arranger, "constantly . . . stressing his presence in the workshop of narration," in Alexis Tadié's terms, Yorick rarely discusses how *A Sentimental Journey* divides across chapters, nor does he bind narrative economy to the material book to the same extent.[8] Yet, as James Chandler notes, *A Sentimental Journey* is, if anything, even more preoccupied with "ambiguities about 'order,' ordonnance, and causality," concerns related to those of narrative distribution.[9] The "order" of its constituent "matter" (*ASJ*, 3) is central from the opening pronouncement that launches Yorick's sojourn in France.

Shifting Sterne's focus from temporal to spatial arrangement, *A Sentimental Journey*'s division into "scenes" or "vignettes" helps form the "*Vehicle*" (*ASJ*, 15) by which Yorick's travels are conveyed. Its boxed divisions, or "frames," construct a productive tension between circulation and stasis; they facilitate narrative movement between scenes while also offsetting them with what Barbara M. Benedict terms a "spectatorial distance."[10] At the same time, focusing *A Sentimental Journey*'s vignettes around particular objects and locales generates another type of narrative "economy," requiring less a stretching of narrative resources and more a stylistic reduction of narrative to scenic arrangement. The adjectival construct of the "sentimental" journey as reconciling emotional with temporal and spatial movement requires that the *Journey*'s chapters also "economize" its relation between inner and outer; in episodes such as "The Sword. Rennes," chapters disconnected by location are placed together to optimize their *affective* value. While we have few insights into Sterne's composition of *Tristram Shandy* beyond his correspondence, the fair copy of *A Sentimental Journey*'s first volume provides a test case as to whether the principles of (o)economy and order that Sterne portrays in his fiction are traceable in the final stages of his manuscript transcription.

Nicholas Dames posits that the origins of the term "chapter" reveal a shift in use.[11] Originally an early type of paratext that indicated how each following segment of text should be read, the term later came to refer to the units of textual division themselves:[12] "The chapter is an invention of antiquity [that] stems from the practice in Roman legal texts of prefacing sections with *capitula* ('head,' or 'heading'), brief introductory summaries of what follows. The notion of the *capitulum* was imported into Biblical manuscripts in late antiquity, and by the early thirteenth century 'chapters' were standardized forms within Western European bibles. A gradual shift took place, in which the term 'chapter' came to refer to the segmented unit of text, while a new term—'argument'—came to refer to the summary heading itself."[13]

Samuel Johnson's *Dictionary* identifies the root of the word in the French *chapitre* (little head) and the Latin *capitulum*. By the middle of the eighteenth century, the movement from paratext to unit of division is nearly complete, Johnson's definition of the chapter being simply "a division of a book."[14] Chaptering outside of prose fiction was thus familiar to most eighteenth-century readers, particularly in relation to Biblical "chapter and verse" readings. Within the context of prose fiction, of the near-five-hundred fictions Leah Orr identifies as published between 1690 and 1730, few considered as bestsellers (by Orr's definition, those that reached five editions) are arranged using chapters.[15] Jonathan Swift's *A Tale of a Tub* (1704), for example, divides across "sections" that alternate between its central mock allegory and various digressions. Defoe notably tells his stories in single blocks divided only into paragraphs. Epistolary works such as Elizabeth Singer Rowe's *Friendship in Death* (1728) are, of course, arranged across fictional letters.

Chaptering, however, is otherwise prevalent at this time in treatises, theological, and philosophical works. Shaftesbury claims its use for "miscellarian authors," arguing that chapters permit readers to "renew their application" after "frequent intervals of repose."[16] This "post way" of writing aligns chaptering, Eve Tavor Bannet notes, with commercial interest: frequent breaks for a change of "subjects or direction" permit readers to commit a business-like "application" to miscellaneous reading.[17] By 1741, the year prior to Henry Fielding's *Joseph Andrews* (often credited as innovating the chapter's use in fiction), Alexander Pope's *Memoirs of Martinus Scriblerus* was already parodying chaptering in the popular subgenre of memoirs, which also frequently used these divisions. Pope promises his reader, perhaps in imitation of Colley Cibber's notoriously disjointed style in his *Apology for the Life* (1740), that "whenever [the reader] begins to think any one Chapter dull, the style will be immediately changed in the next," ironically suggesting a continual shifting of scene, sentiment, and style across chapters as an antidote to readerly malaise.[18]

This brief account of chaptering qualifies two assertions by J. Paul Hunter: (1) that chaptering emerged as a distributive tool just as prose fictions "extended their lengths to match the narrative needs of [private] readers" and (2) that Fielding's apparently innovative use of chapters is "more an adaptation of a feature already standard in Richardson than it is a new discovery."[19] As the long-running success of François Fénelon's *Telemachus* (1699) shows, it was not necessarily the case that lengthy unchaptered works failed to find a market, and, indeed, the use of chaptering did not initially bestow much advantage. While it is correct to view Fielding's chaptering as an adaptation of earlier techniques, there are precedents for its use beyond Richardson's epistolary fiction—not least English translations of Miguel de Cervantes's *Don Quixote* (1605–1615), Cibber's *Apology for the Life* (which became one of Fielding's satirical targets in *An Apology for the Life of Mrs. Shamela Andrews* [1741]), and Fielding's own practices as a dramatist. Although Fielding could by no means claim to have invented chaptering in prose fiction, his authorial practice is closely identified with its popularity. If, as Hunter argues, an increase in extended private reading shaped chaptering as a means of providing respite in the same way that "oral narratives of earlier times took their shape in part from the circumstances of communal gathering," it is Fielding who most strongly identifies this distinction by collapsing it: "These Divisions have the Sanction of great Antiquity. *Homer* not only divided his great Work into twenty-four Books, (in Compliment perhaps to the twenty-four Letters to which he had very particular Obligations) but, according to the Opinion of some very sagacious Critics, hawked them all separately, delivering only one Book at a Time, (probably by Subscription)."[20] Fielding wryly establishes the "Art" of "exhibit[ing] [a work] piece-meal to the public" as one of the time-honored "Mysteries or Secrets" of authorial craft.[21] Common readers labor under the misconception "that by this Art . . . we mean only to swell our Works to a much larger Bulk than they would otherwise be extended to."[22] The very denial of any such attempt to swell the work affirms Fielding's awareness of the increasing "Bulk" of fiction on the market; a well-apportioned fiction can be sold to the reader in greater mass and over longer stretches of time.

Tristram Shandy's chaptering often reframes many of Fielding's and his contemporaries' conceits. Tristram extolls chaptering as a convenience "to relieve the [reader's] mind" (*TS*, 4.10.337), almost certainly a reference to *Joseph Andrews*'s likening of a gap between chapters to an "Inn or Resting-Place."[23] Like Fielding's narrator, Tristram claims to value chaptering as a prudent technique of aeration, breaking up narrative into digestible components and permitting the reader moments in which mentally to regather. He also describes how its use "in a work of this dramatic cast" allows for a "shifting of scenes" (*TS*, 4.10.337) in the same theatrical idiom used in other midcentury fictions such as *The History of Charlotte Summers* (1750).[24] Tristram disarms accusations of indebtedness for these observations by dismissing them as "cold conceits" (*TS*, 4.10.337) in a meaningless "parade of wisdom" (*TS*, 4.10.337), thus allowing Sterne to appropriate their truth while sidestepping charges of plagiarism.

Sterne's theory and practice of chaptering becomes more innovative in its shifting between the "oeconomic" as the husbandry of narrative material and the "economic" as constructing more abstract models of value. Staging scaled-down cycles of obsolescence and renewal, Tristram often interrupts his narration to start afresh, using chapters to contain and thereby license new imaginative flights. For example, volume 1, chapter 23 introduces Tristram's vision of sympathy between Mercury's "vitrified" inhabitants by announcing, "I have a strong propensity in me to begin this chapter very nonsensically, and I will not balk my fancy.—Accordingly I set off thus" (*TS*, 1.23.82). Elsewhere, Tristram broaches a new topic as a chapter develops, only to rein himself in to allow a new chapter to begin. Narrating the news of Bobby Shandy's death, Tristram, having digressed into relating Tacitus's account of Agrippina's grief, decides, "how my father went on, in my opinion, deserves a chapter to itself" (*TS*, 5.2.418). The next chapter opens with the pronouncement, "——— ———And a chapter it shall have, and a devil of a one too—so look to yourselves" (*TS*, 5.3.418).

In both examples, chaptering evinces compositional prowess, albeit contradictorily. In the first, venturing a new chapter stresses Tristram's authorial originality; in the second, ending one allows him to observe a rhetorical rule in relation to the Shandy household. Self-reflexive concern over how copious and how varied the matter apportioned to each chapter should be is not uniquely Sternean. The narrator of *The Life and Memoirs of Mr. Ephraim Tristram Bates* (1756), a well-established antecedent, similarly measures narrative incidents across its divisions, determining, for example, at the end of chapter 2, "What followed would make this chapter too long; and, with a small Addition, is enough for the next."[25] Yet Sterne's Tristram differs in the extent to which his chaptering features explicitly as a tool for domestic management. Tristram uses new chapters to insert documents from the Shandean family archive, such as the "MEMOIRE presenté a Messieurs les Docteurs de SORBONNE" and its "Réponse" (*TS*, 1.20.67–70), Walter's "Cap. XXXV. Excommunicatio" (*TS*, 3.10.202), and most famously Yorick's sermon "*For we* trust *we have a good Conscience*" (*TS*, 2.17.142). Such divisions form what Carol Watts terms Sterne's "montage" effect, a "juxtaposition of temporal zones" and intratexts that distribute "images of social discourse" such as homilies and legal proceedings throughout the tale.[26] Chaptering here functions in Shaftesbury's "miscellarian" sense, allowing Sterne to extend disparate "rolls, records" (*TS*, 1.14.41), and lists into their own segments while sequencing them in a collection.[27]

At the same time, *Tristram Shandy*'s chapters also figure within an economy that seeks to project the text's value. Tristram attempts to auction his "Virgin-Dedication" (*TS*, 1.9.15) to the highest bidder and promises that the dedicatory chapter will be replaced with another of a higher worth. Later, he proffers another chapter for completion to a "*day-tall* critick" for the price of "a crown" (*TS*, 4.13.340). In volume 4, which features a ten-page glitch in its pagination, Tristram justifies his cancellation of the missing chapter so: "[the chapter], upon reviewing it, appears to be so much above the stile and manner of any thing else I have been able to paint in this book, that it could not have remained in it, without depreciating every other scene; and destroying at the same time that necessary equipoise and balance . . . betwixt chapter and chapter, from whence the just proportions and harmony of the whole work results" (*TS*, 4.25.374). As Johnson's *Dictionary* attests, to "depreciate" meant, much as it does now, "to bring a thing down to a lower price" or "to undervalue."[28] Tristram, concerned with establishing a regular economy of style and thereby fixing a more abstract measure of value across his work, insists that even momentary excellence should yield to commercial equipoise.

Tristram Shandy's chaptering thus retains Fielding's focus on how his texts are consumed, while introducing a value form and a conception of market economy to his flat reflexivity. *Tristram Shandy*'s chapters are remarkably fungible in this regard: they are cut, repositioned, put up for auction, even outsourced for completion. The question to consider is whether Tristram's strategies as author-protagonist in any way correspond to Sterne's as author proper. Did Sterne compose his fiction in discrete chapters capable of being switched, traded, or expunged in order to regulate his narrative economy? No extensive surviving manuscripts for *Tristram Shandy* have been discovered beyond volume 6's tale of Le Fever, which Sterne copied out separately as a gift for its dedicatee, Lady Spencer.[29] But perhaps the extant fair copy manuscript in Sterne's hand used by the printer of the first volume of *A Sentimental Journey* can help to answer our question.[30]

A Sentimental Journey introduces some subtle yet important changes in Sterne's chaptering. Sterne handles their distribution across the text with a lesser degree of reflexivity through his central author-protagonist. As Tadié observes, Yorick is rarely situated as an arranger "in the workshop of narration" or of the final printed text to the same extent as Tristram; he rarely vaunts chaptering as evidence of his authorial prowess, discusses when or how to end and begin chapters, or inventories them in the same way as does Tristram.[31] *Tristram Shandy*'s chapters contain no headings unless to indicate the interpolation of a text from the Shandean archive; they are marked sequentially with Roman numerals and usually run contiguously on the page, leaving only a small space after each chapter ends and before the next begins. This presentation aids many of *Tristram Shandy*'s more elaborate japes with the material book, such as the "chasm of ten pages" (*TS*, 4.25.372) in volume 4; it is because Tristram's chapters are clearly numbered in sequence that we notice when they contravene that sequence or appear to have been expunged.

A Sentimental Journey's more subdued approach regarding its internal workings belies an equally mannered and careful structuring. In the first edition, each chapter starts afresh on a new page, which often leaves extensive quantities of white space in the text. In place of *Tristram Shandy*'s Roman numerals, every chapter now has a verbal heading. Some are composed of a prepositional phrase combined with a location, such as "In the Street. Calais" (*ASJ*, 20, 30, 36), orienting the reader within the fiction's geography; others provide a location coupled with an object or character around which the affective action of the scene takes place, such as "Nampont. The Dead Ass." As Tadié notes, the formulation is bifocal: it outlines Yorick's travel itinerary while also unifying the action of each scene.[32] Excepting Yorick's extended preface in the *desobligeant*, *A Sentimental Journey*'s chapters do not vary so widely in length as those in *Tristram Shandy*, providing both a formal regularity to its narrative movement and a sense that, even when we are following Yorick on the open road, we are enclosed in scenes.

A Sentimental Journey's episodes thus appear within textual frames that, in Benedict's terms, apply "spectatorial distance" and aesthetic reflexivity to emotive response. The conventions of travel writing provide a broader generic frame for Yorick's sentimental encounters and these two frames (textual and generic) act in tension, creating "a structural dialectic" between "static" scene and "dynamic narrative."[33] For Chandler, *A Sentimental Journey*'s divisions should therefore not be considered as chapters so much as "brief titled sections," which he elsewhere describes as "vignettes."[34] Even as these sentimental vignettes facilitate movement within *A Sentimental Journey*, the "frame or box" in which they appear also fetishizes and detaches feeling, much like Yorick's snuffbox.[35] One example of this occurs in chapter 5 of volume 1, "The Monk. Calais." Following Yorick's tirade against the Order of St. Francis, the monk departs, and every "ungracious syllable" Yorick has spoken returns to overpower his "imagination" (*ASJ*, 11). The chapter pivots around Yorick's reflective distress in relation to its titular monk, yet it is also filtered to the reader through Yorick's narration. His inability to change his prior treatment of the monk allows his past-tense narrative to linger on the feelings that follow without placing him at fault for not acting on those feelings. In Michael Bell's terms, the frame of the closed vignette grants the reader the "leisure, or freedom, to reflect on the values rehearsed in the narrative" as Yorick interrogates his own behavior before resolving to "learn better manners" as he gets along (*ASJ*, 11).[36] For Yorick and the reader, the ethical and aesthetic are conjoined; what is "seen" by the reader at a certain spectatorial distance is the intimate "scene" of feeling that Sterne frames through Yorick's episodic narration. His resolution provides an impetus to move on to the following vignette, which describes how Yorick's "[discontent] with himself" (*ASJ*, 12) equips his mind to bargain for the *desobligeant*. Yorick's scene of self-scrutiny, which asks the reader to consider feelings in stasis and *in themselves*, returns to narrative movement in Yorick's commitment to resocialize those feelings.

The shift from *Tristram Shandy*'s numerical sequence to organization by location suggests also a new prioritization of spatial over temporal layout. The sense of location conveyed through *A Sentimental Journey*'s headings coheres through parataxis and repetition, wherein key phrases and objects such as "Remise," "Passport," or "Fragment" reappear and lock each other into position. This iterative and more regular structure of discrete episodes and encounters, Tadié argues, more distinctly reflects an act and scene division than Sterne's previous fictions: "These blanks introduce changes of scene, and provide the reader with a visual equivalent of the movements of characters. . . . The different titles can be viewed as contents of chapters, but the juxtaposition of the name of a place in France, with the title, although paying lip service to the fact that this text purports to be a travel book, suggests a setting, as in a play."[37]

Chaptering in *A Sentimental Journey* thus permits each vignette to focus on one or two affecting details while also allowing characters to enter or exit between each scene. The blanks that Sterne leaves between chapters allow for clean and convincing transitions, particularly when shifting from the interiors in which much of the fiction takes place to scenes on the road. White space in the text facilitates another activity: the mind turning in on itself. Yorick explains to his reader that "when your eyes are fixed upon a dead blank—you draw purely from yourselves" (*ASJ*, 21). Ostensibly, the "blank" in question is the *remise* door in the scene on which Yorick's gaze is "fixed," yet, given Sterne's propensity to obscure the line between "text" and "scene," the assertion can also evoke the blank space between chapters.

This interplay between "scene" and "text" is indicative of a fiction that explores how attempting to chart an affective cartography raises issues of mediation, that emphasizes how wordless moments of sympathy must be conveyed to the reader using words and devices that restructure them, and that "encourage[s] readers to look beyond the immediacy of feeling to revisit the material reality that informs it," in Kyoko Takanashi's terms.[38] When Yorick distinguishes himself as a traveler through the "mere *Novelty of [his] Vehicle*" (*ASJ*, 15), he highlights, as Chandler notes, the relation between narrative "movement" and the capacity of the traveler to "be moved" that a "sentimental journey" entails, with much of that movement provided by the transitioning that chaptering affords.[39] The conventional claim to novelty notwithstanding, the design of Yorick's "*Vehicle*" also determines the terrain he traverses, and indeed the ordering of text, thought, and itinerary all intertwine in his opening: "—THEY order, said I, this matter better in France—" (*ASJ*, 3). In driving action from discourse at the *Journey*'s outset, Michael Seidel argues, Sterne "makes the linguistic properties of utterance spatial"; but more importantly, by inscribing "the space for narrative projection" in these terms, he threads the "matter" of what is, or should be, well "order[ed]" into the fiction's textual weave.[40] An instance of metaleptic slippage, it is the order of narrative "matters"—that is, the material arrangement and divisions of the book itself—that Yorick most strongly evokes by asking that his reader interpret the conclusion of a conversation as the beginning of his journey.

Correspondingly, the other extremity of *A Sentimental Journey*—its similarly abrupt aposiopetic ending at an inn in Savoy—also evokes this metalepsis as Yorick's hand reaches out to catch "hold of the Fille de Chambre's // END OF VOL. II" (*ASJ*, 165). Again, Sterne blurs the line between affecting scene and mediating text. Yorick's final reach (or grope) toward the Piedmontese lady in the "parallel" (*ASJ*, 161) bed, which, in true Sternean fashion, appears both deathly and bawdy as the two lie separated side by side in the "damp cold closet" (*ASJ*, 162) like lovers carved on a tombstone, extends out of the diegetic scene and onto its material-textual frame. Scene and text sit in tension on the word "END," which may complete Yorick's final sentence (which otherwise does not conclude with a full stop) or may simply mark a conventional closing of the volume. In breaking off the scene with a punning equivocation that also plays with typographic custom, Sterne encourages us to see *A Sentimental Journey*'s concluding line as a branching off into alternative interpretations. If the *Journey*'s incipit uses a conversational ending to initiate its exploration of material-textual "order," its ending uses an intrusion from the diegetic scene into the text's layout to create new potential narrative openings.[41]

From the fiction's beginning through to its end, then, ordering proves a repeated concern of *A Sentimental Journey* and is closely related to that of narrative economy. Considering the "better order of beings" to which the Lady belongs as axiomatic, or a "general idea," leads Yorick almost to neglect "a more particular inquiry" (*ASJ*, 30) regarding her circumstances before feeling intervenes. However, it is a disordering of those feelings (a "discontented[ness] with himself") that prompts Yorick to retire to the *desobligeant* to compose his "Preface," which itself comes doubly out of sequence. It appears late in the order of the book yet early in the order of composition, a preface being typically a summative paratext composed after a work's completion in order to sell it to the reader. Nature, "prompting us to the thing we are fittest for," reorders "matters" such that Yorick is inspired to write his preface only just after his journey has begun but before he has finished writing it. The preface in part harks back to *Tristram Shandy*'s use of chaptering, allowing Yorick to revert to what Cynthia Wall describes as "detail-oriented description" through listing.[42] Yorick's catalogue inventories various travelers and suggests that traveler-readers can know themselves better by recognizing their type; yet Yorick's own reticence to occupy "a whole nitch entirely to [himself]" (*ASJ*, 15) as a sentimental traveler suggests how this chaptering departs from *Tristram Shandy*'s "miscellarian" uses. Chaptering in the *Journey* attempts to locate and specify affective encounters that threaten to evade even loose categorization. Sterne now economizes his narrative less by stretching its resources, as in *Tristram Shandy*, and more by reducing it to a formal scenic arrangement.

Curiously, *A Sentimental Journey* becomes, in Thomas Keymer's terms, even more "calculable" than Sterne's earlier work concerning what is included in each chapter and what is apportioned to contiguous episodes. When Yorick pronounces in chapter 17 of volume 1 that, despite the length of his opening, he has in fact spent "little more than a single hour in Calais" (*ASJ*, 36), the reader can readily see how Sterne has divided and compartmentalized that hour within fifteen episodes of comparable length (excluding the preface) situated around the monk, the *remise* door, the street, and the snuffbox. The "large volume of adventures" that, Yorick argues, can be arranged from everything that "time and chance . . . perpetually" present to the sentimental traveler is, in one sense, the measurable (in terms of chaptered episodes) rewards of labor for him who "as he journeyeth on his way misses nothing he can *fairly* lay his hands on" (*ASJ*, 36). At the same time, however, the appeal to "time and chance" also suggests that Yorick's sentimental traveler is one who capitalizes on the possibilities of alternate orders or even *dis*ordering. Christina Lupton shows how this apparent contradiction between formal regularity and a sentimentalized appeal to chance is reconcilable through the idea of reading "contingency" (which "exclu[des] . . . impossibility and necessity from a proposition") in the bound codex form: "Sentences and literary forms carry traces of the randomly accessible pool of language from which they are drawn, even as they fix one sentence after another."[43] Read this way, even the closure of chaptered scenes evinces Yorick's openness to the logic that episodes *might have* been arranged otherwise.

Events, qualities, and associations often appear in unexpected arrangements such that they more powerfully affect Yorick. Observing a chivalrous beggar "retiring two steps" from the crowd to withdraw "his claim" for a charitable donation (*ASJ*, 47), Yorick exclaims, "Just heaven! for what wise reasons hast thou order'd it, that beggary and urbanity, which are at such variance in other countries, should find a way to be at unity in this?" (*ASJ*, 47). For this reason, Sterne's concern with narrative ordering predominates even—perhaps especially—during scenes in which his protagonist claims to be "govern'd" by "circumstances" rather than to "govern them" (*ASJ*, 104). Yorick's indecisiveness at Versailles leads to La Fleur's "impossible" discovery of the Chevalier de St. Louis "selling *patès*" (*ASJ*, 104). The Chevalier's tale of declining fortune proves salutary in illustrating how peace after the Seven Years' War led to the reformation of regiments, leaving distinguished soldiers with poor means of subsistence. Yorick concludes the episode nine months from his initial encounter to elide sentimental value with a reversal in the Chevalier's circumstances: his story so moves the various people who pass through Versailles that it "reach[es] at last the king's ears," and the king grants him "a pension of fifteen hundred livres a year" (*ASJ*, 106).

Should we imagine Yorick submitting his own progress to such vagaries of fortune, however, the chapter concludes with him rearranging his sentimental encounters in a quid pro quo bargain: "As I have told this to please the reader, I beg he will allow me to relate another out of its order, to please myself—the two stories reflect light upon each other,—and 'tis a pity they should be parted" (*ASJ*, 106). Yorick's remark concludes one chapter and introduces another "out of its order" and against his direction of travel. The digressive episode is titled "The Sword. Rennes"; if we follow Yorick's journey on a map, its insertion suggests a fully sideways movement rather than simply, in Judith Hawley's terms, a "shuttling back and forth along [the narrative's] temporal line."[44] Indeed, it proves hard to reposition the episode at any point along Yorick's journey given that it marks a detour over two hundred miles each way from Versailles, the most westerly point on his route southeast.

The purpose of this detour, Yorick argues, is to stress the similitude between two tales of declining fortune reversed; each amplifies the other's affective value.

There is, therefore, an intriguing parallel between the detour Yorick takes and the tale he tells in order to take it. Yorick frames the story as another example of the "distress and poverty" that follows when "states and empires have their periods of declension" (*ASJ*, 107), focusing on the Marquis d'E****, whose estate has fallen "into decay" during the ravages of the Seven Years' War. Hoping nonetheless to provide a "*light*" to his two sons, who look to him as an example of nobility, he settles upon the repair of his sword as a symbol of familial regeneration. The sword's mounting, however, proves too costly, "—and simple œconomy was not a match for it—there was no resource but commerce" (*ASJ*, 107). Sterne contrasts "oeconomy" as the management of an estate's resources with the "resource" of the marketplace—the last resort of aristocratic families unable to remain self-sufficient. The Marquis saves his honor by availing himself of a "provision" available only in Brittany: "taking an occasion when the states were assembled at Rennes, the Marquis, attended with his two boys, enter'd the court; and having pleaded the right of an ancient law of the duchy, which, though seldom claim'd, he said, was no less in force; he took his sword from his side—Here—said he—take it; and be trusty guardians of it, till better times put me in condition to reclaim it" (*ASJ*, 107). He preserves his right to the sword by invoking the alternative values of courtly convention and localized codes of honor, which withhold it from circulation across what Deidre Lynch describes as the "heterogeneous spaces" of the market and its abstract "exchange value."[45]

The episode provides an example equal to Yorick's snuffbox of how, as Lynn Festa argues, sentimentalism allows "a society undergoing rapid commoditization to rope off areas that would not be absolutely fungible . . . by stressing the particularity of the feeling self and by withdrawing objects from indiscriminate circulation."[46] It also highlights a paradox that Festa locates as inherent within sentimentalism. The affecting nature of the scene and the social ties of the characters involved appear to bestow on the sword a "singularity that defies the commodity form" and that resists the encroach of "commerce" into life's most private spheres, yet such sentiments are themselves "forged in the smithy of that great commodity the sentimental text."[47] The chapter that frames the episode is an interchangeable component within Yorick's narrative; he bargains with the reader to introduce it "out of its order" so as to optimize its affective worth. As such, it encapsulates the contrary nature of the sentimental commodity, which introduces particularity of feeling as a facet of its exchange value.[48]

We know from the tale's conclusion, where Yorick witnesses the sword's restoration, that the chapter forms part of Yorick's itinerary "out of its order" rather than being a tangential interpolated tale, like that of Abdera featured in the "Fragment." Yorick's presence is important for three reasons: First, it translates the generic "period of declension" that "states and empires" undergo into the specific context of postwar France. Second, it evinces a causal opacity whereby Yorick's almost exclusive concern with scenes of "social intercourse" defines him largely, in Chandler's terms, "through exercises in vicariousness."[49] Yorick's investment in the affairs of others suggests the corresponding ability to augment everyday incidents through his sympathetic imagination, opening him to a flux of potential experiences closed to a Smelfungus or Mundungus. What remains unclear is whether the reflections that open Yorick to this flux "can be supposed to occur on a single plane of circulation, where we all reflect each other," or on "an ascending scale of higher-order recognitions."[50] Yorick asserts, "It was an incident of good fortune which will never happen to any traveller, but a sentimental one, that I should be at Rennes at the very time of this solemn requisition" (*ASJ*, 108), but the precise set of circumstances that led him to be present for the sword's restoration remains mysterious if also determined, evincing again a sentimental contingency.

Finally, Yorick's presence is necessary for his experiential appropriation of the sword. As many critics note, where words often fail to encompass emotional states, visual perspectives and lines of sight remain vital in sentimental literature to the often-delayed triangulation of affecting moments.[51] The criterion for a sentimental object in *A Sentimental Journey* is, according to Festa, its "inalienability": the idea that, "irrespective of its ownership" and in contrast to commodities exchanged in the marketplace, "it cannot be detached from Yorick's subjective experience."[52] Unlike Father Lorenzo's snuffbox, which Yorick incorporates into his daily forays to help "regulate" his spirit (*ASJ*, 27), the sword's only sentimental use lies in later recalling the moment at which it re-enters the newly balanced "oeconomy" of the Marquis's estate. Yorick acknowledges as much when he reflects on his mixed response to the scene as the Marquis leaves with his family in tow and his sword returned to its scabbard: "O! how I envied him his feelings!" (*ASJ*, 108).

Yorick's envy can be read as that of "a peripatetic philosopher" (*ASJ*, 13) continually thrown back into circulation and thereby forced to encounter the limits of a cosmopolitan ethos within its "sphere of contentions and reconciliations" that are never fully resolved, as Shaun Regan has argued.[53] Yorick admits at Versailles, "I seldom go to the place I set out for" (*ASJ*, 103), and the impulses that return him back into circuitous motion through heterogeneous spaces are, as Regan asserts, both "interested and erratic."[54] The *Journey* figures Sterne's own movement between the "oeconomic" management of text and the "economy" as the market's abstract exchange value in Yorick's envy of the Marquis, who redeems his household and withdraws from commerce in the symbolic return of the sword to its scabbard. As Benedict notes, the episode is nostalgic for nobility's ideal relations, evincing in the Marquis's retreat sentimentalism's tension between "static" vignette and "narrative dynamism."[55] The scene provides an archetypal portrait of aristocratic stability, yet it is the mobility that chaptering affords that permits Yorick's attendance at Rennes. Sterne's chapters circulate, can be exchanged, and admit lateral movement in their transition of scenes such that we do not object when Yorick takes us two hundred miles west of his route "out of . . . order," even if he offers us no explanation for the detour beyond it stemming from an "incident of good fortune."

The layout and appearance of the chapters themselves partially facilitates this pose of textual and readerly latitude. Their clean transition, each one beginning afresh on a new page, makes them *appear* interchangeable even as they drive narrative movement. I want to conclude by addressing Tadié's suggestion that this presentation reflects Sterne's practice in the final stage of *A Sentimental Journey*'s transcription: "The careful physical layout of the chapters, in the manuscript as well as in the first edition of the novel, with blanks on the page isolating each chapter, shapes the perception of the text."[56] The manuscript to which Tadié refers is the only lengthy draft entirely in Sterne's hand, a fair copy of the *Journey*'s first volume used by its printer.[57] The corresponding fair copy for volume 2 remains lost and may have been destroyed after printing. This manuscript offers an insight only into the final transcription stage for the *Journey*'s first volume, and it will not be the basis here of speculation as to how Sterne arranged his chapters in earlier stages. The manuscript appears incomplete: of the thirty-eight chapters that appear in the final volume, chapters 14: "In the Street. Calais.," 15: "The Remise. Calais.," and 16: "The Remise. Calais." and the second half of 13: "The Remise Door. Calais.," comprising fols. 56–69, are missing. It provides only a rough guide as to how Sterne wished the volume to appear.[58]

Nonetheless, Tadié's suggestion that the chapters in the manuscript remain discrete and easily separable in appearance at this stage is supported by Gardner D. Stout's description in his edition of *A Sentimental Journey* regarding the way, "as in the first edition, chapters begin at the top of a new folio."[59] It is also important to note that, with the exception of a few explanatory notes and deleted false starts, Sterne only writes on one side of each loose folio leaf, leaving its obverse blank—a detail that, to state the obvious, does not apply to the first print edition. In theory, then, at this final stage of transcription, Sterne's chapters *appear* interchangeable in material if not in narrative terms. Moreover, each chapter's demarcation as a discrete unit of narrative is strengthened by another detail that does not make it into print: each of the manuscript's chapter headings is contained between two horizontal rules, giving them the appearance of intertitles between enclosed, or boxed, scenes (see fig. 5.1).

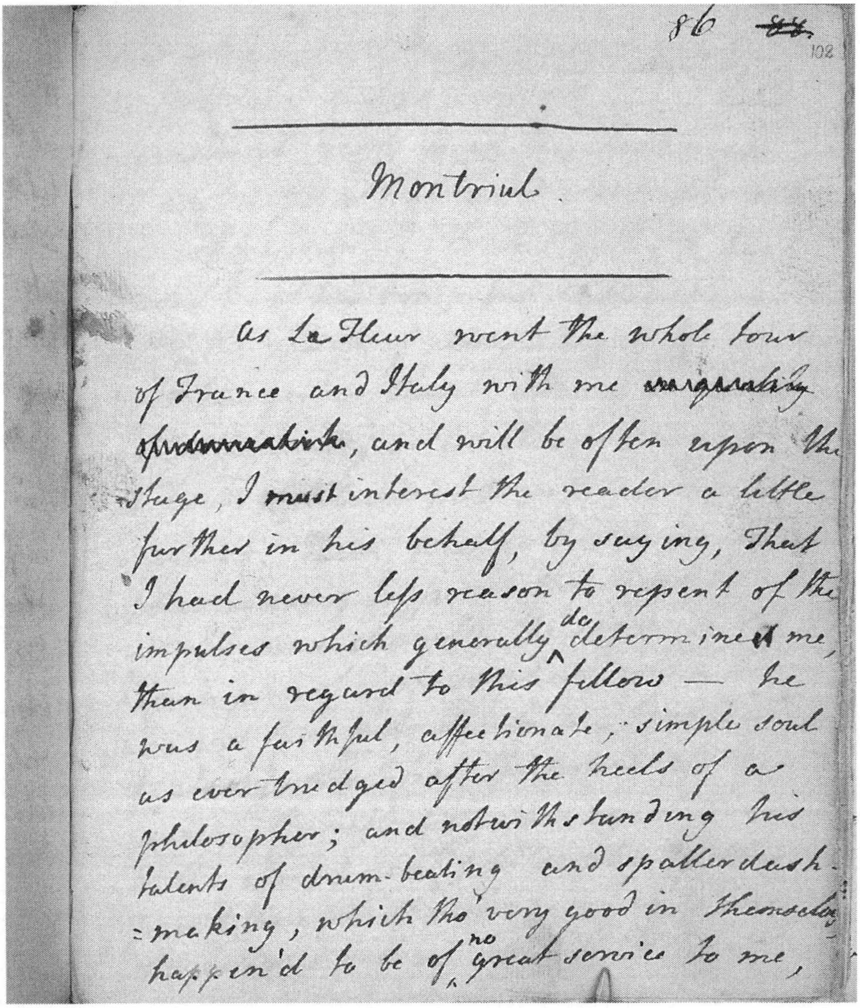
86

102

Montriul.

As La Fleur went the whole tour of France and Italy with me [illegible], and will be often upon the stage, I must interest the reader a little further in his behalf, by saying, That I had never less reason to repent of the impulses which generally do determine me, than in regard to this fellow — he was a faithful, affectionate, simple soul as ever trudged after the heels of a philosopher; and notwithstanding his talents of drum-beating and spatterdash-making, which tho' very good in themselves happen'd to be of no great service to me,

Figure 5.1 *A Sentimental Journey*, *S1*, fol. 86 [108] (British Library, Egerton MS 1610; by permission of the British Library)

The manuscript is not, however, as uniform or schematic in its layout as might at first appear. As Stout further notes, while the majority of chapters do begin at the top of a new folio leaf, five of the thirty-five extant do not (Stout, 298). Each of those chapters runs contiguously on the page from the one preceding it, which accounts for ten chapters in total that are locked into position at this stage of transcription: a statistically high enough figure to make us query whether

TABLE 5.1. Chapter Arrangement in *S1*

Chapters that do not begin at the top of a new fol. (titles as in manuscript; positions as in the first edition)	*Preceding chapters*
The Desobligeant. | Calais. (6)	The Monk. | Calais (5)
The Remise Door. | Calais. (13)	The Snuff Box. | Calais (12)
A Fragment. (23)	Montriuil [*sic*] (22)
Amiens. (28)	Nampont. | The Postillion. (27)
The Letter. (30)	The Letter. | Amiens (29)

Sterne purposed his chapters to be quite as neatly cordoned off from each other as Tadié suggests. Twenty-five of the thirty-five chapters in the manuscript feasibly could thus have been cut or repositioned to any major extent at this stage.[60]

A detailed look at the manuscript's arrangement helps us account for some of the chapters that appear anomalous. Of the five that do not begin on a new folio, two are Shandean interpolated texts: "A Fragment" (23) and "The Letter" (30). Indeed, "A Fragment" begins at the bottom of fol. 91 [114] ~~93~~ (the crossed out folio numbers are in Sterne's hand, whereas those in square brackets were written in pencil at a later date) straight after the preceding chapter; its title is not enclosed within horizontal rules (see fig. 5.2), leading the editors of the Florida edition to query whether Sterne initially intended it as a separate chapter (*ASJ*, 430). Given that Sterne traveled to London to see the first edition of the *Journey* off the press, it is possible that he decided at the last minute to grant these interpolated texts the status of separate chapters; it is also possible that the printer decided on their separation to keep the book's arrangement in line with the layout of the rest of the manuscript. Either way, this can only be speculation.

Of those thirty chapters that do begin on new folios, seven (3, 4, 19, 25, 26, 27, and 38) follow chapters that conclude at the bottom of the preceding folio. Nonetheless, Sterne often left large quantities of paper blank between chapters—sometimes almost three-quarters of a folio leaf (see fig. 5.3)—and on four occasions appeared loosely to signal when the printer should start the next chapter on a new page. These indications do not take the form of written instructions but appear as penned squiggles, which are occasionally used in manuscripts to denote that space should be inserted. The chapters that Sterne concludes in this manner are Yorick's "Preface" (see fig. 5.4), 9: "In the Street. Calais," 19: "Montriul," and "The Letter." The first example is, as we have seen, a paratext folded inward, and the last is an interpolated text; so it may be that Sterne was attempting to specify their offsetting

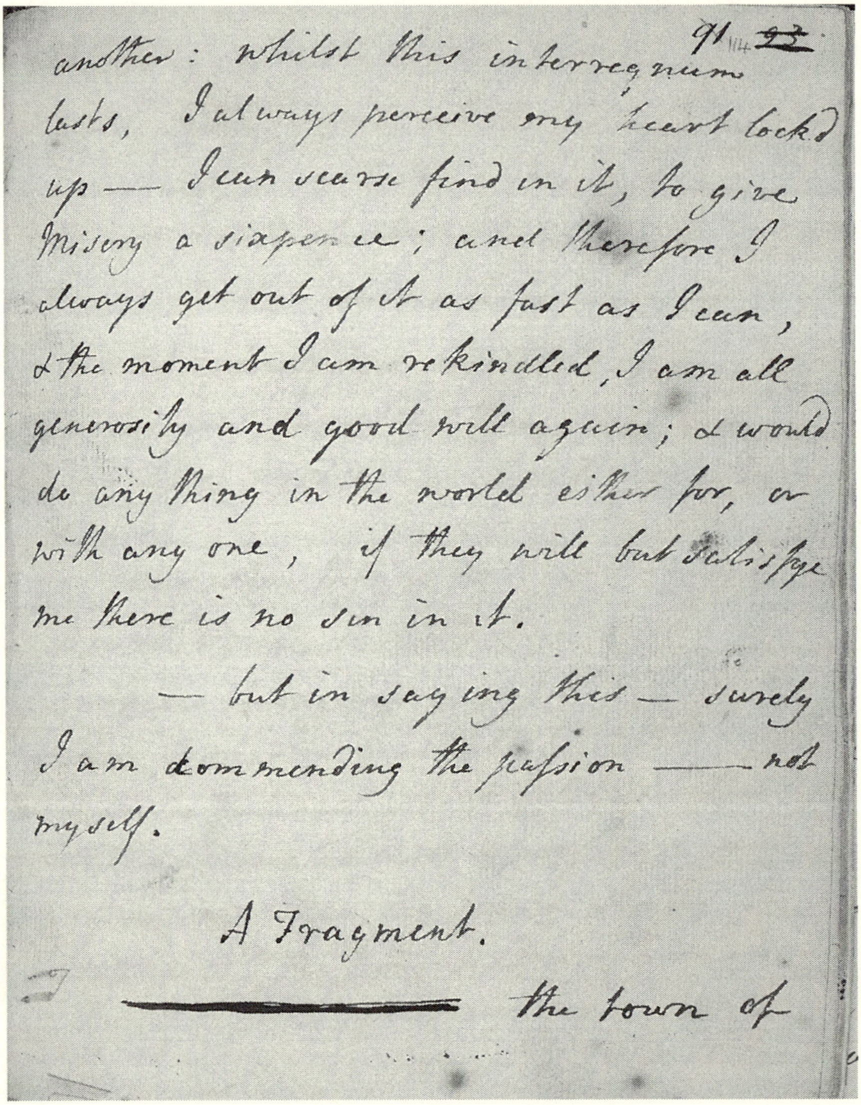

91 114 ~~93~~

another: whilst this interregnum lasts, I always perceive my heart lock'd up — I can scarse find in it, to give Misery a sixpence; and therefore I always get out of it as fast as I can, & the moment I am rekindled, I am all generosity and good will again; & would do any thing in the world either for, or with any one, if they will but satisfye me there is no sin in it.

— but in saying this — surely I am commending the passion —— not myself.

A Fragment.

—— the town of

Figure 5.2 *A Sentimental Journey, S1*, fol. 91 [114] (British Library, Egerton MS 1610; by permission of the British Library)

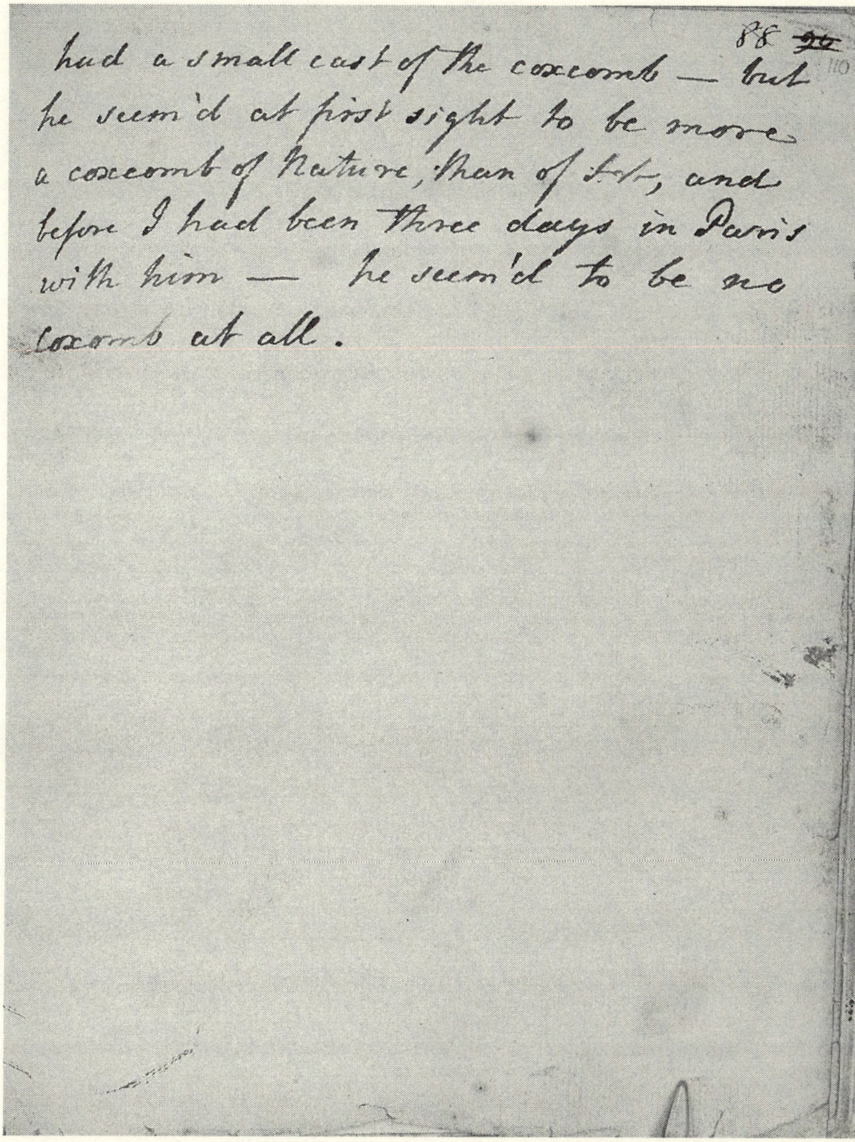
88 ~~90~~ 110

had a small cast of the coxcomb — but he seem'd at first sight to be more a coxcomb of Nature, than of Art, and before I had been three days in Paris with him — he seem'd to be no coxcomb at all.

Figure 5.3 *A Sentimental Journey*, *S1*, fol. 88 [110] (British Library, Egerton MS 1610; by permission of the British Library)

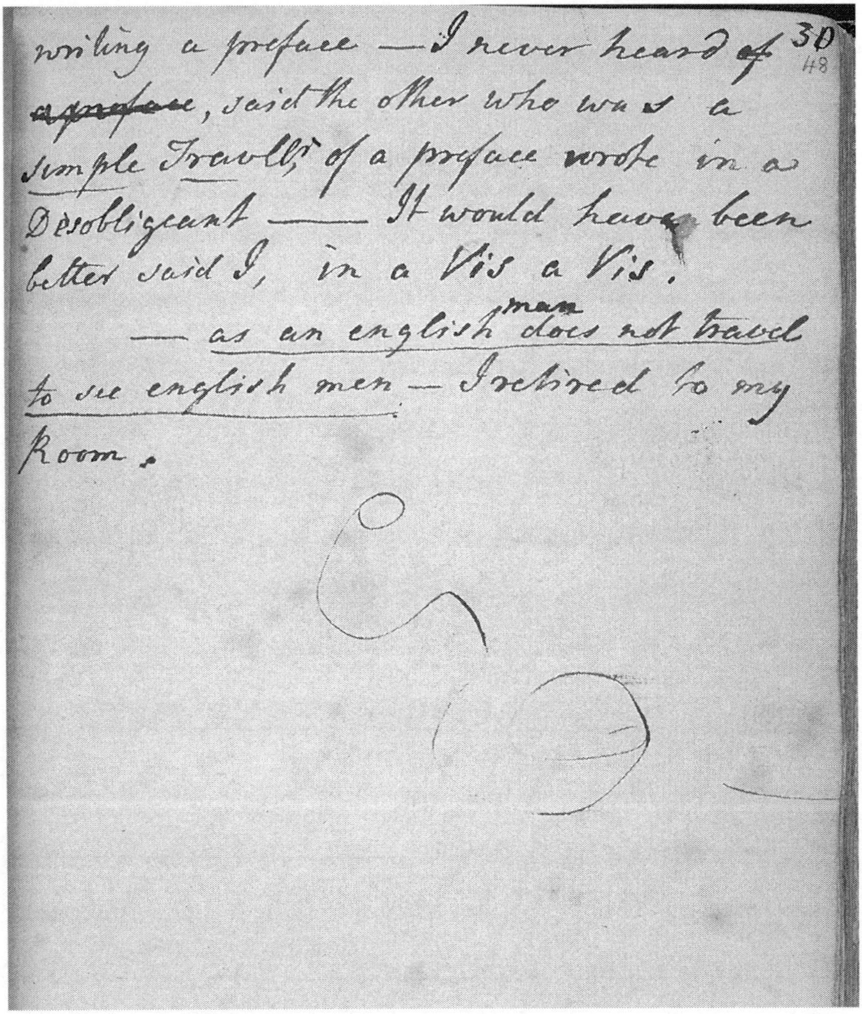

writing a preface —I never heard of ~~a preface~~, said the other who was a simple Travell^r of a preface wrote in a Desobligeant —— It would have been better said I, in a Vis a Vis.

— as an english man does not travel to see english men — I retired to my Room.

30

48

Figure 5.4 *A Sentimental Journey, S1*, fol. 30 [48] (British Library, Egerton MS 1610; by permission of the British Library)

in the text. We cannot conclude that Sterne indicates the beginning of a new page in these instances to allow the chapters in question to remain interchangeable.

There is, however, one instance in the manuscript where Sterne may have moved a chapter from its original position to another; it occurs across the pages marked 72 ~~74~~ [84], 73 ~~75~~ [88], 74 ~~76~~ ~~61~~ [89], ~~7~~75 ~~62~~ [91], 76 ~~78~~ ~~63~~ [92], 77 ~~79~~ ~~64~~

[93] (Stout, 302).[61] These comprise what appears in the first edition as 18: "In the Street. Calais," which concludes with Yorick's famed rebuke of "Smelfungus and Mundungus" (*ASJ*, 38). As Stout observes, the canceled foliation suggests that Sterne positioned the chapter to run up to the folio originally numbered 64, situating its original location somewhere in the gap in the manuscript between the middle of 13: "The Remise Door. Calais." and the beginning of 17: "The Remise. Calais." (Stout, 302). It is not, however, possible to determine from these cancellations on which numbered folio in the manuscript the chapter would originally have begun, given that Sterne may have revised its opening when he opted to reposition it. Stout argues that Sterne may have originally placed it between 13: "The Remise Door. Calais" and 14: "In the Street, Calais"; certainly, the canceled folio numbers support his conjecture. The Florida editors further support this suggestion, arguing that Sterne's awareness of "the play of transition between chapters" may have led him to judge that ending an emphatic apostrophe to Smelfungus and Mundungus "merely to pick up again with the account of Yorick's pursuit of Madame L***" (*ASJ*, xxxviii) would have jarred—hence his eventual decision to conclude Yorick's time in Calais with it instead. Although 14: "In the Street, Calais" is missing from *S1* in Sterne's hand, it appears in *M1*: the manuscript of the first volume in an unknown copyist's hand. In *M1*, the chapter's opening fol. 59 ends with the words "general idea," from the chapter's opening paragraph (*ASJ*, 30), which are, the Florida editors note, "widely spaced on a half line." Fol. 60 opens with the nonindented words "she had scarce," leading the Florida editors to observe that Sterne may have first intended the Smelfungus and Mundungus apostrophe to start on fol. 60 (*ASJ*, 428).

Wherever Sterne originally placed the chapter, marks of the revisions he needed to make in order to reposition it remain visible. Aside from the changes in foliation already mentioned, fol. 74 ~~76~~ ~~61~~ [89] opens with the following crossed-out words:

> ~~—another will—no matter—I get~~
> ~~my Labour for my pains—'tis enough:~~

The canceled script appears to be a first draft of the script that closes fol. 73 ~~75~~ [88], which the first edition retains so: "If this won't turn out something—another will—no matter—'tis an assay upon human nature—I get my labour for my pains—'tis enough" (*ASJ*, 36). That the same script appears at both the beginning of fol. 74 ~~76~~ ~~61~~ and at the end of fol. 73 ~~75~~ suggests that fol. 73 ~~75~~ replaces a different folio page that originally preceded 74 ~~76~~ ~~61~~ and that the chapter as it originally began was of a different length. The first two folios of the chapter do not feature canceled numbers leading up to 61–64, suggesting that these may be newer additions that Sterne rewrote into position.

This reading of the manuscript demonstrates two things: First, Sterne may well have experimented with repositioning or perhaps even replacing certain chapters, although the scope for him to do so at this stage of finalizing *A Sentimental Journey*'s fair copy was more circumscribed than might be assumed from Tadié's description. Second, this reading of the manuscript supports Stout's conjecture that Sterne probably needed to revise the opening of what became 18: "In the Street. Calais" so that he could reposition it in the manuscript, although we may never know how extensive any revisions were. As such, the interchangeability of Sterne's chaptering across a textual model of equivalent value remains more an imaginative leap than a practical reality; it loses little in terms of wit or agility in being so.

NOTES

1. *CH*, 66.
2. *CH*, 122.
3. *CH*, 47.
4. Marc Shell, *The Economy of Literature* (Baltimore: Johns Hopkins University Press, 1978), 89.
5. Karen Harvey, *The Little Republic: Masculinity and Domestic Authority in Eighteenth-Century Britain* (Oxford: Oxford University Press, 2012), 25.
6. Harvey, 26.
7. Charles Taylor, *Modern Social Imaginaries* (Durham, NC: Duke University Press, 2004), 70; Adam Smith, *Inquiry into the Nature and Causes of the Wealth of Nations*, ed. R. H. Campbell and A. S. Skinner, 2 vols. (Oxford: Oxford University Press, 1976), 1:376. John Gray argues that, in Smith's hands, political economy becomes "systematic and comprehensive." Gray, *Liberalism*, ed. Frank Parkin, 2nd ed. (Minneapolis: University of Minnesota Press, 1995), 25. In a recent analysis of "system" as a genre, Clifford Siskin outlines how Smith in *The Wealth of Nations* used "system's scalable architecture" as a means to embed multiple systems of political economy within one single "Master System." Siskin, *System: The Shaping of Modern Knowledge* (Cambridge, MA: MIT Press, 2013), 41, 118.
8. Alexis Tadié, *Sterne's Whimsical Theatres of Language: Orality, Gesture, Literacy* (Aldershot, UK: Ashgate, 2003), 83.
9. James Chandler, *An Archaeology of Sympathy: The Sentimental Mode in Literature and Cinema* (Chicago: University of Chicago Press, 2013), 185.
10. Barbara M. Benedict, *Framing Feeling: Sentiment and Style in English Prose Fiction, 1745–1800* (New York: AMS, 1994), 9.
11. Nicholas Dames, "Trollope's Chapters," *Literature Compass* 7, no. 9 (2010): 855.
12. Gérard Genette defines the "paratext" as a liminal zone of public "*transaction*" and commercial strategy: a "privileged place of a pragmatics." Genette, *Paratexts: Thresholds of Interpretation,* trans. Jane E. Lewin (Cambridge: Cambridge University Press, 1997), 2.
13. Dames, "Trollope's Chapters," 856.
14. Samuel Johnson, *A Dictionary of the English Language in which the words are deduced from their originals and illustrated in their different significations by examples from the best writers* (London, 1755), s.v. "CHA'PTER."

15. Leah Orr, *Novel Ventures: Fiction and Print Culture, 1690–1730* (Charlottesville: University of Virginia Press, 2017), 4, 185–189. Orr's research suggests that during this period at least one-quarter of fictions did not reach a second edition (56).
16. Anthony Ashley Cooper, Third Earl of Shaftesbury, *Characteristics of Men, Manners, Opinions, Times*, ed. Laurence E. Klein (Cambridge: Cambridge University Press, 1999), 460.
17. Shaftesbury, 350; Eve Tavor Bannet, *Eighteenth-Century Manners of Reading: Print Culture and Popular Instruction in the Anglophone Atlantic World* (Cambridge: Cambridge University Press, 2017), 175.
18. Alexander Pope, *Memoirs of the Extraordinary Life, Works, and Discoveries of Martinus Scriblerus*, ed. Charles Kerby-Miller (Oxford: Oxford University Press, 1988), 94.
19. J. Paul Hunter, "From Typology to Type: Agents of Change in Eighteenth-Century English Texts," in *Cultural Artifacts and the Production of Meaning: The Page, the Image, and the Body*, ed. Margaret J. M. Ezell and Katherine O'Brien O'Keeffe (Ann Arbor: University of Michigan Press, 1994), 50–51.
20. Hunter, 50; Henry Fielding, *Joseph Andrews*, ed. Martin C. Battestin (Oxford: Clarendon, 1967), 90–91.
21. Fielding, *Joseph Andrews*, 91, 89.
22. Fielding, 89.
23. Fielding, 89.
24. Anonymous, *The History of Charlotte Summers, the Fortunate Parish Girl*, 2 vols. (London: Corbett, 1750), 1:29.
25. Anonymous, *The Life and Memoirs of Mr. Ephraim Tristram Bates* (London: W. Owen, 1756), 25; Thomas Keymer cites this as an example of how both narrators continually make "calculations about structure." Thomas Keymer, *Sterne, the Moderns, and the Novel* (Oxford: Oxford University Press, 2002), 52.
26. Carol Watts, *The Cultural Work of Empire: The Seven Years' War and the Imagining of the Shandean State* (Edinburgh: Edinburgh University Press, 2007), 56.
27. One contemporaneous reader who treats *Tristram Shandy* as a "ramble" through discontinuous material is Richard Griffith. See Christina Lupton, *Reading and the Making of Time in the Eighteenth Century* (Baltimore: Johns Hopkins University Press, 2018), 116–117.
28. Johnson, *Dictionary*, s.v. "DEPRE'CIATE."
29. Melvyn New, "A Manuscript of the Le Fever Episode in *Tristram Shandy*," *Scriblerian* 23, no. 2 (1991): 165–174.
30. The manuscript is commonly referred to as *S1* in scholarly editions and catalogued in the British Library as Egerton MS 1610.
31. Tadié, *Sterne's Whimsical Theatres*, 83.
32. Tadié, 82.
33. Benedict, *Framing Feeling*, 26.
34. Chandler, *Archaeology of Sympathy*, 5.
35. Benedict, *Framing Feeling*, 41–42.
36. Michael Bell, *Sentimentalism, Ethics and the Culture of Feeling* (Basingstoke, UK: Palgrave, 2000), 71.
37. Tadié, *Sterne's Whimsical Theatres*, 82.
38. Kyoko Takanashi, "Mediation, Reading, and Yorick's Sentimental Vehicle," *Novel: A Forum on Fiction* 49, no. 3 (2016): 488.
39. Chandler, *Archaeology of Sympathy*, 176.
40. Michael Seidel, "Narrative Crossings: Sterne's *A Sentimental Journey*," *Genre* 18 (1985): 2.
41. For a further reading of *A Sentimental Journey*'s ending, see Paul Goring's chapter in this volume. The Florida editors note that later editions contain a dash after "Chambre's" that, while missing from the first and second editions, is "present, interestingly enough, in *M2*"

(*ASJ*, lxvi). The inclusion of the dash adds a typographic obstruction between Yorick's hand and the problematic "END" but does not otherwise resolve the final equivocation.

42. Cynthia Wall, *The Prose of Things: Transformations of Description in the Eighteenth Century* (Chicago: University of Chicago Press, 2006), 21.
43. Lupton, *Reading and the Making of Time*, 99, 100.
44. Judith Hawley, "Digressive and Progressive Movements: Sympathy and Sexuality in *Tristram Shandy*; or, Plain Stories," in *Digressions in European Literature: From Cervantes to Sebald*, ed. Alexis Grohmann and Caragh Wells (Basingstoke, UK: Palgrave Macmillan, 2011), 23.
45. Deidre Lynch, "Personal Effects and Sentimental Fictions," in *The Secret Life of Things: Animals, Objects, and It-Narratives in Eighteenth-Century England*, ed. Mark Blackwell (Lewisburg, PA: Bucknell University Press, 2007), 77.
46. Lynn Festa, *Sentimental Figures of Empire in Eighteenth-Century Britain and France* (Baltimore: Johns Hopkins University Press, 2006), 68.
47. Festa, 69.
48. Festa, 69.
49. Chandler, *Archaeology of Sympathy*, 204.
50. Chandler, 205.
51. Stephanie DeGooyer, for example, argues that the "triangulation of perspective" in the sentimental novel allows sympathetic connections to occur "in the gap of narrative and time rather than through immediacy." DeGooyer, "'The Eyes of Other People': Adam Smith's Triangular Sympathy and the Sentimental Novel," *ELH* 85, no. 3 (2018): 683, 687.
52. Festa, *Sentimental Figures*, 73.
53. Shaun Regan, "Peripatetic Philosophy: Sterne and Cosmopolitanism," *Textual Practice* 31, no. 2 (2017): 277.
54. Regan, 277.
55. Benedict, *Framing Feeling*, 88.
56. Tadié, *Sterne's Whimsical Theatres*, 82.
57. See note 30. As the Florida edition notes, there is another surviving manuscript of the *Journey* at the Morgan Library and Museum that includes both volumes 1 and 2; these are referred to as *M1* and *M2* in scholarly editions. *M1* and *M2* are in two unknown copyists' hands, and the editors of the Florida edition observe that the copyists appear to have "worked directly from *S1–[2]*, attempting to reproduce it page for page." In the case of *M1*, the copyist worked with *S1* "prior to Sterne's final alterations" (*ASJ*, xxxviii).
58. As the Florida editors note, we can reconstruct these missing sections to a certain extent given that they survive as copied in *M1* (*ASJ*, 428).
59. Laurence Sterne, *A Sentimental Journey*, ed. Gardner D. Stout (Berkeley: University of California Press, 1967), 298. Hereafter cited parenthetically as "Stout." I follow the Florida editors in referring to Stout's description of *S1*.
60. The Florida edition's collation of *S1*, *M1*, and *M2* suggests that Sterne's unrevised versions (noted as "*M1*: u.v.") in *M1* do not differ with regard to which chapters run contiguously from each other; no alternative folio endings are indicated (*ASJ*, 472–496).
61. Stout's bibliographic description of the fol. numbers is as follows: "72 <74>; 73 <?75>; 74 <76> <61>; <7 >7^5^ <62>; 76 <78> <63>; 77 <?64>-<79>-."

6

YORICK'S SPEECH AND THE STARLING'S SONG

The Limits of Elocution in *A Sentimental Journey*

FRASER EASTON

THE ROBUST ORALITY OF *A SENTIMENTAL JOURNEY* has long been noted by critics: Sterne's novel famously immerses its reader-listener in a host of speech forms and elements, from double entendre, aposiopesis, and emphasis to apostrophe, soliloquy, and dialogue. Yorick's encounters with monks, opera-goers, shop women, servants, fellow travelers, and nonhuman animals are all dramatically verbal, and much of Yorick's narration is reported speech, including his own soliloquies and monologues. As Jonathan Lamb succinctly puts it, "Yorick *talks* to his reader about a journey whose only notable events have been moments of communication."[1] This chapter builds on (and departs from) some recent studies of the verbal and gestural features of oral language in *A Sentimental Journey* in order to investigate the paralinguistic dimensions of the novel. It argues that Sterne uses Yorick's speech, and the speech of nonhuman animals such as the starling, to rethink and complicate, rather than straightforwardly reproduce or ironize, elocutionary models of communication, especially Thomas Sheridan's.

STERNE'S ELOCUTIONARY PROBLEMATICS

Recent criticism of *A Sentimental Journey* has explored the novel's "moments of communication" (including Yorick's addresses to the reader-listener) in terms of specific period conceptualizations of orality, including elocution. "Elocution" was the eighteenth-century term for the fifth canon of the art of rhetoric, traditionally known as delivery and composed of all the paralinguistic physical elements (gesture and articulation) involved in the verbal performance of speech.[2] For Alexis Tadié, the fundamentally oral nature of Sterne's novels is manifested through their adoption of codified forms of period language usage, such as salon conversation ("the very matrix of Sterne's novels") and sentimental gesture (a form of communication "beyond words").[3] To contextualize the link between gesture and orality, Tadié refers to various eighteenth-century works on embodied communication, including Thomas Sheridan's *A Course of Lectures on Elocution* (1762).[4] Paul Goring extends Tadié's attention to gesture, linking it to an eighteenth-century "*emotionalisation* of oratory" promoted by elocutionists such as Sheridan.[5] According to Goring, Sterne draws on this emotionalized oratory to explore "a language of gesture" made up of "postures, hand movements, looks, and blushes" and to thematize "the difference between polite and impolite ways of writing about the body."[6] For these critics, Sterne treats sentimental communication in terms of a defined elocutionary code that he largely follows rather than troubles.[7]

The present chapter offers a new approach to the relationship between speech and emotion in *A Sentimental Journey* by examining how Sterne foregrounds and even reactivates the problems that elocutionary thought seeks to resolve. For Sheridan, the practical communication of sentiment (the sharing of feeling) is a social phenomenon: "in order to feel what another feels, the emotions which are in the mind of one man, must also be communicated to that of another."[8] This communication occurs via the art of delivery, a nonword language of feeling in which "every passion has its peculiar tone" and "its peculiar look or gesture."[9] Sheridan contends that this nonword language of tone and gesture is necessary to the existence of society because sociality requires sympathy, which in turn requires that feeling be communicable. As a corollary of these claims, spoken communication stands to benefit from the fullest use of tone and gesture. The primary role of the elocutionist is not to create this already effective nonword emotional paralanguage or to study its sources in the mind but to practice, refine, and teach it. As we will see, Sterne's novel does not simply replicate Sheridan's thought; rather, it turns that thought on its head, finding not a need (the sharing of feelings) met by a solution (gesture and articulation) but a solution (gesture and articulation) subject to a host of problems (chance and circumstance).

Of all the elocutionists, Sheridan was by far the most influential and significant, with a career overlapping Sterne's. In the late 1750s and 1760s, he sought, via a considerable campaign of public lectures, private pedagogy, and print publication, to promote specific elocutionary pedagogies as a panacea to all that ailed British education, religion, politics, and law.[10] Johnson joked about Sheridan's ambition and obsession to Boswell and others, but despite this skepticism, Sheridan created a significant popular following, produced a groundbreaking standardized pronouncing dictionary, and was a signal contributor to a movement that went on to inspire the pioneers of modern speech communication technologies, such as Alexander Melville Bell and his son.[11] Even when critical of Sheridan's ideas, contemporary authors responded forcefully to them.[12]

The most famous elocutionary episode in Sterne's corpus is Trim's reading aloud of Yorick's sermon to Walter, Toby, and Dr. Slop in the second volume of *Tristram Shandy*. The Florida editors connect Trim's reading to Sheridan; the scene certainly burlesques his program for the reformation of sermonic delivery, with a comic orator (Trim) in a comic situation (simultaneous with Mrs. Shandy's very different delivery) and a performance that is subject to frequent comic interruptions by Trim's listeners and himself (*TS: Notes*, 168–169).[13] Some interruptions do address or proceed from elocutionary considerations: Walter breaks in on Trim to correct his "accent" and "tone" (*TS*, 2.17.143), for example, while Trim's own emotions lead him to make several interjections, such as his exclamatory cry of "Oh!" (*TS*, 2.17.162). But, by and large, the interruptions focus on theological concepts and concerns, starting with the denominational standing of the sermon's author (*TS*, 2.17.143–145). Debates such as the following (on the sermon's stance toward hypocrisy) are typical: "All this is impossible with us, quoth Dr. *Slop*, turning to my father,—the case could not happen in our Church.——It happens in ours, however, replied my father, but too often.—[such a man] answer'd Dr. *Slop*, he would be denied the benefits of the last sacraments.—Pray how many have you in all, said my uncle *Toby*,—for I always forget?" (*TS*, 2.17.149). Neither Walter, nor Toby, nor Dr. Slop is concerned here with how Trim delivers the sermon; rather, they debate its theological implications. Their interruption directs us not to the details of Trim's elocution but to matters of theological orthodoxy and hobby-horsical trains of thought, focusing attention on the sermon's semantic content and highlighting the theological comedy occasioned by its reading.[14] Here, as elsewhere, *Tristram Shandy* places greater weight on the conceptual than on the sentimental aspects of communication.[15]

In contrast to *Tristram Shandy*'s conceptual emphasis, *A Sentimental Journey* "is not a work of reasoning" (*ASJ*, 80). The elocutionary elements of Sterne's second fiction focus on the communication of feelings that, compared with ideas, are circumstantial and temporal rather than determinant and durable. Sterne is close to Sheridan on this matter.[16] As Goring notes, Sheridan departs from Ciceronian rhetoric through his insistence that orators do not need to follow hoary old codes of gesture and articulation to be effective. Rather, they just need to feel: from authentic, appropriate feeling will come the necessary emphases, tones, postures, and looks for each speech situation.[17] There are, Sheridan claims, "no general practical rules"; delivery, in other words, is situational.[18] *A Sentimental Journey* demonstrates this idea. Some elocutionists, such as John Walker and Gilbert Austin, did seek to conventionalize the emotive performance of speech, developing graphic representations of acoustic and gestural emphasis, for example, which have their counterpoint in the print conventions expressive of sentimental feeling (dashes, fragments, aposiopeses).[19] But from a strict rhetorical perspective, such "grammars" or codes use graphic means to memorialize a performance; as such, they shift delivery into memory and make a score out of an occurrence.[20]

Sterne departs from such memorializing elocutionists.[21] Instead, he builds on Sheridan's ideas to problematize the communication of sentiment by portraying, even exaggerating, the circumstantial nature of Yorick's tones and postures (delivered to others and himself) and of his reception of the tones and postures of others. The key practical obstacle to communicating sentiments, in a theory or practice that conceptualizes elocution as the vehicle of sentiment, is the temporal and situated nature of the elements of delivery. Sterne's critique of elocution picks up on Sheridan's recognition (presumably born of his theatrical background) of the somatic contextuality of passionate speech. The nonword elements of elocutionary communication—tone, posture, and the rest—are by their very nature "the sport of contingencies" and not subject to "regular reasoning" (*ASJ*, 7). Sheridan grapples with this problematic (to which Sterne pays a great deal of attention) when he argues that although elocutionary elements are construable signs, they are best when spontaneous, as with "all other animals."[22] As we will see, Sterne goes so far as to represent Yorick's internal speech, his self-consciousness, as a form of circumstantial self-delivery, with all the problems that such circumstantiality entails for knowing oneself and one's feelings through inner oratory.[23]

Sterne also departs from Sheridan. For example, Sterne dramatizes how the circumstantial, "spontaneous" conditions of elocutionary speech mean that it can always misfire, whether for a human or a nonhuman animal orator. We see this in the unfeeling reception in England of the starling's "little song for liberty" (*ASJ*, 99), where various lords and commoners treat its speech as a mere novelty act. We see it when the Catholic Father Lorenzo's stock "attitude of Intreaty" (*ASJ*, 8) fails to move the Protestant Parson Yorick to charity. For Father Lorenzo, the obstacle to his effective use of visual elocution lies not in the suitability of his choice of supplicant posture but in the recipient's prejudices, not in the code but in the decoder. Sterne's insight is significant: even natural, indexical affect signs (blushes, tears, animal cries) can, when delivered, be misunderstood, taken out of context, or faked. The starling's chant suffers this fate, being misunderstood (by the French), taken out of context (by the English), and faked (by an imagined "vile copy" [*ASJ*, 100]). With deceptive or faked elocution, the obstacle lies in the sender, not the recipient.[24] This is Madame de L***'s concern when she claims that Yorick has been deliberately "making love" to her "all this while" (*ASJ*, 34) with his many, seemingly friendly, little gestures: she is accusing him of being disingenuous.

Sterne's treatment of sexual communication reveals further degrees of complexity in his reworking of Sheridan's ideas. Both thinkers view sexual communication as an essential mode of sentimental communication. Sheridan places the communication of sexual and nonsexual feeling on a common rhetorical ground: according to him, a key acoustic feature of elocution, tone, facilitates sexual "propagation," and it does this for both human and nonhuman animals alike.[25] From the perspective of nature that Sheridan invokes, no form of emotional communication could be more necessary, authentic, or *un*ambiguous than sexual communication, since the continued existence of all animal species (including humans) depends on it. *A Sentimental Journey* follows Sheridan in portraying sexual communication as an elocutionary matter: Sterne, too, gives the animal act of sexual congress explicitly rhetorical features, as with the "caresses" of copulating sparrows (*ASJ*, 116). From the perspective of elocution, then, it does not seem quite fair to claim, as John Mullan does, that Sterne "*conflates* the suggestive and the sentimental" in *A Sentimental Journey*.[26]

However, here too Sterne differs from Sheridan. Sterne, first, gives greater space and attention to the sexual elements in passionate communication: what is briefly treated in Sheridan's *Lectures on Elocution* forms a large part of *A Sentimental Journey*. Second, Sterne recognizes that the elocutionary mediation of sexual feeling is, like the elocutionary mediation of sentiment more generally, *also* situational and liable to misconstruction. Yorick's sexual miscommunications with Madame de L*** are misfires that spring from the same elocutionary ground as the novel's other, sentimental miscommunications. Sterne both appropriates and reverses Sheridan's treatment of sexual sympathy in order to dramatize a larger point: the rhetorical journeying of *all* sentiment, the elocutionary mediation of *all* feeling (sexual or otherwise), must potentially be uncertain.[27] This fundamental uncertainty, highlighted by Sterne through examples of sexual miscommunication, calls into question the sentimental underpinning of sociality through elocution. Yet, far from registering the social consequences of this elocutionary instability as a crisis, Sterne's novel instead makes them out as a comedy—a comedy of self-serving communicational decisions made by self-delivering sentimental/sexual orator-receivers like Yorick.

GESTURE AND ARTICULATION

To appreciate the extent and richness of Sterne's interpretation of elocution in *A Sentimental Journey*, we must consider the significance of the novel's many elocutionary references, encounters, and scenarios. Of central importance is the way in which Sterne's novel presents both gesture and articulation as copresent instruments for the communication of feeling.[28]

The importance of gesture to Sterne's novel has been long established.[29] As Tadié and Goring note, *A Sentimental Journey* is full of visual elements such as blushes and tears and bows; graphic tableaux like the dead donkey, the *grisset*'s shop, or Maria and her dog; and dramatic haptic encounters such as those between Yorick and the *fille de chambre* in his Paris hotel room.[30] As Yorick's mental preparations for a meeting with Monsieur Le Duc de C***** indicate (and as both Goring and Tadié have recognized), *A Sentimental Journey* conceptualizes posture, looks, and touch in classic rhetorical terms as part of verbal delivery. When Yorick encounters the group of beggars, he declares that the "poor tatter'd soul" who bows and steps back "conveyed the sentiment" he sought to communicate through that silent bow better than if "the whole parterre cried out, *Place aux dames*" (*ASJ*, 47). When the French officer seeks to punish the uncouth German at the opera, he simply points the guards in the right direction: "the thing told itself" (*ASJ*, 82). Sometimes the elocutionary force of a gesture invites the laughter of the reader-listener, as when Madame de L*** "disengaged her hand with a look" that Yorick understands to be "a sufficient commentary upon the text" (*ASJ*, 24); at other times, it invites their pity, as with the starling's movement in its cage. Pulses have a "beat" (*ASJ*, 73), of course, but they can also serve as haptic channels of emotional communication: "The pulsations of the arteries . . . told her what was passing within me" (*ASJ*, 25). Sometimes these visual scenes of emotional communion are narrated with a pictorial force; for example, in Yorick's encounter with Maria.[31] But the pictorialism of such scenes is subordinated to an elocutionary structure.[32]

Less well established is the importance of articulation to *A Sentimental Journey*. Of course, Sterne's novel encompasses a host of auditory elements, such as double entendre, aposiopesis, and an overall conversational style. But, crucially, it also describes many specifically elocutionary acoustic elements such as accent, emphasis, and tone. The German owner of the dead ass weeps (an acoustic as well as a visual act) and gives "a sigh" expressive of his "grief" (*ASJ*, 53). Yorick observes the Parisian shop girl's use of "*tones*" (*ASJ*, 70) when she repeats her directions to the *opera comique* to him three times (he underscores their import by asserting that tones "have a meaning . . . to hearts which [do not] shut them out" [*ASJ*, 70]). Madame R****'s *fille de chambre* gives "a low sigh" when Yorick tells her he admires her "innocence" (*ASJ*, 89). And La Fleur, too, responds to paralinguistic cues when Madame de L*** calls him up from the kitchen party at her brother's hotel and interrupts his panicked statements about his master to ask whether he has come with Yorick's response to her letter: "Madame de L*** had said this with such a tone of reliance upon the fact, that La Fleur had not power to disappoint her expectations" (*ASJ*, 60). In this scene, verbal emphasis adds force to the semantic content of Madame de L***'s statement, signaling to La Fleur her feelings on a matter that politeness constrains her from stating directly.

When Sterne pairs gesture and articulation, he follows both classical rhetoric and elocutionists like Sheridan. Recent critics of Sterne, however, focus on the role of gesture in *A Sentimental Journey*, thereby privileging one elocutionary mode at the expense of the other. Further, when they do treat acoustic elements, critics often overlook or downplay the role of nonword sound in the novel, looking instead to speech genres or other language forms rather than to the acoustic dimension of delivery. A critical approach that discounts the elocutionary mode of articulation has significant consequences for understanding communication in *A Sentimental Journey*: it isolates gesture from speech as a physical performance; it implies a contrast between word-based speech and nonword gesture; it sets (conceptual) language against (sentimental) gesture; and it evokes dichotomies such as language versus bodily shorthand or art (language) versus nature (gesture).

Jeffrey R. Smitten's interpretation of Yorick's encounter with the German owner of the dead ass typifies how gesture is often silenced in readings of Sterne's novel, artificially severed from the acoustic dimension of elocution. Smitten explains both the scene's appeal to pathos and how it comically undermines that appeal in terms of what he labels "a pantomime sequence":[33] on the one hand, the old man sits and pathetically laments his dead ass by lifting its bridle up and down, looking at it, shaking his head, laying aside the crust of bread, and finally "look[ing] wistfully at the little arrangement he had made" (*ASJ*, 53). On the other hand, the object of the owner's lament—a lowly ass that is treated very differently in the surrounding two chapters—makes these gestures seem ridiculous. Smitten's reading is perceptive, but it seems wrong to interpret the scene as *silent* ("a pantomime"): after all, the German is telling his tale out loud, and in the course of doing so, Yorick describes him using numerous elements of articulation, including "a sigh," "a vow," an interjection ("Alas!"), and bitter weeping (*ASJ*, 53–54). Smitten excludes these elements from consideration, however, choosing to focus instead on visual elements—"gesture" and "expression" (looks)—which he treats without reference to either elocution as such or to the specific role of articulation in the scene.[34]

Yet acoustic address is a crucial aspect of Yorick's encounter with the old German. The text sketches the general orality of the scene: Yorick tells us that "every body who stood about, heard the poor fellow with concern" and that, by staying in the chaise, he himself "could . . . hear" despite the gathered crowd (*ASJ*, 54, 53). Within this grief-stricken soundscape, Sterne makes one paralinguistic element in particular—"accent"—responsible for Yorick's initial impression that the old man is addressing his dead child: "—AND this, said he, putting the remains of a crust into his wallet—and this, should have been thy portion, said he, hadst thou been alive to have shared it with me. *I thought by the accent,* it had been an apostrophe to his child; but 'twas to his ass" (*ASJ*, 53; emphasis added). The German's "accent" or tone provides the framework for Yorick's initial misunderstanding of the scene. It is on account of this tone that Yorick interprets both the *words* of the German's lament ("—AND this . . . and this, should have been thy portion . . . hadst thou been alive to have shared it with me") and his nonword *gesture* ("putting the remains of a crust into his wallet") as if addressed to a dead child.

Once the real subject of the old German's lament is revealed, Sterne uses Yorick's initial response to it as a standard against which to measure the disproportion between the feelings of the overheard speaker and the lowly creature he is addressing. Only then are reader-listeners invited to reinterpret the German's "pantomime" in comic terms. The transition is abrupt and easy to miss, taking place over the caesura of a single semicolon.[35] Still, despite its brevity, it is enough to establish that the visual field alone does not carry the pathos against which the comedy is subsequently defined. Nor is this scene the novel's only conjunction of animal oratory, suffering innocence, and acoustic elocution: the combination reappears when Yorick thinks he hears the cries of a captive child in an alleyway in Paris (*ASJ*, 95). Provocatively, Yorick's temporary misidentification of the novel's animal orators and receivers as suffering children echoes Sheridan's claim that humans "are moved most by the distressful cries of those animals, that have any similitude to the human voice."[36] Indeed, that Yorick's misidentifications of nonhuman animal speakers and receivers are corrected without leading to a loss of concern for them on his part shows him (and perhaps Sterne) following Sheridan in ascribing an ethical imperative to the rhetorical agency of nonhuman animals.[37]

SELF-DELIVERY AND SELF-CONSCIOUSNESS

Sterne's consistent pairing of articulation and gesture in *A Sentimental Journey* has a significant bearing on the novel's representation of the inner voice. Sterne explicitly references the elocutionary copresence of gesture and articulation in the chapter titled "The Address. Versailles" (*ASJ*, 101–103). Here Yorick visits Monsieur Le Duc de C***** in order to petition for a passport:

> Then nothing would serve me, when I got within sight of Versailles, but putting words and sentences together, and conceiving attitudes and tones to wreath myself into Monsieur Le Duc de C*****'s good graces—This will do——said I—Just as well, retorted I again, as a coat carried up to

> him by an adventurous taylor, without taking his measure—Fool! continued I—see Monsieur Le Duc's face first—observe what character is written in it; take notice in what posture he stands to hear you—mark the turns and expressions of his body and limbs—And for the tone—the first sound which comes from his lips will give it you; and from all these together you'll compound an address at once upon the spot, which cannot disgust the Duke—the ingredients are his own, and most likely to go down. (*ASJ*, 101)

In the self-address of this mental dialogue, Yorick approaches his planned speech to the duke in nakedly elocutionary terms. Like a good orator, he sets out to organize and memorize his appeal for a passport, planning various "tones" (as well as "attitudes") to combine with his "words and sentences," all in order "to wreath [himself] into Monsieur Le Duc de C*****'s good graces" and so emotionally persuade him. Yorick distinguishes here between, on the one hand, the rhetorical canons of arrangement and style ("words and sentences") and, on the other, the canon of delivery ("attitudes and tones"), thereby reserving a distinct space for elocution within the larger practice of eloquence. At the same time, Sterne has Yorick pair the acoustic elements of articulation (such as tone) with the visual components of gesture (such as attitude) as dual aspects of delivery.[38]

Yorick internally debates the matter, persuading himself (self-reflexively addressed as "you") to assess Le Duc de C*****'s mood before determining what he will say, and how. There are two significant consequences of Yorick's self-address. First, Sterne stages self-consciousness as a form of individual elocutionary intersubjectivity; Yorick portrays himself arguing with himself and persuading himself (as in the opening of the novel, although in this case—as far as the reader-listener knows—entirely internally). The oratorical selfhood that Sterne dramatizes here inaugurates a technical innovation that later novelists, such as Jane Austen in her rendering of Emma's mind when she transmits her love for Knightley to herself, were to exploit.[39] Yorick's consciousness is represented using both direct discourse (albeit oscillating between "I" and "you") and elocutionary elements (with typographical cues for paralinguistic interjections ["Fool!"], interruptions ["retorted I"], and pauses ["——"]). In other words, the technical features of Yorick's oratorical self-delivery anticipate the use of free indirect discourse in later novels as a way of representing other consciousnesses.

The second consequence of Yorick's decision to assess Le Duc de C*****'s mood is a clear if comic recognition of the situational nature of delivery; instead of placing a speech in memory, he will improvise, first meeting the duke and then "taking his measure." To what elements will Yorick as oratorical "taylor" apply his metaphorical measuring tape? To Le Duc de C*****'s own elocutionary actions, that is to say, to *his* "face," "posture," and above all "tone." This is not a bad idea in principle, of course, since from Aristotle onward orators were advised to adjust their appeals to suit their audience.[40] Yorick, however, magnifies the circumstantiality of this rhetorical appeal when, in consulting himself about his (planned) address, he claims that, as "for the tone—the first sound which comes from his lips will give it you." He exaggerates his approach further by proposing to copy all of the duke's tones, looks, and gestures and to "compound" them to make his own "address." Because, in this elocutionary bolus, all "the ingredients are [the duke's] own," Yorick judges that the imitation will be "most likely to go down." His plan to mimic the elocution of his interlocutor (recalling the mimicry of the starling's song in the preceding chapter) remains comically ineffective, however, because, despite theoretical sensitivity to circumstance in the form of his interlocutor's tone, Yorick lets slide the occasion for delivery when he instead departs for "the nearest hotel" (*ASJ*, 103).[41]

Sterne foregrounds the circumstantiality of communication throughout *A Sentimental Journey*, beginning with the first sentences of the book. It is difficult for rereaders of the work to recall just how odd its opening is. The first words arrive without context. A nameless, placeless speaker speaks: "—THEY order, said I, this matter better in France—" (*ASJ*, 3). What "matter"? Which "I"? Who are "they"? When, where, why? Some of the reader-listener's questions are answered in the Shandean paragraph that follows: a trip from England to France is proposed and begun with a Dover passage and a Calais arrival, all in time for a three o'clock dinner the next afternoon, to which is added a meditation on death and French law, addresses to the king of France and to Eliza, and a final self-interruption metaphorically alluding to Yorick's foot and anticipating his concluding hand. Even in Shandean terms, the strangeness of the opening remains: it places us in the middle of an unfolding discussion by starting with a retort to an unknown earlier statement.

After the first sentence, Sterne offers the reader-listener a short dialogue as an unnamed manservant responds to Yorick's retort with a question: "You have been in France?" (*ASJ*, 3). On the basis of the elocutionary features of the servant's question, it is not neutral, since when asking it, he "turn[s] quick upon [Yorick] with the most civil triumph in the world" (*ASJ*, 3); the I-thought-so force of this rotation undermines Yorick's opening assertion and his authority. At the end of volume 2, his avowal of authority is comically destabilized by his own elocutionary gesture of "asseveration" (*ASJ*, 164); here it is weakened by the elocutionary gesture of his servant. Yorick responds to this challenge by addressing not the servant or Eliza or even the king of France but himself: "Strange! quoth I, debating the matter with myself" (*ASJ*, 3). Yorick seems to externalize his inner life in both words ("one and twenty miles sailing") and nonword articulation (the emphatic interjection of "Strange!"). His verbal reflections stage a form of public delivery in front of his servant, but they are addressed to himself: "That one and twenty miles sailing . . . should give a man these rights—I'll look into them" (*ASJ*, 3). By contrast, his self-reflection as he plans to speak to Le Duc de C***** is a private version of this public delivery, an internalized moment of self-addressed oratory; in both instances, self-consciousness is represented as a form of circumstantial self-delivery. And that is it: he has persuaded himself, convinced less by argument than by feelings transmitted from and to himself. And so to France.

PROBLEMS OF ELOCUTIONARY TRANSLATION AND RECEPTION

In the chapter titled "The Translation. Paris" (*ASJ*, 76–78), Sterne problematizes commonplace ideas of gestural elocution on the basis of its vulnerability to circumstance and exposes his narrator as naively confident. It is true that, on the heels of an encounter with the "beautiful Grisset" and her gloves (*ASJ*, 74), Yorick boasts that he is able quickly and accurately to translate gestures not only into words but into sentences and even into entire short dramas. Gesture, he claims, is a "*short hand*," one that he has mastered and that he can easily render "into plain words" (*ASJ*, 77). Critics interested in the elocutionary elements of *A Sentimental Journey* have looked to Yorick's shorthand statement as a key to Sterne's understanding of elocution as codified gesture.[42] Tadié, for example, claims that the "episode encapsulates perfectly the whole process of narration in *A Sentimental Journey*, where oral forms of language pass into written English, where visual aspects of communication are translated into 'plain words.'"[43] Indeed, the transtemporal and transnational scope of the chapter may tempt the reader-listener to adopt a universal application of its claims for translation. But the chapter actually shows gesture falling short as a one-to-one equivalent (or shorthand) to spoken or written (word-based) language. Regardless of what Yorick is made to say, in *A Sentimental Journey* Sterne presents gesture as an unstable code because the same gesture can be interpreted in various ways, depending on the circumstances of context and the recipient.

The chapter on translation falls into three parts: (1) a gestural encounter at the *opera comique* in Paris with an "old French officer" (*ASJ*, 76); (2) a boast by Yorick on his success in London at translating gestures; and (3) an anecdote about his translation of the gestures of the Marquesina di F*** at a concert in Milan. In the encounter at the opera, Yorick describes the occupant of the box into which he is shown:

> The old officer was reading attentively a small pamphlet, it might be the book of the opera, with a large pair of spectacles. As soon as I sat down, he took his spectacles off, and putting them into a shagreen case, return'd them and the book into his pocket together. I half rose up, and made him a bow.
>
> Translate this into any civilized language in the world—the sense is this:
>
> "Here's a poor stranger come in to the box—he seems as if he knew no body; and is never likely, was he to be seven years in Paris, if every man he comes near keeps his spectacles upon his nose—'tis shutting the door of conversation absolutely in his face—and using him worse than a German."
>
> The French officer might as well have said it all aloud; and if he had, I should in course have put the bow I made him into French too, and told him, "I was sensible of his attention, and return'd him a thousand thanks for it." (*ASJ*, 76–77)

How is the reader-listener to take Yorick's assertions about the officer's gestures? His action may seem to communicate a warmhearted concern for Yorick as a stranger, and Yorick's bow does appear to express gratitude. But the details of Yorick's translation ("was he to be seven years in Paris"; "using him worse than a German") are hyperbolic and humorously overspecific—they suggest an unfettered invention.

Further, the individual gestural actions on which Yorick's elaboration is based could spring from many causes. We are never told, for example, in what direction the officer is looking and with what demeanor. But that would be key information. The officer puts Yorick in mind of Toby Shandy, who, despite his military background, is a byword for gentle considerateness, even regarding flies (*TS*, 2.12.130–131). But why should the officer share Uncle Toby's character, except that Yorick chooses to think he does? For all the reader-listener knows, Yorick could have irritated the officer when he impolitely "strode over the two back rows of benches" (*ASJ*, 76) and crowded into the box; if so, the officer may have shut his book and removed his glasses out of displeasure or surprise. Yorick is an unreliable recipient of Father Lorenzo's gesture; why not of the old soldier's?

Despite Yorick's exaggerated precision and comic certainty, most critics take Yorick's translation of the officer's gestures at face value,[44] presumably because of the boast that immediately follows it and that forms the second part of the chapter:

> There is not a secret so aiding to the progress of sociality, as to get master of this *short hand*, and be quick in rendering the several turns of looks and limbs, with all their inflections and delineations, into plain words. For my own part, by long habitude, I do it so mechanically, that when I walk the streets of London, I go translating all the way; and have more than once stood behind in the circle, where not three words have been said, and have brought off twenty different dialogues with me, which I could have fairly wrote down and sworn to. (*ASJ*, 77)

As with elocutionary attention to attitudes and postures, facial expression, and demeanor, here gesture comprehends both "looks and limbs"; in this passage, Yorick generalizes his supposed elocutionary expertise from the encounter with the old soldier and positions himself as the ideal receiver of visual delivery.

The thesis that sociality, including that of nonhuman animals, derives from the nonword communication of feeling was a key theoretical claim of elocutionary thinkers such as Sheridan: "it was necessary to society . . . that the language of the animal passions of man . . . should be fixed, self-evident, and universally intelligible [and that humans] should feel much, and have a mutual sympathy."[45] In the passage on the "*short hand*," however, Sterne modifies Sheridan's claim: Yorick asserts that mastery of the gestural shorthand will develop sociality, placing the increase of elocutionary *nous* into a conjectural history of civilization. This might seem to echo Sheridan's program for the advancement of British society through elocutionary pedagogy, but it is not clear if Yorick's shorthand increases sympathy and thus sociality or if it simply replaces scenes of sympathetic gesturing with voyeuristic inscription into words. In any case, Yorick anticipates memorializing elocutionists like Walker and Austin: the scene paints a flâneur Yorick traversing London while using a set code "mechanically" to translate gesture into speech, even "dialogues" (we must imagine him observing both gestural senders and receivers), with a hyperbolic "twenty" conversations that he could have collected, written down, and "sworn to," a dubious juridical testament.

Yorick doth protest too much: the "sworn" assertion that gestures may be understood and "mechanically" translated according to a stable shorthand or code feels like as a red herring, an act of quasi-theoretical misdirection on Sterne's part.[46] Many passages point instead to Yorick engaging in self-serving acts of elocutionary casuistry (starting with his encounter with the monk) and self-delusion (as we will see with the Marquesina di F***). Consider Yorick's encounter with the "beautiful Grisset" in the preceding chapter: "There are certain combined looks of simple subtlety—where whim, and sense, and seriousness, and nonsense, are so blended, that all the languages of Babel set loose together could not express them—they are communicated and caught so instantaneously, that you can scarce say which party is the infecter. I leave it to your men of words to swell pages about it—" (*ASJ*, 74). In this passage, both "men of words" and "all the languages" that use words are held to be inferior to the instantaneous communication enabled by the nonword language of "certain . . . looks." There is a comic slippage, however, from meaningful looks, through communication, to the catching hold of a meaning that is then literalized as a contagion, like venereal disease, with communicators analogized as agents of contagion. The problem from a rhetorical perspective is that it is not clear who is the infector or orator and who is the victim or recipient in this circuit of physical and gestural contagion. Elsewhere, Yorick is seen "*translating* French looks and attitudes into plain English" (*ASJ*, 145): "—THEY order . . . this matter better in France—" (*ASJ*, 3), or at least they order it differently.[47] In the encounter with the *grisset*, Yorick conceives of gesture ("combined looks") as a cultural variable ("Babel"), not a universal code, further questioning its stability as a reliable means of communication when compared to Sheridan's claim that some gestures and tones are "fixed, self-evident, and universally intelligible."[48] The "swell" of the men of letters evokes neither "plain English" nor "Babel" but the verbal play of a double entendre; here, then, as also elsewhere, Sterne's text offers a form of intelligibility to a knowing reader-listener who can grasp the sexual register of a sentimental encounter.[49]

The chapter on translation ends with Yorick's anecdote about an awkward encounter with the Marquesina di F*** at "Martini's concert at Milan" (*ASJ*, 77), where gesture is anything but "fixed, self-evident, and universally intelligible." The anecdote recounts a comical episode in which the Marquesina and Yorick "both blush'd intolerably" (*ASJ*, 77) while attempting to pass each other in the entrance hall of the concert venue. Once they do get around each other, the Marquesina keeps to one side of the hall, with Yorick thinking that she does this for a nonsexual purpose, so that others can go by her to get in. But, on further reflection, with the Marquesina looking back at him, just as the *grisset* had done (*ASJ*, 70), he comes to reject his first interpretation of her "looks and limbs" as a "vile translation" (*ASJ*, 77). Instead, Yorick runs after her, apologizes, and with much sexual innuendo follows her into "her coach," in which "she carried [him] home with her": "I will only add, that the connection which arose out of that translation, gave me more pleasure than any one I had the honour to make in Italy" (*ASJ*, 78). As with Madame de L***, Sterne puts sentimental and sexual communication on an elocutionary continuum, with Yorick tying the successful circumstantial translation of this gesture to the achievement of sexual pleasure, a goal that Sheridan also imagined delivery serving through its facilitation of sexual communication for both human and nonhuman animal orators.[50]

Yorick's two translations of the Marquesina's gesture once again exemplify the process of self-consciousness as circumstantial self-delivery and show how his purposes and sentiments as a listener-observer are mediated through self-address.[51] Across the three parts of the chapter, Yorick comically asserts his theoretical mastery of a code for the elocutionary translation of gesture *and* comically celebrates his practical agency in determining gestural meaning according to the translation he spontaneously prefers, simply disavowing as "vile" the application of any code or normative expectation when his own purposes are better served by something else. Yorick's change of understanding illustrates his active role in the circuits of elocution and reaffirms the circumstantiality of sentimental/sexual communication in relation to a receiver's rhetorical relationship with themselves. Yorick translates the Marquesina's gesture twice, he himself is translated to her home, and behind it all are the sexual feelings (blushes) and satisfactions (pleasures) that are translated between them. We do not know for certain, focalized as we are in Yorick's consciousness, whether the Marquesina's glance back began as one of desire—or if it ever truly became one; nor do we know if it was meant by her from the start as a visual double entendre in order to test Yorick's sexual sophistication and interest. But even if Yorick has managed a successful second translation of the Marquesina's elocutionary actions, the chapter undermines his vaunted expertise in the gestural "*short hand*" by highlighting the circumstantial limits that are determinative to elocution, beginning and ending with the narrator's own changeable self-delivery.

PROBLEMS OF ELOCUTIONARY CARRIAGE AND CONTEXT

When sentiments travel, they may, like people, get into scrapes; carriages may overturn, passengers may land in unexpected situations. The tone of the German mourner misleads Yorick; Yorick refuses Father Lorenzo's attitude of entreaty. Sometimes the elocutionary mediation of feeling succeeds, whether immediately (as with Madame de L***'s tone) or on reflection (as with the Marquesina's attitudes and looks). But just as often it can fail or issue in an impasse, as with the "beautiful Grisset." Sometimes it can both succeed and fail, as with the starling's song.

In contrast to the instability of delivery in Sterne, elocutionary doctrine holds that tones, postures, and looks do effectively communicate feelings; for Sheridan, this is especially so if elocutionary elements are produced extemporaneously. Sheridan replaces reliance on specific encodings, as seen in memorializing elocutionists, with a doctrine of spontaneous legibility; for Sheridan, nature stabilizes elocutionary meaning within the vagaries of circumstance. Sterne, by contrast, in the chapter on translation, plays with both conventional gestures and Yorick's claims to a natural understanding of them. An implication of Sterne's play on elocutionary elements (both natural and conventional, sexual and nonsexual, produced by human and by nonhuman animals) is that they are not stable or stabilizable.

From the start of the novel, Sterne dramatizes how the successful mediation of feeling is guaranteed neither by the intention of the elocutionary sender nor by the elocutionary devices a sender employs. Instead, Sterne shows how the emotional condition and agency of a receiver of sentimental communication contributes to shaping elocutionary transmission, as with Yorick and the Marquesina or with the starling and its audiences. And this in turn opens another way of thinking about the reception of *Yorick's* narrative: how can it ever be possible for reader-listeners to come to a stable understanding of the gestures and articulations that Yorick himself describes and enacts—whether they are natural or artificial, polite or bawdy, "heartfelt" or subject to "mockery"—given that a key driver of elocutionary response (both sentimental and sexual) is the recipient's own feelings?[52] The reader-listener of *A Sentimental Journey* is, after all, also the recipient of Yorick's speech.

Yorick explicitly reflects on the determining role of context and chance in elocutionary communication (and by implication on the reception of his own speech by reader-listeners) at the start of the "Preface In the Desobligeant" (*ASJ*, 13–17), which cleverly sets his reflections on traveling and on sentimental communication (the traveling of feeling) in a physical vehicle.[53] The *desobligeant* symbolizes both the isolation of the individual sensibility ("our own sphere" [*ASJ*, 13]) and the physicality of elocution through the muscular movements of a writer-speaker. The chapter opens with a jest about travel abroad as sexual adventuring: it is only "sometimes" that we find ourselves able to spread "our happiness . . . beyond *her* [nature's] limits"; rather "'tis so ordered, that from the want of languages, connections, and dependencies, and from the difference in education, customs and habits, we lie under so many impediments in communicating our sensations out of our own sphere, as often amount to a total impossibility" (*ASJ*, 13). As a description of the limits on the communication of a traveler's feelings, this passage brings together mediation as an ontological problem with mediation as an intercultural one, since it applies to the communication of feeling out of the "sphere" of the human head or body as well as to the limits on communication set by knowable as well as unknowable "impediments" or contextual spheres such as nation, custom, language, and animal species.[54] In any event, "It will always follow from hence, that the balance of sentimental commerce is always against the expatriated adventurer" (*ASJ*, 13).

Mistakes in passionate communication due to features of the traveler's context arise comically at the end of the preface. Yorick unexpectedly begins a long passage about the virtues of *not* traveling and turns this into praise of England and then into a criticism of the would-be English traveler. As the topic starts changing, so does the language form, shifting imperceptibly from written exposition to spoken declamation. This shift is crucial because the question that concludes the preface, "—Where then, my dear countrymen, are you going—," suddenly jolts the reader-listener into a new frame of reference when it is answered by two passing Englishmen: "—We are only looking at this chaise, said they—Your most obedient servant, said I, skipping out of it, and pulling off my hat" (*ASJ*, 17). We realize that Yorick is, as it were, writing aloud. His speech was not intended for these listeners; indeed, he does not know he is being overheard when he starts speaking. Still, *they* do not know that they are not his addressees, *they* feel confident in the way they have been hailed, and thus, by a contextual chance, *they* speak as if he had meant to address them. As a scene of communication, the singular "*Vehicle*" (*ASJ*, 15) is, as it were, invaded by the ears of others, with neither the carriage nor the soliloquy remaining private.

The miscommunications with the English travelers are not limited to the words of Yorick's utterances; Sterne also shows nonword elocutionary elements leaking into unexpected and unintended contexts between them when they run into Yorick in the Calais carriage yard a second time and observe him deep in conversation with Madame de L***. Here, the travelers interpret the hand-holding and other "communications" between Yorick and Madame de L*** as indicating that they are "*man and wife* at least," something that they "naturally took . . . into their heads" when "passing by" (*ASJ*, 28). On the one hand, holding hands appears to be a natural sign of marriage: Adam and Eve in *Paradise Lost* exit the garden in just this fashion. On the other hand, given that Yorick and Madame de L*** are not married, indeed have just met, we see Sterne again bawdily reminding us that there are no natural (meaning universal) gestures. Rather, what is natural is context.

Sterne has Yorick communicate this last insight in the parable of the Burgundy grapes. The story of these grapes, "transplanted . . . to the Cape of Good Hope," teaches that the traveler cannot know what he will become when he changes scenes and travels abroad: "it did not depend upon his choice, but . . . what is generally called *chance*" (*ASJ*, 16). In the parable, the transplanter "never dreamt of drinking the same wine at the Cape, that the same grape produced upon the French mountains" (*ASJ*, 16). This "Dutch man" (*ASJ*, 16) is not to be confused with travel writers like Smelfungus and Mundungus, each of whom in his own way is unmoved by what he sees and travels through: for them, context counts for nothing; they are "without one generous connection or pleasurable anecdote to tell of," and indeed, were they in heaven, they "would do penance there to all eternity" (*ASJ*, 37–38). It is unnatural, then, not to respond to situational signals, including those of travel. At the same time, as the scene with Yorick and the two Englishmen makes clear, the ability to manage the fluid circumstances of elocution will always be subject to uncertainty and serve as an endlessly fruitful source of comic miscommunication.

RHETORICS OF BIRDSONG AND BIRDSCRIPT

Sheridan claimed that the expression of feeling through tone is a capacity shared by all animals, human and nonhuman; that it serves to communicate feeling between individuals in a species and so to socialize them; and finally that humans understand the tones and thus feelings of other species, including birds.[55] Sterne's key example of a nonhuman animal orator in *A Sentimental Journey* is the starling that Yorick encounters in Paris. Just as the reception of Yorick's speech in the *desobligeant* oscillates between pathos and comedy, so too does the starling's "song" (*ASJ*, 99)—a fitting emblem of elocution, its problematization, and its performance in the novel. The bird is the secret sharer of Yorick's mantle as an orator: both are English travelers who use elocution; both are passionate communicators who succeed in moving others; both appear at times to be mechanical reproducers of elocutionary elements; and both have their delivery misunderstood.[56]

The starling chapters of *A Sentimental Journey* build on the novel's earlier treatments of the reception and context of elocution and develop its thinking about the limits of elocutionary response by engaging with the canon of memory. As with the old German's apostrophe and the Marquesina's posture, the starling's elocution is interpreted twice by Yorick: first naively and then with comic sophistication. Yorick receives the starling's speech in two modes: as performance and as legend. The legend of the starling—the "story" Yorick tells about it, its own recitation of its "song" (*ASJ*, 99), and the chance that other birds may "copy" (*ASJ*, 100) it without feeling—develops in the aftermath of Yorick's travels, on his return to England. So too does the version of the legend the reader-listener receives, the "short history of this self-same bird" (*ASJ*, 99) that Yorick includes in *A Sentimental Journey* itself. As we will see, Yorick's stance toward the legend, "story," or "history" of the starling—that is, his stance toward its various memorializations—is ambivalent. He is not at all ambivalent, however, when he first encounters the bird's musical performance: "I *never* had my affections *more* tenderly awakened" (*ASJ*, 95; emphasis added). Sterne ties Yorick's hyperbolic claim directly back to the German's apostrophe through Yorick's misidentifications: at that time he initially misidentified the addressee (really an ass) as a child; now he initially misidentifies the speaker (really a starling) as one.

Yorick first hears the starling when he is musing on the Bastille and is "interrupted" by "a voice . . . which complained 'it could not get out.'—" (*ASJ*, 95). His concern only heightens when he discovers the speaker to be a caged bird, which he tries to free:

> The bird flew to the place where I was attempting his deliverance, and thrusting his head through the trellis, press'd his breast against it, as if impatient—I fear, poor creature! said I, I cannot set thee at liberty—"No," said the starling—"I can't get out—I can't get out," said the starling.
>
> I vow, I never had my affections more tenderly awakened; [n]or do I remember an incident in my life, where the dissipated spirits, to which my reason had been a bubble, were so suddenly call'd home. Mechanical as the notes were, yet so true in tune to nature were they chanted, that in one moment they overthrew all my systematic reasonings upon the Bastile; and I heavily walk'd up stairs, unsaying every word I had said in going down them. (*ASJ*, 95–96)

The dialogue between Yorick and the starling is an elocutionary one: it is not the words or inscribable "notes" of the starling's speech that carry its feelings (its impatience) but its gestures and "chant[ing]"; it is not Yorick's reason that the bird addresses but his passions; the bird is not a musical monad but a rhetorical agent whose tones and gestures draw on physical interaction to successfully create cross-species sympathy and society.[57] When Yorick vows that he "never had [his] affections more tenderly awakened," the reader-listener is invited to believe him (regardless of Yorick's dubious earlier claims to expertise as a translator of gestures) because on this occasion the elocution (the chant) is "in tune to nature." Yorick *feels* that the bird wants out.

The communicational circumstances in Paris also favor sensitivity to the bird's plight: Yorick himself faces confinement in the Bastille. Those circumstances are very different later on, in England:

> In my return from Italy I brought him with me to the country in whose language he had learn'd his notes—and telling the story of him to Lord A—Lord A begg'd the bird of me—in a week Lord A gave him to Lord B—Lord B made a present of him to Lord C—and Lord C's gentleman sold him to Lord D for a shilling—Lord D gave him to Lord E—and so on—half round the alphabet—From that rank he pass'd into the lower house, and pass'd the hands of as many commoners——But as all these wanted to *get in*—and my bird wanted to get out—he had almost as little store set by him in London as in Paris.

> It is impossible but many of my readers must have heard of him; and if any by mere chance have ever seen him—I beg leave to inform them, that bird was my bird—or some vile copy set up to represent him. (*ASJ*, 99–100)

The idea of Yorick's starling as an imitator of its first instructor's "tongue" (*ASJ*, 99) whose mimicry may itself be imitated is a theoretical crux, but the purpose here is to set this crux in an elocutionary framework. First, the comic/pathetic fate of the eloquent starling is that men come to treat it as a fashionable and replaceable automaton without emotional, political, or other import. Yorick's use of the modifier "vile" reflects his discomfort with the bird's English reception and provocatively reminds us of his "vile" first translation of the Marquesina's backward glance. Second, although birdsong often evokes a spontaneous or natural utterance, the shift in context and thus in the reception of the bird's words (from elocutionary occasion to memorial repetition) is what makes it "mechanical" (*ASJ*, 95) in the sense of artificial (not the mere act of repetition alone). Third, the specific source of the artificiality of the bird's song is the repetition of a word formula ("I can't get out") without context or sentimental freight, so that even the "vile copy" of another bird can stand in for it, much like one insensitive auditor may stand in for another (Lords A to Z). At the same time, this "vile" copying memorializes how the "notes" are "chanted," making them available for any context as well as any auditor; in that sense they are denatured elocution-wise.[58] The same repetition that earlier transmitted the bird's unhappiness (as emphasis) now expresses the bird's lack of true feeling (as script).

One of the central implications of Sheridan's argument, that verbal elocution is to written words as musical performance is to musical notation, can help us understand the changing reception of the starling.[59] Notes, like words, can be memorized or—what is a form of memorialization—written down; but neither memorization nor inscription is to perform or deliver them. From the rhetorical perspective that Sheridan promoted, moving from performance (in context) to script or score (out of context), that is, from delivery to memory, is a shift from sentimental communication to conceptual inscription.[60] The same process is present in Yorick's claim that he could "mechanically . . . translat[e]" the gestures of the circle into "twenty . . . dialogues" (*ASJ*, 77). It is not just that his claim is comically exaggerated or that, as with the Marquesina, it is vulnerable to the impact of circumstances; rather, as with the Burgundy grapes, without the circumstantiality that is consequent on performance, gesture and articulation are no longer elocutionary, and, in Sheridan's view, feeling cannot be shared. Without elocutionary sympathy, social bonds are lost, too: between Yorick and the starling, between Yorick and the various lords and commoners, and even between the "vile copy" and Yorick's "readers." Unfeeling social competition ("all these wanted to *get in*" [*ASJ*, 100]) and the vaunting of social status replace sympathetic sociality.[61]

Memorial decontextualization also endangers Yorick's speech about the starling: the "telling [of] the story" (*ASJ*, 99) is itself inscribed first as a mental script that the various owners repeat to each other and second through print publication when Yorick informs his reader-listeners about the starling in the book of his travels. When Yorick adds, "from that time to this, I have borne this poor starling as the crest to my arms" (*ASJ*, 100), Sterne provides the legend of the starling with a graphic emblem ("the crest") that cleverly reframes memorialized elocution in relation to social sympathy. A drawing of Yorick's coat of arms (based on Sterne's) appears directly in the text, re-enforcing the starling's passage from delivery to memory, joining the flow of Yorick's written words to an unsayable graphic emblem (a silent bird), and mocking the graphic codes of memorializing elocutionists in the persons of the herald's officers: "let [them] twist his neck about if they dare" (*ASJ*, 100). Here unfeeling inscriptions of social status replace felt performances of sympathetic sociality. Shockingly, the chapter titled "The Captive. Paris" (*ASJ*, 97–98), which separates the two treatments of the starling, traces a similar memorial logic when, Yorick says, "THE bird in his cage pursued me into my room" (*ASJ*, 97). In that chapter, Yorick's attempt to "sustain" a mental "picture" (*ASJ*, 98) of a human captive overwhelms, rather than enables, his ability to feel either for the captive or for "the millions of [his] fellow creatures born to no inheritance but slavery" (*ASJ*, 97).[62]

MEMORY AND DELIVERY

The dynamic interplay between elocutionary performance and memorializing inscription in *A Sentimental Journey* is highlighted in the much-commented-on, brilliant aposiopesis that concludes the work. As Yorick tells it, he is reaching out to make a point in the midst of a late-night dispute with a female fellow traveler. After he suddenly shouts out, "O my God!" they debate what has happened: she claims he has used words ("an entire infraction of the treaty" they made when they agreed to share the room); he claims it is just an exclamation, "no more than an ejaculation" (*ASJ*, 164). Yorick employs elocutionary casuistry in his defense, asserting that his outburst was in substance a nonword cry expressive of his feelings of frustration and exhausted patience. While swearing to the lady that he has not violated the accord, he draws his reader-listener into the elocutionary scene by telling us how he "stretch[ed his] arm out of bed, by way of asseveration" (*ASJ*, 164). This act both references a stock gesture of sweeping out an arm to assert something and slyly offers a bawdy suggestion about what he may have "caught hold of" (*ASJ*, 165).[63]

How can the force of this rhetorical action best be delineated? It is true that Sterne engages with what Tadié calls "the forms of the book"; what matters most here, however, is the scene's elocutionary structure, not its "heterogeneity" of language forms.[64] First, the declamatory motion is faintly ridiculous, as if a lady in this "delicate" (*ASJ*, 164) circumstance is to be moved by formal oratory. Second, the gesture is ineffective because the bedroom is pitch black. This is why Yorick does not see the maid when she comes between the two beds, "so that," as he famously tells it, "when I stretch'd out my hand, I caught hold of the Fille de Chambre's // END OF VOL. II" (*ASJ*, 165). Third, while we never find out what part of the *fille de chambre*'s body, clothing, or accoutrements Yorick has "caught hold of," the action tips the scene into bedroom farce. The physical comedy has a further rhetorical consequence inasmuch as, among the various figures of speech, orators frequently used aposiopesis to achieve emphasis by instigating a gap in speaking. As M. Wade Mahon observes, "a figure like *aposiopesis* has more to do with a dramatic break in delivery than with diction or syntax," so that it may simultaneously serve both style and delivery.[65] In this case, the interruption draws attention to whatever it is that Yorick actually catches hold of by leaving it unspecified, although the bawdy play on "END" supplies the fourth dimension of the episode, the interlinking of a speech gesture with a print artifact: a double entendre is created through the material context of the physical volume in which the aposiopesis occurs. Enacted by the performance of the text as an utterance, as reader-listeners temporalize the novel through their reception of it (getting to the "END OF VOL. II"), the double entendre traces the reverse of the starling's fate: an escape from graphic constraint rather than a memorial confinement.

Comic use of the material form of printed works was commonplace among the novelists of the 1750s, as Thomas Keymer has shown,[66] and Sterne readily drew comic attention in his narratives to the material form of printed works, a point that Tadié examines in some detail.[67] What matters most in "The Case of Delicacy" (*ASJ*, 160–165), however, is how Sterne enlists a paratextual element into the service of an elocutionary experience: earlier the crest froze elocution by memorializing the starling-orator in an image; here Yorick's hand bursts onto the printed page as we read, linking the complex occasionality of both *print* performance and *nonword* memorialization in the experience of the reader-listener.

THE LIMITS OF ELOCUTION

Thomas Sheridan's approach to the resources of verbal delivery sought radically to sever the relationship between communication based on memory (writing) and communication based on delivery (speech). However much this move may be philosophically suspect or the result of a failure to understand Locke, Sheridan's revival of delivery wrenched the terms by which the sharing of feeling could be discussed away from the inside-outside dynamics of natural signs (problems of sensible feeling, of the embodiment of feeling, and of mediation) to the outside-outside dynamics of spaciotemporality (problems of elocutionary technique, circumstance, and attention). Sheridan placed the agents of communication, the orator and recipient, at the center of sentimental mediation and highlighted the animal nature of elocution. This turn to delivery was, in other words, a fresh intervention into contemporary philosophical and physiological thinking about the sharing of feeling within and between species.

Sterne's genius was to take Sheridan's fresh approach, which ascribed successful emotional communication to spontaneous delivery, as an opportunity to experiment with the limits of elocution deriving from spontaneity: circumstance, self-address, and the dynamics of memory and delivery. Within the field of unlimited articulations and gestures posited by Sheridan, Sterne's narrative explores what such paralinguistic variability entails for the way feelings are sent and received, tracing the comic uncertainty of their transits, and offering new literary techniques to map the communicational flow of emotional consciousness. And because *A Sentimental Journey* is both a retrospective account of the narrator's elocutionary experiences and an embodied print artifact communicating them to its reader-listeners, Sterne's novel has the further effect of problematizing any straightforward division of writing and speaking, memory and delivery.

In this manner, *A Sentimental Journey* both puts delivery back in relation with the other canons of rhetoric and solicits the agency of its own receiving reader-listener. First, against the reduction of gesture and articulation to a code, Sterne's novel experiments with the use of print as a physical, even elocutionary, performance. It is a timely reminder that the canons of rhetoric are an artificial decomposition of actual communicational events. Sheridan is fully aware of this practical point, both criticizing the limits of writing, famously calling it "dead" compared with speech, and defending its importance as an aid to effective oral communication.[68] Second, as an elocutionary performance, *A Sentimental Journey* models its own unstable historical reception—for example, through Yorick's changing responses to the starling's song or to the Marquesina's glance. Depending on the reader-listener's own condition and agency, the novel's weaving of memory and delivery will resolve in different patterns with different affects. This variable resolution is not the result of a defect in Sterne's text, Yorick's speech, or even the starling's chant. Rather, it is a demonstration, through and to the work's reader-listeners, of the problematics of elocution that *A Sentimental Journey* sets out to explore.

NOTES

I would like to thank Chris GoGwilt, Melanie Holm, and, especially, Camie Kim for their comments on an earlier version of this chapter.

1. Jonathan Lamb, "Language and Hartleian Associationism in *A Sentimental Journey*," *Eighteenth-Century Studies* 13, no. 3 (Spring 1980): 285.
2. The five canons of classical rhetoric are invention, arrangement, style, memory, and delivery. "Elocution" (delivery) is not a synonym for eloquent oratory; it is a component of oratory's successful execution, "the just and graceful management of the voice, countenance, and gesture in speaking," in Thomas Sheridan's formulation. Sheridan, *A Course of Lectures on Elocution* (London, 1762), 19. Further, elocutionary thought treats gesture (the elements of visual action in delivery, such as looks, postures, and touches) and articulation (the elements of acoustic vocalization in delivery such as accent, emphasis, and tone) as copresent features in the performance of speech. Influential scholars of sentimentalism sometimes obscure these rhetorical matters by writing as if the two modes of elocution were easily separable or as if eloquence were a synonym for elocution; see, for example, John Mullan, *Sentiment and Sociability: The Language of Feeling in the Eighteenth Century* (Oxford: Clarendon, 1988), 16. The present chapter seeks to avoid these confusions by adhering to a rhetorical understanding of elocution and the sentimental communication it enables.
3. Alexis Tadié, *Sterne's Whimsical Theatres of Language: Orality, Gesture, Literacy* (Aldershot, UK: Ashgate, 2003), 17, 18. Note that, for Sheridan, both the visual field of gesture and the acoustic field of articulation are "beyond words."
4. Tadié, 62–63.
5. Paul Goring, *The Rhetoric of Sensibility in Eighteenth-Century Culture* (Cambridge: Cambridge University Press, 2005), 39.
6. Goring, 197, 189.
7. Thus Tadié: "Authors of treatises on rhetoric devoted parts of their books to defining gestures, giving precise and normative instructions. . . . gestures must be codified"; when Yorick encounters a mourner, the "attitude of grief is ritualized" (*Sterne's Whimsical Theatres*, 63, 65). Goring considers *A Sentimental Journey* "a rendering into words of a catalogue of eloquent gestures" (*Rhetoric of Sensibility*, 197).
8. Sheridan, *Lectures on Elocution*, 99.
9. Sheridan, 114. I use the term "nonword" because Sheridan draws a bright line between linguistic material used to communicate ideas (word-based language) and paralinguistic material used to communicate feelings (articulation- and gesture-based delivery): "the passions and the fancy have a language of their own, utterly independent of words" (x). The present chapter uses the term "nonword" for all the paralinguistic elements of elocution, both visual (nonacoustic) gesture and acoustic (nonvisual) articulation.
10. On Sheridan's impact, see Goring, *Rhetoric of Sensibility*, 91–113; Conrad Brunström, *Thomas Sheridan's Career and Influence: An Actor in Earnest* (Lewisburg, PA: Bucknell University Press, 2011); and Paula McDowell, *The Invention of the Oral: Print Commerce and Fugitive Voices in Eighteenth-Century Britain* (Chicago: University of Chicago Press, 2017),

174–184. On Sterne's own well-documented fame seeking, see Thomas Keymer, *Sterne, the Moderns, and the Novel* (Oxford: Oxford University Press, 2002), 155–156.

11. On Sheridan's dictionary, see Goring, *Rhetoric of Sensibility*, 106–107; Brunström, *Thomas Sheridan's Career*, 88; and McDowell, *Invention of the Oral*, 184. On Alexander Melville Bell's elocutionary work, see Jed Rasula, "Understanding the Sound of Not Understanding," in *Close Listening: Poetry and the Performed Word*, ed. Charles Bernstein (New York: Oxford University Press, 1998), 247–251. Melville was Alexander Graham Bell's father.
12. Fraser Easton, "Christopher Smart's Elocution," in *Reading Christopher Smart in the Twenty-First Century*, ed. Min Wild and Noel Chevalier (Lewisburg, PA: Bucknell University Press, 2013), 63–84.
13. According to Sheridan, the "Divine Service in general is not performed with . . . solemnity, distinctness, and propriety . . . nor discourses delivered from the pulpit, with such powers of persuasive, or forcible elocution, as alone can make them produce their intended effects" (*Lectures on Elocution*, 1).
14. Of course, as with the mock-erudite discussion of the angles of Trim's body, the interruptions also burlesque the art of elocution. See Mullan, *Sentiment and Sociability*, 179; and Goring, *Rhetoric of Sensibility*, 190–191. Hogarth's decision to portray Trim from behind focuses the viewer's attention on the reaction of Trim's audience, who are "each engaged in their own activity," as W. B. Gerard notes, instead of attending to the orator's delivery. Gerard, *Laurence Sterne and the Visual Imagination* (Aldershot, UK: Ashgate, 2006), 61.
15. Keymer identifies delivery as one "of the many undeveloped nodules for continuation" that Sterne salted away in *Tristram Shandy* (*Sterne, the Moderns, and the Novel*, 146); the present chapter posits that *A Sentimental Journey* returns to this nodule as its raison d'être.
16. Sheridan associated ideas with the durability of written words on the basis of his reading of Locke's interest in "words, as symbols of our ideas" that can be inscribed, and Sheridan contrasted this durability with the ephemerality of tone and gesture as "signs of internal emotions" that cannot be inscribed (*Lectures on Elocution*, 97).
17. Goring, *Rhetoric of Sensibility*, 110–111; Sheridan, *Lectures on Elocution*, 121.
18. Sheridan, *Lectures on Elocution*, 118.
19. See, for example, John Walker, *Elements of Elocution* (London, 1781), plate 1, graphing "the inflexions of the voice" (1:136); and Gilbert Austin, *Chironomia; or A Treatise on Rhetorical Delivery* (London, 1806), plate 3, "The Systematic Positions of the Arms" (figs. 19–33), graphing movements of the arms.
20. For an example of such a score, see Joshua Steele's illustration of the measure, accent, and quantity of the nonword acoustic elements of Garrick's performance of Hamlet's "To be or not to be" speech in *An Essay towards Establishing the Melody and Measure of Speech to be Expressed and Perpetuated by Peculiar Symbols* (London, 1775), 47–48.
21. For an early English example of the sort of memorializing elocution that Sterne departs from, see the illustrations cataloguing various hand gestures in John Bulwer, *Chironomia; or, The Art of Manual Rhetorique* (London, 1644).
22. Sheridan, *Lectures on Elocution*, 105. With respect to tone, Sheridan writes that "man, in his animal capacity, is furnished, like all other animals, by nature herself, with a language . . . which spontaneously breaks out in the exactest expressions"; for this and other reasons, including the way in which customary affect signs form a "second nature" in elocution, "extemporaneous speaking" is best because the "exact" gestures and tones will then "spontaneously start forth" (105, 107, 12).
23. This inner orator is acknowledged early on: when Yorick is confronted by his servant's challenge, he describes the flow of his thoughts as "debating the matter with myself" (*ASJ*, 3).

24. The possibility of deceitful elocution is anticipated in Sterne's sermon on prayer: although there is "a strong sympathy and union between our souls and bodies," although "Nature has assigned a different look, tone of voice, and gesture, peculiar to every passion and affection we are subject to," and although "our heart and affections [should] go along with [prayer]," which should never be "dispassionate," Sterne notes that "it is possible, and often happens, that this external garb of religion may be worn, when there is little within of a piece with it" (*Sermons*, 402, 406, 407). For the feeling supplicant, however, Sterne posits no such obstacles to delivery: "The mind will shine through the veil of flesh which covers it" (407). The sermon, then, focuses on inside-outside matters of religious sincerity. In contrast, *A Sentimental Journey* focuses on outside-outside factors such as context and chance, factors which in Sterne's novel amount to a necessary limit on the elocution of even a sincerely feeling orator.
25. According to Sheridan, the sympathetic responsiveness of nonhuman animals to the tones of their own species, and their antipathy to those of other species, "shews us, that the auditory nerves of animals, are constructed in such a way, as to be affected only with such sounds, as immediately regard the two chief ends of their being; the propagation, and preservation of their species" (*Lectures on Elocution*, 102–103). Humans, in contrast, understand the tones of all species (including, implicitly, sexual tones) as part of their own "animal capacity" (105).
26. Mullan, *Sentiment and Sociability*, 189, emphasis added.
27. The literature on mediation in Sterne is extensive; in general, it focuses on embodiment, or the relationship between mind and matter, as an epistemological and ontological problem, often referencing issues in Locke. David Fairer, for example, argues that "the literature of Sensibility is interested in those moments when the transfer between mind and matter is made" and that such a "sentimental translation" is confirmed when a man of feeling experiences a "*frisson* of physical arousal," whether sexual or spiritual. Fairer, "Sentimental Translation in Mackenzie and Sterne," *Essays in Criticism* 49, no. 2 (April 1999): 136. For Sheridan, in contrast, such philosophical enquires can never bear on the practice of effective delivery, since Locke does not treat "the seat of the passions" in "the human mind," commonly and "unphilosophically" known as "the heart"; and, even if he had, "little or no benefit in point of practice, has resulted from a display in theory" such as Locke's analysis of word usage (*Lectures on Elocution*, ix). Although aware of the influence of Locke on Sterne, and of Sterne's interest in period physiological ideas, the present chapter approaches sentimental mediation (the traveling of feeling) as a rhetorical issue for Sterne, by way of Sheridan's presentation of elocution.
28. The copresence of both modes was a common assumption in discussions of delivery: John Mason defined elocution or "*Pronunciation*" as "the Art of managing the Voice, and Gesture in speaking." Mason, *An Essay on Elocution, or, Pronunciation* (London, 1748), 4. According to Sheridan, "As every passion has its peculiar tone, so has it, its peculiar look or gesture" (*Lectures on Elocution*, 114). Tadié cites Hugh Blair making a similar point: "strong tones, and animated gestures, we may observe, always go together" (*Sterne's Whimsical Theatres*, 63n22).
29. See, for example, Mullan, *Sentiment and Sociability*, 158.
30. Goring, *Rhetoric of Sensibility*, 196–197; Tadié, *Sterne's Whimsical Theatres*, 51–53.
31. See Gerard, *Laurence Sterne and the Visual Imagination*, 135–173.
32. For example, Yorick's encounter with Maria, which cheekily pictures their emotional communication in a sexualized interaction, adheres to an elocutionary framework. When Maria says of her dog, "Thou shalt not leave me, Sylvio," Yorick calls attention to the paralinguistic "tears [that] trickled down her cheeks" (*ASJ*, 150) in order to justify his claim that she is actually mourning her father's death, not the loss of her goat. Who knows if he

is correct? What we do know is that Yorick's elocutionary interpretation of her statement recalls Sheridan's observations about the power of paralinguistic elements to determine the semantic content of an utterance (*Lectures on Elocution*, 58). The exchange of tears on Yorick's handkerchief (*ASJ*, 151) further echoes Sheridan's claim about "tears" as "of all parts of language, the most expressive" (*Lectures on Elocution*, 114) and contrasts with Yorick's insincere mirroring of the sentiments of others in Paris, which he does for personal advantage and considers a form of "vile prostitution" (*ASJ*, 148). In whatever way a reader-listener understands the sexual references and sexual irony in the Maria episode, a sympathetic-sentimental dimension persists in how Yorick acts companionably when with her and, once he resumes his tour, continues to express sorrow for her when it can do him no sexual good (*ASJ*, 155). For an alternative view, see Thomas Keymer, "Marvell, Thomas Hollis, and Sterne's Maria: Parody in *A Sentimental Journey*," *Shandean* 5 (1993): 9–31.

33. Jeffrey R. Smitten, "Gesture and Expression in Eighteenth-Century Fiction: *A Sentimental Journey*," *Modern Language Studies* 9 (1979): 91.
34. By "expression," Smitten means "facial expression" (85), what Sterne calls "looks" (*ASJ*, 77).
35. "I thought [it was] an apostrophe to his child; but 'twas to his ass" (*ASJ*, 53).
36. Sheridan, *Lectures on Elocution*, 104.
37. The old German's relationship with his ass is rhetorical because, on his account, the animal when alive had been weighed down by his master's expression of his feelings about his dead sons: ironically, the animal's death is taken as proof that the owner successfully communicated his "afflictions" to it. Rather than the old German's grief provoking Yorick's ridicule, Yorick responds sympathetically, calling his bitter weeping for his dead "friend" (the ass) a "tribute" to "nature" and famously declaring, "Did we love each other, as this poor soul but loved his ass—'twould be something.—" (*ASJ*, 54).
38. The layout of Sterne's page also seems to notate acoustic elements, using dashes, asterisks, and other marks of punctuation to indicate verbal pauses and elocutionary emphasis (rather than following semantics). See Michael Vande Berg, "'Pictures of Pronunciation': Typographical Travels through *Tristram Shandy* and *Jacques le fataliste*," *Eighteenth-Century Studies* 21 (1987–1988): 21–47; and Christopher Fanning, "On Sterne's Page: Spatial Layout, Spatial Form, and Social Spaces in *Tristram Shandy*," *Eighteenth-Century Fiction* 10 (1997–1998): 429–450. Whether these notations amount to an inscribed code of articulation or are rather a set of variable cues to inspire reading aloud is matter for further consideration.
39. Describing Emma as stuck "in a fixed attitude," Austen narrates how she became "aquainted with her own heart" only when, "with the speed of an arrow" that "darted through her," Emma receives her own feelings and is thereby persuaded that Knightley "must marry no one but herself!" Jane Austen, *Emma*, ed. James Kinsley (Oxford: Oxford University Press, 2008), 320.
40. Aristotle, *The "Art" of Rhetoric*, ed. and trans. John Henry Freese (Cambridge, MA: Harvard University Press, 1926), 169–263.
41. As a "dirty address" (*ASJ*, 101) meant to manipulate the Duc de C***** for a passport, the scene anticipates Yorick's later practice of rhetorical "prostitution" (*ASJ*, 148) in Paris high society and contrasts with his interactions with the starling and Maria.
42. See, for instance, Goring, *Rhetoric of Sensibility*, 197.
43. Tadié, *Sterne's Whimsical Theatres*, 68.
44. For example, *Tadié, Sterne's Whimsical Theatres*, 56. In a rare dissent, Shaun Regan views Yorick's response to the officer as involving "projection." Regan, "Peripatetic Philosophy: Sterne and Cosmopolitanism," *Textual Practice* 31, no. 2 (2017): 274.
45. Sheridan, *Lectures on Elocution*, 101.
46. Gestural code is an old idea among English rhetoricians: see, for example, Bulwer, *Chironomia*. One can go back further still, to Quintilian's remarks on specific hand gestures

and their meanings in *The Orator's Education*, vol. 5 (books 11–12), ed. and trans. Donald A. Russell (Cambridge, MA: Harvard University Press, 2001), 133–147. Sheridan, however, eschews such codings, arguing that there are "no general models for imitation," and accordingly he provides no catalogue of specific gestures in his chapter on them (*Lectures on Elocution*, 119, 126, 113–134).

47. It was commonplace to contrast French and English uses of elocutionary gesture; Adam Smith, for example, in his lectures on rhetoric, sets the "thousand gestures and contortions of [a Frenchman's] face" against the behavior of an "Englishman," who will speak "without altering a muscle in his face." Smith, *Lectures on Rhetoric and Belles Lettres*, ed. John M. Lothian (London: Nelson, 1963), 192. See also Sheridan, *Lectures on Elocution*, 118.
48. Sheridan, *Lectures on Elocution*, 101.
49. The Earl of Clonmell comments in his copy of *A Sentimental Journey*, "This Chapter is A Master Piece of familiar painting, & sagacious Observation, The Scene is A Glover's Shop ye 2 Ideas are Gallantry on ye Man's Part Extortion on ye Lady's. . . . ye fair Translation is, these Gloves give an Excuse for doing what we both desire, but ye Place is too publick." Transcribed in Paul Franssen, "'Great Lessons of Political Instruction': The Earl of Clonmell Reads Sterne," *Shandean* 2 (1990): 172.
50. Sheridan, *Lectures on Elocution*, 102–103. As Debra Hawhee observes about ancient and medieval rhetorical treatises, "nonhuman animals turn up in rhetoric's theoretical and instructional texts when sensation matters the most." Hawhee, *Rhetoric in Tooth and Claw: Animals, Language, Sensation* (Chicago: University of Chicago Press, 2017), 2.
51. Sterne provides examples of the multi-interpretability of gestural elocution in *Tristram Shandy* but without making the same point about self-delivery; see, for example, the "different springs" of Walter's and Toby's "shaking of heads" (*TS*, 4.12.340) and the three sources of Trim's tears: "bashfulness . . . gratitude . . . sorrow" (*TS*, 9.5.746). Sterne problematizes the distinctness of the elements of elocution when Trim drops his hat: "Nothing could have expressed the sentiment of mortality . . . like it . . . [although] Ten thousand, and ten thousand times ten thousand . . . are the ways by which a hat may be dropped upon the ground, without any effect.—" (*TS*, 5.7.432–433).
52. The quoted terms are from Thomas Keymer, "*A Sentimental Journey* and the Failure of Feeling," in *The Cambridge Companion to Laurence Sterne*, ed. Thomas Keymer (Cambridge: Cambridge University Press, 2009), 90.
53. See Danielle Bobker, "Carriages, Conversation, and *A Sentimental Journey*," *Studies in Eighteenth-Century Culture* 35 (2006): 243–266.
54. For a recent account of national and cosmopolitan concern in *A Sentimental Journey*, see Regan, "Peripatetic Philosophy." As for animal species, the dilemma of the starling is both that it is caged and that it cannot (generally) share its feelings: neither it nor its feelings (whatever success it has with Yorick aside) successfully "get out" (*ASJ*, 95).
55. For a fuller account of Sheridan's views on animals, birds, tone, and sociality, see Fraser Easton, "Smart's Professors: Birdsong and Rhetorical Agency in *Jubilate Agno*," in *Mocking Bird Technologies: The Poetics of Parroting, Mimicry, and Other Starling Tropes*, ed. Christopher GoGwilt and Melanie D. Holm (New York: Fordham University Press, 2018), 83–85. For studies of the place of nonhuman animal communication in rhetorical thought more generally, see Hawhee, *Rhetoric in Tooth and Claw*; Diane Davis, "Creaturely Rhetorics," *Philosophy and Rhetoric* 44, no. 1 (2011): 88–94; and George A. Kennedy, "A Hoot in the Dark: The Evolution of General Rhetoric," *Philosophy and Rhetoric* 25, no. 1 (1992): 1–21. Although none of these scholars take up the work of Sheridan or of other eighteenth-century elocutionists, they are helpful in thinking about the role of delivery in nonhuman animal communication; for, as Hawhee notes, "animals repeatedly call attention to rhetoric's visual, aural, and tactile capacities" (*Rhetoric in Tooth and Claw*, 9). Sterne himself is part of a devel-

oping awareness of animal nature and animal communication in the eighteenth century, and recent work in animal studies has placed his starling in a larger cultural context; see, for example, Tobias Menely, *The Animal Claim: Sensibility and the Creaturely Voice* (Chicago: University of Chicago Press, 2015), 195–198.

56. For other important affinities between Yorick and the starling, see Melinda Alliker Rabb, "Engendering Accounts in Sterne's *A Sentimental Journey*," in *Johnson and His Age*, ed. James Engell (Cambridge, MA: Harvard University Press, 1984), 538–540; and Jim Owen, "Laurence Sterne and the Caged Starling of *A Sentimental Journey*," *CEA Critic* 64, nos. 2–3 (Winter–Spring/Summer 2002): 30–33.
57. Compare Sheridan, *Lectures on Elocution*, 104–105. As Hawhee notes of ancient rhetorical works, "When animals show up in treatises with an educational purpose . . . they often function to activate sensation [and] inspire a kind of kinetic mimicry" (*Rhetoric in Tooth and Claw*, 9).
58. Sheridan does not always reject memory. For example, he sees it as supporting delivery when "comedians" (actors) and readers "get the words by rote," the better to deliver a set speech feelingly rather than coldly (*Lectures on Elocution*, 13, 80). Sterne reverses this relationship in the possible coldhearted copying of the starling.
59. Sheridan, 101–102.
60. We can "utter" a document (delivery); we can document an utterance (memory); the distinction between memory and delivery helps us to differentiate these two language states that differ in degree but not in kind. For an influential argument identifying them, see Jacques Derrida, "Signature Event Context," trans. Jeffrey Mehlman and Samuel Weber, in *Limited Inc.*, ed. Gerald Graff (Evanston, IL: Northwestern University Press, 1988), 1–23.
61. Tadié argues insightfully that, for Sterne, "it is the book, conceived as object, which enables the connection between the narrator and the reader" (*Sterne's Whimsical Theatres*, 145), a connection that compensates for the loss of the physical proximity of speaker and listener in oral storytelling. However, in *A Sentimental Journey* the starling serves to trouble the social value of memorial forms (of which "the book, conceived as an object," is one), perhaps especially for Yorick's "readers" (*ASJ*, 100).
62. In "The Captive. Paris," Sterne seems to adopt, and then to reject, the viability of the Smithian idea of a theatrical social sympathy. Amit Yahav nicely distinguishes between "the visceral model of sympathy" entailed in elocutionary thought and the "theatrical model" made famous by Smith. Yahav, "The Sense of Rhythm: Nationalism, Sympathy, and the English Elocutionists," *Eighteenth Century* 52 (2011): 181.
63. Memorializing elocutionists list the gesture: for example, Austin describes a movement in which "the arm is projected forwards in authority" (*Chironomia*, 483). The use of the gesture here once more (comically) highlights the common elocutionary ground of sexual and sentimental communication.
64. Tadié, *Sterne's Whimsical Theatres*, 149.
65. M. Wade Mahon, "Making the Green One Red: Elocution, Emotion, and the Impact of Print Literacy," *Eighteenth Century* 58 (2017): 329.
66. Keymer, *Sterne, the Moderns, and the Novel*, 67–72.
67. Tadié, *Sterne's Whimsical Theatres*, 147–148.
68. Sheridan, *Lectures on Elocution*, xii, 13.

7

THINGS OF THE SPIRIT

Vibrant Matter in *A Sentimental Journey*

JENNIFER PRESTON WILSON

UNLIKE THE VERBOSE BUT METHODICAL sign-posting in *Tom Jones* or the sequential correspondence of *Clarissa*, chapter titles in Laurence Sterne's *A Sentimental Journey* offer sparse information, usually only noting a place and a main character as if setting up the scene of a play. Approximately one-sixth of these titles, however, break the pattern and instead cite inanimate matter as the principal element—be it a door, a snuffbox, a letter, a wig, or another property—situating the thing as the central focus of observation. *Tristram Shandy*, of course, includes a whole "chapter of THINGS" but uses the term to designate topics that Tristram will alternately "name . . . lament . . . hope . . . promise" (*TS*, 4.32.400)—and the list goes on, adding to the comedy of Tristram's ever-faltering race to bring his narrative up to the present day.

The significance of things in *A Sentimental Journey* is less about the challenges of authorial digression than about those of the physical and temporal world we must navigate. Yorick's narrative is staged so that it repeatedly butts up against the material reality that we habitually manipulate to serve our ruling passion and sense of pride. The things in Sterne's final work tend to subvert their use-values and fall apart, calling attention to themselves and enacting their problematic entanglement with human lives, prompting readers to become salvagers in the wake of Yorick's progress. When we notice a thing in his narrative, it manifests something excessive, liminal, or nonfunctional that draws both it and its relations with subjects to our attention.

Just as Sterne's sermon "The parable of the rich man and Lazarus" exhorts parishioners actively to "look into the world" to see how "inclinable" men are to commit and defend evil (*Sermons*, 216), his last fiction pushes us to examine the springs of human behavior in their material contexts. Compared with the wide circulation of customary objects in the moneyed and sentimental economies of *A*

Sentimental Journey, things appear only rarely to Yorick, but when they do, they offer an indirect route around the ambiguities of Yorick's autobiographical narration to consider more fully the self-deceit that troubles his conscience.

Thing theory rests on the distinction between object and thing, with the latter serving as "limit cases at which our ordinary categories for classifying signs and substances, meaning and materiality, appear to break down."[1] Since Bill Brown's 2001 groundbreaking issue of *Critical Inquiry*, thing theory has flourished in multiple disciplines, especially anthropology, art history, and literary studies.[2] While there are now many branches to this critical approach, this reading of *A Sentimental Journey* is interested in the way thing theory reorganizes Yorick's experience away from the object-oriented projection of the sentimental traveler into moments of enchantment with things that erupt unexpectedly and facilitate spiritual choice. In this pursuit, I follow the theorizing of Jane Bennett on "embodied sensibility" as an impetus for the enactment of moral codes.[3] The historio-autobiographical rationale for adopting this method includes Sterne's friendship and convivial exchange of ideas with Baron d'Holbach and his circle, which brought him into familiarity with materialist philosophy, the "thing theory" of his own time, and encouraged a deepening of arguments for his own Anglican faith in response.[4]

D'Holbach's town house in the Rue Royale Saint-Roch provided a gathering place for many artists and intellectuals including Sterne and became particularly known as the epicenter of mid-eighteenth-century materialist thought. This philosophical school follows Spinoza's rejection of Cartesian dualism but inverts his contention that nothing could exist outside of God's substance to argue that nothing exists besides matter.[5] Julien Offray de La Mettrie exemplifies this mode of thinking in *L'homme machine* (1747), claiming that his observations as a physician had convinced him of an indissoluble connection between bodily and mental illnesses. D'Holbach's *Système de la nature* (1770) further employs materialist arguments to call for the clear separation of rational discourse from religion and other supposed illusions. While Sterne remained the friend and correspondent of the Parisian materialists, engaging with their idea that everything can be understood through close attention to matter, he complicated their determinist philosophy by putting forward his own themes of free will and divine grace.

Yorick begins his travels positioned between two things, the *desobligeant* and Lorenzo's snuffbox, that place him in the middle of opposing attitudes of shame and emulation, a dialectic that probes the depth to which he feels his own insufficiencies. In this portion of the text, he clings to the very materials that might prompt him to become a better Christian but uses them to proceed into further error. His attraction to the *desobligeant*, for example, at first seems auspicious as an indicator of his contrition. Yorick encounters the one-man carriage when, embarrassed by his ungenerous conduct to the monk, he literally and figuratively wants to move on from his misbehavior. He walks out into the coach yard in search of a vehicle to purchase and encounters "an old Desobligeant in the furthest corner of the court": "[It] hit my fancy at first sight, so I instantly got into it, and finding it in tolerable harmony with my feelings, I ordered the waiter to call Monsieur Dessein the master of the hôtel" (*ASJ*, 12). The brokenness of the vehicle renders it difficult to categorize: Can it really still be called a carriage if it is so derelict? As such, and because it "hits" Yorick's fancy with its odd and independent state of being, it exists as a thing rather than a culturally assimilated object or a projection of Yorick's mind. Its surprising, two-toned "harmony" with Yorick's unexpected state of being gives it a new life. This coach is *not* fit for travel, having been taken to pieces multiple times in previous "adventures"; its unsuitability has landed it in the farthest corner of the court, rotting away with every rainy night that passes.

Following a pattern in *Tristram Shandy* traced by Paul Goring, in which "tragi-comical and tragi-farcical sequences are underpinned or set in motion by a human-thing relationship in which the conventional use-value of the thing is disturbed," this carriage that will not carry has more "misuse" than use-value.[6] Bill Brown's articulation of thing theory depends precisely on such misfunction; he argues that "we begin to confront the thingness of objects when they stop working for us. . . . The question is less about 'what things *are* for a given society' than about what claims on your attention and on your action are made on behalf of things."[7] Yorick pays special attention to the carriage in part because of the name of this particular type of transport. The sense of the *desobligeant* as an asocial way to travel may appeal to his conscience after his own petty lecturing of the monk, itself a disobliging motion (*ASJ*, 9–11). Yet it is the thing, not the word, that first strikes Yorick; he does not project this title and attitude onto the vehicle but merely sees the thing performing its lack of sociality—narrow, set apart, collapsing in on itself—and he has an uncanny experience as he feels its nearness to his own interior state.

Aligned with the attitude of the *desobligeant*, Yorick seems positioned to learn and move on from his unthinking conduct; however, Sterne complicates his protagonist's interaction with the possible vehicle of his spiritual growth to dramatize human fallibility. While Yorick is struck by the coach's shabbiness—and his own—and is poised for change, he notices the monk talking with "a lady just arrived, at the inn" and assumes that their topic is his mistreatment of the mendicant (*ASJ*, 12). Eager to escape the scorn of the attractive newcomer, Yorick leaps inside the carriage. The possibility of the hero's advance through a spiritual threshold thus becomes literalized as the lowly physical movement of dodging through a ramshackle door. Yorick chooses to hide from the monk in this emblem of his shame with only the measly protection of its "taffeta curtain" (*ASJ*, 12). Yorick's attitude as he occupies the *desobligeant* also shifts, becoming cheerfully unmindful of his asocial situation: in his perspective, this thing is *obligeant*, accommodating his need to avoid the lady's potentially disdainful glance. The metamorphosis of his feelings from the shock of exterior recognition to the contentment of inward escape echoes warnings in Sterne's "Abuses of Conscience" sermon about the dangers of placidity, where he argues that while the accuracy of a guilty conscience is generally reliable, an undisturbed mind does not always indicate innocence (*Sermons*, 257–258). Yorick briefly recognizes his sinfulness for what it is in his initial response to the *desobligeant*, but when he hides within it to protect his self-pride, he curtails his own better guidance and rests secure in what literally and metaphorically will not carry him forward.

Sterne frames Yorick's backsliding as an aspect of our free will in working toward grace. Although his hero does not seek immediate change, Sterne points to shame's potential to set one on a new course by humbly admitting to one's sins and praying for forgiveness and help. This attitude was consistent with his religion, which "supported the pre-Augustinian, Erasmian, and Arminian view that man's will is free, that God's grace is given to all, and that man can work with or against it as he chooses."[8] By stalling Yorick in the *desobligeant*, Sterne satirizes the wrongheaded obstinacy of his pride, pinpointing the moment when Yorick turns away from other possible responses. This crisis is signaled in the play between motion and stasis throughout the episode. Yorick's physical shutdown of contact, "I drew the taffeta curtain betwixt us," is suggestive of the end of a theatrical performance; at the same time, it is a willed gesture that opens a new scene, witnessed when he says, "determined to write my journey, I took out my pen and ink, and wrote the preface to it in the *Desobligeant*" (*ASJ*, 12). Yorick is simultaneously liberated and caught in his choice, as he moves beyond his own "sphere" in traveling and writing about travel but paradoxically only does so from a position of physical and moral confinement.

Arthur Hill Cash and Martin C. Battestin observe that such entrapment in repeated behaviors provides the crux of Sterne's moral comedy. The former suggests that benevolence is Yorick's hobbyhorse and that he "fails to govern himself" according to reason, which "ought to sanction every moral decision."[9] The latter argues that *A Sentimental Journey* dramatizes the philosophes' dictate that "the human animal acts strictly according to the impulse of whichever passion happens to be uppermost," with sentimentalized eroticism as the only passion that can lead one away from the self.[10] Yorick's encounter with the *desobligeant* suggests a further option: that human intuition might mediate between reason and passion to provide tempered guidance. His instantaneous fascination with the carriage provides him with a flash of insight into his own ontology, a truth that comes from neither reason nor self-interest. While the mechanical aspects of Yorick's behaviors do seem to engage with French materialism, as Battestin suggests, such spontaneous moments of realization upset systemic thinking about Sterne's text. Yorick's failure to weigh these insights sufficiently does not negate the fact that he senses and records them, allowing Sterne's audience to reflect on their significance.

That Yorick seeks refuge within the dangerously dilapidated carriage offers an absurd image, a fact that even he seems to glimpse in his later disavowal that his "Preface" "would have been better [written] in a *Vis a Vis*" (*ASJ*, 17). The *desobligeant* is a comically broken-down, awkward thing, and when Yorick steps within it, he retreats from the sensory impression that strikes him on its first appearance. To better understand Yorick's withdrawal, his reaction might be contrasted with a scene from volume 5 of *Tristram Shandy* where the full weight of a thing is not only felt but allowed to resonate. As Trim discourses on time and the death of Tristram's brother, he drops "his hat plumb upon the ground" (*TS*, 5.7.432) in a manner so expressive of loss that the customary item of clothing transforms into a thing, moving "from a mere object into a ritualized presence."[11] Tristram asks readers to pause over "the mortality of *Trim*'s hat" (*TS*, 5.7.432) and to consider what could have made it such a profound sight. Bennett identifies these types of affective response as moments of enchantment, "to be struck and shaken by the extraordinary that lives amid the familiar and everyday."[12] In the hat's fall, it changes from an accessory item into a resounding expression of communal loss.

Tristram's own analysis of the hat's significance incorporates language from Sterne's sermon "The Efficacy of Prayer" that ponders the connection of body and soul: "We are not angels, but men cloathed with bodies, and, in some measure, governed by our imaginations, that we have need of all these external helps which nature has made the interpreters of our thoughts" (*Sermons*, 402). The mysteriousness of God's design in making us "men cloathed with bodies" not only involves our "need" for divine grace but also calls us to "interpret" our subjective experience in striving toward virtue. The God-given interrelationship of our body and soul is an idea that features prominently in all of Sterne's writings and in seventeenth- and eighteenth-century religious discourse more generally (*Sermons: Notes*, 433–436). As the churchman Robert South counsels, "since God has placed the Soul in a Body, where it receives all things by the Ministry of the outward Senses, he would have us secure these *Cinque-ports* . . . against the Invasion of vain thoughts, by suggesting to them such Objects as may prepossess them with the contrary."[13] The bodily senses and the soul work in conjunction in ways the human understanding cannot fathom,[14] so South cautions the believer to be alert to those sensory encounters that may "prepossess" us toward spiritual growth.

Yorick struggles to follow South's advice, showcasing his ongoing difficulty with adherence to his religious creed. He suppresses his first instantaneous impression that the dilapidated coach symbolizes his own transgressions, caring more for the way he will appear to a beautiful woman than fearing for his soul, but at least he belatedly sees how confined his vision has been. When he later notices "another old tatter'd *Desobligeant*" in the coach yard, the memory of the earlier object and its associations means that "the very sight of it stirr'd up a disagreeable sensation" within him (*ASJ*, 32). Yorick is aware that ideally he should live openly and connectedly, as if sitting together in a *vis-à-vis* with another person. However, that harmonious connection only rarely happens in *A Sentimental Journey*. Sterne's sermon "The case of Elijah and the widow of Zarephath, considered" presents these fugitive instances of unalloyed sympathy as moments of grace; for instance, full sympathy suddenly shines forth in the Widow of Zarephath, who "must have been wrought upon by an unmixed principle of humanity.——She look'd upon [Elijah] as a fellow-partner almost in the same affliction with herself" (*Sermons*, 44). To find such an uncommon moment of "unmixed" compassion is miraculous in a world where there is "nothing unmixt" (*ASJ*, 116); most often we act out of pride, as Yorick has already encountered with the monk. While Yorick shuns the initial vision of his own spiritual shabbiness that he derives from the broken *desobligeant*, retreating inside its decaying frame, when he moves beyond it and the self-defensive structure it had provided, he also becomes more amenable to larger ideas of social connection. In waiting for Monsieur Dessein—a character whose name, "Mr. Design," alludes to a real-life innkeeper but might also be taken as a euphemism for God—Yorick rebuilds an openness to what may come next that his earlier predeterminism had denied. In this unconfined space and time, the possibility of emending his response to the monk opens up.

As Yorick accepts Lorenzo's snuffbox, however, he once again veers into error. He tightens his grip and attitude, all too eagerly embracing its supposed access to the giver's humble spirit. Between the two containers of carriage and snuffbox, Sterne sets up a dichotomy of negative and positive symbolism, alternating between the unsociable and the social. Both items communicate with Yorick, but he is much more interested in the horn box as a positive reminder of tolerance and forgiveness that travels with him but remains "withdrawn from the ordinary rules of commodity circulation."[15] The box is a metonym for Lorenzo, whose gentleness is represented simply and directly in the text. Yorick takes the monk's personal token seriously, "guard[ing]" it "to help [his] mind on to something better" (*ASJ*, 27). Building on this avowal, Battestin likens the snuffbox to a "homely thurible" that prepares Yorick's spirit for religious devotion.[16] Because Lorenzo is tolerant and modest and the horn box is of him and from him, it seems directly to stand for those qualities. Yet Yorick clings to and sentimentalizes the snuffbox, decontextualizing it from the lessons of the *desobligeant* and the rest of his experience.

Excessively touted by Yorick, the horn box departs from the simplicity of its giver and comes to resemble the complexity of later Victorian "portable properties" that John Plotz identifies as "at once priceable and invaluable, fungible and nonfungible."[17] The complicated dialectic of the snuffbox traveled beyond fiction and into worldly economies with the Lorenzo Cult. This movement's origins are described in the *Hamburgischer Correspondent* of April 4, 1769, which documents how the reading circle of the poet Johann Georg Jacobi, inspired by the Father Lorenzo passage, purchased horn boxes and vowed to use the items to emulate the monk's spirit. Jacobi thereafter received a letter informing him of the mass manufacture of such *Lorenzodosen*, and "references to this *Lorenzo-Kult* started to appear in German Sternean imitations."[18] Critics have since noted the irony of commodifying a figure who has renounced the worldly path, describing the cult as a market surge where merchants capitalized upon consumers' desire to act out Lorenzo's and Yorick's sentimental exchange.[19] On the one hand, the snuffbox is a gentleman's essential accessory for the stylish consumption of tobacco; on the other, it stands as a nostalgic memorial for a particular good man.[20] W. G. Day adds a further dimension to this standoff; asking why none of these once-faddish snuffboxes survives today, he concludes that perhaps the "cult was a carefully cultivated figment of J. G. Jacobi's imagination."[21] Even granting that the story itself might be invented, though, the consequent vogue for sentimentalizing Lorenzo's horn box renders it a complicated symbol, far different from the mild artlessness of its owner.

When Yorick produces the horn box at the *opera comique* in Paris, he reveals its paradoxical role: it is vibrant matter and yet stimulates sensations that are insufficiently assimilated with others filtered through what South terms the "*Cinque-ports*" of his senses. Both the object itself and the situation in which it finds itself seem to make this an even more complicated matter. In this venue, Yorick expatiates on the short stature he has observed of many Parisians and the possible theories to explain dwarfism, leading to his "disgust" at any unmerciful treatment of "a poor defenceless being of this order" and his witnessing of just that in the parterre of the opera (*ASJ*, 80–81). By chance and association of ideas, he is at that moment taking a pinch of snuff and imagines with what mercy Lorenzo would have given "an ear to this poor soul's complaint!" (*ASJ*, 81). Yorick enjoys this fantasy so much that he renders his thoughts at the time in three sequential exclamations: "And how would thy meek and courteous spirit, my dear monk! so temper'd to *bear and forbear!*—how sweetly would it have lent an ear to this poor soul's complaint!" (*ASJ*, 81). His body also registers these conceits as he lifts his eyes "with an emotion" that is noticed by his companion, an old French officer. While Yorick cherishes his relic and watches the scene, noting, "I could have leaped out of the box to have redressed [the wrong]" (*ASJ*, 81), his French companion actually takes action to stop the abuse of the dwarf. Yorick's troubling auxiliary verb, "I could have . . . ,"[22] indicates his critique of his own performance, a slippage between sentiment and action.

In this test case of the snuffbox's influence, rather than prompting Yorick immediately to emulate Lorenzo, Yorick uses the horn box merely to stimulate his emotions as he finds pleasure in the scene of distress and its resolution.[23] Although Yorick says that he values the box as he does "the instrumental parts of [his] religion, to help [his] mind on to something better" (*ASJ*, 27), suggesting that like religious rites, it guides him toward embodying the precepts of his faith, in practice it seems to turn him toward inward indulgence of sentiment. Yorick experiences his vision of Lorenzo's imagined aid to the dwarf in a social context, however, and in the larger fabric of the scene, his visible emotion effectually prompts the neighboring officer to action. Even further, Yorick's self-reflection, compared with the officer's ethical response, primes him for later selfless charity of his own.

This aftereffect occurs when, roving the streets of Paris, Yorick sees a "boy" in the gutter and swoops down to help him, only to realize that his beneficiary is actually a short, middle-aged man of "about forty" (*ASJ*, 80). Yorick's good deed in this moment occurs as an instinctual act of his already-moving body—instantaneous, unthinking, and part of a charitable economy that we all hope will one day pay back some of our contributions. The horn box's influence depends on just such a humble willingness to see others' needs as an extension of one's own. Even though Yorick's professions about the horn box may seem superficial and hypocritical, underneath those imperfect words, he turns to Lorenzo as a reflected, ideal self: an impetus to be a better human, if still an imperfect one. The enchantment effect of Lorenzo's influence depends on Yorick's "being on his feet," mentally and physically, as witnessed in his subsequent dissatisfaction with his behavior at the opera and his immediate responsiveness on the street.

Yorick's wavering virtue underscores the perpetual encroachments of sin, dramatizing his need for socioreligious support. Sterne clearly contrasts worldly and spiritual stances in his sermon "The House of Feasting and the House of Mourning Described"; yet in *A Sentimental Journey* those "houses" are not so easily delineated (*Sermons*, 12–20). Yorick, for example, should exemplify the mind-set of the house of mourning at the grave of Lorenzo by engaging in serious reflection on the brevity and vanities of life. His account of this moment instead registers the flux of his emotions: "I had a strong desire to see where they had laid him—when, upon pulling out his little horn box, as I sat by his grave, and plucking up a nettle or two at the head of it, which had no business to grow there, they all struck together so forcibly upon my affections, that I burst into a flood of tears—but I am as weak as a woman; and I beg the world not to smile, but pity me" (*ASJ*, 27). Rather than serving as a "help" to his mind in this context, the box acts as a prop enabling Yorick's "strong desire," unchastened by thoughts of Lorenzo but filled with tears at the loss suffered by his own "affections." The graveside scene showcases Yorick's isolation and mawkish plea for audience response. His attitude ironically corresponds to that of the house of feasting, which cultivates "loose and unguarded moments [when] the imagination is not always at command—in spite of reason and reflection, it will forceably carry him sometimes whither he would not" (*Sermons*, 16). Yorick's spiritual laxness occurs without the social undergirding that informs the scene with the French officer; it is also without a troubled conscience. His mind-set is mechanical, and Sterne underscores that point by offering a sentimentally formulaic graveside performance.

Ultimately, Sterne's equivocal treatment of the snuffbox can be traced back to the very moment of gift-giving and its associated problems of authenticity. Ambiguity creeps into the interchange of boxes due to the presence of a witness, the lady of Brussels, who has attracted Yorick's interest but whom he fears has heard a detrimental account of his own character from the monk. Does he perform his apology and bestowal of his snuffbox to impress her, as he seems to admit when he says, "I set myself to consider how I should undo the ill impressions which the poor monk's story, in case he had told it her, must have planted in her breast against me" (*ASJ*, 25)? If so, does that motive lessen the significance of his gesture or the reciprocal one made by Lorenzo? Jakub Lipski contends that the lady's presence changes the scene into a "public performance" that follows one of Erving Goffman's categories of "idealization," "misrepresentation," or "mystification." Yorick thus performs "in the 'mask of sentiment' with some hidden agenda," leading readers to weigh whether his ends suit their means.[24] Elizabeth Kraft, by contrast, understands Yorick's behavior at this moment as proceeding from inward transformation rather than strategic performance. She notes that before he even sees Madame de L***'s face, he is convinced that she is "of the better order of beings" (*ASJ*, 30), causing him to generate "an entire history for her, a history that touches his heart," a generative impulse infused with biblical allusions. Kraft argues that such spontaneous "alchemical change can occur with any desire," even though these are only transitory, imperfect glimpses of divine love.[25]

Yorick himself is aware at some level of the selfish appearance of his behavior and gilds it in the language of chivalric service to "one princess or another," which purportedly makes him "all generosity and good will" (*ASJ*, 44). Reviewing his first meeting with the monk, though, we find that this theory of the transformative power of courtly love does not hold up over time: Yorick rebuffs Lorenzo while pledged in devotion to Eliza, even as he carries her image about with him; and yet her influence only goes so far. It would be more accurate to say that the immediate presence of any desirable woman affects Yorick. Even then, in the exchange scene it is impossible to gauge the degree of Madame de L***'s sway over him versus that of his own conscience in evaluating his conciliatory action toward the monk. Similarly, Bennett acknowledges in her case for enchantment that other forces might intrude on its operation, specifically aesthetic cravings, an obliviousness to economic and social conditions, and a susceptibility to disciplinary regimes, but she overrides these dangers with the argument that "as long as affect remains an indispensable part of human life, it makes more sense to discipline it into a magnanimous sensibility than to try to ban it from ethical life."[26] In portraying the vagaries of Yorick's motivations and behaviors, Sterne both entertains Bennett's idea and shows its limitations. Yorick's attempts to enact a more virtuous self occasionally do create breakthrough instances of charity, but to build a whole doctrine of self-fashioning on that foundation would counteract the humility needed to be truly responsive to the vital matters at hand.[27]

By dramatizing such convoluted causations, Sterne stresses the inescapability of the self and its games of rationalization and flattery. Even the seemingly charitable rite of gift exchange, as Lynn Festa observes, necessarily involves aspects of the self, entailing "a desire to produce relations while maintaining difference."[28] The entity of the gift is perpetually marked by its transfer—it is yours but not yours—and thus presents problems of authenticity that also adhere to the sentimental text, which "performs emotions on behalf of its audience, feeling in our stead."[29] Sterne drives his readers up against uncertainties that, indeed, pervade all forms of representation by maximizing ambiguity and irony of language. Donald R. Wehrs analyzes the resultant unresolvable textual riddles as instances of the rhetorical technique of *epoché*, or suspension of judgment;[30] Yorick's interpretation of the snuffbox offers one of many instances when we cannot verify his claims of brotherly love.

It is particularly noticeable that throughout Yorick's interaction with things in volume 1 of *A Sentimental Journey*, Sterne writes with what Jonathan Lamb terms a "double vision" to block a congruous account of the self.[31] For instance, Yorick registers one response to the outside and another to the inside of the *desobligeant* and later presents a completely different reaction to another such vehicle. In a similar fashion, sometimes the horn box serves as a meditative focus for Yorick, and at other times it is just a snuffbox. These shifting meanings are not solely mechanical, a facet of Yorick's eccentricity, or a sign of Yorick's insular "relationship with a knowing and exceptional reader."[32] Rather, they intersect at a nexus of contextual, performative, cognitive, and conscientious influences that move us toward the necessary yet inconsistent mediations provided by the text's religious themes.

Once Yorick is in Paris, his capacity to draw intuitive insight from surrounding things diminishes amid the proliferating wares of this cosmopolitan setting. The metropolis teems with material goods, especially the textiles and currency that surround Yorick's interactions with women, servants, and the poor. As this imagery of consumption and circulation builds in the text, it is easy to grow skeptical and feel disgust for the self-serving side of moneyed sentimental exchanges. Yorick's repeated engagements with the object-oriented economy lead not to societal improvements, as Robert Markley points out, but "to self-absorbed and self-congratulatory mystifications of inequality."[33] Thomas Keymer concurs but adds that "Yorick's failure to move from exquisite sympathy to practical action may have been exactly Sterne's point."[34] While Yorick's self-reflexive and indulgent emotional interactions with the things he meets suggest a satire against sentimentality, these encounters are drawn with a potential rooted in his genuine insight or charity. These glimpses of sentimental potential do not approach anything like Shaftesburian benevolence, but they do hint that skepticism, or what Bennett calls "disenchantment," is not a complete answer either.[35]

Although we become inured to the many objects that intertwine in suggestive ways with Yorick's socializing in Paris, we can join him in amazement and puzzlement before the pastry seller adorned with an incongruous thing, a cross of honor. As Yorick pauses before this figure, stock still with a *patè* in hand, he contraposes his usual restless mode of being, dramatized only moments before with his admission, "I changed my mind a second time—In truth it was the third. . . . I am govern'd by circumstances" (*ASJ*, 104). The *croix* worn by the *pattiser* stands forth as a thing because it does not appear to belong to the tidy, aproned world of the food vendor. Yorick is transfixed by this contrast, recounting, "the more I look'd at him—his croix and his basket, the stronger they wove themselves into my brain—I got out of the *remise* and went towards him" (*ASJ*, 105). Bennett identifies such experiences as a state of wonder, a "temporary suspension of chronological time and bodily movement."[36] In this and the ensuing chapter, Sterne gives a nod to the vital elements of our world that might exist with a self-sufficiency separate from their associations with people. They are at once entities of their own and marked by histories; one could imagine spin-off it-narratives that feature their independent voices, suggested by the fact that they are, like Achilles's shield, ripe with meaning. With the *croix* of St. Louis and the sword of "the house d'E**** in Britany" (*ASJ*, 107), the thing is at once dislocated from and awaiting reunion with its human reference; the chevalier who earned the *croix* through loyal service to his country becomes "*le patisser*," and the marquis of an ancient house in Brittany sets aside his birthright in the form of a sword to transform into a merchant in Martinique (*ASJ*, 107–108). The thing in each case, however, keeps living in the absence of its referent, its "owner." It is the coherent element, especially when seen against the shakiness of human fortunes. Standing at what Plotz calls "the vexed boundary between self and world," the thing continues and awaits the return of its distressed owner, who must work his way back to it through stoic resolve.[37]

While the *croix* and sword appear in adjacent chapters, united under the idea of "things symbolic of honor," Sterne depicts the rarity of such tidy focus in the human consciousness. More often, the human mind elides the current moment of being as it processes the language of everyday transactions, although travel can help to counteract this tendency. A telling example of this cognitive glossing occurs when Yorick's Parisian barber asserts that the buckle of his new wig will withstand immersion in the ocean. This boast makes Yorick think of how he might get to that thing, the ocean, by "run[ning] post . . . a hundred miles" to test the claim (*ASJ*, 67). Thus, on the very first night that Yorick arrives in the great metropolis, his thoughts return to his embarkation point of Calais. As he muses on oceans, however, he realizes that they are merely contained vats of water: "the grandeur is *more* in the *word*; and *less* in the *thing*" (*ASJ*, 67). Accepting a humbler alternative, he alights on a nearby thing that happens to fit this definition equally well: the simple pail. His movement toward that which might be overlooked because of its ordinary qualities foregrounds issues of perspective, proximity, and feeling. As an English traveler in France, Yorick has a double awareness of the idioms of both countries, hearing the words and imagining the referents that would be used in each context. His alighting on the nearby pail bridges national differences by side-stepping a literal insistence on language and simply considering things that resemble each other. This seemingly insignificant hypothetical dilemma models the adaptability, spontaneity, and humility that also informed his "on his feet" moment of assisting the dwarf caught in the gutter.

Despite such rare breakthroughs of unselfconscious responsiveness, the Parisian chapters more generally show that relationships with things are undergirded by fears. We see this underlying apprehension when Yorick is enticed and astonished by a lost thing that smuggles its way onto his breakfast table, an ephemeral piece of text severed from its fellow pages. The scrap paper seems to be a mere nothing that had provided extra protection for La Fleur's hand while transporting a pat of butter on a currant leaf (*ASJ*, 134). Nevertheless, it surprises Yorick: "When I had finish'd the butter, I threw the currant leaf out of the window, and was going to do the same by the waste paper—but stopping to read a line first, and that drawing me on to a second and third—I thought it better worth" (*ASJ*, 134). Unlike the obvious strengths inherent in the *croix* and sword, this flimsy orphan of a page has somehow survived life's depredations for over two hundred years but is now on the verge of extinction. Its Old French and "Gothic letter" proves irresistible to Yorick, who, trapped indoors, engages in hours of effort to translate and understand its import. Like the *croix* and sword, this page has been severed from its human context (like the leaf from its natural environment), but its loss has occurred over generations, to the point that it may become something else: unwanted waste. Perhaps fear of this outcome underlies Yorick's daylong exertions to save the document, just as the terror of wasting away in the Bastille informs his interpretive urgency with *croix* and sword. Yorick's efforts have an effect but do not pay off as he hopes. The thing, however, produces a major change within him. As he labors over the manuscript, Yorick enters a state of flow unusual to his typical experience of time: "it kept hold of me; and the difficulty of understanding it increased but the desire" (*ASJ*, 134). The aim of his desire is not so much to be with this thing that he has resuscitated from death but to determine its identity completely, to fix it within a system of pages that he hopes La Fleur will assist him in recovering. Sterne shapes these chapters near the end of Yorick's time in Paris, suggesting the folly of his hero who valiantly tries to erase the effects of time so that he can possess a pristine, completely restored manuscript. Yorick burns with his preoccupation, happy in his pursuit, supporting the Erasmian Folly's logic that "the saddest thing is not to be deceived."[38] Even though finally thwarted in this particular scheme, Yorick soon finds another outlet for his energies. Not long after this day of frantic scholarship, he discovers the powers of flattery and overindulges in its determined, oleaginous rhetoric.

By the time Yorick leaves Paris, sickened by the artificiality of flattery and the vacillating persona it forces on him, he has had numerous opportunities to heed the intimations of things. They stand out in their thingness as puzzles to our feelings and understanding, offering opportunities to pause, meditate, and re-evaluate habits. While Yorick is not insensitive to their potential, he usually submerges his intuitive awareness of things beneath accessory fears and desires. His most significant encounter with things occurs in a literal resting spot, a farmhouse where he finds nonegoistic and nondeterministic harmony with a host family that gives him shelter. These penultimate chapters, "The Supper" and "The Grace," confirm that responsiveness to things can lead us into a devout state of being. Yorick's access to "Grace" occurs from an awareness of need: "The poor devil [of a thill horse] lost a second shoe, and from off his other fore-foot; I then got out of the chaise in good earnest; and seeing a house about a quarter of a mile to the left-hand, with a great deal to do, I prevailed upon the postilion to turn up to it. The look of the house, and of everything about it, as we drew nearer, soon reconciled me to the disaster" (*ASJ*, 157).

Yorick seeks and instantly finds shelter in a home surrounded by "every thing which could make plenty" (*ASJ*, 157). He walks through the door as if invited and finds a "feast of love" waiting on the table (*ASJ*, 158). Such a serendipitous arrival and simple bounty of food suggests a very different tenor of social interaction than that which Yorick has found so far in his travels; its resemblance to the Last Supper, as noted by some critics, reinforces its symbolic embodiment of the Christian tradition of *agape*.[39] On being welcomed, Yorick moves without hesitation toward the table and borrows "the old man's knife" to cut a piece of bread (*ASJ*, 158), sensible that any reticence would give pain to his hosts. His assuredness in taking the father's knife, a household item associated with multiple functions (carving meat, chopping, possibly even defense) shows that Yorick recognizes it as a significant thing. His use of it places him under the protection of the familial roof. Indeed, Bill Brown associates such resonant things with "what is excessive in objects, . . . an 'all-at-onceness'" that speaks to Yorick's intuitive gravitation toward the communal spirit of the family.[40] We see the knife's role as the central thing of the house when, the supper over, "the old man gave a knock upon the table with the haft of his knife" (*ASJ*, 159). The blade of the knife had apportioned material sustenance during the meal; now, the "haft" acts as a signal for the dance, like a church bell tolling to summon parishioners to worship.[41]

During the dance, Yorick practices a situated observance very different from his earlier behavior. First he takes a seat of honor "betwixt" the old man and his wife "upon a sopha of turf by the door" (*ASJ*, 159), a placement symbolic of indeterminacy. This seat is both a manmade and a natural thing; customarily an interior, domestic comfort, here the "sopha" is outside and formed of raised turf (*ASJ*, 378n159.9). The reference both assigns Yorick the status of honored guest and foreshadows his eventual mortal rest underneath a mound of earth. He is grouped with the old married couple, rather than among the children and grandchildren who dance, and yet he is placed "betwixt" the father and mother as if he were their child. From this vantage, Yorick believes he sees Religion herself "mixing in the dance," but he is also aware that he is merely witnessing the ordinary lives of a family: "this was their constant way" (*ASJ*, 159). With this paradox, Yorick achieves the insight offered by the sermon "Inquiry after Happiness," in which the much-sought-after good of happiness can only be found when everyday life synchronizes with "religion . . . in the consciousness of virtue—and the sure and certain hopes of a better life" (*Sermons*, 10). He sees this truth simply and does not overelaborate it as a sentiment as he shares in a joyous religious practice that transcends the individual. New and Day interpret "The Grace" as enacting "the notion that religion's 'ways are ways of pleasantness, and all her paths are peace' (Proverbs 3:17)," a major theme of the Anglican pulpit in Sterne's era (*ASJ*, 379n159.15–27).[42] With its pleasing embodiment of proverbial wisdom, the chapter invites all to partake of its happiness.

Yorick's balanced in-betweenness as he comes to this realization is mimicked by the formal qualities of the chapter, which step back and forth in a pattern of indoor/outdoor, old/young, grace/jollity, grave/life, and constancy/dance. The sound of the father's instrument, an old French fiddle with a hand-cranked wheel, adds to the pulse. The vielle's double structure, hinted at in its alternate title, the hurdy-gurdy, consists of a rosined wheel that vibrates the drone strings while the player presses keys to articulate the melody strings (*ASJ*, 378n159.11). Altogether, it creates a full sound akin to that of a wind instrument, the bagpipe. In principle, anyone could pick up and play the instrument, but the beauty of the music comes from the practiced coordination of left and right hands to produce harmony, which in this passage is complemented by the line of the melody woven into it by both husband and wife, probably from their memory of traditional tunes. The performance serves as a vivid example of Bennett's concept of enchantment, to "surround with sound or incantation; hence to cast a spell with sounds" or, in other words, be drawn out of one's typical egocentric behavior into an affective union.[43] The experience for Yorick is physically visceral, as he directly experiences the vibrating sensations of sensibility once again: sitting between these two music makers, he would undoubtedly feel the throb of the vielle's vibrating bridge while immersing himself in the surrounding sound of the singers' voices. In contrast to his earlier outcry to sensibility and the "great—great Sensorium of the world!" in "The Bourbonnois" (*ASJ*, 155), replete with visions of Maria and the "generous swain," here Yorick directly experiences the pulsations of the music in the context of pious familial love.

For all the symbolism of balance that might come from this imagery, it is worth noting the troubled history of the vielle. As Robert A. Green documents, "in the thirteenth and eighteenth centuries it was found in the most musically cultivated circles," but "in the [intervening] fourteenth through the seventeenth centuries, it was played by the lowest classes."[44] In the trough of its reputation, the vielle "became associated with blind beggars. Blindness was regarded as a physical manifestation of inner or moral blindness, and, therefore, the very appearance of the instrument in a painting suggested sin."[45] Although the father in "The Grace" has played the vielle for over fifty years and would not be influenced by its resurgence of popularity among wealthy amateurs during his lifetime, his association with an instrument identified with sin adds to the moral message of his performance. Like the *croix* and the sword, the historical vielle has known both highs and lows.

Until the last pages of *A Sentimental Journey*, Yorick's encounters with things show his obtuseness to those promptings he most needs to heed. In Calais, through Yorick's interactions with the *desobligeant* and the horn box, Sterne stages the problem of self-delusion, while in Paris, he represents Yorick's relations with the *croix*, sword, and butter wrapper as unwise attempts to wrest control from the rule of providence. Sterne portrays all these things as uncanny and allows many of them to flicker back and forth in our perception, rendering them so split in their composition that we must pause and ask, "What is it?" In the final stage of the narrative, Yorick comes across the multipurpose knife and multisensory vielle, things whose complex structures resemble humanity's own mixed, fallen nature. In the rare moments when Yorick does move toward a better self via material interactions with things such as these, he does so in a spirit of adaptability and humility. However, Sterne's text, significantly, does not conclude with one of these breakthroughs of spirit but humorously returns to problems of embodiment. This structural emphasis marks the divergence of Sterne's and Bennett's paths. Whereas Bennett advocates enchantment as a weak ontology that "might be deployed to propel ethical generosity" and effect social change, Sterne's project differs in its estimation of humankind, in its Christian rather than Epicurean roots.[46] He portrays states of enchantment as moments of potentiality that bring about openheartedness only inconsistently due to human shortcomings. That such enchanted moments exist, however, and sometimes carry us beyond our usual limitations gives us cause to tune in to them as opposed to other calls on our attention. Sterne builds this tempered insight into the nonresolution of his plot. Despite the social harmony Yorick has experienced in the previous chapter, "The Grace," he is not done with his journey or with the same old familiar difficulties of communication and embodied life, of our nearness and distance from one another.

The last chapter, "The Case of Delicacy," is set on the downhill side of Mount Taurira, requiring a "journey of caution" rather than of repletion (*ASJ*, 160). The difficulty of traversing this rocky terrain stands in for Yorick's awkward situation at the inn, where he must share a room with an unknown woman. The bed curtain loosely held together with corking pins represents a comically flimsy attempt to guard appearances, recalling the earlier "flimsy" curtain of the *desobligeant*, and provides a solution that leads to the very problem it is designed to avert. This, then, is the setup for the conclusion. In these surroundings, corking pins, recriminations, and finally hands fly around in the dark. Yorick ends his narrative on a joke about his recurrent problem: intending to gesture meaningfully, he accidentally grasps a thing. The refusal of full resolution and the punning on the very idea of "end," amid this much ado about "no-thing," rejects attitudes of rest and complacency, sending the audience back into the text to find meaning. Is this a sign of his development or his continued evasiveness? It depends how we interpret things.

NOTES

The title of this chapter reprises that of a volume edited by my valued colleague Kristina K. Grover, *Things of the Spirit: Women Writers Constructing Spirituality* (Notre Dame, IN: University of Notre Dame Press, 2004). Many thanks, as well, to the editors and reviewers whose judicious suggestions have shaped my argument.

1. John Plotz, "Can the Sofa Speak? A Look at Thing Theory," *Criticism* 47, no. 1 (Winter 2005): 110.
2. Bill Brown, "Thing Theory," *Critical Inquiry* 28, no. 1 (Autumn 2001): 1–22. For more general background on thing theory, see Brown, ed., *Things* (Chicago: University of Chicago Press, 2004); Brown, *Other Things* (Chicago: University of Chicago Press, 2015); Plotz, "Can the Sofa Speak?," 109–118; and Ileana Baird and Christina Ionescu, eds., *Eighteenth-Century Thing Theory in a Global Context: From Consumerism to Celebrity Culture* (New York: Routledge, 2013).
3. Jane Bennett, *The Enchantment of Modern Life* (Princeton, NJ: Princeton University Press, 2001), 131.
4. For a complete discussion of these friendships and influences, see Martin C. Battestin, "Sterne among the *Philosophes*: Body and Soul in *A Sentimental Journey*," *Eighteenth-Century Fiction* 7, no. 1 (October 1994): 17–36.
5. Philipp Blom, *A Wicked Company: The Forgotten Radicalism of the European Enlightenment* (New York: Basic Books, 2010), 83.
6. Paul Goring, "'Into What a Delicious Riot of Things am I Rushing?': Material Things and Humour in *Tristram Shandy*," in *Hilarion's Asse: Laurence Sterne and Humour*, ed. Anne Bandry-Scubbi and Peter de Voogd (Newcastle, UK: Cambridge Scholars, 2013), 82–83.
7. Bill Brown, "Thing Theory," in *Things*, 4, 9 (emphasis mine).
8. Isabel Rivers, *Reason, Grace, and Sentiment: A Study of the Language of Religion and Ethics in England, 1660–1780*, vol. 1, *Whichcote to Wesley* (Cambridge: Cambridge University Press, 1991), 73.
9. Arthur Hill Cash, *Sterne's Comedy of Moral Sentiments: The Ethical Dimension of the Journey* (Pittsburgh: Duquesne University Press, 1966), 105, 108.
10. Battestin, "Sterne among the *Philosophes*," 30.
11. Ileana Baird, "Introduction: Peregrine Things: Rethinking the Global in Eighteenth-Century Studies," in *Eighteenth-Century Thing Theory in a Global Context: From Consumerism to Celebrity Culture*, ed. Ileana Baird and Christina Ionescu (New York: Routledge, 2013), 3.
12. Bennett, *Enchantment of Modern Life*, 4.
13. Robert South, *Twelve Sermons Preached upon Several Occasions*, 2 vols. (London, 1692), 1:358–359, quoted in *Sermons: Notes*, 434.
14. Bennett argues the same point in delineating the truths accessible to disenchantment from those found by enchantment, observing, "I am less [disenchantment's] critic than its trash collector" (*Enchantment of Modern Life*, 8).
15. John Plotz, *Portable Property: Victorian Culture on the Move* (Princeton, NJ: Princeton University Press, 2008), xiv.
16. Battestin, "Sterne among the *Philosophes*," 34.

17. Plotz, *Portable Property*, xiv.
18. W. G. Day, "Sternean Material Culture: Lorenzo's Snuff-Box and His Graves," in *The Reception of Laurence Sterne in Europe*, ed. Peter de Voogd and John Neubauer (London: Thoemmes Continuum, 2004), 250.
19. *CH*, 429–431.
20. Rudi Mathee, "Exotic Substances: The Introduction and Global Spread of Tobacco, Coffee, Cocoa, Tea, and Distilled Liquor, Sixteenth to Eighteenth Centuries," in *Drugs and Narcotics in History*, ed. Roy Porter and Mikuláš Teich (Cambridge: Cambridge University Press, 1997), 39.
21. Day, "Sternean Material Culture," 252.
22. Volume 5 of *Tristram Shandy* concludes with Walter Shandy's educational theories involving auxiliary verbs (*TS*, 5.43.486–487).
23. Sterne also mixed sensory influences in his own snuffbox, which contained a portrait of Eliza Draper (*LY*, 275).
24. Jakub Lipski, "The Masquerade Metaphor and the Paradoxes of Sentiment in *A Sentimental Journey*," in *Sterne, Tristram, Yorick: Tercentenary Essays on Laurence Sterne*, ed. Melvyn New Peter de Voogd and Judith Hawley (Newark: University of Delaware Press, 2016), 191.
25. Elizabeth Kraft, *Laurence Sterne Revisited* (New York: Twayne, 1996), 110–112.
26. Bennett, *Enchantment of Modern Life*, 132.
27. Bennett's work, seen in larger grain, does grapple further with this problem (one that for Sterne would have been known as "Pelagianism"). She acknowledges the polemical nature of her theory, poised as it is against the disenchantment of modernity, and in subsequent writing develops a more complex framework, moving from "the vitality of a discrete thing to vitality as a (Spinozist) function of the tendency of matter to conglomerate or form heterogeneous groupings." Jane Bennett, *Vibrant Matter: A Political Ecology of Things* (Durham, NC: Duke University Press, 2010), xvii.
28. Lynn Festa, *Sentimental Figures of Empire in Eighteenth-Century Britain and France* (Baltimore: Johns Hopkins University Press, 2006), 76.
29. Festa, 79.
30. Donald R. Wehrs, "Levinas and Sterne: From the Ethics of the Face to the Aesthetics of Unrepresentability," in *Critical Essays on Laurence Sterne*, ed. Melvyn New (New York: G. K. Hall, 1998), 320.
31. Jonathan Lamb, *Sterne's Fiction and the Double Principle* (Cambridge: Cambridge University Press, 1989), 29–30.
32. John Mullan, *Sentiment and Sociability: The Language of Feeling in the Eighteenth Century* (Oxford: Clarendon, 1988), 198.
33. Robert Markley, "Sentiment as Performance: Shaftesbury, Sterne, and the Theatrics of Virtue," in *Critical Essays on Laurence Sterne*, ed. New, 288.
34. Thomas Keymer, "*A Sentimental Journey* and the Failure of Feeling," in *The Cambridge Companion to Laurence Sterne*, ed. Thomas Keymer (Cambridge: Cambridge University Press, 2009), 88.
35. Cash, *Sterne's Comedy of Moral Sentiments*, 38.
36. Bennett, *Enchantment of Modern Life*, 5.
37. Plotz, "Can the Sofa Speak?," 114.
38. Desiderius Erasmus, *The Praise of Folly*, trans. Hoyt Hopewell Hudson (Princeton, NJ: Princeton University Press, 1941), 63.
39. Battestin, "Sterne among the *Philosophes*," 35; Martin C. Battestin, "*A Sentimental Journey* and the Syntax of Things," in *Augustan Worlds*, ed. J. C. Hilson, M.M.B. Jones, and J. R. Watson (New York: Barnes and Noble, 1978), 234.
40. Brown, "Thing Theory," in *Things*, 5.

41. The happy scene of the peasant family at supper with the knife foregrounded on the table as multitool harks back to the resignation of the Marquis d'E**** from sword, title, estate, and homeland for a score of years. The things of peasant life, in comparison, appear just as noble and much more sustainable than those of the aristocracy.
42. New and Day assess Gardner Stout's analysis of intertextualities between this chapter and sermon 20, "The return of the prodigal son," and sermon 28, "Temporal advantages of religion." They also find that "[Edward] Young's entire sermon 'The safe way to happiness' is a very useful gloss to 'The Grace'" (*ASJ*, 379).
43. Bennett, *Enchantment of Modern Life*, 6.
44. Robert A. Green, *The Hurdy-Gurdy in Eighteenth-Century France* (Bloomington: Indiana University Press, 1995), ix.
45. Green, 2.
46. Bennett, *Enchantment of Modern Life*, 3.

Part Three

HISTORICAL CONTEXTS, REWRITTEN TEXTS

8

BOSWELL AND STERNE IN 1768

MELVYN NEW

On earth the righteous man takes the form of a tedious Grandison, in whose eyes even a Venus of the streets would be sexless.

—Balzac, *Cousin Pons*

IT HAS OFTEN BEEN OBSERVED that 1759 was a banner year in literature, producing three masterpieces that seem to have much in common, most pertinently, perhaps, that in the so-called age of the novel not one of them fits comfortably into that genre. I refer, of course, to Voltaire's *Candide*, Johnson's *Rasselas*, and the first two volumes of *Tristram Shandy*. We know there were hundreds if not thousands of literary publications in 1759 but only a very few of equal genius. Adam Smith's *Theory of Moral Sentiments* might thus qualify but certainly not *Memoirs of the Celebrated Miss Fanny Murray*. Both, however, are quite rightfully assigned chapters in *Reading 1759: Literary Culture in Mid-Eighteenth-Century Britain and France*.[1] In celebrating Sterne's final year, 1768, I prefer to eschew the notion of "culture," literary or otherwise, that makes Fanny's *Memoirs* includable and concentrate instead on a genius equal to Sterne's, pursuing my belief that some writers influence each other because when we read their work we inevitably put them into an overheard conversation.[2] At times that intercourse can involve authors widely separated by time and space, authors who have never actually talked to each other; at other times, as in the present instance, they may be contemporaries or neighbors, intimate or distant as the case may be. What distinguishes the conversation I am listening to, in other words, is not any actual or conscious dialogue but rather one that emerges from works of genius put in proximity to each other. Obviously, readers are the ones overhearing this conversation, indeed creating it, but I invoke the too-often-slighted concept of *literary genius* to validate their reports: genius does not find itself justly reflected in conversations with mediocrity but only with another genius. That, at any rate, is the premise of the conversation I overhear when I bring James Boswell and Laurence Sterne into proximity for the sole reason that both created works of genius in 1768.[3]

A project of this sort clearly requires a certain amount of blindness or deafness. Sterne was writing his final work while staving off death, in part by clinging to the fantasy-driven hope of "new love." He survived only long enough to finish two of the projected four volumes of *A Sentimental Journey*. Boswell, on the other hand, was still a very young man, reluctantly beginning his career in law, dreaming of an alternative career as a famous writer, falling in and out of love with great (ir)regularity but convinced that marriage was the only cure for his appetite for life—and women. These highly significant differences matter little once we put Boswell's *Account of Corsica* into proximity with *A Sentimental Journey*.[4] Our deafness will also extend to the historical events and the social and economic innovations of the 1760s and, even more pertinently given my literary emphasis, to the many voices clamoring for recognition in 1768. Francis Burney began her journals this year, Gibbon started and abandoned his "History of the Swiss," and Mackenzie began writing *The Man of Feeling* (published in 1771). Oliver Goldsmith, Hugh Kelly, George Coleman, Richard Cumberland, and David Garrick all had new plays staged during the 1767–1768 season. Poets we might have listened to would include the undervalued Francis Fawkes, a Yorkshire resident, to whose first collection (1761) Sterne had subscribed; this year he published his fine edition of the *Poems of Theocritus*. That the internet allows us to recover tens of thousands of pages of "literature" written in any given year tempts us to believe we can derive from it the year's "literary culture." I suspect, however, that what we will actually derive from this access to an unmanageable wealth of information is evidence only for our preconceived notions, the thousands of pages being irreducible to meaningful interpretation of the actual content of literature.

For example, if I have the opinion that "Scriblerian" satire did not exist, I could sort through a thousand documents with a title that includes "satire" or "satiric" and point to many of them that pay no attention to Swift or Pope: QED. On the other hand, if I believe that the term "Scriblerian" captures a unifying element of the genius of those canonized authors and helps to define the age, I can put them into relationship with another genius and find their existence documented to my own satisfaction. In the two months preceding Boswell's *London Journal*, from September 14 to November 13, 1762, he recorded a journey from Auchinleck to Edinburgh en route to London, his so-called Harvest Jaunt.[5] For his entertainment on the road, Boswell armed himself with several volumes of the Pope-Swift *Miscellanies* (1727), along with Orrery's biography of Swift (1751). On September 17, he refers to "Memoirs of P. P. Clerk of the Parish" (probably by Pope) (46), and five days later, to Swift's "Letter to a Young Lady Newly Married" (56). Then, on September 30, he entertains Lord Kames by reading *The Art of Sinking in Poetry*, "a performance which cannot be too often read, as its inimitable humour must always please" (65). All are in *Miscellanies*. That Boswell in 1762, at the age of twenty-two, found the collection worth taking on his journey suffices in my judgment to indicate the reality—indeed the vitality—of the Scriblerians into midcentury—and, of course, our own present day.

Donald R. Wehrs has beautifully confronted this problem in reviewing a book based on electronic research, Brad Pasanek's *Metaphors of Mind: An Eighteenth-Century Dictionary*, a work celebrating "surfing the web, wandering wither the search engine listeth." The results, Wehrs argues, can be useful for readers and scholars but may also "encourage confusion of appearances of learning with its substance, and invite mistaking industry for achievement. These dangers are prominently satirized by Sterne, Swift, Cervantes, Rabelais, and Erasmus and associated by those writers with reservations about modernity that one might expect eighteenth-century scholars to be cognizant of when they reflect on digitized modernity." Wehrs goes on to note that "availability is no guarantee of significance" and that being able to locate "long unread, out-of-print texts" by using a search engine and "keyword" (e.g., 1768) and grant such works posthumous recognition is "the scholarly equivalent of a trophy for participation." Rather, he suggests, "the work of time and judgment in regulating forgetting" should not be undone.[6] With this in mind, I want to listen to the conversation Sterne and Boswell had in their works of 1768, the year of the death of one and the first literary triumph of the other.

It is important to preface my account by acknowledging the fully valid argument of James J. Caudle that much if not all the legend of a Boswell-Sterne relationship in London in 1760 was a construct of Boswell's imaginative mind, a "cock-and-bull story."[7] Boswell would spend much of the ensuing decade in Europe, while Sterne traveled abroad first between January 1762 and June 1764, then again between November 1765 and June 1766. Some cities they had in common but at different times: for example, Boswell was in Turin in January 1765, Sterne ten months later; in Naples they missed each other by eleven months, in Rome by a full year. We have some letters written by Sterne during his travels but nothing that compares to Boswell's records. Still, while Sterne would have had little if any reason to think about the young man he may or may not have encountered in his whirlwind days in London, in Utrecht Boswell characterized his journal-keeping by recalling Sterne's masterpiece: "I can never resist anything laughable that presents itself, whether there is occasion for it or not. In this I follow the example of Rabelais, Tristram Shandy, and all those people of unbridled imagination who write their books as I write my themes—at random, without trying to have any order or method; and for that reason they have acquired great reputation among people of unregulated vivacity who do not wish to give themselves the trouble of thinking even in their amusements."[8]

A second mention of Sterne during the decade also occurred in Utrecht, when Boswell was in the company of Robert Brown (1728–1777), a fellow Scot and minister of the English Presbyterian Church, who was "a useful and reasonably sympathetic friend" to him during his year of legal studies.[9] Brown is known to Sterne scholars as the author of perhaps the most perceptive and enthusiastic response to the first two volumes of *Tristram Shandy* that we know of: "Never did I read any thing with more delectation. What a comical Fellow the author must be! & I may add also what a Connoisseur in Mankind!" (*Letters*, 691).[10] One may at least hope that Brown and Boswell held some discourse about Sterne during their many hours together, but the only other mention is that Brown shared Sterne's correspondence with him on March 13, 1764. Whether it was Sterne's reply on September 9, 1760, to the July letter or to more recent letters we do not know.[11]

This is rather scant documentary evidence on which to construct a relationship between the two authors, and especially if we elaborate on the many and enormous differences already suggested. During the 1760s, while Sterne was writing seven more volumes of *Tristram Shandy*, Boswell first studied law in Utrecht before proceeding on a prolonged Grand Tour through Germany and Switzerland (1764–1765), then to Italy and France (1765–1766), all the while—in the telling modern title of the final journal volume of the decade—"in search of a wife." Sterne traveled for his health, in part to pursue his wife, who had decided that life in France was better than life with him, in part to keep distance between them. After a bout of severe depression in Utrecht, Boswell was a hale and hearty twenty-something (except for his many episodes of sexually transmitted diseases—or, as he would have put it, "clapt again!"). Sterne, on the contrary, was a wasted body, fleeing from death across the Continent, as he reveals in a telling autobiographical detail at the opening of volume 7 of *Tristram Shandy*; he was also, it might be mentioned, trying to convince Eliza, if not himself, that he was not being treated for a venereal disorder (*BJ*, 176–177).

Boswell fell seriously in love with several women during the decade and engaged in sex with countless others, important experiences that filled him with guilt and an abiding concern with the mysteries of free will, sin, and final judgment. The counterweight to this worrisome state of being was an equally abiding faith that he was destined to atone for his weaknesses with great accomplishments. Sterne's sexual activity in the decade, so far as we know, was more limited but culminated in a love affair with a married woman half his age; he left behind some letters and a portion of his one-sided journal to her, a journal that opens to us one strain of the conversation between Sterne and Boswell: the inclination to chronicle their days in terms of their encounters with women. As has been often observed, it is a structuring frame in *A Sentimental Journey*, which was written alongside the *Bramine's Journal*. Finally (although it would be impossible to exhaust all the differences between them), Sterne was to publish his second masterpiece on February 27, 1768, just three weeks before his death—his "work of redemption" as he is said to have labeled it.[12] Nine days before *A Sentimental Journey* appeared, Boswell had published his first masterpiece (February 18), a work that would make him an instant celebrity ("Corsica Boswell") and also one we might accurately label—if we accept its probable motives—a "work of redemption."[13]

Prior to Boswell's experiences in Corsica, the highlight of his travels was his meeting with Rousseau and Voltaire, both living in Switzerland at the time. Setting aside his ever-present urge to meet famous men and his concomitant desire to be praised by them, one might posit a third motive, already evident in his seeking Johnson's company at the beginning of the decade. More than most men, Boswell was enormously disturbed by the question of free will for the very obvious reason that his life to this point was one in which he constantly willed himself to have control over his sexual and social practice and, with equal constancy, acted otherwise. He had already quickly entered and exited the Roman Catholic Church, which has its own solutions to the problem—namely, celibacy and confession; the first he found impossible, the second was precisely what led him to Johnson, Rousseau, Voltaire, and a host of friends, male and female, to whom he revealed his weaknesses and sought both advice and reassurance.

We have Boswell's scattered notes of his conversation with Voltaire on December 29, 1764, during which the conversation took a turn indicative of these concerns, one that offers a most useful intersection with Sterne.[14] Pursuing his desire to be known to everyone as the most open and frank young man ever to seek an audience with fame, Boswell tells Voltaire that he had expected to find him great but "very bad," an expectation that sincerity makes him admit; now, although finding him more virtuous than he thought he would, he nevertheless confronts Voltaire with his entry on "Soul" in the *Dictionnaire philosophique*. It had bothered Boswell, and he refuses to accept Voltaire's judgment that it was "a good article." Boswell objects most particularly to the notion that immortality is just a "pleasing imagination," insisting instead on its reality: "It must be so." Boswell was quite proud of himself in this encounter and wrote about it to Voltaire a few weeks later (January 15, 1765): "You may remember that I showed no mean timidity; and while I maintained the immortality of my soul, did I not glow with a fire that had some appearance of being divine? I am exceedingly happy that I have had an important conversation with you. . . . Although I am sincerely sorry at your being prejudiced against the doctrines of consolation and hope."[15] Again, in April, he returned to this discussion in a second letter to Voltaire: "It is curious after all to reflect that the Soul is really the All, the man, the thinking principle, the source of everything noble and elegant. . . . (You must forgive my zeal for immortality. I am a melancholy man, I know not how. In this world my prospect is clouded. I cheer my hours of gloom with expectations of a brighter scene after death, and I think I have a strong probability that I shall not be deceived)."[16]

Where Boswell had written "It must be so," Pottle has interpolated into the text, "Like Cato, we all say. . . ." Most readers of *A Sentimental Journey*—and most literate people of the eighteenth century—would not have needed the prompt. Yorick comes to the same passage from Joseph Addison's *Cato* (1713) late in *A Sentimental Journey* and for the same reason Boswell has invoked him. A few pages earlier, Yorick's meeting with Maria, and his sympathy for her, had culminated in precisely the assertion of positive belief that Boswell wants for himself and finds lacking in Voltaire:

> I felt such undescribable emotions within me, as I am sure could not be accounted for from any combinations of matter and motion.
>
> I am positive I have a soul; nor can all the books with which materialists have pester'd the world ever convince me of the contrary. (*ASJ*, 151)

This is soon followed by his apostrophe to "Dear sensibility," the "divinity which stirs within" him, although at times this evidence for the existence of a soul is overwhelmed by "sad and sickening moments," when his soul "'*shrinks back upon herself, and startles at destruction*'—mere pomp of words!" (*ASJ*, 155). The Florida editors provide context for the quoted material (*ASJ*, 372–373). The lines from *Cato* occur at the opening of the fifth act when Cato sits with "Plato's Book on the Immortality of the Soul" in his hand and a sword in front of him, contemplating suicide:

> It must be so—Plato, thou reason'st well!—
> Else whence this pleasing hope, this fond desire,
> This longing after immortality?
> Or whence this secret dread, and inward horror,
> Of falling into nought? Why shrinks the soul
> Back on herself, and startles at destruction?
> 'Tis the divinity that stirs within us;
> 'Tis heaven itself, that points out an hereafter,
> And intimates eternity to man.
> Eternity! Thou pleasing, dreadful thought![17]

Equally telling are these lines from Nicolas Rowe's *The Fair Penitent* (1703), also, it would seem, on Sterne's mind when constructing the passage: "Hast thou e'er dared to meditate on death? . . . Say, has thou coolly thought? / 'Tis not the stoic's lessons got by rote, / The pomp of words, and pedant dissertations / That can sustain thee in the hour of terror."[18]

Thomas Keymer finds both "sentiment and satire" in *A Sentimental Journey*'s encounter with Maria and in Yorick's assertion of a soul, a combination of "casual sympathy and smug self-approval."[19] I would suggest instead that Yorick and Sterne—and even Boswell—might have considered the "failure of feeling" as the universal failure of Christians when they measure themselves against what they believe is expected of them, both by God and by the soul (conscience) they believe He planted within them. In this process of self-examination, with eternity at stake, the mixture of righteous and condemned behavior in almost every encounter with reality would seem to preclude smugness (or "callous egotism," as Keymer amplifies his disapproval of Sterne), an attitude directly opposed to those who seek salvation with fear and trembling. Of course, this entails reading their writings as if they believed in the soul, in eternity, and in judgment, which is the argument of this chapter.

For both Boswell and Sterne, I suggest, the existence of a soul and an afterlife is consistently and frighteningly connected to the possibility of free will. Simply put, both men—one entering his prime, the other sharply aware of impending death—knew that despite every effort, their bodies had triumphed over their better intentions with too-frequent regularity. If they indeed had a soul looking toward immortality, it was in dire straits. Boswell's well-chronicled bouts of dark despair were manifestations not of religious doubt but rather of his worthiness or, more to the point, his unworthiness for religion's promise of immortality. This overt distress helps us toward an understanding of the dying Sterne, who left behind far less by way of personal confessions but in their place a work that transforms Boswell's journalized anxieties into a fictionalized confession of faith, a final statement on the end of a Christian's life. Immersed in both loneliness and illness, when juxtaposed to Boswell, Sterne is an old man confessing to the world what Boswell, as a young man, confessed to Johnson, to Voltaire, to Rousseau, indeed to anyone who would listen: his life was too often a contradiction to his beliefs—and hence to his hopes for immortality.

The suggestion that Boswell, and especially Sterne, would agonize over theological issues is somewhat less suspect than it was a few decades ago, although perhaps we still tend to evaluate their religious faith through secular eyes. Putting the two authors in proximity may encourage us to improve our perspective on what can be so difficult for the modern mind to grasp, that belief in Christian dogma is neither a sign of imbecility nor hypocrisy, neither the privilege of immaturity nor the desperation of the deathbed. With rare exceptions, those who were born in that time and place considered themselves bound by Christianity's truths. Whatever the French Enlightenment produced (and both Sterne and Boswell touched its headsprings, the one with visiting Diderot and d'Holbach, the other with Voltaire and Rousseau), it did not free the vast majority of the British population, and among them the most profound geniuses of the day, into the slumber of secularism[20] that has all too often characterized literary and historical studies of the eighteenth century.[21]

Without doubt, every age adds something to the crucible of Christianity, and the eighteenth century was no exception; but its contribution was something far more important than the rational or empirical knowledge that Enlightenment has come to signify as being essentially hostile to religion. Sterne apostrophizes this new "discovery": "Dear sensibility! source inexhausted of all that's precious in our joys, or costly in our sorrows! thou chainest thy martyr down upon his bed of straw—and 'tis thou who lifts him up to HEAVEN—eternal fountain of our feelings!" (*ASJ*, 155). Thus opens the paragraph that winds its way to Cato's theorizing of a world without that divine spark of sympathy the soul shares with the "great—great SENSORIUM of the world! Which vibrates, if a hair of our heads but falls upon the ground." The Florida annotators suggest that "Sterne's argument—we awaken to God's presence through our most generous feelings—is well within orthodox boundaries" (*ASJ*, 373), and indeed it is; I would also suggest, however, that orthodoxy itself subtly shifted from one end of the century to the other, so that now a religion of the heart has, for many people, replaced one of the head.[22] Boswell's primary love while in Holland (and for some time thereafter), Belle du Zuylen (Zélide), seems to have anticipated Sterne by some four years: "Blest Sensibility! Zélide will never disown thee, thou sole offset for the misfortune of nice discernment and exacting taste. Thou who causest her to cherish the sweets of Nature, thou who dost bind her to the Arts."[23] That she summons Rousseau's *Émile* at the end of her invocation perhaps separates her from the providentialism of Sterne's expression,[24] but the distance is a narrow one. Sensibility, from the Cambridge Platonists at the end of the seventeenth century to Rousseau at the end of the eighteenth, was an incorporation of the divine within the human, a turning of Jesus into the original "man of feeling." The reasonableness of self-interest and the urgency of physical desire both had to be overcome by a counter-intuitive and disruptive force that embodied belief in an immaterial and immortal essence characterized by its essential distinction from both reason and appetite.[25] Those virtues the self and body could not practice were nonetheless the passport to eternal life, and for Boswell and Sterne the soul became the repository of whatever hopes they retained for an eternity spent in the presence of God.

Boswell wonderfully embodies this most difficult conflict again and again in his travels but perhaps never so starkly as in the following few entries made while he was still in Holland (and trying to practice celibacy). On Sunday, April 15, 1764, he writes in his journal, "Think if God really forbids girls,"[26] and two days later he writes to his good friend (and another confessor) William Johnson Temple, "Sometimes I think myself good for nothing, and sometimes the finest fellow in the world. . . . I, who am conscious of changes and waverings and weaknesses and horrors, can I look upon myself as a man of dignity?"[27] This attitude pervades much of his Utrecht journal, his periodic "dismal" periods, but we must pay equal attention (and credence) to the path by which he overcomes these moments: "I am now again at rest. I view Deity as I ought to do, and I am convinced that Jesus Christ had a divine commission, that through him the justice of God is satisfied; and that he has given us the most exalted morality: 'To love God with all our heart, and our neighbour as ourselves.'"[28] What I would stress here is that for both Boswell and Sterne, confrontation with one's own devices and desires, and one's hope to overcome them and achieve promised salvation, leads to the most mundane and fundamental doctrines of belief: providential care and the Golden Rule—both involved with caring for others more than for oneself.

We have come to think of Sterne as proleptically engaged with theories of the mind, struggling to unravel the novelistic practices by which thought could be displayed on the page. Boswell may help us to see that ideation was not Sterne's preoccupation but that of the age, including those who were never preoccupied with narrative technique: "How strange is the mind of man! How are our ideas lodged? How are they formed? How little do they depend upon realities!"[29] The problem returns frequently because of Boswell's journalizing; for example, "I find it is impossible to put upon paper an exact journal of the life of man. External circumstances may be marked. But the variations within, the workings of reason and passion, and, what perhaps influence happiness most, the colourings of fancy, are too fleeting to be recorded. In short, so it is that I defy any man to write down anything like a perfect account of what he has been conscious during one day of his life, if in any degree of spirits."[30] Where most Sterne scholars would immediately cite John Locke's *Essay Concerning Human Understanding* at this point, Boswell might more pertinently have had Montaigne in mind—or even Augustine's *Confessions*, since the impetus for Boswell's puzzlement is as ethical as it is aesthetic, returning us again and again to his struggle with a will that seems anything but free and most particularly when he deals with desire: "I must observe of myself that from my early years I have never seen an agreeable lady but my warm imagination has fancied as how I might marry her and has suggested a crowd of ideas."[31] We might observe a very similar attitude in Yorick, as with his first encounter with a woman in France: "—Good God! how a man might lead such a creature as this round the world with him!—." In a gesture that he will repeat again and again in *A Sentimental Journey*, the thought then leads him to justify his soul: "In a word, I felt benevolence for her; and resolved some way or other to throw in my mite of courtesy" (*ASJ*, 22–23), only to allow the body to be reasserted by bawdy innuendo: ". . . if not of service."[32] As Boswell could tell him, he could tell Boswell: the promise of Heaven depends on a will that seems irrepressibly self-destructive, a central mystery of a religion that embraces both omnipotence and free will, divine goodness and the presence of mundane evil. A secular mind may simply dismiss as willful abstraction the desire for immortality and salvation, as Voltaire seems to have done but as Sterne and Boswell are unable to do.

However, the two men order things better in France. Boswell, too, was enamored of the idea that a change of place could renew his life: "had I been told that by being drawn some hundreds of miles in a certain machine, seeing another assemblage of houses and some more of those miserable two-legged animals called human . . . I should feel myself a happy man, should view the Creation in an agreeable light . . . I should most certainly have treated him who told me so . . . a very ignorant fellow."[33] But the old Boswell, filled with regrets and dismal thoughts, never quite disappears, and the usual culprit is temptation: "Bless me, have I now committed adultery? . . . Should I now torment myself with speculations on sin, and on losing in one morning the merit of a year's chastity. No: this is womanish. . . . Let it go. I'll think no more of it. Divine Being! Pardon the errors of a weak mortal. Give me more steadiness. Let me grow more perfect."[34] We might try to resist the secular instinct to dismiss these moments as hypocrisy or as self-deceiving and smug pieties. Instead, if we are willing to rouse ourselves from the dogmatic slumbers of secularism and return to those of Christianity (a fair-enough exchange to make when trying to overhear conversations taking place among believers), we will find in Boswell an honest and painful awareness of his inability to control himself and an often-incapacitating (if increasingly "old-fashioned") dread of final judgment because of it. We might be influenced by different dogmas but still no more able to control our desires than was Boswell. When, therefore, we suspend our secular dismissal of Boswell's anguish and our tut-tutting at Sterne's unclerical conduct, we may then be better prepared to overhear a conversation about being human, still meaningful to the modern reader although it took place 250 years ago.

We left Yorick before the *remise* door, hand in hand with the woman in Calais, contemplating whether he could be of "service" to her. His next words are, "Such were my temptations—and in this disposition to give way to them, was I left alone with the lady with her hand in mine" (*ASJ*, 23). It is a scene often repeated in *A Sentimental Journey*, tactile encounters where approach and avoidance wrestle with each other.[35] Yorick does not have Boswell's futuristic hope to "mature" and become virtuous. Rather, conflated with Sterne, he is a dying man, painfully aware that his hope is lodged in a Heaven more understanding of weakness than is human judgment. When Yorick first dismisses the *fille de chambre*, it is with a "kiss of charity, as warm and holy as an apostle" (*ASJ*, 90), but when he meets her a second time, with thoughts "not in strict unison with the lesson of virtue" (*ASJ*, 124) of their first meeting, and finally tumbles her on the bed, he rises to the occasion with a dramatic apostrophe: "Yes——and then—Ye whose clay-cold heads and luke-warm hearts can argue down or mask your passions—tell me, what trespass is it that man should have them" (*ASJ*, 124). Sterne did believe they were a trespass, however, and the rest of the chapter wrestles with the hope that "providence" will take into account the interweaving of body in the same narrow space occupied by head, heart, and soul; his language, typically enough, mirrors exactly this "entangled" web, a plea to God: "Let me feel the movements which rise out of it [the situation], and which belong to me as a man—and if I govern them as a good one—I will trust the issues to thy justice, for thou hast made us—and not we ourselves" (*ASJ*, 124). The challenge when reading *A Sentimental Journey* is to find in "movements," "as a man," and "issues" not disqualifying bawdry but rather the very essence of the anxieties and fears of Sterne's final illness. We will return to this encounter shortly, but here it suffices to indicate that Sterne's invocation at this point to the "great governor of nature" is really a plea to his God to forgive his lifelong inability to disentangle the conflicting threads of inclination and conscience. For those who believe in possible eternal separation from the Creator, this is a persistent anxiety; and for those who believe they have no such conflict to deal with, I might suggest a rereading of Sterne's "Abuses of Conscience" sermon.[36]

For Boswell, almost every encounter with a woman entailed a decision and hence a question of his free will. One such occasion, when Boswell is presented by Louis Dutens[37] to the French ambassador's wife, will bring Yorick immediately to mind:

> I had the honour to hand her to her coach. About the middle of the stair we were met by a marquise, who of course was to turn back. But the great question was, who should be led first to her coach? *Madame la marquise!*

> *Madame l'ambassadrice!* I was simple enough to be tossed from the one to the other, as I did just what I was bid; while the rogue Dutens enjoyed my perplexity and probably studied from it something to insert among his notes on Leibnitz on determining motives. At last her Excellency of France took the *pas*.[38]

The question of protocol here becomes more overtly sexual in Yorick's meeting on the stairs in Milan with another marquise, the Marquesina di F*** (*ASJ*, 77–78); in both instances one sees an everyday encounter turned into a puzzle that the mind alone seems unable to solve, a mundane puzzle of motivation as Boswell astutely observes in this instance, even while he admits to feeling so helpless a depression over the incident that it spoils the remainder of his evening.

At the end of the seventeenth century, the journeys of Boswell and Sterne might well have been written under the sign of John Bunyan's *Pilgrim's Progress*, wherein each encounter is a temptation to overcome. We tend to slight Bunyan today, but as Samuel Johnson noted in 1773, "It has had the best evidence of its merit, the general and continued approbation of mankind. Few books, I believe, have had a more extensive sale."[39] Not coincidentally, the *Divine Comedy* is part of this same conversation, another literary classic that reflects the pervasiveness of journeying as Christianity's predominant metaphor for each individual existence. When Johnson accepted the task of accompanying Boswell as far as Harwich to begin his travels in 1763, I suspect he saw himself setting the young man forth on a pilgrimage into adulthood. While there, they attend church, and, Boswell writes, "Johnson . . . sent me to my knees, saying, 'Now that you are going to leave your native country, recommend yourself to the protection of your Creator and Redeemer.'"[40] That the conversation then turned to Berkeley's immateriality and Johnson's famous kick is significant because if Berkeley was correct, the struggle Boswell felt between his physical and metaphysical parts would have seemed meaningless.[41] Given the challenge of Berkeley, however, and of Locke and Descartes before him, we might suggest that for eighteenth-century Christian travelers, neither Dante nor Bunyan but Miguel de Cervantes created their model in the knight of La Mancha, Don Quixote. Much has been made of the shifting interpretation of Cervantes's hero during the eighteenth century, whereby the ludicrous madman becomes the idealist creating a better world, but it is worth noting that *Don Quixote* was written some seventy-five years before *Pilgrim's Progress* and in a Roman Catholic country. It is, I suggest, as Christian a work as *Divine Comedy* and *Pilgrim's Progress* and one that spoke with pertinent significance to mid-eighteenth-century travelers.

Sterne's many allusions to Cervantes have often been commented on, and indeed Gardner Stout sees *Don Quixote* as central to *A Sentimental Journey*.[42] In

Yorick's meeting with Maria, during which (as noted) he asserts his assurance that he has a soul, he had begun the episode by picturing himself "like the Knight of the Woeful Countenance, in quest of melancholy adventures" and then had added, "but I know not how it is, but I am never so perfectly conscious of the existence of a soul within me, as when I am entangled in them" (*ASJ*, 149). Boswell is not as multifold in his allusiveness to Cervantes, but on the day he sat down to begin writing his *Account of Corsica* (March 27, 1767), he reports that his father was reading *Don Quixote* and was "much entertained with him": "Joked on my Account; called it quixotism."[43] Earlier in the same month, he had written to Temple, "You say well that I find mistresses wherever I am. But I am a sad dupe, a perfect Don Quixote."[44] Nine years earlier, at the age of eighteen, Boswell had already recognized something quixotic in his relationship to women, again in his correspondence with Temple on July 29, 1758: "You used to admonish not to turn an Old Man too soon, dont be thunderstruck, if this same fellow, should all at once, subito furore obreptus, commence Don Quixote for his adorable Dulcinea. But, to talk seriously, I at first fell violently in love with her."[45]

While both Sterne, especially with his letters and journal to Eliza, and Boswell, with almost every woman he meets, partake of Quixote's imaginary romance with Dulcinea, it is in the *Account of Corsica* and *A Sentimental Journey* that we find the most striking influence of Cervantes. Early in Cervantes's opening volume, Quixote recites at length to a company of shepherds the perfections he plans to restore, creating a world in which there is "no fraud, no deceit, no malice intermixed with plain-dealing truth: justice . . . undisturbed and unbiassed by interest and favour, which now impair, confound, and persecute her."[46] The speech precedes the first of several similar inset tales, often masterful versions of the idyllic fictions Cervantes parodies through his woeful knight: in this particular romance, the shepherd Chrysostom dies of love, rejected by the beautiful Marcella. Both Quixote and Chrysostom are willing to die for the cause of a beautiful, harmonious, and peaceful world, whether found in the books read by Quixote or in the woman loved by the shepherd, but their desire for a return to Edenic purity entails no reciprocal response from those whom they encounter. Indeed, as Quixote all too often discovers, his attempts arouse hostility or comic dismissal from those whom he intends to convert to his own vision of the good.

On the other hand, Cervantes and his readers surely knew these scriptural verses: "Where is the wise? . . . Hath not God made foolish the wisdom of this world?" (1 Corinthians 1:20), a verse at the heart of Erasmus's *Praise of Folly* and still foundational, if reluctantly so, to the ethics of the Enlightenment. Erasmus states the proposition thus: "The entire Christian religion seems to bear a certain natural affinity to folly, and to relate far less clearly to wisdom. . . . You see that no fools are more distracted than those whose ardent zeal for Christian piety has wholly eaten them up. They discard their belongings, swallow insults, put up with trickery, . . . subsist on fasts, vigils, tears, toils, and humiliations. They shun life, seek death . . . as if their souls existed somewhere else, not in their bodies."[47] The conclusion of *Praise of Folly* is replete with difficult ironies and paradoxes, but importantly it opens a counterintuitive pathway for the appraisal of Quixote as a character quite other than a mere fool; he now becomes, theologically, a "fool for Christ."

As the Enlightenment progresses, the two "fools" will merge into a composite whole, Quixote becoming an admired, indeed beloved, but *secular* idealist, a stubborn reformer who, in the words of his twentieth-century incarnation, will dream "impossible dreams." Where Erasmus's fool attempts to gain salvation by reenacting the simplicity and sacrifice of Christ, Enlightenment's fool wages war on the ills of the world in the belief that humankind will be saved by human effort. No longer a fool, no longer a fool for Christ, the new Quixote will eventually become a force for social and political good (and, sadly enough, for totalitarian states, an embodiment of their own versions of what is good for others). For Boswell and Sterne, however, in the middle of the eighteenth century, the fool melds the two strands of reformer and soul seeker into the figure of sensibility. We can see this in one of Boswell's laments while in Turin, a hotbed of sexual temptations: "I saw that amongst profligate wretches a man of sentiment could only expose himself."[48] Or again, "My sensibility is so delicate that I must fairly own it to be weak and unmanly. It prevents me from having a decent and even conduct in the course of ordinary life."[49] Boswell sees "sensibility" as a cause both of strength and of weakness, a duality he confronts most cogently when deriving from Pasquale Paoli's character a lesson for life:

> I saw from Paoli's example the great art of preserving young men of spirit from the contagion of vice, in which there is often a species of sentiment, ingenuity and enterprise nearly allied to virtuous qualities.
>
> Shew a young man that there is more real spirit in virtue than in vice, and you have a surer hold of him, during his years of impetuosity and passion, than by convincing his judgment of all the rectitude of ethicks.[50]

One has in this character of Paoli the essence of what Boswell wanted to learn on his Grand Tour, his own quixotic search for self-control on the one hand, greatness on the other. The quixotic at midcentury is, I am suggesting, the visionary future in which all evils will be overcome by enlightenment, including the evils of sickness, sinfulness, separation, even death—and, in contrast, a continuing belief in the truth of a religion that considers sin and death inherent to the human condition and hence a fool's or madman's errand (knight errantry)[51] to reform oneself or the world. Reformation is embodied for both authors in the failures of their wills; Enlightenment, in their desire to assert their souls.[52]

On the Friday Sterne died (March 18, 1768), Boswell was once again traveling, this time from Edinburgh to York; he made no inquiry after the Yorkshire native but on Saturday visited York Minster ("Saw the cathedral. It is a prodigiously noble Gothic edifice"), where Sterne preached at times, and on Sunday went to a play at the York Theater and then had an excellent supper.[53] Between these activities, he also pursued a very young girl, Mary—"a pretty, lively little girl whom accident had thrown in my way a few days before"[54]—whom he has decided to save from profligate men after first testing her "virtue": "I find I am still somewhat of a Don Quixote, for now am I in love with perhaps an abandoned, worthless being."[55] A second encounter then calls forth this exclamation: "How strange is this! The author of the *Account of Corsica* the sport of a frivolous passion. Shall my mind ever be all solid and rational? Yes. A room which is hung with the slightest chintz and gaudiest paper may by and by be hung with substantial velvet or even thick arras hangings with scripture stories wrought upon them. My walls are good, so they will bear any sort of hangings."[56]

The juxtaposition of Mary and Corsica is what at the outset of *Tristram Shandy* Sterne calls the "*cervantick* tone" (*TS*, 1.12.34),[57] which might be simplified, for the present purpose, as a voice aware of the conflict between vision and reality, between a desire to improve ourselves and our world and the persistent resistance to that desire. Boswell's brief time in York is part of his journey to London to celebrate the publication of his *Account*. Johnson was in Oxford at the time, but he sent Boswell a most typical letter of deflation: "I wish you would empty your head of Corsica, which I think has filled it rather too long."[58] Boswell's epistolary response soars to quixotic heights:

> But how can you bid me "empty my head of Corsica?" . . . Consider fairly what is the case. The Corsicans never received any kindness from the Genoese. . . . They owe them nothing; and when reduced to an abject state of slavery by force, shall they not rise in the great cause of liberty and break the galling yoke?[59] . . . Empty my head of Corsica! Empty it of honour, empty it of humanity, empty it of friendship, empty it of piety. No! while I live, Corsica and the cause of the brave Islanders shall ever employ much of my attention, shall ever interest me in the sincerest manner.[60]

A very useful discussion of the meaning of Corsica to Boswell and his age can be found in the introduction to the Boulton-McLoughlin edition, as well as an awareness of the conflict I am exploring: "One of the compelling reasons for Boswell to visit Corsica was that he wanted to see for himself the native islanders who were fighting for their freedom. Rousseau was perhaps the first to bring him to focus on this singular example in Europe of a people striving for nationhood. . . . There are aspects of Boswell on the Grand Tour that bring him close to Pope's caricature, 'The Stews and Palace equally explor'd / Intrigu'd with glory, and with spirit whor'd.' But the seriousness of his curiosity about Corsica more than makes up for this."[61]

Despite the "best intentions" of the Corsicans and Boswell, General Paoli was defeated by the French in May 1769, and Corsica became a French territory (and remains so today); six months after that, Boswell married his cousin Margaret Montgomerie (November 1769), was reconciled to his father, entered seriously into the profession of law, and paraded his Corsican outfit at Garrick's Shakespeare festival. In quixotic terms, the world reasserted itself—and the fate of human will in its struggle with the realities of body and mind remained unresolved, if not defeated. And yet, when we position ourselves to listen to a conversation between Boswell and Sterne, are we not saying, as did Addison's Cato, "it must be so"? Are we not, when overhearing any conversation from the past, listening to a "divinity that stirs within us," providing an "intimation of eternity"—or, as Wordsworth would phrase it, "intimations of immortality"? Stripped of the Christian promise, our only access to what Boswell and Sterne thought when they invoked "this pleasing hope, this fond desire, / This longing after immortality" (their "souls") is our capacity to overhear the sensibilities of one enduring author conversing with another. Indeed, it seems quite possible that just such dialogues have always been what humanity has taken (and mistaken) to be the voice of God.

Boswell would live the second half of his life after 1768, and his major literary achievement was still ahead of him. In the same month that he began writing *Corsica*, Sterne began a journal to Eliza Draper, whom he had met some three months earlier: "you shall see it, for if I live not till your return to England, I will leave it you as a legacy" (*Letters*, 550). Whatever flights of fancy Sterne indulged in when writing to Eliza, his dying is the final truth to which all his dreams revert. And he does dream excessively, much induced by illness we can assume, but certainly a portion of his desire for Eliza was to justify his sexual life with a final bodiless encounter with his own Dulcinea; she is, after all, "not handsome" but still appeals to a "man of sense, tenderness, and feeling"; in short, she possesses "that bewitching sort of nameless excellence, that men of *nice sensibility* alone can be touch'd with" (*Letters*, 553). This chord is struck again and again in his address to her, entwined with biblical snatches, prayers for her safe passage, and dreams of his wife's demise, with Eliza's husband also fading from the scene and a future idyllic life for the two of them, happily forever after. The quixotic underwrites the entire affair, as Sterne caroms between his own dying body and his desire for justification.

What appears in rather naked and desperate openness in the *Bramine's Journal* and Sterne's letters to Eliza is given aesthetic cover in *A Sentimental Journey*, but it is an often-committed error of interpretation to overlook the biographical fact that its author was a dying man, fearful, even as a good Christian still has to be, of the righteous judgment awaiting him. He had been sanctified to preach this day of judgment to others for more than thirty years, but as with his congregants, he had too often ignored in life what he preached in church. Nowhere is this conflict more evident than in his sermon "The Levite and his concubine," wherein he preaches three different lessons: (1) It is very difficult for a body to live without human companionship; (2) a loving God understands this and forgives weaknesses of the body; and (3) that same God is far more forgiving (and virtuous) than one's gossiping neighbors.

The first truth returns us to the struggle between our will and our reason: thus, when Sterne presents the "concubine," he asks his congregation to consider that "our actions stand surrounded with a thousand circumstances which do not present themselves at first sight; . . . the difficulties and temptations under which they acted,——the force of the passions,——the suitableness of the object, and the many struggles of virtue before she fell,———may be so many appeals from justice to the judgment seat of pity" (*Sermons*, 168).[62] When he turns to the Levite, his justification echoes the writings of John Norris of Bemerton, whose presence in both *Tristram Shandy* and *A Sentimental Journey* has come to be recognized as central to Sterne's theology. Thus, where Sterne writes, "Yet still, '*it is not good for man to be alone*:' nor can all which the cold-hearted pedant stuns our ears with upon the subject, ever give one answer of satisfaction to the mind; in the midst of the loudest vauntings of philosophy, Nature will have her yearnings for society and friendship" (*Sermons*, 169–170), he is copying from Norris's discourse "Of Solitude": "We all . . . stand in need of one anothers help at every turn, both for the *Necessities* and *Refreshments* of Life. And therefore I am very far from commending the undertaking of those *Asetics*, that out of a pretence of keeping themselves *unspotted from the World* . . . abandon all Human Society." Unless one is a God, he continues, "*It is not good for man* (tho in *Paradice* it self) *to be alone*."[63] Sterne was preparing this sermon for the press even while writing *A Sentimental Journey*, as reflected in the words of Yorick's second encounter with the *fille de chambre*, already quoted: "Yes——and then—Ye whose clay-cold heads and luke-warm hearts, etc."[64]

In the sermon's next paragraph, Sterne gives yet another version of the "cold-hearted pedant," the "*Asetics*," the "clay-cold heads": "Let the torpid Monk seek heaven comfortless and alone——God speed him! For my own part, I fear, I should never so find the way: let me be wise and religious—but let me be MAN: wherever thy Providence places me, or whatever be the road I take to get to thee——give me some companion in my journey" (*Sermons*, 170). The road and the journey come naturally to the sermonizer as images for life itself and return us to Quixote and Boswell as well as to the man Sterne as opposed to the priest. All three wanted to do more than seems possible for a man to do, all three are again returned to the world and its realities.

Still, Quixote's dream of correcting the injustices of the world becomes part of the Enlightenment dream of progressive amelioration of ourselves and others, and Boswell's own knight-errantry entitles him to a sense of accomplishment and achievement that endures to this day: in Corsica's struggles, he had placed himself and the Corsicans on the right side of history. As for Sterne, his Eliza was perhaps just another Dulcinea, a work of an overheated imagination; and his letters and journal to her, just his own attempt at knight-errantry, replete with language using the clichés from those books Cervantes both satirized and, in his interpolated tales, imitated. Sterne's final exploit, however, is the writing of *A Sentimental Journey*, a work that makes him, perhaps, the most quixotic hero of the three. It is a book written with all the marks of the author's humanity about him, a man still striving toward forgiveness and immortality but staking his claim not on a reformation that eludes him but rather on an insistence that his God would know him for the divided being He had created. Sterne's *Journey* is the final heroic declaration he left behind for us all, but particularly in conversation with Boswell, assuring him that for the duration of his journey or pilgrimage through life, every moment of Grace (as in the title of its penultimate chapter),[65] every connection in life where we believe we can, with awakened sensibility, perceive "*Religion* mixing in the dance," will be followed by a "Case of Delicacy," his final chapter. Ever and again, the body will be confronted by irresistible temptations in defiance of our reason and our piety, and we will end with our hand stretched across the empty space surrounding us, seeking whatever solace we hope is out there. For Sterne, facing his own death and judgment, *A Sentimental Journey* is a particular act of quixotic heroism, a final assertion that being human, all too human, can also promise immortality, or, "in the tender strokes of nature which the poet has wrought up in that pathetic speech of Perseus: '*O Cupid, prince of God and men &c.*'" (*ASJ*, 45).

NOTES

1. Shaun Regan, ed., *Reading 1759: Literary Culture in Mid-Eighteenth-Century Britain and France* (Lewisburg, PA: Bucknell University Press, 2013); respectively, Nigel Wood, "Adam Smith's *The Theory of Moral Sentiments* in 1759: Spectatorship, Duty, and Social

Improvement," 57–74; and Mary Peace, "'On the soft beds of luxury most kingdoms have expired': 1759 and the Lives of Prostitutes," 75–91.

2. I have pursued this line of inquiry over three decades, beginning with "Proust's Influence on Sterne: A Remembrance of Things to Come," *Modern Language Notes* 103 (1988): 1031–1055; and more recently in "A Genius of that Cast: Celebrating Sterne," *Shandean* 26 (2015): 9–26; and "*Sir Charles Grandison* and Laurence Sterne: A Study in Influence," *Modern Philology* 115, no. 2 (2017): 213–243.
3. Concomitant with the concept of "genius" is that of literary canonization, which, as with its religious counterpart, remains for me a telling act of spiritual belief. The capacity to be canonized derives from an achievement that measures itself against those who are already canonized and should (although it rarely does) remain beyond all the social or political considerations that might motivate those who are empowered to add to—or subtract from—the canon. Despite efforts, early and late, e.g., F. R. Leavis's "irresponsible (and nasty) trifling" (*The Great Tradition* [New York: Doubleday, 1954], 11n); or Donald Greene's "The World's Worst Biography" (*American Scholar* 62, no. 3 [1993]: 365–382), Sterne and Boswell remain canonized literary geniuses, whose conversation we can hear if we quiet contemporary conversations about our own predilections and concerns.
4. The best edition of *Account of Corsica* is edited by James T. Boulton and T. O. McLoughlin (Oxford: Oxford University Press, 2006). It contains both the *Account* and *The Journal of a Tour to That Island*; hereafter cited as *Tour*.
5. See Frederick A. Pottle, introduction to *London Journal*, by James Boswell (London: William Heinemann, 1951; numbered edition only), 10–11; hereafter cited parenthetically in text.
6. Donald R. Wehrs, review of *Metaphors of Mind: An Eighteenth-Century Dictionary*, by Brad Pasanek, *Scriblerian* 50, no. 1 (2017): 78–81. The concept of rightful and necessary "forgetting" is Nietzsche's, what Wehrs characterizes as "an evolutionarily valuable skill."
7. James J. Caudle, "'Fact' or 'Invention'?: James Boswell and the Legend of a Boswell-Sterne Meeting," *Shandean* 22 (2011): 30–55.
8. James Boswell, *Boswell in Holland, 1763–1764*, ed. Frederick A. Pottle (New York: McGraw-Hill, 1952), 68–69 (November 1763); hereafter cited as *Holland*. Boswell refers specifically to the daily exercises he wrote in his journal in the languages he was, at that moment, trying to master. It is important to note that throughout this chapter, I have consulted only the "trade" edition of Boswell's writings; generalizations, therefore, await final validation from the "research" edition.
9. *Holland*, 23n7.
10. That Brown singled out the influence of Montaigne ("he is no stranger to Montaigne; nay . . . he is full as well acquainted with him, as with the book of common prayer") is noteworthy; Perhaps only Boswell among eighteenth-century authors exhibits an equal engagement with *Essais*.
11. *Holland*, 180.
12. The comment was reported by Richard Griffith in *A Series of Genuine Letters between Henry and Frances*, vol. 5 (London, 1770), 83: "It has all the Humour and Address of the best Parts of Tristram, and is quite free from the Grossness of the worst. . . . He . . . calls it his *Work of Redemption*."
13. Boswell wrote to his friend William Johnson Temple on May 3, 1769, "Never did there live such a man as myself. I beseech you write to me without delay: Dublin is address enough for *Corsican Boswell*." James Boswell, *Boswell in Search of a Wife, 1766–1769*, ed. Frank Brady and Frederick A. Pottle (New York: McGraw-Hill, 1956), 202; hereafter cited as *Search*. Typically enough, Boswell was on his way to Ireland to court the latest of his possible wives, Mary Ann Boyd, traveling with his cousin Margaret Montgomerie, to whom he

would propose a few months later and marry in November 1769. We recall that Sterne too was so popular that it was rumored that "A Letter addressed to Tristram Shandy in Europe shou'd reach him" and indeed did, if we believe for once the usually unreliable John Croft. Croft, "Anecdotes of Sterne," *Shandean* 19 (2008): 54; originally published in *The Whitefoord Papers*, ed. W.A.S. Hewins (Oxford: Clarendon, 1898), written by Croft in 1795.

14. James Boswell, *Boswell on the Grand Tour: Germany and Switzerland, 1764*, ed. Frederick A. Pottle (New York: McGraw-Hill, 1953), 303–304; hereafter cited as *Germany*.
15. *Germany*, 319.
16. *Germany*, 322.
17. Here quoted from Joseph Addison, *Cato: A Tragedy and Selected Essays*, ed. Christine Dunn Henderson and Mark E. Yellin (Indianapolis: Liberty Fund, 2004), 88 (5.1.1–10); the editors point out that Cato is reading Plato's *Phaedo*.
18. Nicholas Rowe, *The Fair Penitent*, ll. 77, 79–82, ed. Malcolm Goldstein (Lincoln: University of Nebraska Press, 1969), 63.
19. Thomas Keymer, "*A Sentimental Journey* and the Failure of Feeling," in *The Cambridge Companion to Laurence Sterne*, ed. Thomas Keymer (Cambridge: Cambridge University Press, 2009), 90–91.
20. I allude to Kant's famous awakening from the "dogmatic slumber" induced by Hume's dismissal of metaphysics, without engaging with the arguments of either; suffice to say, the dogmatic slumbers of religious faith can too easily be replaced with the dogmatic slumbers of secularism, both equally smug in their certainties. Enough scholarly progress has been made in recent years toward modifying our secularist views so that younger scholars may feel I have exaggerated our past smugness. An exchange between myself and an unnamed scholar fictionalized in my introduction to *Theology and Literature in the Age of Johnson: Resisting Secularism*, ed. Melvyn New and Gerard Reedy, S.J. (Newark: University of Delaware Press, 2012), xiv–xvii, will suggest the atmosphere twenty-five years ago when the actual exchange took place in the pages of *Eighteenth-Century Life* in 1992–1993.
21. Boswell's account of Voltaire's direct encounter with disbelief is telling: "He expressed his veneration—his love—of the Supreme Being, and his entire resignation to the will of Him who is All-wise. He expressed his desire to resemble the Author of Goodness by being good himself. . . . He does not inflame his mind with grand hopes of the immortality of the soul. He says it may be, but he knows nothing of it. And his mind is in perfect tranquility" (*Germany*, 294). But then, in asserting his sincerity of belief, Voltaire goes on, "I suffer much. But I suffer with patience and resignation; not as a Christian—but as a man." Perhaps we should take Boswell's account of Voltaire cum grano salis, but the opposition between tranquility and suffering, between being a Christian and a man, is certainly present in both Boswell and Sterne, if not in Voltaire, who, we must remind ourselves, when told by Boswell that Johnson was "orthodox," replied, "He is then a dog. A superstitious dog. No worthy man was ever superstitious" (*Germany*, 300).
22. My longtime colleague Richard E. Brantley, over a course of seven full-length studies of nineteenth-century British and American authors, has argued with cogency for an evangelical (Methodist) merger of mind and heart, studies that culminate with a reading of Emily Dickinson: "The poet collapses distinction between mind and heart and creates thereby an uneasy but sympathetic composite of common humanity." Brantley, *Transatlantic Trio: Empiricism, Evangelicalism, Romanticism* (Ames, IA: Culicidae, 2017), 34. For Sterne and Boswell, such a "collapse" of distinction was not possible, because their minds and hearts rarely merged. Sensibility was the century's fresh attempt to reconcile mind and heart by turning from oneself to others, an attempt codified, e.g., in *Theory of Moral Sentiments*. It was enthusiastically preached from Anglican as well as Dissenting pulpits, with a stress on caring for rather than judging others (emulating God's mercy rather than justice).

This shift in emphasis between two teachings both easily derived from scripture was Christianity's attempt to reconcile religious faith with empirical knowledge (the challenge of Enlightenment), but an "empirical faith" seems remote from both Sterne and Boswell; Sternean ironies and Boswellian fear and trembling reflect far more Kierkegaard's impasse than the age's embrace of sensibility.

23. *Holland*, 188. Cf. Boswell's friend George Dempster to Boswell, August 22, 1763: "Adieu, thou mass of sensibility!" (*Holland*, 11).
24. I.e., Matthew 10:29–31, the most fundamental providential assertion in scripture.
25. One will recognize in this formulation a dependence on the excellent work of Donald R. Wehrs, "Levinas and Sterne: From the Ethics of the Face to the Aesthetics of Unrepresentability," in *Critical Essays on Laurence Sterne*, ed. Melvyn New (New York: G. K. Hall, 1998), 311–329; and Wehrs, "Anarchic Signification and Motions of Grace in Sterne's Novelistic Satire," in *Sterne, Tristram, Yorick: Tercentenary Essays on Laurence Sterne*, ed. Melvyn New, Peter de Voogd, and Judith Hawley (Newark: University of Delaware Press, 2016), 77–99.
26. *Holland*, 222.
27. *Holland*, 223.
28. *Holland*, 282 (to Temple, June 11, 1764).
29. *Germany*, 16.
30. *Search*, 242.
31. *Germany*, 23.
32. The biblical echo, "And there came a certain poor widow, and she threw in two mites" (Mark 12:42), is played against "service," a word Sterne well knew could evoke the Shandy bull kept "for the service of the Parish" (*TS*, 9.33.807).
33. *Germany*, 35.
34. *Germany*, 91.
35. Ray McDermott, applying his training as an ethnologist, examines in minute detail the complexity of Yorick's interaction with his partner in this scene; see "Yorick's Ethnographic Journey," in New, de Voogd, and Hawley, *Sterne, Tristram, Yorick*, 169–186, esp. 180. See also Anne Bandry, "Les livres de Sterne: Suites et fins," *XVII–XVIII: Revue de la Société d'études anglo-américaines des XVIIe et XVIIIe siècles* 50 (2000): 132–133, where she notes that in *A Sentimental Journey* Sterne uses the word "hand" more often than "heart" (107 occurrences to 62) or any other common noun except "man." Sterne's tactile sensitivity, a hyperawareness of human touch, is matched by Boswell's: e.g., "I sat [at the opera] vis-à-vis to her and pressed her legs with mine, which she took very graciously." James Boswell, *Boswell on the Grand Tour: Italy, Corsica, France*, ed. Frank Brady and Frederick A. Pottle (New York: McGraw-Hill, 1955), 28 (January 10, 1765); hereafter cited as *Italy*. Or again, "I sat close behind the Princess, and at the most affecting scenes [of *Othello*], I pressed my hand upon her waist. She was in tears, and rather leaned to me" (*Search*, 109; December 24, 1767). A distinction between touching and groping might not have occurred to either party, although Boswell does seem more culpable than Yorick—we do not know about Sterne. At a time of increased social isolation, it is perhaps well to recall one of Boswell's astute comments about his social nature: "in the immense multiplicity of human beings, the more attachments we can form, the better" (*Search*, 116).
36. I think it no accident that Sterne published this sermon three times, once in 1751 in a pamphlet, then in volume 2 of *Tristram Shandy* (1760), and a third time in volume 4 of the *Sermons of Yorick* (1766). It is, perhaps, his most complete statement of what he perceived to be the basis of human nature, his own included: in a word, self-deception.
37. This is the same Louis Dutens who met Sterne at a dinner in Paris and was amused by Sterne abusing him to the guests, not realizing he was at the table (*Journey*, 278, n. to 40.2); he subscribed to *Sermons* in 1769. As Boswell and Sterne crisscrossed Europe, they often

encountered the same people, including many English travelers; Boswell, however, had far more contact with the nobility than did Sterne, wealth and property (and the title Baron) having more sway than genius, then and now.

38. *Italy*, 30.
39. James Boswell, *Life of Johnson*, ed. R. W. Chapman and Pat Rogers (Oxford: World Classics, 1980), 529.
40. Boswell, 333.
41. What could Boswell (or Sterne) do with this typical conclusion from Berkeley: "Not to mention that the apprehension of a distant deity, naturally disposes men to a negligence in their *moral* actions, which they would be more cautious of, in case they thought him immediately present, and acting on their minds without the interposition of matter, or unthinking second causes." George Berkeley, *Three Dialogues between Hylas and Philonous*, ed. Robert Merrihew Adams (Indianapolis: Hackett, 1982), 90.
42. Gardner D. Stout, introduction to *A Sentimental Journey through France and Italy*, by Laurence Sterne (Berkeley: University of California Press, 1967), 44–46.
43. *Search*, 45.
44. *Search*, 35.
45. In James Boswell and William Johnson Temple, *The Correspondence of James Boswell and William Johnson Temple, 1756–1795*, vol. 1, ed. Thomas Crawford (New Haven, CT: Yale University Press, 1997), 6.
46. Miguel de Cervantes, *The History and Adventures of the Renowned Don Quixote*, 1.2.3, trans. Tobias Smollett, ed. Martin C. Battestin (Athens: University of Georgia Press, 2003), 74.
47. Desiderius Erasmus, *The Praise of Folly and Other Writings*, trans. Robert M. Adams (New York: Norton, 1989), 82–83.
48. *Italy*, 39.
49. *Italy*, 112.
50. *Tour*, 180.
51. Cf. Temple to Boswell, January 8, 1768: "Undoubtedly . . . my dear Boswell; the romance of knight-errantry is no more. . . . Does not this shock the sensibility of your enthusiastic soul?" (*Search*, 120). Temple, as he often does, confronts Boswell with his weakness: "The great Baron, the friend of Rousseau and Voltaire, the companion of Paoli, the author of that immortal work, the Account of Corsica, is dwindled into a whining, fawning lover, the slave of a fair hand and a pair of black eyes" (119).
52. I deliberately invoke the capitalized terms, Reformation and Enlightenment, to suggest that, as Erasmus perceived, both movements contained within themselves the countermovements, if not self-destructive impulses, that twentieth-century modernism, in art and literature, had to confront.
53. *Search*, 135–136.
54. *Search*, 135.
55. *Search*, 135. *O tempora! O mores!* Today we are often appalled, as here, by Boswell's (and Sterne's) rather overt objectification and demeaning of women; it is quite impossible to predict what will appall readers 250 years from now about our own age, but, again, Sterne's sermon on conscience and "self-deception" might provide one clue.
56. *Search*, 137. In one of those eerie moments of confluence, Boswell engages in a coffeehouse discussion about Corsica with Sir George Armytage, MP for York, 1761–1768, and receives Armytage's compliments on the *Account of Corsica* ("authentic and very accurate") without revealing his identity as the author. Sir George had subscribed to Sterne's *Sermons* in 1760; one suspects his name never came up in their conversation.

57. The Florida annotation to this passage (*TS*, 3:75n34.25) indicates the far greater complexities triggered by Sterne's several allusions to Cervantes and his tone; see also 3:216n200.6.
58. *Search*, 164 (March 23, 1768).
59. Sterne's own brief encounter with the issue of slavery has received outsized attention in recent years, both favorable and unfavorable, indicative of our proclivity to enlist past authors into our own party—or to exclude them. Here we shall simply note Boswell's own reflection on sighting prison ships in the harbor of Marseilles, imagining how the prisoners might think: "If we could escape, we should certainly do it. A bird shut up in a cage desires freedom, and so much the more should a man desire it" (*Italy*, 243); I am inclined to praise their sensibility, but of course we tend to believe our own sensibilities far better honed than those of the past.
60. *Search*, 164–165. Corsican tradition, it is worth noting, considerably helped Boswell to leave his whoring behind: "They told me that in their country I should be treated with the greatest hospitality; but if I attempted to debauch any of their women, I might expect instant death" (*Tour*, 165). It is worth noting that *An Account of Corsica* had every bit as much success as the first two volumes of *Tristram Shandy* a decade earlier. It was quickly translated into Dutch, French, German, and Italian; and Benjamin Franklin "did not find it difficult to draw political analogies between the Corsicans and the American colonists on the subject of liberty" (*Tour*, li). One might also claim for the *Account* an influence on Byron's fierce interest in Greek independence.
61. *Tour*, xxxi.
62. As has often been observed, Sterne does not pursue the quite horrid subsequent events of Judges 19.
63. John Norris, *A Collection of Miscellanies*, 2nd ed. (London, 1692), 159; quoted from *Sermons*, 5:208. Some very good work has been done on Norris and Sterne in recent years, but for the present subject, perhaps the most pertinent is Geoff Newton, "Divine and Human Love: Letters between John Norris and Mary Astell, Laurence Sterne and Eliza Draper," in New and Reedy, *Theology and Literature in the Age of Johnson*, 183–201. Significantly, another important borrowing from Norris in *Journey* concerns the unfitness for Heaven of Smelfungus and Mundungus (*ASJ*, 38; see also 273n38.4–13). See also Melvyn New, "Job's Wife and Sterne's Other Women," in *Out of Bounds: Male Writers and Gender(ed) Criticism*, ed. Laura Claridge and Elizabeth Langland (Amherst: University of Massachusetts Press, 1990), 55–74.
64. The Florida annotations (*Sermons: Notes*, 208) point significantly enough to the opening paragraph of Johnson's sermon on marriage: "That society is necessary to the happiness of human nature, that the gloom of solitude, and the stillness of retirement . . . neither extinguish the passions, nor enlighten the understanding, that discontent will intrude upon privacy, and temptations follow us to the desert, every one may be easily convinced, either by his own experience, or that of others." Samuel Johnson, *The Sermons of Samuel Johnson*, ed. Jean Hagstrum and James Gray (New Haven, CT: Yale University Press, 1978), 3. Surely when Boswell confessed his failures in 1762, Johnson provided just such consolation to him.
65. Cf. *Tour*, 165, when Boswell is sailing to the island of Corsica: "At sunset all the people in the ship sung the Ave Maria, with great devotion and some melody. It was pleasing to enter into the spirit of their religion, and hear them offering up their evening orisons."

9

THE SHADOW OF ELIZA

Sterne's Underplot in *A Sentimental Journey*

Peter Budrin

L'esprit est toujours la dupe du cœur.
—François de La Rochefoucauld, *Maximes*

LAURENCE STERNE HAS OFTEN BEEN regarded as a great innovator of literary form. In his first work, *Tristram Shandy*, the narrator seems to lay bare his literary techniques, the form constituting an integral element of its design. The Shandean narrative's self-reflexivity, however, is notably absent in *A Sentimental Journey*; at first reading, the structure of Sterne's travel narrative seems more conventional and linear. Nevertheless, Sterne's last work contains a set of narrative techniques that are no less intricate and original. Unlike in *Tristram Shandy*, these techniques are not foregrounded or reflected on in the text but rather concealed from the reader. The present discussion addresses an important formal structure, a subtextual "underplot" that organizes the seemingly random and episodic encounters of *A Sentimental Journey*.

The word "underplot"[1] here defines a second, buried layer of the narrative that develops independently from the main (overt) plot, which, in the case of *A Sentimental Journey*, is often described as a series of vignettes, a set of scenes loosely connected by the consciousness of the traveling protagonist.[2] While remaining just below the structural surface, the underplot creates the emotional background for the narrative and, in certain instances, directly influences the events of the fiction, serving as a bridge between otherwise separated episodes. The notion of "burying" referred to here is used in critical literature as a narrative technique especially common in genres such as the detective story. Catherine Emmott and Marc Alexander, for example, analyze different techniques for concealing the elements of the plot whereby readers may or may not notice such buried elements in the course of reading and their importance is only revealed at the end, when they are used to solve the mystery.[3] In contrast to such conventional narrative techniques, however, the buried elements in *A Sentimental Journey* are structured so as to remain unnoticed by the implied general reader. The well-known ambiguities in Sterne's text (for instance, the matter of Yorick's argument with his "gentleman" in the introductory chapter of the book or the nature of his "conquest" in his little adventure with the *fille de chambre* in Paris) remain subject to debate, inspiring critics to offer different, and at times conflicting, interpretations. Buried meanings for some of these episodes can be uncovered with the light provided by the supposition of an underplot. Central to this underplot is the woman named Eliza, a figure simultaneously absent and present in the text of *A Sentimental Journey.* Although she is not an active character in the narrative, there are five places where Eliza's name is mentioned directly (six, if we consider the manuscript of *A Sentimental Journey*), those mentions evenly punctuating the narrative. There are also phrases and episodes in which Eliza is not mentioned explicitly but that can be read as the author's hidden conversation with her.

Eliza, of course, refers to Eliza Draper, an actual person who played a key role in Sterne's life during its final year. His relationship with her has been described in various scholarly studies, including Arthur Cash's account in the second volume of his biography of Sterne (*LY,* 250–304).[4] To summarize, Eliza was born in India to a family of British East India Company officials. At the age of fifteen she married an employee of that company, Daniel Draper, with whom she had two children. When Sterne met Eliza in London, presumably in January 1767, he was living separately from his wife and daughter, who had settled in France several years previously. Sterne was fifty-three, Eliza twenty-three, and both were alone in London. Sterne is known for his roguish correspondence with different women, but none of his previous relationships seems to have affected him to the same extent as that with Eliza. Two months into their acquaintance, Eliza left England for India. She promised Sterne that she would return to him after informing her husband of their relationship, having convinced Sterne that her rather unhappy marriage with Draper had long been a mere formality.

We know the details of the relationship from Sterne's perspective thanks to the miraculously preserved part of the diary that he kept for Eliza, hoping that she would read it after her return. In *Bramine's Journal,* Sterne calls himself either Yorick or Bramin and sometimes addresses Eliza as Bramine, alluding to both her Indian origin and his clerical profession.[5] The *Journal* exhibits Sterne suffering from his real and soon-to-be-fatal illness and either a real or imagined (or, indeed, *both* real and imagined) longing for Eliza and her expected return. We will never know how sincere Eliza was, but it was over five years after Sterne's death before she returned to England.

Since the first publication of *Bramine's Journal* in 1904, there has been some debate as to whether this journal is a genuine product of the heart or rather a consciously constructed literary work intended for publication. Central to this discussion is the question of Sterne's sincerity and how we should understand the descriptions of his feelings in the text. Arthur Cash and the Florida editors argue that this document was not meant for publication.[6] At the same time, we cannot ignore the fact that Sterne was an artist and that all his texts, whether public or personal, are written in the language of a highly self-conscious writer. It therefore holds considerable potential to inform discussion of the narrative composition of *A Sentimental Journey*, the literary work that was composed simultaneously with the *Journal*.

Indeed, the Florida editors suggest that *A Sentimental Journey* "cannot be sufficiently understood" (*ASJ*, xxvii) without considering *Bramine's Journal*, which Sterne himself called a "Diary of the miserable feelings of a person separated from a Lady for whose Society he languish'd" (*BJ*, 169). Many studies devoted to Sterne and Eliza discuss the emotional and ethical aspects of their relationship; the primary focus here is on how Sterne's encounter with Eliza influenced the form of his second fictional work.[7]

THE "FEVER OF THE HEART"

According to both *Bramine's Journal* and Sterne's letters, he started to work on the manuscript of *A Sentimental Journey* in June 1767 after his arrival in Coxwold, which followed an extended period spent in London (*ASJ*, xxii–xxiv). The early period of composition coincides with the regular chronological entries of his *Journal*. His state of mind after Eliza's departure in March 1767 can best be described by Sterne's own metaphor of the "fever of the heart" that he uses in his *Journal* entry for April 15: "worn out with fevers of all kinds but most, by that fever of the heart with w[ch] I'm eternally wasting, & shall waste till I see Eliza again—dreadful Suffering of 15 Months!—it may be more— . . . —What a change, my dear Girl, hast thou made in me!—but the Truth is, thou hast only turn'd the tide of my passions a new way—they flow, Eliza to thee—& ebb from every other Object in this world—" (*BJ*, 171–172).

On the textual level, the "fever" creates a sense of impulsiveness and rapid "change" to Sterne's emotions. Ian Campbell Ross remarks that "Sterne's moods . . . fluctuated rapidly. On his first day in Coxwold he imagined Eliza inhabiting his cottage with him; on the second he tormented himself by imagining that Daniel

Draper's behaviour to his wife would be so different from what she had previously experienced that she would not return to England at all. Convinced once more that Eliza would come back, Sterne dwelt . . . on the time that must elapse before they were united."[8] The impression of overwhelming impulsiveness endures but also informs the processes of literary composition. Further in the *Journal*, Sterne repeatedly points out that all his thoughts are constantly directed toward Eliza: he is unable to put his passion aside, causing difficulties in writing *A Sentimental Journey*. In his entry for June 3, he writes,

> —Cannot write my Travels, or give one half hours close attention to them, upon Thy Acc^{t}, my dearest friend—Yet write I must, & what to do with You, whilst I write—I declare I know not—I want to have you ever before my Imagination—& cannot keep You out of my heart or head—In short thou enterst my Library Eliza! (as thou one day shalt) without tapping—or sending for—by thy own Right of ever being close to thy Bramine—now I must shut you out sometimes—or meet you Eliza! with an empty purse upon the Beach—(*BJ*, 194)

The publication of *A Sentimental Journey*, a book Sterne had already promised to his subscribers, was supposed to become a source of income for his future life with Eliza on her return, as his fears for his "empty purse" suggest. Sterne intended to part with his wife by giving her a portion of his money and dividing their property between them. However, *Bramine's Journal* shows that he was suffering from constant oscillations between anticipation and anxiety, hopes for future happiness with Eliza and fears of possible disappointment; as New notes, "whatever else Eliza Draper was, she was not 'up to the ears' in love with Sterne as he had forced himself to believe."[9] Quite possibly, it was during this period that Sterne came up with the idea of an underplot in which he could leave an imprint of his constantly changing state of mind. Again, on June 3, 1767, he complained of his inability to write. Several entries later, on June 17, he mentions that he has introduced Eliza's name into his work: "I have brought y^{r} name *Eliza!* and Picture into my work—where they will remain—when You & I are at rest for ever—Some Annotator or explainer of my works in this place will take occasion, to speak of the Friendship wch Subsisted so long & faithfully betwixt Yorick & the Lady he speaks of—" (*BJ*, 202).

Apparently, after Sterne introduced Eliza's name into *A Sentimental Journey*, he began making progress in his writing and no longer lamented his inability to work. He may have been inspired by the fact that Eliza, who appears on the list of subscribers—"a List which I am most proud of because my Eliza's name is in it" (*BJ*, 221)—would be able to see that he thought about her while writing his *A Sentimental Journey*, even if she never received the *Journal* he kept for her.

The early sections of the book were written at a time when Sterne lacked correspondence from Eliza, who was then on her way to India. He bought a map on which he traced the route of her ship, hoping that returning vessels would carry some letters from Eliza back to him. Each new disappointment made Sterne worry for Eliza's health and anxious about their relationship, as he writes on July 3: "Doubt! did I say—but I have none—and as soon w^{d} I doubt the Scripture I have preach'd on—as question thy promisses, or Suppose one Thought in thy heart during thy absence from me, unworthy of my Eliza.—for if thou art false, my Bramine—the whole world—and Nature itself are lyars—and—I will trust to nothing on this side of heaven—but turn aside from all Commerce with expectation, & go quietly on my way alone towards a State where no disappointments can follow me—" (*BJ*, 212–213).

At the end of July 1767, Sterne received a package of letters from Eliza and very soon after ceased to keep his *Journal*. Both Cash and the Florida editors (*ASJ*, xxv) suggest the contents of the package brought Sterne bitter disappointment. Nevertheless, as Cash puts it, even after breaking off the *Journal* "for good," Sterne still "kept it by him as he worked on his novel" (*LY*, 303). The Florida editors give various examples of direct textual repetitions and parallels between the two texts. Some of these can be explained by the fact that they are commonplaces of Sterne's speech; for instance, the "ebbs and flows" metaphor can be found in *Tristram Shandy*, the *Sermons*, and throughout *A Sentimental Journey*.[10] Virginia Woolf, who was interested in the personal aspect of Sterne's work almost as much as its artistic merit, described the *Journal* as a sort of notebook that he reused while drafting his *A Sentimental Journey*: "*Journal to Eliza* in which the most secret passions of his heart are laid bare is but the note-book for passages in *The Sentimental Journey* which all the world may read. Sterne himself, no doubt, scarcely knew at what point his own pain would be dissolved in the joy of an artist."[11] Sterne did not, however, simply recycle "the most secret passions of his heart" for creative purposes; rather, one might suggest that he used the text of *A Sentimental Journey* as an extension of his *Journal*, inscribing it within his book in what we might think of as "invisible ink." Interestingly, Sterne himself provides an indirect clue for this reading. In his penultimate entry of the *Journal* he tells Eliza, "At present all I can write would be but the History of my miserable feelings. . . . I will give you one gen^{l} Acc^{t} of all my sufferings together—but not in Journals—I shall set my wounds a-bleeding every day afresh by it—& the Story cannot be too short.— . . .

farewell—every Moment will I have thee present—& sooth my sufferings, with the looks my fancy shall cloath thee in.—" (*BJ*, 224). If we read this entry literally, Sterne promises to continue the description of his feelings, but not in the form of a journal. His decision to introduce Eliza into the text of *A Sentimental Journey* marked the start of the book's "double life."

THE INTRODUCTORY CHAPTER OF *A SENTIMENTAL JOURNEY*

Beginning episodes with a decontextualized phrase or exclamation is a typical device in Sterne's prose and is found in both *Tristram Shandy* and *A Sentimental Journey*. In most instances, the context is later revealed to the reader, and the inversion creates an additional comic effect and gives depth to the episode.[12] The opening of *A Sentimental Journey* employs a seemingly similar technique, though the subject matter of Yorick's argument with his gentleman remains undefined and his interlocutor never resurfaces. Michael Seidel persuasively argues that this uncertainty is intentionally used by Sterne as a structural device.[13] More to the point, any attempt to find a rational answer for it must also take into account the unnatural speed with which Yorick departs to France following this conversation. On hearing the gentleman parrying his words, Yorick goes straight to his "lodgings," packs his portmanteau, and takes a stage coach to Dover; in the morning he crosses the Channel and by midafternoon finds himself having a meal in Calais. The narrative speed of Yorick's transit notably exceeds Tristram's during his metaphorical "flight from Death" in the seventh volume of *Tristram Shandy*. Moreover, in the second volume of *A Sentimental Journey* the reader is reminded of Yorick's rushed departure: because of it, he had forgotten about the war then taking place between England and France and, without attempting to obtain a passport, crosses the Channel illegally.

The unnatural rapidity of Yorick's movement is emphasized by the sharp contrast with the lengthy description of his stay in Calais, which follows the introductory chapter and unfolds over eighteen chapters (that is, about a fifth of *A Sentimental Journey*). In the final chapter of the Calais sequence, Yorick hears the town clock strike four and realizes that he "had been little more than a single hour in Calais" (*ASJ*, 36). This syncopated perception of time suggests a specific logic within the underplot. In the sections of the *Journal* that temporally coincide with Sterne's work on the early sections of *A Sentimental Journey*, he alludes to his own sense of time in that period, describing it using spatial metaphors.

For example, on June 30 he writes:

> —the Space between is a dismal Void—full of doubts, & suspence—(*BJ*, 210)

And later, on July 2:

> —Time goes on slowly—every thing stands still—hours seem days & days seem Years whilst you lengthen the Distance between us—from Madras to Bombay—I shall think it shortening—and then desire & expectation will be upon the rack again——come—come———(*BJ*, 212)

If in "real" life time stands still, it seems the author intentionally gives his protagonist this hyperbolic push to start his *Journey*. The direct metaphor of Tristram's flight from Death in Sterne's first work of fiction can here be read as being replaced by a buried metaphor for the flight from an unbearable period of anticipation and doubt: while Sterne remains at Shandy Hall, Yorick embarks on his imaginary travels.

In the text, this effect of rapidity is visually intensified by a syntactic device. All Yorick's actions in this first chapter are compressed into five phrases, four of which are short. The central long sentence, however, is both stretched and convoluted, constructed of several distinct independent clauses brought together by dashes and semicolons:

> —Strange! quoth I, debating the matter with myself, That one and twenty miles sailing, for 'tis absolutely no further from Dover to Calais, should give a man these rights—I'll look into them: so giving up the argument—I went straight to my lodgings, put up half a dozen shirts and a black pair of silk breeches—"the coat I have on, said I, looking at the sleeve, will do"—took a place in the Dover stage; and the packet sailing at nine the next morning—by three I had got sat down to my dinner upon a fricassee'd chicken so incontestably in France, that had I died that night of an indigestion, the whole world could not have suspended the effects of the *Droits d'aubaine*—my shirts, and black pair of silk breeches—portmanteau and all must have gone to the King of France—even the little picture which I have so long worn, and so often have told thee, Eliza, I would carry with me into my grave, would have been torn from my neck. (*ASJ*, 3)

This long sentence acts as a bridge that directly connects Yorick's London lodgings to Calais and his room at the inn. In the main plot of Sterne's travel narrative, this textual metaphor can be interpreted as an image of the geographical proximity of England and France, while the reference to "the *Droits d'aubaine*" demonstrates that they are, nevertheless, two very different countries with completely different laws and customs. In the underplot, however, this phrase contains additional connotations. Here, the contents of Yorick's portmanteau are rhythmically listed twice: six shirts and "a black pair of silk breeches," to which is added, in the second listing, Eliza's portrait, which he wears around his neck. The sudden appearance of the portrait reveals it to be the most valuable of Yorick's possessions, since he would not expect to carry his six shirts and portmanteau to his grave.[14]

The way that Sterne introduces the name of Eliza into his text constitutes a specific literary technique, and most other direct references to her follow the same structural pattern. In most cases, the name appears—with seeming spontaneity—at the end of passages that are initially unrelated to her. With these references, as well as with other, less obvious allusions, Sterne shows Eliza that she is present in his mind while he is working on his book and that Yorick, his protagonist, remembers Eliza even when he is seemingly concerned with other matters. Of course, Sterne could have invented a fictional name for Yorick's Dulcinea or turned her into a purely literary abstraction (like Jenny in *Tristram Shandy*)—that way, he would not have had to constrain the expression of his feelings. Instead, Sterne implemented a different strategy. Eliza's presence, as structured by Sterne, is thus able to provide two distinct dimensions: she is the beautiful damsel addressed by Yorick the knight-errant, and she is also the author's secret interlocutor.

The name of Yorick itself and its role in Sterne's fiction and biography—however unsteady such borderlines are in the case of this writer—have been addressed by multiple critics. As is well known, Sterne had two fictional personas, Tristram Shandy and Mr. Yorick, each containing traits of authorial self-portraits. Sterne used both names in his correspondences and emphasized his analogy with Yorick by printing his *Sermons* under both names (Mr. Yorick and Laurence Sterne). As has been mentioned, Sterne used the name of Yorick to sign most of his letters to Eliza and called himself Yorick in the journal that he kept for her. As we do not know exactly when Sterne selected the name of his protagonist, it seems possible that his choice was related to the introduction of Eliza's name into his work.

The resonances between past and present writing, after all, pervade Sterne's output. An attentive reader of *Tristram Shandy* would notice that the contents of Yorick's portmanteau are listed in a similar way to the contents of the cloak bag belonging to Diego, the protagonist of "Slawkenbergius's Tale," whose unnaturally long nose becomes an obsession among the citizens of Strasbourg. Significantly, the list of Diego's belongings is mentioned repeatedly throughout the tale as he comically unpacks and repacks his cloak bag and laments the burden his mule must bear, observing, "there's nothing in my cloak-bag but two shirts—a crimson-sattin pair of breeches, and a fringed—Dear Julia!" (*TS*, 300). As with so many of Sterne's aposiopeses, the list's conclusion must be reached in the imagination, although it inevitably returns to the "breeches" and "fringed cod-piece" Diego had worn earlier. The Florida editors point to this textual parallel in their notes (*ASJ*, 230–231n3.10–11), although not to the latent relationship between these two texts that continues throughout *A Sentimental Journey*; the "inventory" (*ASJ*, 44) of Yorick's portmanteau, after all, resurfaces several times, the "breeches" making their most notable reappearance in the inn on the road to Lyon at the end of the second volume (*ASJ*, 163).[15] What is the function of this parallel? The Florida editors observe how Diego is also "a most sentimental traveler" (*ASJ*, 231); but, while he eventually reunites with his Julia, the narrator hints that the "Intricacies" of their union do not bring the couple the desired happiness (*TS*, 4.1.326). In the context of Yorick's meditations in *Bramine's Journal*, it may suggest an undertone of the author's self-irony and an allusion to his quixotic quest for happiness with Eliza.

Thus, even in the first chapter of *A Sentimental Journey*, we see an interplay of two layers: the reality of Yorick, the sentimental traveler, and the reality of the author, which is realized by Sterne dropping into his fictional work the real name of his love interest, alongside the introduction of an intertextual allusion—a recollection of the unsentimental conclusion to Diego's amours, adding a note of sad irony that is most fully grasped by those who are able to bring both *Tristram Shandy* and *Bramine's Journal* to the opening of *A Sentimental Journey*.

UNCOVERING THE UNDERPLOT

Addressing Eliza and mentioning her portrait in the introductory chapter does not prevent Yorick from expressing interest in the Flemish lady whom he meets at Calais. Various critics have compared her with Eliza (*ASJ*, 256n23.10). Indeed, Yorick describes the lady's features in a manner similar to how Sterne praises Eliza in his letters: "You are not handsome, Eliza, nor is yours a face that will please the tenth part of your beholders,—but are something more; for I scruple not to tell you, I never saw so intelligent, so animated, so good a countenance" (*Letters*, 553). As he describes the Lady, "—it was a face of about six and twenty—of a clear transparent brown, simply set off without rouge or powder—it was not critically handsome, but there was that in it, which in the frame of mind I was in, which attached me much more to it—it was interesting" (*ASJ*, 23). Although some of her features are indeed similar to Eliza's, she is not Eliza's double. As will later become apparent, subject to the changeable "ebb and flow" of feeling, Yorick is interested in the Flemish lady up until the moment he faces a choice between her and Eliza.

As for the author, his dialogue with Eliza is covertly present in the underplot of almost every episode of the Calais section. When Yorick encounters the Franciscan monk, for instance, he notes that his head "would have suited a Bramin." If this reference is just the author's covert greeting to his Bramine (*ASJ*, 8), the following biography of the monk, who turns out to be the author's namesake, may contain hidden hints at Sterne's melancholic account of his own circumstances: Lorenzo's life changed following "a disappointment in the tenderest of passions" after which he took sanctuary, "not so much in his convent as in himself" (*ASJ*, 27). Perhaps Sterne was convinced that his perceptive friend would easily guess at these hints, hidden from the general reader. The manuscript version of the flash-forward to Yorick visiting Lorenzo's grave originally contained the following line, which is absent in the published version: "I wept over him, as a widow" (*ASJ*, 478). The word "widow" is present in Sterne's correspondence with Eliza in some of his more bittersweet jokes—he could never forget about the age gap between them; Yorick also projected this quality onto Madame de L*** (the Flemish lady), persuading himself that she too is, probably, a widow. In the only known letter to Eliza signed "Tristram," Sterne addresses the subject in a typically Shandean fashion: "Talking of widows—pray, Eliza, if ever you are such, do not think of giving yourself to some wealthy nabob, because I design to marry you myself— . . . —'Tis true, I am ninety five in constitution, and you but twenty-five; . . . but what I want in youth, I will make up in wit and good humour—" (*Letters*, 565). The Calais section, written in the period when he was still hoping that Eliza would eventually return to him, is therefore particularly dense with covert addresses to her, which would be perceived very differently by the general reader.

An echo of Eliza's absent presence can also be heard in the celebrated preface in the *desobligeant*. That vehicle's design for a single traveler and its name alike represent Yorick's solitude and internal discomfort: by closing the door and drawing the curtains, he isolates himself in an uncomfortable and confined space. This chapter ends with a bawdy innuendo, as Yorick is suddenly interrupted by two Englishmen who express their surprise at the *desobligeant*'s vibrating motions: "—We are only looking at this chaise, said they—Your most obedient servant, said I, skipping out of it, and pulling off my hat—We were wondering, said one of them, who, I found, was an *inquisitive traveller*—what could occasion its motion.—'Twas the agitation, said I coolly, of writing a preface—I never heard, said the other, who was a *simple traveller*, of a preface wrote in a *Desobligeant.*—It would have been better, said I, in a *Vis a Vis*" (*ASJ*, 17). In this period, *vis-à-vis* chaises were often the subject of erotic jokes and double entendres. However, in light of Sterne's hidden conversation with Eliza, the obvious erotic reference of the episode gains an additional level of meaning. In his *Letters* and in *Bramine's Journal*, Sterne, who always had Eliza's portrait in front of him on his desk, repeats multiple times that his writing would improve greatly if he had a real Eliza before him. If we consider how the space is organized in a *vis-à-vis* (with the passengers facing each other), the erotic joke can be read as a metaphor for Sterne's longing for Eliza. As he notes in *Bramine's Journal*, "I want You to be on the other side of my little table, to hear how sweetly y[r] Voice will be in Unison to all this—I want to hear what You have to say to Yorick upon this Text" (*BJ*, 212).

CORRESPONDENCES

The outlook of the early sections of *A Sentimental Journey* is relatively optimistic. Although Yorick the knight-errant is missing his lady, he still hopes he can be reunited with her. His peak optimism occurs in the episode in Amiens, which describes Yorick's inability to respond to the letter of the Flemish lady, who demonstrates her receptiveness to his courtship in Calais with an invitation to visit her in Brussels. He first exults, saying he would be happy to make this detour in order to hear her sad story and wipe her tears: "'twill scarce be ten posts out of my way; but were it ten thousand!" (*ASJ*, 57). However, almost immediately afterward, Yorick reproaches himself, informing readers that, three months earlier, he had lit up his "flame" at the "pure taper of Eliza": "swearing as I did it, that it should last me through the whole journey" (*ASJ*, 58). As soon as Eliza is mentioned, this being the second direct reference to her in the book, Yorick not only decides not to go to Brussels but abandons his pursuit of the Flemish lady entirely, a change that has a direct impact on the development of the plot; thus, in the next episode, Yorick is unable to come up with a polite response to her letter: "In short, I was in no mood to write" (*ASJ*, 61). In the manuscript of *A Sentimental Journey*, this fragment reads, "In short, I was in no mood to write, except to Eliza—" (*ASJ*, 585). Sterne had crossed out this phrase in the manuscript, perhaps deciding to bury the direct motivation of the episode (being unable to write to women other than Eliza), but only partially hiding the motive in the underplot (addressing Eliza as a faithful lover). The subsequent scene transposes the episode into a comic register: La Fleur gives Yorick a template, a love letter written by a drummer to a corporal's wife. Yorick, who at this point is seemingly more concerned about the risk of displeasing his servant than the Flemish lady herself, takes "the cream gently off," whips it up in his own way, and sends La Fleur to deliver it (*ASJ*, 64). After this episode, Madame de L***, the Flemish lady, disappears from the plot and is only mentioned because of the letter of recommendation to her Parisian friend Madame de R*** that she gives to Yorick.

Madeleine Descargues, in her analysis of this episode, argues that Sterne, on a metafictional level, demonstrates to the reader a writer's challenges in overcoming his unwillingness to write.[16] This observation resonates with the previously cited *Journal* entries where Sterne describes his difficulties in starting to write *A Sentimental Journey*. Moreover, in the underplot, this scene possibly contains another biographical aspect: Cash indicates that in June 1767 Sterne received a letter from his wife and daughter, informing him of their intention to return to England. Sterne—allegedly—responded to them but later claimed that his letter went astray. In the *Journal*, as well as in his correspondence, he alludes to the disappearance of this letter. At the same time, according to Cash, even after he found out about this incident, he did not take any further action for seven weeks (*LY*, 305). Only on August 24, 1767, in a response to his daughter, who expressed bewilderment at not hearing from him, did Sterne apologize, assuring Lydia that he was not responsible for the loss of the letter (*Letters*, 612). Cash expresses doubts as to whether it was ever sent: "Something in him did not want to welcome them" (*LY*, 306). Indeed, considering Sterne's state of mind as it is presented in the *Journal*, it is feasible to make an assumption that it was unbearably difficult for him to write a polite response to his wife, though other explanations are of course possible. However, other correspondences with Sterne's *Journal* and his letters of that period reinforce this idea.

By the time Sterne replied to Lydia, his hopes for future happiness with Eliza were dashed, and he rarely kept his *Journal* after that point; however, he had previously written in its pages that his wife's visit was motivated mainly by vested interests and that she was going to take with her all the valuables in the house except for Eliza's portrait. On June 2, Sterne wrote, "I shall be pillaged in a hundred small Item's by them—wch I have a Spirit above saying, *no*-to; as Provisions of all sorts of Linnens—for house use—Body Use—printed Linnens for Gowns—Magazeens of Teas—Plate, all I have (but 6 Silver Spoons)—In short I shall be pluck'd bare—all but of y^{r} Portrait & Snuff Box & y^{r} other dear Presents" (*BJ*, 193–194). Perhaps it was this remark in the *Journal* that suggested to Sterne the thought of the "*Droits d'aubaine*" and the image of the French king, who would certainly tear the portrait of Yorick's beloved from his neck. The same thought is repeated in Sterne's letter to Anne James of August 10: "She [Elizabeth Sterne] takes back sixteen hundred p^{ds} into france–with her—and will do me the honour, likewise to strip me of every thing I have—/—except Eliza's Picture" (*Letters*, 607).

Given these circumstances, Yorick's "intricacies" with the letter to the Flemish lady may provide an interesting key for better understanding the internal connections between the first and second volumes of *A Sentimental Journey*, namely, a second incident in which Yorick avoids writing another polite letter, this time to Madame de R***, Madame de L***'s friend. In this scene, the *fille de chambre* of Madame de R*** comes to Yorick's hotel and insists that he should write a letter to her mistress, while Yorick claims he has no paper to carry out this task. The fair *fille de chambre*, however, seems unwilling to leave his room and continues to insist that he should write this letter "upon anything" (*ASJ*, 122). What follows remains a secret, but in the context of the underplot, this time Yorick is clearly a victor, in that the *fille de chambre*, unlike La Fleur in the first volume, leaves the hotel without a letter to her mistress.

In the Paris section of *A Sentimental Journey*, Yorick's hidden conversations with Eliza become less frequent, and their tone changes. After parting with the *fille de chambre*, our protagonist spends a sleepless night thinking exclusively, and perhaps surprisingly so, about the clever beggar whom he spotted on his return to the hotel, bemused by his persuasive solicitation of women's charity (*ASJ*, 125–126). The motif of India reappears: "a secret, I thought, which so soon and so certainly soften'd the heart of every woman you came near, was a secret at least equal to the philosopher's stone; had I both the Indies, I would have given up one to have been master of it" (*ASJ*, 130). It is interesting to note that the beggar's secret engages Yorick, despite the fact that he has repeatedly demonstrated to the reader his own self-described ability to engage (if not seduce) women. In Calais, for example, he demonstrated his skills by holding the Flemish lady's hand in what might be considered a textbook account of the approach/avoid technique of all intrapersonal relations (*ASJ*, 24–28).[17] Why, then, is Yorick ready to give one of his Indies (if he had any) to learn how to influence women's hearts? As early as June 13, Sterne made the following entry in his *Journal*: "I have had a present, Eliza! this year, of a Heart so finely set—with such rich materials—& Workmanship—That Nature must have had the chief hand in it—If I am able to keep it—I shall be a rich Man;—If I lose it—I shall be poor indeed—so poor! I shall stand begging at y^{r} gates" (*BJ*, 201). Yorick's insomnia and the mention of two Indies can be interpreted not as another covert salutation to Eliza but as a response to his growing awareness that his dream of Eliza's return to him was, indeed, a form of self-deception. As we know from the later development of the plot, the explanation of the beggar's secret (which turns out to be base flattery) helps Yorick ascend to the top of Parisian society.

However, before Yorick is accepted into Paris's high society, he has to face difficulties due to his lack of a passport. Often overlooked, this episode from the first half of the second volume contains the third direct reference to Eliza in *A Sentimental Journey*. As soon as Yorick interiorizes the risk of being arrested and sent to prison, his nonchalance gives way to anxiety. Hoping for an audience with the Duc de C***** in Versailles, Yorick realizes that he will never achieve anything in such an emotional state. Before he enters the duke's salon, Yorick finally manages to come to terms with himself: "I neither ascended the steps like a victim to justice, who was to part with life upon the topmost,—nor did I mount them with a skip and a couple of strides, as I do when I fly up, Eliza! to thee, to meet it" (*ASJ*, 102). The technique used in the first chapter reappears, with Eliza capping the end of the sentence. Yorick recalls how, when they were together, he ran up the stairs to regain life in her company, and here it may seem as though Yorick's feeling for Eliza is elevated to the extreme. The context of the phrase, however, suggests a different metaphorical reading: a hope for reciprocal feeling when a person surrenders to his feeling and opens his heart too trustingly is as ungrounded as the hope for mercy experienced by someone who is sentenced to death. Yorick therefore manages to regain self-control and takes on the mask of the charming and witty interlocutor and eventually achieves the result he sought for: he receives the passport.

Thus, in the second volume, the underplot of *A Sentimental Journey* attains a new quality. Up to a certain point, when Sterne was still making records in *Bramine's Journal* simultaneously with his work on *A Sentimental Journey*, he used the underplot as a means of direct communication with Eliza. It was the need to maintain this hidden dialogue that led to the creation of the unusual form of his literary work. After Sterne realized that Eliza was not going to return and stopped making entries in his *Journal*, the underplot acquired the features of covert records of the author's reflections on his emotional experiences. Therefore, while, in the first volume, Yorick hopes to be reunited with Eliza, and this expectation is reflected in the overt plot of his *Journey* (Yorick refuses to accept Madame de L***'s invitation to Brussels, "unless Eliza went along" with him [*ASJ*, 58]), this theme is absent in the later sections of the *Journey*.

Although Yorick continues to mention Eliza as his beloved and writes letters to her and to Eugenius, the general mood is different: Yorick begins to doubt if he knows how women's hearts work, whereas his interest in women of his social circle seems to vanish. Under various pretexts, he avoids meeting with Madame de R***, making the *fille de chambre* forget about the letter that she had asked him to write to her mistress. After entering the salons of Parisian nobility, Yorick does not seem to express much interest in the aristocrats who surround him and so greatly enjoy his company.

Sterne's gift for sociability, which was universally renowned and brought him great success in both London and Paris, is also inherent in Yorick. However, after being adopted by the best houses of the aristocracy, Yorick suddenly "grows sick" of socializing and its "*beggarly system*" of self-promotion (*ASJ*, 148) and sets out to continue his journey. Although Yorick's road leads him further, the form of Sterne's fiction suggests that the story of Yorick's journey "in pursuit of Nature, and those affections which rise out of her" (*ASJ*, 111) is rapidly nearing its end. Thus, the entire narrative of the protagonist's brilliant victories in various salons is compressed into one short chapter. In the chapter that follows, the reader is informed that only a "few small pages" are left in the book to fit in the rest of his journey across France.

MIRRORS AND REFLECTIONS

The final reference to Eliza is found in the celebrated scene with Maria of Moulins, which refers to a similar episode in *Tristram Shandy*. Melvyn New points to the fact that Maria's and Yorick's movements reflect each other; when Yorick weeps with Maria in those "mirrored, balanced actions, . . . he discovers in a convincing manner the strongest sense of identity, not simply with Maria, but with himself."[18] Here, I would add, Maria becomes a mirror in which Yorick sees a reflection of his own broken heart: "could the traces [of her lover] be ever worn out of her brain, and those of Eliza's out of mine, she should *not only eat of my bread and drink of my own cup*, but Maria should lay in my bosom, and be unto me as a daughter" (*ASJ*, 154). Yorick equates himself with Maria, seeing both of them as abandoned lovers and, thus, he indirectly informs the reader about his own failure in the "tenderest of passions." The journey could have been continued, but the underplot comes to its conclusion.

After leaving Maria, Yorick addresses "Dear sensibility!" and the "great—great Sensorium of the world" and feels "some generous joys and generous cares" beyond himself (*ASJ*, 155). His apostrophe serves as the emotional peak of his journey across France and concludes many of the work's leitmotifs. In this invocation, Yorick once again mentions his friend Eugenius, returning to a scene of friendship in *Tristram Shandy*, and once again he makes Eugenius his bedside comforter. It would be possible to imagine Eliza in his place, but her name is noticeably absent in this passage: "Touch'd with thee [sensibility], Eugenius draws my curtain when I languish—hears my tale of symptoms, and blames the weather for the disorder of his nerves" (*ASJ*, 155). This is followed by the scene of rural dance. Whereas in the seventh volume of *Tristram Shandy* the protagonist "dances it away" through the south of France (*TS*, 7.43.651), the Yorick of *A Sentimental Journey* acts as a passive observer, seated between the elderly couple; the theme of age is again at play. While in the overt plot this scene may appear full of optimism, comparing this episode with Sterne's dream of the "golden Age" of his reunion with Eliza, when she will "govern the rural feast" and will be the "Mistress" of Yorick's table (*BJ*, 211–212), reinforces Yorick's increasing loneliness not just in this chapter but throughout the final part of the book.

A Sentimental Journey begins in daylight and ends in the dark of night, in an uncomfortable inn in Savoy where Yorick reluctantly shares a bedroom with another traveler, a Piedmontese lady who, like Yorick, is trying to escape the cold and severe weather. The motifs from the book's central scenes are repeated, creating an underlying effect of what Hegel termed "bad" or "spurious" infinity: the indeterminate and formless infinity that is nothing but the possibility of always adding one more.[19] While the presence of the lady's *fille de chambre* alludes to the Parisian sequence, the encounter with her mistress parallels the Calais section where Yorick meets the Flemish lady. Yorick admires the features of the Piedmontese lady, but it seems that this time he is not inclined to engage the lady in conversation. He claims that it is only thanks to the wine that they managed to break the awkward silence: "had we not had more generous wine to it than a little inn in Savoy could have furnish'd, our tongues had been tied up, till necessity herself had set them at liberty" (*ASJ*, 162).

The contents of Yorick's portmanteau are mentioned again—invoking once more "Slawkenbergius's Tale," with its suggestions of romance about a knight-errant separated from his damsel. This time the items in Yorick's luggage are listed during the composition of the "nonaggression pact" that is drawn between Yorick and the lady. Thus, the lady demands that he sleeps in his "robe de chambre," a request he must reject because he "has nothing in his portmanteau but six shirts and a black silk pair of breeches" (*ASJ*, 163). The function of this treaty is mutually to isolate the man and the woman who find themselves in an embarrassing situation. The "ejaculation" (*ASJ*, 164) with which Yorick breaks this treaty is the exclamation of a "way-worn traveller" (*ASJ*, 160) exhausted by insomnia, an uncomfortable bed, and the awkwardness of the situation.

What if the unintended "encounter" that follows Yorick's final gesture is only parodying frivolity, and, just as in the case of La Fleur's letter template in Volume 1, the mechanical comedy of the chapter is used to conceal the underlying sense of emptiness and discomfort? In this light, the ambiguous ending of the novel can be interpreted as simultaneously melancholic and optimistic. The reader—even if aware of the circumstances in which *A Sentimental Journey* was written, including the death of the author that followed soon afterward—will close the book with a smile.

In this chapter, I have suggested that *A Sentimental Journey* contains an underplot that is directly connected to the events of Sterne's life as they emerge from Sterne's *Journal* and letters. The text is constructed in such a way that, apart from addressing the general reader,[20] it contains hidden messages addressed to another implied reader: Eliza Draper. Moreover, if in the earlier sections of the novel, written in parallel with *Bramine's Journal*, such hidden salutations are quite frequent, in the later parts of the book the author no longer seems to be hailing his lover but rather reflecting on his failure as well as her unwillingness to be returned to him. Thus, the underplot of this *Journey* can be read as metaphorically reflecting the author's hopes, fears, doubts, and disappointments, as well his struggle against the blows of fate, which he opposed with his literary craft.

NOTES

I would like to thank M-C. Newbould, Melvyn New, W. B. Gerard, and Thomas Keymer for their invaluable feedback on this chapter at various stages. I am also grateful to Peter Buchanan, Madeleine Chalmers, Elizabeth Ramsey, and Pany Xenophontos for their support and assistance.

1. This use of the word is suggested by Sterne himself: "How my uncle *Toby* and Corporal *Trim* managed this matter,—with the history of their campaigns, which were no way barren of events,—may make no uninteresting under-plot in the epitasis and working up of this drama" (*TS*, 2.5.113–114).
2. See James Chandler, "The Novelty of Laurence Sterne," in *The Oxford History of the Novel in English*, vol. 2, *English and British Fiction, 1750–1820*, ed. Peter Garside and Karen O'Brien (Oxford: Oxford University Press, 2015), 112.
3. Catherine Emmott and Marc Alexander, "Foregrounding, Burying and Plot Construction," in *The Cambridge Handbook of Stylistics*, ed. Peter Stockwell and Sara Whiteley (Cambridge: Cambridge University Press, 2014), 329–343.
4. See also the introduction to the Florida edition (*ASJ*, xi–lxxii) and Ian Campbell Ross's interpretation of this episode in *Laurence Sterne: A Life* (Oxford: Oxford University Press, 2001), 360–403. The only book-length biography of Eliza is Arnold Wright and William Lutley Sclater's *Sterne's Eliza: Some Account of Her Life in India: With Her Letters Written between 1757 and 1774* (London: W. Heinemann, 1922). Another useful source is L. P. Curtis's edition of Sterne's correspondence in which the entries of the *Bramine's Journal* are interspersed between Sterne's letters. It is important to keep in mind that some of Curtis's attempts at dating the entries were later corrected by Cash and the Florida editors.
5. Jakub Lipski writes, "The characters of the sentimental Mr. Yorick and the bawdy Tristram Shandy were the two literary masks Sterne would alternatively wear not only on social occasions but also in his literary endeavors (depending on his mood and circumstances)." Lipski, "'Too much for Nature': Laurence Sterne's *Continuation of the Bramine's Journal* and the Language of Theatre," *New Review: An International Journal of British Studies* 5 (2015): 54.

6. It is important to remember that Cash's view of *BJ* evolved throughout his career as a Sterne scholar. His 1966 *Sterne's Comedy of Moral Sentiments: The Ethical Dimension of the Journey* (Pittsburgh: Duquesne University Press, 1966) argued for the literariness and calculated nature of the *Journal*, but Cash modified this view in the course of writing his biography; he alludes to this change in *LY*, 285. See also *BJ*, xxi–xxvii.
7. See, for example, Serge Soupel, "*The Journal to Eliza* (13 Avril–1er Novembre 1767) de Sterne: Mémoire et imagination," *XVII–XVIII: Revue de la Société d'études anglo-americaines des XVIIe et XVIIIe siècles* 26, no. 1 (1988): 25–35; Elizabeth K. Goodhue, "When Yorick Takes His Tea: Or, the Commerce of Consumptive Passions in the Case of Laurence Sterne," *Journal for Early Modern Cultural Studies* 6, no. 1 (2006): 51–83; and Geoff Newton, "Divine and Human Love: Letters between John Norris and Mary Astell, Laurence Sterne and Eliza Draper," in *Theology and Literature in the Age of Johnson: Resisting Secularism*, ed. Melvyn New and Gerard Reedy S.J. (Newark: University of Delaware Press, 2012), 183–202. A useful overview of different approaches can be found in Eva C. van Leewen's *Sterne's "Journal to Eliza"; A Semiological and Linguistic Approach to the Text* (Tübingen: G. Narr, 1981), 45–67.
8. Ross, *Laurence Sterne*, 396. Throughout the *Journal*, Sterne alludes to the novelty of his feelings for Eliza, claiming that he has never felt this way about any other woman. Regardless of whether such statements were a form of self-deception, it is interesting to compare Sterne's letters to Eliza with his much cheekier letters to Catherine Fourmantel in 1760 (*Letters*, 100–147).
9. Melvyn New, "Job's Wife and Sterne's Other Women," in *Laurence Sterne*, ed. Marcus Walsh (London: Routledge, 2002), 78. As Cash puts it: "Eliza, in all probability, was less in love with Sterne than he with her, and she may not have been fully aware of his desires" (*LY*, 279).
10. Indeed, "ebbs and flows" appears three times in *A Sentimental Journey* and can serve as a useful metaphor for the narrator's constantly fluctuating emotional state.
11. Virginia Woolf, "Eliza and Sterne," *Times Literary Supplement*, December 14, 1922, 839.
12. This can be said of several episodes in *TS*. This device is also found in *ASJ*, for instance, at the beginning of "The Dead Ass." With regard to *Tristram Shandy*, George P. Landow describes the device as follows: "With everything shown as becoming, as in process, the novel groups into scenes which are shown with little explanation, the significance becoming apparent from the context. This occurs in the Phutatorius episode, where 'Zounds!' first is heard, and then the explanation follows, tracing what has happened by making it happen again, this time from an accessible point of view. Once again, context furnishes meaning." Landow, "*Tristram Shandy* and the Comedy of Context," *BYU Studies Quarterly* 7, no. 3 (1966): 222.
13. Michael Seidel, "Narrative Crossings: Sterne's *A Sentimental Journey*," *Genre* 18 (1985): 2.
14. Sterne constantly refers to Eliza's portrait in his journal and letters to Eliza. See Harriet Guest, "Sterne, Elizabeth Draper, and Drapery," *Shandean* 9 (1997): 8–33.
15. Another echo of Slawkenbergius's Tale can be found in the "Fragment" episode in the first volume of *ASJ*, a parallel between the citizens of Strasbourg, who become obsessed with the stranger's nose, and the inhabitants of the ancient town of Abdera, whose morals were changed by the theatrical performance of a play by Euripides.
16. Madeleine Descargues, "Fonctions d'un lettre d'amour, de la correspondance de Sterne à *A Sentimental Journey*," *XVII–XVIII: Revue de la Société d'études anglo-américaines des XVIIe et XVIIIe siècles* 31, no. 1 (1990): 143–157.
17. See the fine essay by Ray McDermott, "Yorick's Ethnographic Journey," in *Sterne, Tristram, Yorick: Tercentenary Essays on Laurence Sterne*, ed. Melvyn New, Peter de Voogd, and Judith Hawley (Newark: University of Delaware Press, 2016), 169–186.

18. Melvyn New, "Proust's Influence on Sterne: Remembrance of Things to Come," *Modern Language Notes* 103, no. 4 (1988): 1049.
19. Robert Urquhart, "Accumulation as Eternal Recurrence: Theology of the Bad Infinity," *International Review of Economics* 63, no. 1 (2016): 13; and G.W.F. Hegel, *Hegel's Logic: Being Part One of The Encyclopaedia of the Philosophical Sciences (1830)*, trans. William Wallace (Oxford: Clarendon, 1975), 137–138.
20. Thomas Keymer suggests that Sterne's view of the *Journey* as "likely to take in all Kinds of readers" does not suggest a hoax but rather a "catering or providing for all in an open or ambiguous text." Keymer, "*A Sentimental Journey* and the Failure of Feeling," in *The Cambridge Companion to Laurence Sterne*, ed. Thomas Keymer (Cambridge: Cambridge University Press, 2009), 89.

10

DEBT, DEATH, AND LITERARY INHERITANCE

The Ends of Sterne and *A Sentimental Journey*

PAUL GORING

"WHAT A JOVIAL AND A MERRY WORLD would this be, may it please your worships, but for that inextricable labyrinth of debts, cares, woes, want, grief, discontent, melancholy, large jointures, impositions, and lies!" (*TS*, 6.14.520). Thus Tristram, with his characteristic energy and underlying joie de vivre, bemoans the pitiful situation of the modern subject. He catalogues ten causes of misery—some timeless, others consequences of the burgeoning capitalism of his era—and a treatise could probably be written about the wider significance of each of them within Sterne's writing. This chapter is concerned with the thorn in the flesh to which Tristram gives pride of place: debt. It will attempt to chart some of the different types of debt to which Sterne's narrators give attention—monetary debts, emotional debts, narrative debts, "book-debts," and more—and it will consider how ideas of indebtedness in the fiction intersect with Sterne's long-recognized interest in death and its transcendence.

It is well known that the age of Sterne was an age of unprecedented debt, both for the British nation and for many who were a part of it. As economic historians have shown, from the 1680s the economy underwent what may fairly be deemed a financial revolution, and an increasing use of credit was a key part of it. The "extent and forms [of credit use] multiplied considerably" between 1680 and 1790, Julian Hoppit has written, and this occurred at all levels: "public, corporate and private."[1] The sovereign debt, as John Brewer demonstrated in his classic study of England as a "fiscal-military state," grew markedly with every international conflict (not least, in Sterne's time, the Seven Years' War), and the deficit financing of the nation's wars and imperial ambitions would come to touch the entire population through the numerous taxes that had to be introduced to keep up with repayments to creditors.[2] The "sinews of power," to use Brewer's phrase, enmeshed debt within a truly "inextricable labyrinth," to repeat Sterne's phrase, and historians are still facing the challenges of unpicking the complexities of how the market in debt functioned and was administered. The growth of the Bank of England—it had swollen to become "the world's largest white collar employer at the start of the nineteenth century"—is just one sign of how deeply ingrained in the workings of the nation debt and debt administration had become.[3]

Meanwhile, the debtors' prisons were doing brisk trade. There was nothing new about such prisons—they had been around since the thirteenth century—but a rising culture of payment through credit produced a consequent growth in failures to meet repayments, and the use of debtors' prisons became institutionalized as a means by which creditors would get back, or at least attempt to get back, what they were owed.[4] Depicted vividly by William Hogarth in the seventh plate of *The Rake's Progress* (1735), debtors' prisons cast their shadows across Britain and British culture long before Charles Dickens produced literary history's most extended exploration of incarceration for debt in *Little Dorrit* (1855–1857). Daniel Defoe was locked up in debtors' prison during his turbulent business career—it was an experience that doubtless informed his extensive writing about credit and debt in *Roxana* (1724), in *The Complete English Tradesman* (1725), and in his journalism. There were other notable figures who served time as a consequence of credit culture's precariousness, among them John Cleland, who famously wrote his pornographic *Memoirs of a Woman of Pleasure* (1748) while serving a spell in Fleet Prison.

Laurence Sterne was never so unlucky. Furthermore, unlike Defoe and Dickens, it cannot be said that Sterne gave *extended* attention to debt and its consequences in his writing. But there is nonetheless an ongoing concern with debt in his fiction that has tended to be passed over by critics, despite long-standing interest in the literary debts that underpin Sterne's writing and in the idea of "commerce" as a way of perceiving social interaction, particularly in *A Sentimental Journey*.[5]

What is it that brings about Yorick's death? It is actually debt, yet this is rarely noted, probably because the reason for Yorick's death, explained in Scriblerian fashion at the beginning of chapter 12 of *Tristram Shandy*'s first volume, has been overshadowed (almost literally) by the end of that chapter, where we find the endlessly referenced black page: proto-modernist typographical play has trumped *après-garde* satire, and debt has been eclipsed in the process. Another question: What was the final expression from Sterne to be printed in his lifetime? Something about catching hold of part of a *fille de chambre*? No, it was actually the declaration of a debt, but again this is rarely noted. These moments in Sterne's writing will be considered at greater length later; his last published gasps in *A Sentimental Journey* are, in fact, the final destination of the discussion, but the journey there will involve reaching into Sterne's writing from the first installment of *Tristram Shandy* in 1759 to *A Sentimental Journey*'s publication in 1768. In fact, since *A Sen-*

timental Journey in some ways both begins and ends in *Tristram Shandy*—with the introduction of Yorick and the narration of his death—the eleven volumes of fiction will be treated here more as an organic whole than as two discrete works. Two broad observations will govern the discussion: Firstly, Sterne's interest in debt stretches far beyond its financial forms, and we see different types of debt mingling with one another in his writing; his fiction, in fact, substantiates Margaret Atwood's idea of debt, formulated in *Payback: Debt and the Shadow Side of Wealth*, as "that peculiar nexus where money, narrative or story, and religious belief intersect."[6] Secondly, the fiction discloses a particular interest in the ways in which the idea of debt can structure interpersonal relations that are more than fleeting and play out over time.

Debt (from the Latin *debere*: to owe) creates a relationship: it involves a lender and a borrower, and it defines the connection between them. A debt relation is one of imbalance, and it endures until the debt is waived or repaid, as acknowledged by both parties. There are some similarities to ritual gift exchange within debt relations, but giving, where reciprocation is ultimately voluntary, does not carry expectation of return as strictly as lending does: obligation carries more weight than gratitude, requiring action to be discharged. The terms of a debt relation may be formalized, as with a mortgage, and particularly where money is concerned may be calculated to the final groat. Other forms of debt, however, such as obligations that are felt in response to a service or favor, are much less precise with regard to the nature of both relationship and repayment. Indeed, there is a fluidity within the nature of debt that may create obligation without any conscious action by the lender; a feeling of being in debt, particularly in a mediated relationship, may arise distinct from the source of what has been borrowed. In this way, a debt can pass through the barrier of death, either from the living to the dead or from the dead to the living. Like a fortune, debt may be inherited from the dead, and the living, as the philosopher Bob Brecher has argued, may feel obliged to the dead and indeed may develop new debts to those who have long been dead.[7] In the literary world, this is seen in the idea of literary influence, as in Harold Bloom's notion of the "anxiety of influence," whereby living authors may accrue literary debts to their forebears and be weighed down by them.[8]

Sterne's works display an ongoing interest in debt relations among the living, as, for example, when Yorick, in a scene of flirtation, tells the *grisset* in Paris how much he is "obliged to her" (*ASJ*, 70)—a moment suggesting that there can be pleasure as well as pain in the business of debt. But while Sterne attended to the diverse debts of the living, he was also interested in the ways in which debt may cross the divide of death. He preached a religion that taught a sense of indebtedness to Christ, while as an author he was keenly aware of what he was inheriting, together with feelings of obligation, from literary history—from Rabelais, Cervantes, Shakespeare, Pope, Swift, and many others.

"Neither a borrower nor a lender be"—so insists the officious Polonius in a speech mentioned explicitly among *A Sentimental Journey*'s several references to *Hamlet* (*ASJ*, 87).[9] Sterne, we know, did not follow the warning. As a writer he was an extraordinarily keen borrower; indeed few writers of fiction have plundered their bookshelves more avidly than Sterne. He probably had his own habits of composition in mind when he has Tristram express his lament that modern authors are merely like apothecaries making "new mixtures, by pouring only out of one vessel into another" (*TS*, 5.1.408), a sentence appropriately enough lifted from Robert Burton's *Anatomy of Melancholy*, and it is such open pointers to the derivative nature of his writing that make Sterne appear more a borrower than a thief. He did not declare all his sources, but he acknowledged his fundamental status as a literary debtor, presenting indebtedness as a condition of authorship. Of course, this aspect of Sterne's relationship to debt has been much studied, his numerous borrowings having provided fodder for scholarly sleuths ever since John Ferriar's *Illustrations of Sterne* (1798) set in motion the enterprise of Shandean source detection. The title of a 1928 essay by Edward Bensly—"A Debt of Sterne's"—would accurately fit many dozens of scholarly studies, while the copious notes to the Florida edition of Sterne's works convey the extent of his reach as he gathered material for absorption within his own writing.[10]

Sterne sought, though, to be on the lending as well as the borrowing side of the literary debt relation—to attain literary longevity by becoming a writer whose works would keep on offering something to those who came after him. "Quand Je serai mort," he wrote to Elizabeth Montagu in one of his last letters, "on mettra mon nom dans le liste de ces Heros, qui sont Morts en plaisantant"—his name, he suggests, will endure after his death in a list of jesting heroes (*Letters*, 658). This desire for a form of immortality (an "anxiety to influence" perhaps) is a recognized aspect of Sterne's character as a writer, addressed notably by William V. Holtz, who examined the complex outpourings of Sterne's visual imagination to argue that Sterne was swayed by a strong sense of posthumous selfhood.[11] More recently, Emily Hodgson Anderson has argued convincingly that Sterne's attention to *Hamlet* in his fiction was part of a project of personal "memorialization," while Celia Barnes has suggested that Sterne nourished his backward gaze to his literary predecessors (notably Pope) while marking out a place for himself within the future through his erotic correspondence with women so as "to guarantee himself a place in literary history . . . [and] to ensure his name will survive."[12] This chapter will also be considering Sterne's attention to his posthumous status, augmenting the arguments of Holtz, Anderson, and Barnes by suggesting that an idea of debt, involving the building up of an inexhaustible stock of literary capital that could be lent freely from the grave, was part of Sterne's conception of literary history and of his attempt to insert himself within it. From the dead Shakespeare, Sterne borrowed Yorick. Identifying with this escapee from the grave, Sterne sought to make his own successors his debtors, casting himself as a fellow who could lend infinite jest to the reading and writing public, not only of his present but also of the future. This authorial hope for futurity is reflected, it will be argued, in his ongoing concern throughout his fiction with the intricacies of being and feeling obliged.

A "CURSED THING": MONETARY DEBT

The first associations of debt are typically monetary, and it is worth considering, before we turn to Sterne's fiction and to wider notions of obligation, that while Sterne can never be placed in the pantheon of author-debtors alongside Defoe, Cleland, and others, his circumstances and desires in life were such that he was no stranger to pecuniary borrowing and the perils of debt. In his pre-fame years he was willing to take on debt to improve his situation, as when he and his wife borrowed money to buy Tindal Farm in 1744 (*EMY,* 146). Some years later his mother, who had long suffered poverty, was imprisoned in York, probably for debt, although there is some uncertainty around this (*EMY,* 236–238). In the 1760s, when his clerical income was supplemented with proceeds from his writing, he was no longer poor, but he was by no means as rich as those with whom he now wanted to keep company, and in this "middle state," aggravated by his foreign travel, he would sometimes touch others for cash or credit. When he traveled to France in 1762, for example, he borrowed £20 from David Garrick—a loan that ultimately would cause the two to fall out. In 1765 Sterne had still not paid the money back, and a testy exchange of letters ensued when Garrick pressed for the return of what was a significant sum. Whether it was ever repaid is not entirely clear (*LY,* 214).

In these dealings with Garrick, Sterne was engaging in (and possibly abusing) a type of semicasual borrowing common in the period. Margot Finn has shown in *The Character of Credit: Personal Debt in English Culture, 1740–1914* that the eighteenth century saw only a partial movement toward a contract-based economy of borrowing, and there remained a significant culture of lending by means of private arrangement. Less formalized debts were not without a sense of contract—they were surrounded by "a scaffolding of extra-legal customs, obligations and expectations"—but in the arrangement of such debts, the agreement was often tacit.[13] Whether or not Sterne ever repaid Garrick, he no doubt had a good grasp of the conventions and silent rules, as we see particularly in his correspondence from abroad, where the management of his finances was more challenging than when on home turf. Letters written during his travels are peppered with detailed remarks and instructions concerning the movement of money, and they also show a good deal of caution with regard to the accumulation of debts.

Stranded in Toulouse in 1763 because of a lack of funds, Sterne wrote of having "a letter of credit for two hundred pounds from a person [he] never saw," but he was reluctant to employ it "out of a nicety of temper" (*Letters*, 331; the editors assume it was from his Montpellier banker, Alexander Ray). It was also in Toulouse that Sterne gave considerable aid to George Oswald, a young tourist who was dying of tuberculosis, and his letters at the time show his careful attention to both Oswald's debts and his own expenses. When Oswald died, Sterne meticulously tallied his debts and informed a correspondent of all that was "wanting to clear our poor friend with this side of the world" (*Letters*, 312). Furthermore, it fell to Sterne to break the news of the death to Oswald's father, but he took it on himself also to inform him of the young man's credits and debts. "In short he owed it," Sterne explained of a £100 sum that had been sent by the father, "& had borrow'd the money before he got the Credit—& the Moment he rec[d] the Obligation from You, he discharge[d] his Obligations to Others with it" (*Letters*, 320).[14] Sterne was clearly attentive to the details of who owed what to whom, and as such letters suggest, had he not found more interesting pursuits, he could well have been an effective bookkeeper. As a backdrop to his literary authorship, though, his personal attentiveness to debt is important for its demonstration of a keen sensitivity to the idea of a fair and proper balancing of obligation and repayment. It is not simply "sentimental commerce" but the "*balance* of sentimental commerce" that Yorick is repeatedly drawn to document as he makes his way through France (*ASJ*, 13; emphasis added).

In the fiction it can be difficult at times to separate quantifiable debts (measured in pounds and shillings, *louis d'ors* and *livres*) from those fuzzier debt relations (for example, obligations of feeling) that resist meticulous accounting yet are still subjected to precisely that by Sterne's narrators. When monetary debts are given narrative space, they are often enmeshed in relations that have complex nonmonetary dimensions. A financial debt, for example, becomes part of the fraternal relation between Tristram's father and uncle, when Walter bails out his brother, whose income cannot support his military obsession. In volume 3 of *Tristram Shandy*, Walter warns Toby of the costs of his hobbyhorse:

> Brother *Toby* . . . you care not what money you dissipate and throw away, provided . . .'tis but upon a SIEGE.—Have I not one hundred and twenty

> pounds a year, besides my half-pay? cried my uncle *Toby.*——What is that,—replied my father, hastily,—to ten pounds for a pair of jack-boots?——twelve guineas for your *pontoons*;——half as much for your *Dutch*-draw-bridge;— . . . —these military operations of yours are above your strength;—you mean well, brother,—but they carry you into greater expences than you were first aware of,—and take my word,——dear *Toby*, they will in the end quite ruin your fortune, and make a beggar of you. (*TS*, 3.22.242)

This passage may appear to present a financially astute rationalist speaking to an innocent, but Walter's acumen is put into doubt when later we find him mentioning to Toby the £100 that, he says, "*I lent thee to carry on these cursed sieges*" (*TS*, 6.32.555), surely a benevolent version of "subprime lending" with little prospect of repayment. Such is the power of affection that, for Walter, fraternal love can overwhelm fiscal reason. He will not have his brother begging, and yet he provides a loan rather than a gift (he is not *that* benevolent), which locks the pair in a debt relation. However, Sterne does not suggest that Toby, with his insulating simplicity, suffers badly from the pressure and pain of financial debt. In *Tristram Shandy*, it generally falls to Tristram himself to feel and communicate the sting of debt.

Tristram is in many ways a lonelier, less well-supported character than most of those he writes about, and he is vulnerable to the harshness of debt when, unlike Toby's borrowing, it stretches beyond the family circle. His famous lament in volume 8 regarding unsold copies of earlier volumes is prompted by frustration with debt: "Is it not enough that thou art in debt, and that thou hast ten cart-loads of thy fifth and sixth volumes still—still unsold, and art almost at thy wit's ends, how to get them off thy hands" (*TS*, 8.6.663). Here debt retroactively defines and diminishes the nature of the work to which Tristram has dedicated his efforts. It is not a problem of *unread* books that he faces; the indebted author needs buyers more than readers, and the offspring of Tristram's labor is reduced, from a debtor's viewpoint, to mere saleable commodities measured not by literary standards but by the cartload. Tristram's situation is no better when he reaches his next and final volume, where he complains of owing his tailor "some five and twenty pounds at least" and declares it to be "a cursed thing to be in debt." His reflections on his financial situation show him to be an early proponent of the type of "debt-free dream" that financial gurus and lifestyle columnists now dangle before the largely debt-laden readers of newspaper supplements. "There is not any one prince, prelate, pope, or potentate, great or small upon earth," Tristram declares, "more desirous in his heart of keeping streight with the world than I am" (*TS*, 9.17.769). Typical of Tristram, though, the reality of his situation falls short of his aspirations.

Sterne's other narrative persona displays a comparable interest in "keeping streight with the world," albeit with less focus on financial debt. Yorick is a humble but solvent traveler, not a lavish grand tourist, but nonetheless one able to buy gloves and ruffles and, when his conscience has a hand in the accounting, to hand out coins to beggars. The monetary debt that enters the narrative lies in the short-term transactions of someone on the move, but it is not without significance. In "The Case of Conscience," for example, when Yorick is accused by his hotelier of impropriety with a young *fille de chambre* and asked, at evening time, to leave his lodgings, an assertion of his honest approach to debt becomes a part of his self-exoneration. Indeed it stands in for a declaration concerning whatever has happened on Yorick's rumpled bed: "I exhorted him to let his soul sleep in peace, as I resolved to let mine do that night, and that I would discharge what I owed him at breakfast" (*ASJ*, 127). Avowing his reliability as a short-term debtor, Yorick is indirectly insisting on his respectability in his dealings with the *fille de chambre*. At the same time, though, he is pointedly directing his discourse away from that uncomfortable topic ("my pride not suffering me to enter into any detail of the case" [*ASJ*, 127]), and he is working hard to avoid a change of lodging as night approaches. And the maître d'hôtel—who, it emerges, is more concerned with money and the appearance of decency than with decency per se—is willingly persuaded by Yorick's appeal. In this chapter's knowing exchange between Yorick and the maître d'hôtel, an ability to pay a debt is allowed by both parties to stand metonymically for a more general steadfastness, while also giving confidence to the hotelier (who soon arranges for a *grisset* to visit Yorick, ostensibly to sell lace) that his guest may be touched for more money. As in *Tristram Shandy*, the introduction of a financial debt is not merely incidental (there are other ways in which Yorick could have insisted on another night's stay). Sterne, it may be admitted, does not introduce many monetary debts into his fiction, but when he does, they carry significance beyond themselves and are tied to nonfinancial motives or feelings, akin to the interplay of the fiscal and emotional in Sterne's dealings with George Oswald, where sorrow and sympathy for the dying young man are intertwined with financial accounting. As Yorick remarks, "there is nothing unmixt in this world" (*ASJ*, 116).

ENDURING DEBTS AND MORAL EDUCATION

A debt may have no tangible connection to money, though, and in both *Tristram Shandy* and *A Sentimental Journey*, as characters engage in varied forms of exchange, obligations of a nonfinancial kind often result. In *A Sentimental Journey* Yorick's perception of himself as traveling within a country that orders "matter" better than at home renders him obliged as he experiences a type of personal education. He remarks to the Count de B**** in Versailles, "A polish'd nation . . . makes every one its debtor" (*ASJ*, 118), and through his self-improving encounters with the French, he accrues a series of emotional and moral debts. For example, he sees himself as changed by his contact with La Fleur and observes, "it always mortifies the pride of the conceit, by reflecting how much I *owe* to the complexional philosophy of this poor fellow, for shaming me into one of a better kind" (*ASJ*, 43; emphasis added). Such is the additional service that may be provided by a servant—inadvertently—when the employer has the openness to moral development that Yorick, as he travels, comes to foster within himself. Yorick is going beyond his early resolution to "learn better manners" (*ASJ*, 11); he charts a development that runs deeper than that, and his recording of what he *owes* becomes an important part of that process.

Yorick calls again on the language of debt when describing the influence of the caged starling that has "tenderly awakened" his "affections" through its utterance of "I can't get out": "four simple words—(and no more)—to which I own'd myself so much its debtor" (*ASJ*, 95, 99). The feeling of debt here is an acknowledgment of the depth of the starling's impact: it is the starling that prompts Yorick's reflections on the miseries of captivity and thereafter his resolve to obtain a passport; listening to the bird is pivotal for Yorick's emotional state, his journey, and thereby his narrative. But the declaration of the debt is at the same time a display of Yorick's improved or improving nature, suggesting not simply appreciation of the starling's effect on Yorick but a deeper and more lasting recognition of one's dependence on others. As noted earlier, obligation is stronger than gratitude, and here and elsewhere Sterne's fictions seem to recognize this distinction.

The debts to La Fleur and the starling are both reminiscent of Tristram's reflections on the emotional and moral education that he gained when, at the age of ten, he witnessed his Uncle Toby catch and release a fly: "I often think that I *owe* one half of my philanthropy to that one accidental impression" (*TS*, 2.12.131; emphasis added). Nothing is consciously lent in any of these exchanges; but a debt has been felt, and significantly, that debt has the power of endurance. The transactions are not rapidly completed—indeed, a sense of having paid the debt may never be felt—and so the feeling of obligation becomes an undying strand of the debtor's character. Melinda Alliker Rabb, in a study of the nexus of money and gender in *A Sentimental Journey*, has considered how the characters encountered en route "constantly participate in 'sentimental commerce'" with Yorick: "They sell, spend, give, or take."[15] This is true, but the observation emphasizes only those transactions that have rapid completion—or "closure"—while overlooking Sterne's interest in the idea of debt as a long-term form of commerce and in the capacity to feel obligation as a lasting marker of virtue. Tristram thinks "often" about what he owes to Toby and the fly; Yorick's reflections on what he owes La Fleur "always" have the same effect on him. Both experience felt debts that recur, exhibiting an enduring power to nourish an individual's sense of connection—of being, in John Donne's terms, not an island but "a part of the main."

TRIBUTES DUE AND "BOOK-DEBTS"

In addition to charting those debts that may be amassed between individuals in the passage through life, at a more existential level Sterne's fictions also incorporate the idea of life itself as a debt, as something borrowed from nature that must be paid back. As Walter Shandy remarks, "*To die*, is the great debt and tribute due unto nature" (*TS*, 5.3.421). He is reiterating a commonplace here, one that Sterne had used in his sermons ("to die, was the necessary and unavoidable debt of nature" [*Sermons*, 145]) but that already had a long heritage. Ben Jonson, for example, drew on the idea in his elegy "On My First Son": "Seven years thou wert lent to me, and I thee pay / Exacted by thy fate, on the just day." It is also seen in the meditation on transience in Shakespeare's "Shall I compare thee to a summer's day": if immortalized in verse, the loved one would not "lose possession of that fair thou ow'st." Indeed in this sonnet, summer is also on a "lease": a calling in of debts is part of "nature's changing course."[16] A powerful and comforting way of thinking about mortality, the commonplace is also voiced by Tristram in a hectic passage on gambling and debts of different kinds. Writing of his time in Boulogne, when he sees himself among "debtors and sinners before heaven," he declares, "I have no debt but the debt of Nature, and I want but patience of her, and I will pay her every farthing I owe her" (*TS*, 7.7.585).

But can this debt of life be paid only through death, or are there preparatory forms of repayment that may be made by means of actions performed while living? Sterne's writing holds up various serious and seriocomic responses to these questions. His religion maintains the value of living within a code of ethics and performing good works as a form of down payment before death; a place in heaven was not predestined. His fiction, with its attention to benevolence and charity, largely follows the precepts of compassionate Christianity, yet it does so within a framework that comically asserts the challenges involved in knowing and doing what is right. Nature bestows the debt of life but suggests no obvious repayment plan; religion might proffer guidance, but it does not provide answers to all questions: How do we know what we owe, what is due, and what—to take a short etymological step–our duties are?

A payment of dues—or rather their mispayment—is, in fact, what sets in motion *Tristram Shandy* (and Tristram as a character). In the work's celebrated first sentence, Tristram complains of his parents failing in their congress to "duly" consider "how much depended upon what they were then doing"; they had not "duly weighed and considered" what hinged on the act in which they "were in duty equally bound" (*TS*, 1.1.1). Three times in that remarkable sentence, Tristram points to the failures to respect what was "due" in the act of his begetting, a form of self-diagnosis that readily connects with Tristram's own preoccupation with the dues and duties that surround his acts of creation. As the parent of narrative, Tristram is acutely conscious of the duties that his chosen endeavor imposes on him, while his recognition of forever falling short in the performance of authorial duty constitutes a key part of his comic failure.

A state of narrative debt is indeed one of the constants of *Tristram Shandy*. The nature of Tristram's project—with its unattainable goal of autobiographical completeness—has debt at its core. Tristram's belief that his readers, as Tita Chico puts it, need "to know *everything* to be able to understand *anything*," means that there cannot not be matters untold.[17] There will always be an act of telling that is due or overdue. Tristram, in an often cited passage, dubs these untold matters "book-debts," giving an alternative meaning to a term that in normal usage in Sterne's time referred simply to a debt noted in a ledger: "Amongst many other book-debts, all of which I shall discharge in due time,—I own myself a debtor to the world for two items,—a chapter upon *chamber-maids and button-holes*, which . . . I promised and fully intended to pay off this year" (*TS*, 5.8.434). The absurd aspiration that Sterne plants within his narrator makes an overarching sense of the not-yet-told—here framed pointedly in the language of fiscal debt—a defining feature of *Tristram Shandy*. But it is not only Tristram who displays this sense of debt; another narrative debtor emerges in *A Sentimental Journey* when Yorick is informed that Madame de L*** owes him a story. This feeling of debt is expressed in a letter that Yorick reads in Amiens: "She was sorry . . . that she had been prevented telling me her story—that she still owed it to me; and if my rout should ever lay through Brussels, and I had not by then forgot the name of Madame de L***—that Madame de L*** would be glad to discharge her obligation" (*ASJ*, 57).

Beyond the portrayal of the extreme case of Tristram, then, Sterne's fiction suggests that stories—like explanations and apologies—are matters that may be owed; narrative may be the currency of a debt relation. This is distinct from the idea of a story that simply must be told, such as in the myth of Midas: when punished with ass's ears, Midas keeps the signs of his shame secret from all but his wife, who then finds herself with a story she is unable not to tell. Midas's wife unburdens herself without having recourse to a human listener when she shares the secret with the reeds in a meadow—for her there is an obligation in the telling, but it is the expression, not the reception, that is important. For Sterne, the expression of a story, driven by an obligation to another rather than oneself, is motivated by the reception. This is narrative as a relational, social bond, a payment from the self to others. For Madame de L***, the obligation is to the singular Yorick, while for Tristram, it is to his imagined community of readers: "Sir," "Madam," and "dear Jenny" and also those unnamed figures who constitute that more diffuse idea of a readership to which a commercial author feels a sense of obligation.

What of Sterne himself? With Tristram he created one of literary history's greatest narrative debtors, but we cannot know the degree to which he shared that sense of obligation to provide others with stories, albeit that he did so for many years as a clergyman and then devoted the last decade of his life to doing so as a professional author. What we do know, however, is that at the end of Sterne's life he placed himself in a state of eternal narrative debt.

A DEBT AT THE END OF THE JOURNEY

Little attention has been given to the fact that Sterne concluded his literary career with a published admission of a debt. To be fair, there are good reasons for this. Readers and critics understandably have been captivated by the last scene of *A Sentimental Journey* and have treated it as the concluding public expression of Sterne's life—one that, far from placing him in debt, gave him ongoing credit in the ledger of literary life. In "The Case of Delicacy" Sterne offered all the ingredients but not the performance of a sexual threesome, and the pent-up bawdiness of this final chapter initially drew criticism from some readers. Sterne was unable, one early critic lamented, to "take leave of his readers without some pleasantry of the *lower species*."[18] Over time, though, general admiration of the chapter's ingenuity and craft has come to overshadow this prudish critique that found too much sensuality in the last literary breath of Sterne the clergyman. The final sentence of the work—"So that when I stretch'd out my hand" and so on (*ASJ*, 165)—has been particularly celebrated, not only for its sly offer of a choice between a bawdy reading and an innocent one but also for an open-endedness that allows interpretation to range beyond those binary options. Sterne ended his career with something inconclusive: no full stop on the printed page and a subtle invitation to his readers to waver over what has gone before, to read beyond the absent punctuation down to "END OF VOL. II" and thereafter into the empty future of the unwritten with all its unknown potential. He presented an end but not a conclusion, a text that stops but also gestures forward. It makes readers work for their pleasure and at the same time still hands something to them—making them indebted, we might say—as it passes on the baton of creation by offering a gap to be uncertainly filled.

The unspecific pregnancy of the "END OF VOL. II," though, is thrown into a curious form of relief by the fact that Sterne had placed himself in authorial debt during his final months of writing when, dogged by ill health, he found himself rather less productive than he had predicted. His debt was to his roughly two hundred subscribers and was acknowledged in the "Advertisement" that was issued together with *A Sentimental Journey* on February 27, 1768:

> THE Author begs leave to acknowledge to his Subscribers, that they have a further claim upon him for Two Volumes more than these delivered to them now, and which nothing but ill health could have prevented him, from having ready along with these.
>
> The Work will be compleated and delivered to the Subscribers early the next Winter. (*ASJ*, xxx)

This pledge was printed on a single sheet inserted into subscription copies as an extra leaf at the start of volume 1; it was a postscript among the prelims.[19] Single-leaf additions of this kind—usually witnessed with prefatory errata slips—make possible the disruption of the relationship between time and textual production as reflected in the linear progression of the physical book. They allow a "finished" printed volume to be declared unfinished and for further material to be inserted at any chosen point. In this case, at the beginning of *A Sentimental Journey* readers were confronted with another end of sorts: a text produced after that which it was placed before.

This placement of the "Advertisement" may be seen simply as a diplomatic strategy of placating, sooner rather than later, potentially disgruntled subscribers. Sterne was literally in debt to them; he had taken money on the promise of four volumes and was only providing two. But perhaps the positioning was, for Sterne, another toying with narrative chronology and the form of the printed book following his eight-year career in textual play in *Tristram Shandy*. Sterne had very pointedly worked with the insertion of extra material for volume 3 of *Tristram Shandy* in order to accommodate his tipped-in marbled page, invoking as he did so "the knowledge of the great saint *Paraleipomenon*," a name that at least some of Sterne's more learned readers would have seen springing from "paraleipomena": matters omitted from a work and added as a supplement (*TS*, 3.36.268).[20] The marbled page—*Tristram's* "motly emblem"—is emblematic of Tristram's project in part because it embodies temporal disruption in relation to book production; it is a material counterpart to the asynchrony of the narrative. Did the positioning of *A Sentimental Journey*'s "Advertisement" carry any comparable significance? Should Sterneans add "the loose page" to their discussions of the better-known "black page," "marbled page," and "blank page"?

In fact, we cannot be entirely certain as to the extent of Sterne's involvement in the "Advertisement." Presented as the pledge of "The Author" and passed on by a third party, the text itself was perhaps the work of Thomas Becket, the publisher of *A Sentimental Journey*, but the nub of the message certainly appears to have come from Sterne. The promise to have the missing volumes ready by the following winter points clearly to an authorial plan, while also showing that Sterne, accustomed to being seriously ill, was not expecting to die just three weeks after *A Sentimental Journey*'s publication. But whether a direct or indirect expression from the author, the "Advertisement" plainly indicates Sterne's consciousness of his duties and obligations, while also making clear to subscribers at the outset that *A Sentimental Journey* was unfinished. It cast the shadows of debt and incompletion over the entire work. For three weeks after its publication, readers who internalized the "Advertisement" may have read *A Sentimental Journey* with a sense of "more is to come." Then on March 18, 1768, the day of Sterne's death, this framework for reading changed, and the work became locked in its unfinished state. Alas, poor readers—denied whatever Yorick might have got up to in Italy.

But readers were not denied the opportunity to speculate on what was unwritten, and for some enthusiasts—the would-be Yoricks of the world—the work's unfinished status offered an irresistible occasion for producing an eighteenth-century equivalent of "fan fiction." "Eugenius," the name appended to *Yorick's Sentimental Journey, Continued* (1769), is the most renowned of those imitators who took a cue from what one critic, writing in the *Monthly Review*, had seen as the "ludicrous hiatus" at the end of the work, but there were a good many further attempts by other authors (or "reader-authors") to use Sterne's final ellipsis as an entry point into a creative collaboration of sorts with the dead author.[21] M-C. Newbould has shown, in a broad study of "Sterneana," that *A Sentimental Journey*'s open end was a particular spur to imitative action. Works such as the anonymous *Continuation of Yorick's Sentimental Journey* (1788) and, by "Mr. Shandy," *A Sentimental Journey: Intended as a Sequel to Mr. Sterne's* (1793) specifically manipulated "the provocative nothingness of the final page of *A Sentimental Journey*."[22]

Of course, though, the writers of these continuations, however accomplished their efforts, were not paying off Sterne's debt or doing anything that would come to be recognized as truly filling the gap, despite a number of readers and booksellers treating some imitations as Sterne's own writing well into the nineteenth century.[23] Sterne's imitators could never *be* Sterne, but, motivated by pleasure, money, or whatever, they could *use* him and capitalize on what he had left behind by aping his characters, narrative ploys, idiosyncratic humor, and other literary characteristics. What is most significant about the phenomenon of Sterneana here is that Sterne's imitators, by their borrowing, were not paying Sterne's debt but were declaring themselves indebted.

THE SENSE OF UNENDING

When Sterne died, then, we may say—adopting the metaphor that he himself used—that he paid his debt to nature, but by doing so before concluding *A Sentimental Journey*, he created a major outstanding "book-debt." At the same time, his imitators provide an obvious pointer to ways in which "payments" can continue to be made from the grave—that is, if you have contributed something with enduring value to culture while living. In conclusion, I suggest that an internalization of this idea of literary immortality exists within Sterne's fiction: notions of debt and obligation are found functioning there as tools for imagining and articulating the literary exchange that may occur between the living and the dead.

Ideas of the continuing fecundity of the dead artist have, of course, a long history, reaching back way beyond Sterne. We may return to Shakespeare's self-referential "Shall I compare thee to a summer's day?" for a classic expression of the idea of literature's power to give indefinitely: "So long as men can breathe, or eyes can see / So long lives this, and this gives life to thee."[24] For living readers, the work of a dead author may continue to live and, in the process, sustain the quickness of the dead. For an equally powerful, if less direct, illustration of the idea—and one of undoubted importance to Sterne's authorship—we might turn to Hamlet's reflections on the unearthing of Yorick's skull:

> Alas, poor Yorick! I knew him, Horatio. A fellow of infinite jest, of most excellent fancy. He hath borne me on his back a thousand times, and how abhorred my imagination is. My gorge rises at it. Here hung those lips that I have kissed I know not how oft. Where be your jibes now? Your gambols? Your songs? Your flashes of merriment that were wont to set the table on a roar? No one now to mock your own jeering? Quite chopfallen? Now get you to my lady's chamber and tell her, let her paint an inch thick, to this favour she must come. Make her laugh at that.[25]

The scene has become established as a classic meditation on death: a dramatic memento mori that visually and verbally points to where all lives are heading. It is also, however, a scene of reanimation in which something dead is imaginatively revived and passed on to the living. There is an important turn in the speech: Hamlet begins by addressing Horatio and discussing Yorick in the third person, but he then engages Yorick himself in conversation: "Where be your jibes now?" Yorick is brought to life as a conversational partner, and the questions Hamlet asks him regarding the fate of his humor are important because, while they may not exactly point to life beyond the grave, they demonstrate the idea of posthumous influence. Where are Yorick's "flashes of merriment"? One place where they may immediately be identified is within Hamlet himself, as he jests with the "chopfallen" skull, adopting and perpetuating the jester's witty discourse, and this resolves a paradox in Hamlet's opening description of Yorick as a "fellow of infinite jest." Yorick's skull is a stark reminder of the finite nature of his life. How can such an obviously transient being have anything of the infinite about him? The scene suggests that Yorick attains this by passing on his wit to members of the next generation, such as Hamlet. It is a depiction of a cultural chain in which Hamlet, who recalls a literal form of support from Yorick when he was borne on his back, appears through his own wit to acknowledge a deeper and more enduring form of debt to his jesting forebear.[26]

Sterne, seeking to attach himself to that same cultural chain, has his own Yorick identify more than closely with his Danish predecessor. When Yorick meets the Count de B**** in Versailles, with a set of Shakespeare volumes before him, and is asked to identify himself, he takes up *Hamlet*: "and turning immediately to the grave-diggers scene in the fifth act, I lay'd my finger upon Yorick, and advancing the book to the Count, with my finger all the way over the name—*Me, Voici!* said I" (*ASJ*, 112). Sterne's Yorick is fully identified with Shakespeare's Yorick—at least momentarily, before Yorick finds himself obliged to explain to the bewildered Count that "there are two Yoricks" (*ASJ*, 112). Here the fictional Yorick makes a play with the fictional basis of his own existence, suggesting that while the later Yorick is distinct from the skull in *Hamlet*, at some level they are the same; an essence of Shakespeare's Yorick lives in Sterne's character and by doing so enables, for the benefit of readers, a fresh scattering of wit and humor, of gibes and jests. And while the Danish Yorick is continuing to make payments from the grave both in *Hamlet* and in Sterne's work, so too is Shakespeare, and this is underlined explicitly by the Count, who declares "how much he stood *obliged* to Shakespear for making [Yorick] known to him" (*ASJ*, 111; emphasis added). It is another expression that connects enduring literary capital with debt and suggests a transcendence of death across a lender-borrower, author-reader relation. Here and elsewhere

Sterne's invocations of the literary past and his references to dead writers—not only Shakespeare but also "beloved Cervantes," Rabelais, and others—collectively show the bountiful nature of literary history and that there is much that one can inherit by opening a book. Was Sterne aiming to build up a stock of literary capital with his own cultural contributions that would similarly have posthumous value—that could be, like the story of the poor gentleman in "The Fragment," "a legacy to the world" (*ASJ*, 138) and could increase his credit "so long . . . as eyes can see"?

Perhaps such an aim informed the entire literary enterprise of this author who wrote "not to be *fed*, but to be *famous*" (*Letters*, 116), but there are also particular strategies within the fiction that seem pointedly to stage a resistance to finality, specifically to the finality of death, and to maintain a form of credit through inconclusiveness. "Closure" and "lack of closure" may have become hackneyed concepts within literary critical discourse, but it is difficult not to find in Sterne's work some passages—including the end of *A Sentimental Journey*—that seem intent on not letting readers settle with a clear sense of completion or resolution. James Joyce said of *Ulysses* that he had "put in so many enigmas and puzzles that it will keep the professors busy for centuries. . . . That's the only way of insuring one's immortality."[27] Sterne did not exactly trade in enigmas and puzzles, but, like Joyce, he shaped his fiction in such a way that many readers and critics have found it difficult to be completely finished with it and consequently finished with their obligations to him.

Alongside the irresolvable ambiguity, various closure-resistant techniques may be identified, but perhaps most important here is Sterne's obsession with non-sequential time schemes—let us call it his "anachrophilia." The vigorous refusal of correspondence between *fabula* and *sjuzet* legislates against stops within the world of the fiction falling at stopping points within the form of the book, and this has particular significance with regard to the effects of narrated deaths. In Sterne's work, the death of a character does not bring with it an absence in the narrative. By means of anachrony, his characters (like Christ and Shakespeare's Yorick before them) enjoy a form of resurrection when the *sjuzet* allows them to breathe again. Sterne could not apply such narratological medicine to himself, but he could at least imagine immortality and arrest any sense of stoppage where his fictional characters were concerned.

The prime locus of this technique is, of course, the character of Yorick, and if we look back to his death in *Tristram Shandy*, we find not only a case of rapid resuscitation by means of anachrony but also a return to the issue of debt. Yorick's demise in *Tristram Shandy*'s first volume, written eight years before Sterne failed to finish *A Sentimental Journey*, presents an interplay of the issues of death, debt, and, soon after, narrative resurrection. His death is induced by a curious kind of debt, and the chapter in which he dies opens boldly, if obscurely, with reflections on how "the *Mortgager* and *Mortgageé* differ the one from the other, not more in length of purse, than the *Jester* and *Jesteé* do, in that of memory. . . . The one raises a sum and the other a laugh at your expence, and think no more about it. Interest, however, still runs on in both cases" (*TS*, 1.12.30).[28] From Latin via Old French, a mortgage—or "mort gage"—is a "death pledge": debt and death have long been bedfellows. Sterne would almost certainly have been aware of this etymology as he developed the narrative of Yorick's death through debt. With Scriblerian slippage between the cultures of finance and wit, it is Yorick's humor that draws him into fatal debt, the result of too many laughs at the expense of others. He has "wantonly involved himself in a multitude of small book-debts of this stamp" (*TS*, 1.12.30), and as his creditors unite against him, he is brought down by their attacks: "he threw down the sword; and though he kept up his spirits in appearance to the last,—he died . . . quite broken hearted" (*TS*, 1.12.33).

Yet as the chapter presents the debits inscribed on Yorick's account sheet, there are also suggestions of the continuity of culture *through* Yorick—that there are credits to be associated with his name and that, to misquote Hamlet's dying words, the rest is *not* silence. We may note how at the point of dying he appears as a link in the chain of literary history. His last utterance to Eugenius "was utter'd with something of a *cervantick* tone;—and as he spoke it, *Eugenius* could perceive a stream of lambent fire lighted up for a moment in his eyes;—faint picture of those flashes of his spirit, which (as *Shakespear* said of his ancestor) were wont to set the table in a roar!" (*TS*, 1.12.34). We may also note how in death—laid "under a plain marble slabb" but more importantly under his Shakespeare-derived epitaph, "Alas, poor YORICK!"—he continues to contribute something to the world. Significantly this occurs through the act of reading: "Ten times in a day has *Yorick*'s ghost the consolation to hear his monumental inscription read over" (*TS*, 1.12.35). The scene positions Sterne's alter ego as an active part of literary history—a borrower from Shakespeare but also a benefactor for the future—and as the character is revived for readers through anachrony, his credit continues to rise. In terms of *fabula*, Yorick's death-through-debt may, in fact, be seen as the true end of *A Sentimental Journey*, since it depicts the moment that the first-person narrator is silenced, but Sterne wisely dispatched that matter early and was thus able to pursue altogether more life-affirming, death-denying writing concerning Yorick thereafter.

Indeed, if we return to "The Case of Delicacy," we might well see the final scene as a rewriting and wish-fulfilling reimagining of the death of Yorick in *Tristram Shandy*. There are certainly a number of suggestive parallels and reversals. At the conclusion of both episodes, Yorick is prone on a bed and positioned behind a curtain: in *Tristram Shandy*, Eugenius draws "*Yorick*'s curtain" to connect with him (*TS*, 1.12.33); eight years later, Sterne places Yorick behind "curtains . . . of a flimsy transparent cotton" (*ASJ*, 163). Furthermore, the parting of curtains in both scenes is followed by Yorick connecting with others by means of his hand. With Eugenius, we know exactly what Yorick does with his hands: "I beseech thee, *Eugenius*, quoth *Yorick*, taking off his night-cap as well as he could with his left hand,—his right being still grasped close in that of Eugenius" (*TS*, 1.12.34). In "The Case of Delicacy," we are famously left wondering what Yorick catches hold of: readers are handed the task of imaginative creation by Sterne. If we have him grasp the *fille de chambre*'s hand, we gain another parallel with the death scene in *Tristram Shandy*. But there are many things that might be grasped, and we are, of course, invited to think that Yorick's groping in the dark may have resulted in a far more intimate contact. Such a reading produces a fertile image—one suggestive of literary reproduction, as his hand, that essential bodily part of a writer, makes contact with what Gustave Courbet would later call "L'Origine du Monde." We do not need to decide, however, what Yorick touches to find fertility in the conclusion; it is found *because* it is inconclusive and thus leaves readers unable to be finished with Sterne—unable to close him in his grave. As Rabb writes of the final sentence, "By leaving Yorick in the dark bedroom at the inn and obscurely joining his hand with 'the *fille de chambre*'s,' Sterne . . . engender[s] an unending account that earns him immortality."[29]

"A Case of Delicacy" may be read as a life-affirming rewriting of Yorick's death-bed scene, and it concludes with a passage of text that has made generations of readers and critics obliged to Sterne. It should have been a midpoint and not an end, but perhaps Sterne—with his interest in balancing the accounts—was thinking of it as an insurance policy, just in case he would not live to accompany Yorick through Italy. Sterne, like Yorick, died in debt, but by aiming for and securing a place in literary history, he ensured that he was at the same time, like Yorick, in the black.

NOTES

1. Julian Hoppit, "Attitudes to Credit in Britain, 1680–1790," *Historical Journal* 33 (1990): 306.
2. John Brewer, *The Sinews of Power: War, Money and the English State, 1688–1783* (Cambridge, MA: Harvard University Press, 1990).
3. Anne L. Murphy, "Making the Market: Trading Debt at the Eighteenth-Century Bank of England" (EABH Papers 14-05, European Association for Banking and Financial History, 2014), 7, https://ideas.repec.org/p/zbw/eabhps/1405.html.
4. See Alexander Wakelam, *Credit and Debt in Eighteenth-Century England: An Economic History of Debtors' Prisons* (London: Routledge, 2020).

5. On commerce, see, for example, Melinda Alliker Rabb, "Engendering Accounts in Sterne's *A Sentimental Journey*," in *Johnson and His Age*, ed. James Engell (Cambridge, MA: Harvard University Press, 1984), 531–558.
6. Margaret Atwood, *Payback: Debt and the Shadow Side of Wealth* (London: Bloomsbury, 2008), 2.
7. Bob Brecher, "Our Obligation to the Dead," *Journal of Applied Philosophy* 19, no. 2 (2002): 109–119.
8. Harold Bloom, *The Anxiety of Influence: A Theory of Poetry* (New York: Oxford University Press, 1973).
9. The prominent position of the reference to this speech—in the first sentence of volume 2—suggests that Sterne saw "Polonius's advice to his son" upon traveling (*ASJ*, 87) as a significant counterpart or reference point for his own fictional travel writing.
10. Edward Bensly, "A Debt of Sterne's," *Times Literary Supplement*, November 1, 1928, 806. Bensly examines aspects of Sterne's use of Ephraim Chambers's *Cyclopaedia*.
11. William V. Holtz, *Image and Immortality: A Study of "Tristram Shandy"* (Providence, RI: Brown University Press, 1970).
12. Emily Hodgson Anderson, "Theatrical *Tristram*: Sterne and *Hamlet* Reconsidered," *Eighteenth-Century Fiction* 27, nos. 3–4 (2015): 661–680; Celia Barnes, "Orna Me: Laurence Sterne's Open Letter to Literary History," *Authorship* 5, no. 2 (2016): 2, https://doi.org/10.21825/aj.v5i2.3878.
13. Margot Finn, *The Character of Credit: Personal Debt in English Culture, 1740–1914* (Cambridge: Cambridge University Press, 2003), 95.
14. Sterne displayed a rather different attitude in his correspondence with Eliza Draper, condemning Eliza's husband for being concerned about debt: "I am credibly informed, that his repugnance to your living in England arises only from the dread which has enter'd his brain, that thou mayest run him in debt. . . . That such a creature should be sacrificed, for the paltry consideration of a few hundreds, is too, too hard!" (*Letters*, 564). Had he not been smitten, he may well have shared the husband's point of view.
15. Rabb, "Engendering Accounts," 534.
16. Ben Jonson, *The Works of Ben Jonson, Volume the Sixth* (London, 1756), 238; William Shakespeare, *The Sonnets*, ed. G. Blakemore Evans, introduction by Stephen Orgel, 2nd ed. (Cambridge: Cambridge University Press, 2006), 35.
17. Tita Chico, "'The More I Write, the More I Shall Have to Write': The Many Beginnings of *Tristram Shandy*," in *Narrative Beginnings: Theories and Practices*, ed. Brian Richardson (Lincoln: University of Nebraska Press, 2009), 84.
18. Ralph Griffiths, *Monthly Review*, April 1768, in *CH*, 201.
19. Five hundred copies of the "Advertisement" were printed by William Strahan. See *ASJ*, 461.
20. On this aspect of the marbled page, see Shaun Regan, "Print Culture in Transition: *Tristram Shandy*, the Reviewers, and the Consumable Text," *Eighteenth-Century Fiction* 14, nos. 3–4 (2002): 308.
21. Griffiths, *Monthly Review*, in *CH*, 201.
22. M-C. Newbould, *Adaptations of Laurence Sterne's Fiction: Sterneana, 1760–1840* (Farnham, UK: Ashgate, 2013), 21. For further studies of Sterneana, see René Bosch, *Labyrinth of Digressions: "Tristram Shandy" as Perceived and Influenced by Sterne's Early Imitators*, trans. Piet Verhoeff (Amsterdam: Rodopi, 2007); and Warren L. Oakley, *A Culture of Mimicry: Laurence Sterne, His Readers and the Art of Bodysnatching* (London: Maney, 2010); plus the many articles in *The Shandean* on creative responses to Sterne. Bosch focuses on imitators of Sterne who were active during Sterne's lifetime and so is not concerned with those who were inspired by *A Sentimental Journey*. A specific study of continuations of *A Sentimental Journey* is found in W. B. Gerard, "'Betwixt One Passion and

Another': Continuations of Laurence Sterne's *A Sentimental Journey*, 1769–1820," in *On Second Thought: Updating the Eighteenth-Century Text*, ed. Debra Taylor Bourdeau and Elizabeth Kraft (Newark: University of Delaware Press, 2007), 123–138.

23. Gerard discusses how the continuation by "Eugenius" was quite commonly accepted as the work of Sterne in the late eighteenth century ("Betwixt One Passion and Another," 129).
24. Shakespeare, *The Sonnets*, 35.
25. William Shakespeare, *Hamlet: The Texts of 1603 and 1623*, ed. Ann Thompson and Neil Taylor (London: Arden Shakespeare, 2006), 335. Quoted from the 1623 text.
26. For a more extensive consideration of how Sterne uses Yorick's unearthing and *Hamlet* more broadly to perform the work of memorialization, see Anderson, "Theatrical *Tristram*."
27. Quoted in Richard Ellmann, *James Joyce*, 2nd ed. (Oxford: Oxford University Press, 1982), 521.
28. That this is not the most lucid of Sterne's comic passages was pointed out by the anonymous author of *The Clockmakers Outcry against the Author of "The Life and Opinions of Tristram Shandy"* (Dublin, 1760): "There may be humour and great pleasantry concealed under 'the mortgager and mortgagee differ the one from the other not more in length of *purse*, than the *jester* and *jestee* do in that of memory. &c.' but our dull knobs cannot reach it; nor can we find any of those who laugh so inconsiderately at this and many other equally brilliant Strokes, able to give us a reason why" (27–28).
29. Rabb, "Engendering Accounts," 558.

AFTERWORD

Pat Rogers

ANNIVERSARY MOMENTS

This volume commemorates events that took place in the closing days of Sterne's life. Anniversaries are curious things, sometimes celebrating incidents for the arbitrary reason (and no other) that a certain time span has elapsed. But they can illuminate both the past and the present, if the connection remains a meaningful one. A hundred years or so ago, not much fuss was made about the Sterne anniversaries that fell in the second decade of the twentieth century, though there was an article in the *Edinburgh Review* in 1913 to mark the author's birth date. Interest in the writer had been growing since 1900, with collected editions meant for bibliophiles, accompanied by serviceable lives from Percy Fitzgerald, "Lewis Melville," and Walter Sichel, and the entry of *Tristram Shandy* into Everyman's Library (a sure guide to popular taste of the era). However, just one work had appeared that today retains a place in the scholarly canon, *The Life and Times of Laurence Sterne* by W. L. Cross (1862–1948), with its first version dated 1909. Later editions were published by Yale University Press in 1925 and 1929, prior to the biographer's election as governor of Connecticut from 1931. The Great War slowed the pace, though reprints of the novels appeared occasionally. Then, in 1918, the world had more important things to deal with—the end of the war in November, preparations for the Versailles Peace Conference, and the Spanish flu pandemic that was raging across half the globe. It was only in the following decade that major advances in understanding were permitted by critical works such as Viktor Shklovsky's essay on *Tristram Shandy* and the theory of the novel (1921), as well as biographic aids such as *Sterne's Eliza* by Arnold Wright and William Lutley Sclater (1923).

Things were different by the time that 1968 came around. Notable for other reasons, the year saw a major conference held in and around Sterne's home territory at Coxwold and York, from which an influential volume of essays was assembled, *The Winged Skull*, edited by Arthur H. Cash and John M. Stedmond in 1971. This collection reflected the great growth in scholarship and criticism that had taken place over the previous generation, with the first serious attempts at scholarly editions of the fiction and the novels. Formalist readings were creeping in, with a more sophisticated sense of the narratological issues raised both by *Tristram Shandy* and by *A Sentimental Journey*. Still, by current standards, the "modernist" elements in the book seem tentative and provisional. This stands out if we compare *The Winged Skull* with a similar collection of essays, *Sterne, Tristram, Yorick: Tercentenary Essays on Laurence Sterne*, edited by Melvyn New, Peter de Voogd, and Judith Hawley (2016), which had its origin in a conference marking Sterne's birth held three years earlier at the University of London. The differences are striking. Not only do the contributors belong to a different breed from their predecessors, having imbibed theoretical idiom almost with their mother's milk, but they also had available a number of remarkable resources denied to those working in the 1960s.

Some of these resources were gains specific to the world of Sterne studies: the existence of the Florida edition edited by Melvyn New and others; the presence of a house journal, *The Shandean*, under the general editorship of Peter de Voogd; and the authoritative life in two volumes by Arthur Cash. Almost all subsequent biographic work has struggled to avoid coming over as a rehash of Cash, and this present chapter is of course no exception. Other advances relate more generally to a huge leap in the ease and speed with which students are able to access books and manuscripts thanks to electronic aids. The scale of this change may be fully apparent only to those who undertook research fifty or more years ago, when that activity meant copying out materials laboriously by hand after cross-country journeys to remote libraries and archives. Sometimes it was necessary to go by what John Betjeman, in his poem "A Subaltern's Love Song" (1941), called "roads 'not adopted,' by woodlanded ways." Perhaps such experiences helped a little to put the scholar back into the world that Sterne knew on his own, sometimes wild, excursions.

In any case, we are better now at planning commemorations, as we have these enhanced routes to obtain instant access to memorials of the past. So it is little surprise that, this time in 2018, more notice was taken of the 250th anniversary of some key events—the writer's death, of course, but also the publication of *A Sentimental Journey*. The preceding year had seen the ninth and last volume of *Tristram Shandy* come before the public, as well as the composition of the *Journal to Eliza* (or *Bramine's Journal*, as Sterne and the Florida editors call it). Thus 1767 and 1768 form a bibliographical climax to Sterne's writing career, and they are bookended by his collected sermons—volumes 3 and 4 having appeared in 1766, with the posthumous volumes 5, 6, and 7 to follow in 1769. Behind this story lie the facts that defined the culmination of the clergyman-novelist's stay on earth, sometimes comically enlivening, sometimes hectically overstrained, sometimes morbidly fascinating, sometimes excruciatingly pathetic—much like the content of his writings, in other words.

Here we have a mixture of literal and virtual realities. The first was acted out on the streets of London and in the byways of the north of England, when Sterne journeyed to and from York, Coxwold, and Crazy Castle (his friend's medieval fortress near the coast of what is now Cleveland, a structure that itself perished within a few years). The second involved the reconstructed memories of earlier journeys on the Continent, as well as the fantasies of an idyllic life with Eliza Draper, with the harsh contingencies imposed by a wife, money problems, and, so far as he could, a terminal illness all magicked out of sight. This collection celebrates the conjunction of biographic and bibliographic aspects of Sterne's last two years, as had a gathering that along with other meetings marked the date of his death. Held at the novelist's alma mater, Jesus College, Cambridge, it was titled "'Alas, Poor Yorick!': A Sterne 250-Year Anniversary Conference," and as that suggests, it placed a special emphasis on *A Sentimental Journey*.

The later part of this chapter will attempt to provide a short survey of the events that took place in Sterne's life at this juncture, along with the progress of his writing. But first we need to look at what else was going on in the world, something very seldom undertaken by those who discuss the works.

CONTEXTS

At one time, when an older version of literary history prevailed, Sterne did not have many rivals among his contemporaries for canonical status. According to this reading of the eighteenth century, the rise of the novel was followed by a drab age—a period of stasis in which those who were dubbed "the early masters" (Defoe, Richardson, Fielding) had few successors of comparable innovative skill. Apart from the works of Smollett and Sterne, with an outrider in *The Vicar of Wakefield* (1766), little was happening on the scene to change the main course of fiction. This situation went on until Frances Burney began to prepare the way for the next generation of major writers at the start of the new century, including Scott, Austen, and maybe Edgeworth. Minor exceptions were allowed for a few marginal categories: novels of sensibility, such as Henry Mackenzie's *Man of Feeling* (1771), Oriental tales such as William Beckford's *Vathek* (1786), and fiction of political and social ideas, which more often included William Godwin's *Caleb Williams* (1794) than *Mary* (1788) by his wife, Mary Wollstonecraft. On the whole, Gothic novels could be safely consigned to a top shelf of the bookcase, where they would not spread their rotting contents to more polite literature housed below. Thus Horace

Walpole, Clara Reeve, and Ann Radcliffe could be ghettoized within the genre of horror and terror.

We have changed all of that: in particular, genres such as the Gothic have been allowed to flow into the mainstream. Fables and romances are no longer deemed automatically less worthy of attention than strictly "realistic" works are. In the process, we have rediscovered many writers, some of whom enjoyed considerable popularity in their own day. Titles once held to belong to the category of "popular literature" have been admitted to the fold. Women writers have come much more into their own, leading to a re-evaluation, among others, of Frances Sheridan, author of *Memoirs of Miss Sidney Bidulph* (1761); Sarah Scott, *A Description of Millenium Hall and the Country Adjacent* (1762); Frances Brooke, *The History of Lady Julia Mandeville* (1763); and Charlotte Smith, *The Old Manor House* (1794). No longer does Sarah Fielding always have to tag onto the coattails of her brother Henry, with the recognition of books such as her last novel, *The History of Ophelia* (1760). Similarly, there have been efforts to reinstate less familiar items by Charlotte Lennox, including *Sophia* (1762). But male novelists have benefited too, with a greater willingness to pay attention to works that once lay on the fringe of critical discourse, for instance, *The Spiritual Quixote* by Richard Graves (1773) or even the Rousseauesque children's book *Sandford and Merton* (1783–1789), which was exceedingly popular into the nineteenth century and shared with *Robinson Crusoe* the honor of being translated into words of one syllable. The desire to incorporate the ideas of *Émile* or Goethe's *Werther* no longer looks as inherently absurd as it did to an older generation of historians.

These developments have altered our sense of where the novel was going in the third quarter of the century. Their effect has been paradoxical in some respects. Sterne and Smollett no longer loom on the skyline like lonely monuments. We realize that other writers, both women and men, attempted formal innovations, experimented with narrative methods, adopted the voice of a contrived persona, and felt influence from Continental models. To that extent, Sterne in particular seems less of a one-off figure standing outside tradition. Yet the comparisons that are now easier to make serve in another way to redefine his eccentricity and his difference. The many efforts at reproducing his style just demonstrate that you can copy mannerisms, borrow linguistic turns, and parody the broken progress of his narration—and yet end up with a text that no one would confuse with the real thing. Like Dickens in the Victorian era, Sterne became "the inimitable" as a result of so many failed attempts at imitation.

Even when he utilized literary mechanisms favored by many other writers, Sterne never operated in quite the same way. For example, a large number of authors from Swift and Defoe onward had taken over some of the conventions and concerns of travel writing; they appear in fictional narratives such as *Candide* and *Rasselas*. Most obviously in the mid-1760s, Smollett blurred the generic lines when he turned his *Travels* into the rumbustious self-satire of a pathologically splenetic character (almost a figure from Ben Jonson) and then later made *The Expedition of Humphry Clinker* into a kind of survey of Britain, not just topographic but also social and political. Yet no one went as far as Sterne, for *A Sentimental Journey* is less a trip across France (where it scarcely reaches first base) than a revelation of personality. As readers have always appreciated, the book is only incidentally concerned with national differences, despite its arresting opening. The vacillations of mood it dramatizes in Yorick could have been experienced years before among the inns and highways of Sterne's home country, as he made his obligatory peregrinations on pastoral duties or bumped along the Great North Road to London (still not fully turnpiked until the last stretches were completed in 1766 and 1776).

As for wider events, it should be recalled that high politics took no respite at this time. In 1767 Charles Townshend had introduced his hugely unpopular duties on imports into the American colonies. The following year saw the end of the Chatham administration, led by Pitt the Elder, to whom Sterne had dedicated volumes of *Tristram Shandy* in 1760 and then, obliquely, in 1766 when the ministry took over. As the novelist lay on his deathbed, the year also witnessed further episodes in the career of John Wilkes, a friend of Sterne, culminating in his triumph at the Middlesex election, prior to his imprisonment and his expulsion from the Commons twelve months later. In May came the notorious "massacre of St. George's Fields," when a large crowd of Wilkes's supporters held a rally in South London. When the Riot Act was read and the crowd failed to disperse, troops opened fire and killed between ten and twelve of those who were present. Demonstrations continued throughout the year, a sign of what has been called "a disastrous breakdown in the much-vaunted Hanoverian stability." Coal heavers, tailors, and silk weavers were among many groups to clash with the authorities. At one time all the merchant ships on the Thames were strikebound. "Even the whores in London brothels rioted over the exorbitant 'cuts' demanded by bawds, pimps, panders, tavern-keepers, and waiters."[1]

The events of recent months were well chronicled in the press, and though Sterne died before they came fully to a head, he must have been aware of the looming course of events as he spent his final weeks at the center of the city in Bond Street. He was in touch with as prominent a politician as Lord Shelburne, secretary of state and Chatham's anointed successor in the Rockingham faction of Whigs. Sterne never mentions any of these things in his letters, though he saw the lead-up to them after Wilkes's return from exile in the previous December, but of course that does not mean that he was oblivious to the state of the nation.

WORKS AND DAYS

The year 1767 began with a nightmare journey Sterne made to London from Coxwold. A blizzard sprang up as he left, and on the coach southward the travelers encountered "such a terrible Hurricane of Wind & snow" (*Letters*, 515). The immediate purpose of the trip was to superintend the publication of the ninth and final volume of *Tristram Shandy*, which would take place on January 30. Sterne had begun this segment in July 1766 after returning from his long sojourn on the Continent. At this stage he seems to have believed that he would return to Shandy's life story once he had completed a new project, a book planned in four volumes that would eventually turn into *A Sentimental Journey*. He thought that he might die with his pen in his hand but hoped that he might "live these ten years," a sadly optimistic forecast (*Letters*, 502, 489). In this volume there are a few proleptic hints of the later fiction, such as the "Invocation" in chapter 24 (*TS*, 9.24.780–784), which obliquely criticizes Smollett's *Travels through France and Italy* (published in May 1766), foreshadowing comments in his new book, and tells the story of the peasant girl Maria, reprised in a section near the end of *A Sentimental Journey* (*ASJ*, 37–38, 149–154).

With Sterne having rid himself for the time being of *Tristram Shandy*, he was looking to push ahead with his new venture while in London. His wife and daughter had remained in the south of France to winter in a balmier climate. He made some progress in collecting subscribers: "the undertaking is protected & highly encouraged by all our *Noblesse*—& at the rate tis subscribed—for, will bring me in a thousand guineas (au moins)—twil be an Original—in large Quarto—the Subscription half a Guinea" (*Letters*, 533). As it turned out, this was an unduly roseate estimate. In any case, he suffered a number of distractions as he began to write. One factor was an ominous decline in his health. In April, he felt pains severe enough to give rise to a fear that they might herald his imminent dissolution. "Death knocked at my door," he told Lord Shelburne on May 21 (*Letters*, 579). Two doctors diagnosed the problem as "a venerial Case" and recommended the standard treatment of "a Course of Van Sweetens corrosive Mercury" (*ASJ*, 177–180).[2] Sterne did not agree with their diagnosis, as he claimed to have abstained from sex for fifteen years (unlikely to be true). Arthur Cash has produced medical testimony to suggest that he was probably right about his condition: the symptoms all point to tuberculosis as the underlying cause of his malady (*LY*, 290).

The other distraction was less malign, though it would end in unfulfillment and regret. Late in January he met Elizabeth Draper, a woman of about twenty-three. She had returned to London with her two children temporarily from Bombay, where her husband, Daniel, was an East India Company official. Her marriage was unhappy, while Sterne's own had long been less than satisfying to both parties. He immediately began a tempestuous courtship, though one centered more on a vein of sentimental excess than any known physical relations. Eliza soon had to return to her hated husband, sailing from Deal on April 3, 1767. By that time the besotted Sterne had written her ten letters sharing intimate details of his life that even he kept from other people. After her departure, he embarked on his famous *Journal to Eliza* (entitled *Continuation of the Bramine's Journal* in the manuscript), a series of daily entries running from April 12 to August 4, a mixture of intense feeling with sometimes banal "dear Diary" material covering everyday happenings. Eliza wrote some letters back, if not a full-scale journal, but these are lost. The messages Sterne wrote before her departure were purloined by an unscrupulous bookseller and published in 1773: several forgeries and imitations would follow. Eliza eventually left her husband and came back to England, where she died in 1778. The manuscript of the *Bramine's Journal* disappeared before it was fortuitously rescued by a small boy playing in an old storeroom. Some years afterward, the finder lent it to W. M. Thackeray, who cited it at some length in his *English Humorists of the Eighteenth Century* (1853). It was printed in 1904 as part of the York edition (rather misleadingly titled, as it was issued in New York), with an introduction by the then-little-known Wilbur L. Cross. With some justice, he described the materials used in this volume, which included other letters and papers of the principals, as "by far the most important Sterne discovery of the nineteenth century."[3]

In late May it was time to head back to Yorkshire, again by means of a ponderous journey that took five days rather than the three usually allocated to the trip. The summer proved unproductive. Sterne had excuses ready. One of them was his continuing obsession with his platonic mistress: as he wrote in his journal to Eliza on June 3, "Cannot write my Travels, or give one half hours close attention to them, upon Thy Acc^{t}, my dearest friend" (*BJ*, 194). Or again: "this very morning that I set about writing my Sentimental Journey through France—have I received a letter from my wife, who is at Marseilles, advertising, that she is going (not to write,—but what is a much better thing) that she is going to make a Sentimental Journey through France, and post it a thousand miles, merely to pay me a visit of three months.—The deuce take all Sentimental Journeys!!" (*Letters*, 592). Elizabeth and Lydia Sterne did not arrive until the end of September. Meanwhile Laurence had paid visits to Byland Abbey near Coxwold; found time for a short stay with his friend John Hall-Stevenson at Crazy Castle; attended the York race meeting; and drank the waters at an inland spa, Harrogate, and a coastal resort, Scarborough. But that is the way writers often work. It was not until September that he managed to finish some of the early scenes and confidently told his publisher, Thomas Becket, on September 3, "my Sentimental Journey goes on well—and some Geniuses in the North declare it an Original Work, and likely to take in all Kinds of Readers" (*Letters*, 616). His faith in the project was on the rise: on November 12 he told Eliza Draper's friend Anne James, "My Sentimental Journey will please Mrs. James, and my Lydia—I can answer for those two. It is a subject which works well, and suits the frame of mind I have been in for some time past" (*Letters*, 629). He even began to make financial provisions for his family, including an alimony payment to his wife. As Cash shows, his ideas of what was possible were a little inflated (*LY*, 311). For a brief period, the sense of having to outrun his own mortality, which had long haunted his mind, seemed to recede a little. But another bout of sickness, with bleeding from his lungs, caused further delay in December, and he now realized that he must abandon the plan of a work in four volumes that he had dangled before subscribers. The only thing left was to publish the book as far as he had been able to take it.

Once the new year arrived, there was only a very short period remaining to Sterne. He left Yorkshire for the last time on December 30 or 31 in company with Hall-Stevenson and arrived in a damp London some three days later. As well as working on proofs, he tried at first to bustle around town in the old way. He went to see Sir Joshua Reynolds, then at the peak of his influence as president of the Royal Academy, who had painted an almost diabolic image of the writer in 1760. The first edition of *A Sentimental Journey* appeared on February 27. Becket announced the publication in the press, along with a reminder that the nine volumes of *Tristram Shandy* and the four volumes of *Sermons of Mr. Yorick* were available. Sterne survived long enough to write to Lydia, "My Sentimental Journey, you say, is admired in York by every one—and 'tis not vanity in me to tell you that it is no less admired here" (*Letters*, 656). There was a second edition on March 29, but by that time Sterne was dead. The end came on March 18, when the tuberculosis had done its full damage: "His disintegrated lungs had filled with fluid, bringing oxygen starvation, often a euphoric condition, and finally heart failure" (*LY*, 327). Somehow the idea of euphoria bursting into a scene of grief and pathos seems aptly Sternean.

Controversy and confusion did not die away with the author. There was the final batch of sermons in 1769; innumerable editions, legitimate or otherwise; parodies and continuations, all spurious; and collections of letters, of which the most authentic was the one made in 1775 by Lydia Sterne (now Medalle), on a brief visit from her home in France. Her mother had died in 1773. The writer left no will, and some predictable legal consequences ensued. Sterne's personal possessions were auctioned off at Coxwold, among them a cow near calving.

CONCLUSION

Sterne achieved an amazing amount in his relatively short literary career, which blossomed only in the last decade of his life. The range of activity he got through in 1767 and the early weeks of 1768 is remarkable, in view of his failing health, his marital difficulties, and his taste for social pleasures—not to mention his potentially comic involvement at fifty-four with a woman less than half his age. We can be grateful for the resilience that allowed him to complete the ninth segment of *Tristram Shandy*, which may or may not have been intended as bringing the work conclusively to its destination. Critics have long debated this question: I am inclined to agree with Marcia Allentuck, the author of a defense in *The Winged Skull* of an unfinished *Tristram Shandy*, that the book observes the protocol of *il non finito*. She distinguished between "a work which was moving towards a declared end but was aborted by its creator's death" or "a work interrupted, either by the ghost of the person from Porlock or by any other extraneous influences," and "a work with its own complete expressive value . . . which the artist *intended* to leave unfinished, like a torso or a sketch, a work still whole within itself."[4] This is in addition to the creation of *A Sentimental Journey*, a book that Sterne would surely have enlarged if he had been granted the opportunity; and the *Bramine's Journal*, a splendid miniature that could never be taken any further because of the most cogent "extraneous influences," imposed by geography, marital circumstances, and ultimately death. As this collection demonstrates, the writings that emerged within a period of just fifteen months, amid so many difficult circumstances, still have the power to excite and engage modern readers.

NOTES

1. Frank McGlynn, *Crime and Punishment in Eighteenth-Century England* (Oxford: Oxford University Press, 1991), 227–228.
2. A solution of mercury chloride, less toxic than the conventional dosage, was recommended by Gerard van Swieten (1700–1772), the Dutch physician to Empress Maria Theresa and perhaps the most distinguished pupil of Herman Boerhaave.
3. Wilbur L. Cross, introduction to *The Journal to Eliza and Various Letters by Laurence Sterne and Elizabeth Draper*, by Laurence Sterne (New York: J. F. Taylor, 1904), xv.
4. Marcia Allentuck, "In Defense of an Unfinished *Tristram Shandy*: Laurence Sterne and the *Non Finito*," in *The Winged Skull: Papers from the Laurence Sterne Bicentenary Conference*, ed. Arthur H. Cash and John M. Stedmond (Kent, OH: Kent State University Press, 1971), 147.

ACKNOWLEDGMENTS

The editors are grateful to Paul Goring, who offered invaluable input in the early stages of assembly, to Peter de Voogd, for his contributions to the bibliography, and to Melvyn New for his ongoing advice and support. We also are in great debt to the family and friends who have been supportive throughout this project.

BIBLIOGRAPHY

Addison, Joseph. *Cato: A Tragedy and Selected Essays*. Edited by Christine Dunn Henderson and Mark E. Yellin. Indianapolis: Liberty Fund, 2004.

Ahern, Stephen. *Affected Sensibilities: Romantic Excess and the Genealogy of the Novel, 1680–1810*. New York: AMS, 2007.

Allentuck, Marcia. "In Defense of an Unfinished *Tristram Shandy*: Laurence Sterne and the *Non Finito*." In *The Winged Skull: Papers from the Laurence Sterne Bicentenary Conference*, edited by Arthur H. Cash and John M. Stedmond, 145–155. Kent, OH: Kent State University Press, 1971.

Anderson, Emily Hodgson. "Theatrical *Tristram*: Sterne and *Hamlet* Reconsidered." *Eighteenth-Century Fiction* 27, nos. 3–4 (2015): 661–680.

Anderson, Fred. *Crucible of War: The Seven Years' War and the Fate of Empire in British North America, 1754–1766*. London: Faber and Faber, 2000.

Andrew, Donna. *Aristocratic Vice: The Attack on Duelling, Suicide, Gambling, and Adultery in Eighteenth-Century England*. New Haven, CT: Yale University Press, 2013.

Andrews, John. *An Account of the Character and Manners of the French; with Occasional Observations on the English*. 2 vols. London, 1770.

———. *Reflections on the Too Prevailing Spirit of Dissipation and Gallantry; Shewing its Dreadful Consequences to Publick Freedom*. London, 1771.

Anonymous. *The Clockmakers Outcry against the Author of "The Life and Opinions of Tristram Shandy."* Dublin, 1760.

———. *The History of Charlotte Summers, the Fortunate Parish Girl*. 2 vols. London: Corbett, 1750.

———. *The Life and Memoirs of Mr. Ephraim Tristram Bates*. London: W. Owen, 1756.

———. *Sterne's Maria: A Pathetic Story; With an Account of her Death, at the Castle of Valerine*. London: Rusted, [1800?].

Aristotle. *The "Art" of Rhetoric*. Edited and translated by John Henry Freese. Cambridge, MA: Harvard University Press, 1926.

Asfour, Lana. *Laurence Sterne in France*. London: Continuum, 2008.

Atwood, Margaret. *Payback: Debt and the Shadow Side of Wealth*. London: Bloomsbury, 2008.

Austen, Jane. *Emma*. Edited by James Kinsley. Oxford: Oxford University Press, 2008.

Auster, Paul. *In the Country of Last Things*. London: Faber, 1989.

Austin, Gilbert. *Chironomia; or A Treatise on Rhetorical Delivery*. London, 1806.

Bachelard, Gaston. *The Poetics of Space*. Translated by Maria Jolas. Boston: Beacon, 1994.

Bagehot, Walter. *The Works and Life of Walter Bagehot*. Vol. 4. London, 1915.

Baird, Ileana. "Introduction: Peregrine Things: Rethinking the Global in Eighteenth-Century Studies." In *Eighteenth-Century Thing Theory in a Global Context: From Consumerism to Celebrity Culture*, edited by Ileana Baird and Christina Ionescu, 1–16. New York: Routledge, 2013.

Baird, Ileana, and Christina Ionescu, eds. *Eighteenth-Century Thing Theory in a Global Context: From Consumerism to Celebrity Culture*. New York: Routledge, 2013.

Bandry, Anne. "First Reactions to *Tristram Shandy* in the Oates Collection." *Shandean* 1 (1989): 27–47.

———. "Imitations of *Tristram Shandy*." In *Critical Essays on Laurence Sterne*, edited by Melvyn New, 39–52. New York: G. K. Hall, 1998.

———. "Later Reactions to *Tristram Shandy* in the Oates Collection." *Shandean* 2 (1990): 27–44.

———. "Les livres de Sterne: Suites et fins." *XVII–XVIII: Revue de la Société d'études anglo-américaines des XVIIe et XVIIIe siècles* 50 (2000): 115–136.

Bandry-Scubbi, Anne, and Peter de Voogd, eds. *Hilarion's Asse: Sterne and Humour*. Newcastle, UK: Cambridge Scholars, 2013.

Bannet, Eve Tavor. *Eighteenth-Century Manners of Reading: Print Culture and Popular Instruction in the Anglophone Atlantic World*. Cambridge: Cambridge University Press, 2017.

Barker-Benfield, G. J. *The Culture of Sensibility: Sex and Society in Eighteenth-Century Britain*. Chicago: University of Chicago Press, 1992.

Barnes, Celia. "Orna Me: Laurence Sterne's Open Letter to Literary History." *Authorship* 5, no. 2 (2016): 1–10. https://doi.org/10.21825/aj.v5i2.3878.

Batten, Charles L., Jr. *Pleasurable Instruction: Form and Convention in Eighteenth-Century Travel Literature*. Berkeley: University of California Press, 1978.

Battestin, Martin C. "*A Sentimental Journey* and the Syntax of Things." In *Augustan Worlds*, edited by J. C. Hilson, M.M.B. Jones, and J. R. Watson, 223–239. New York: Barnes and Noble, 1978.

———. "Sterne among the Philosophes: Body and Soul in *A Sentimental Journey*." *Eighteenth-Century Fiction* 7, no. 1 (October 1994): 17–36.

Baugh, Daniel. *The Global Seven Years War, 1754–1763*. New York: Longman, 2011.

Bekoff, Marc. *The Emotional Lives of Animals*. Novato, CA: New World Library, 2007.

Bell, Michael. *Sentimentalism, Ethics and the Culture of Feeling*. Basingstoke, UK: Palgrave, 2000.

Benedict, Barbara M. *Framing Feeling: Sentiment and Style in English Prose Fiction, 1745–1800*. New York: AMS, 1994.

Bennett, Jane. *The Enchantment of Modern Life*. Princeton, NJ: Princeton University Press, 2001.

———. *Vibrant Matter: A Political Ecology of Things*. Durham, NC: Duke University Press, 2010.

Bensly, Edward. "A Debt of Sterne's." *Times Literary Supplement*, November 1, 1928.

Bentham, Jeremy. *An Introduction to the Principles of Morals and Legislation*. Edited by J. H. Burns and H.L.A. Hart. London: Athlone; Oxford: Clarendon, 1970.

Berger, John. "Why Look at Animals?" In *About Looking*, 3–28. New York: Pantheon Books, 1980.

Berkeley, George. *Three Dialogues between Hylas and Philonous*. Edited by Robert Merrihew Adams. Indianapolis: Hackett, 1982.

Black, Jeremy. *The British Abroad: The Grand Tour in the Eighteenth Century*. Stroud, UK: Sutton, 1992.

Blom, Philipp. *A Wicked Company: The Forgotten Radicalism of the European Enlightenment*. New York: Basic Books, 2010.

Bloom, Harold. *The Anxiety of Influence: A Theory of Poetry*. New York: Oxford University Press, 1973.

Bobker, Danielle. "Carriages, Conversation and *A Sentimental Journey*." *Studies in Eighteenth-Century Culture* 35 (2006): 243–266.

Bosch, René. *Labyrinth of Digressions: "Tristram Shandy" as Perceived and Influenced by Sterne's Early Imitators*. Translated by Piet Verhoeff. Amsterdam: Rodopi, 2007.

Boswell, James. *An Account of Corsica, the Journal of a Tour to That Island, and Memoirs of Pascal Paoli*. Edited by James T. Boulton and T. O. McLoughlin. Oxford: Oxford University Press, 2006.

———. *Boswell in Holland, 1763–1764.* Edited by Frederick A. Pottle. New York: McGraw-Hill, 1952.

———. *Boswell in Search of a Wife, 1766–1769.* Edited by Frank Brady and Frederick A. Pottle. New York: McGraw-Hill, 1956.

———. *Boswell on the Grand Tour: Germany and Switzerland, 1764.* Edited by Frederick A. Pottle. New York: McGraw-Hill, 1953.

———. *Boswell on the Grand Tour: Italy, Corsica, France.* Edited by Frank Brady and Frederick A. Pottle. New York: McGraw-Hill, 1955.

———. *Life of Johnson.* Edited by R. W. Chapman and Pat Rogers. Oxford: World Classics, 1980.

———. *London Journal.* Edited by Frederick A. Pottle. London: William Heinemann, 1951.

Boswell, James, and William Johnson Temple. *The Correspondence of James Boswell and William Johnson Temple, 1756–1795.* Vol. 1. Edited by Thomas Crawford. New Haven, CT: Yale University Press, 1997.

Bourdieu, Pierre. *Outline of a Theory of Practice.* Translated by Richard Nice. Cambridge: Cambridge University Press, 1977.

Brady, Frank. "*Tristram Shandy*: Sexuality, Morality, Sensibility." *Eighteenth-Century Studies* 4, no. 1 (1970): 41–56.

Brandtzæg, Siv Gøril, M-C. Newbould, and Helen Williams. "Advertising Sterne's Novels in Eighteenth-Century Newspapers." *Shandean* 27 (2016): 27–57.

Brantley, Richard E. *Transatlantic Trio: Empiricism, Evangelicalism, Romanticism.* Ames, IA: Culicidae, 2017.

Brecher, Bob. "Our Obligation to the Dead." *Journal of Applied Philosophy* 19, no. 2 (2002): 109–119.

Brewer, John. *The Sinews of Power: War, Money and the English State, 1688–1783.* Cambridge, MA: Harvard University Press, 1990.

Brissenden, R. F. *Virtue in Distress: Studies in the Novel of Sentiment from Richardson to Sade.* London: Macmillan, 1974.

Brown, Bill. *Other Things.* Chicago: University of Chicago Press, 2015.

———. "Thing Theory." *Critical Inquiry* 28, no. 1 (Autumn 2001): 1–22.

———. "Thing Theory." In *Things*, edited by Bill Brown, 1–22. Chicago: University of Chicago Press, 2004.

———, ed. *Things.* Chicago: University of Chicago Press, 2004.

Brunström, Conrad. *Thomas Sheridan's Career and Influence: An Actor in Earnest.* Lewisburg, PA: Bucknell University Press, 2011.

Bryson, Anna. *From Courtesy to Civility: Changing Codes of Conduct in Early Modern England.* Oxford: Clarendon, 1998.

Budrin, Peter. "The Shadow of Eliza in *A Sentimental Journey*." Paper presented at "Alas, Poor Yorick!": A Sterne 250-Year Anniversary Conference, Cambridge, UK, March 18–21, 2018.

Bullard, Paddy. "*Tristram Shandy*, Lord George Sackville, and Uncle Toby's Apologetical Oration." *Shandean* 14 (2003): 94–103.

Bulliet, Richard W. *Hunters, Herders, and Hamburgers. The Past and Future of Human-Animal Relationships.* New York: Columbia University Press, 2005.

Bulwer, John. *Chironomia; or, The Art of Manual Rhetorique of the Hand; Composed of the Speaking Motions, and Discoursing Gestures Thereof. . .* London, 1644.

Burns, Robert. *The Letters of Robert Burns.* Edited by J. DeLancey Ferguson and G. Ross Roy. Vol. 1. Oxford: Oxford University Press, 1985.

Butler, Judith. *Giving an Account of Oneself.* New York: Fordham University Press, 2005.

———. "Restaging the Universal." In *Contingency, Hegemony, Universality: Contemporary Dialogues on the Left*, by Judith Butler, Ernesto Laclau, and Slavoj Žižek, 11–43. London: Verso, 2000.

Cardwell, M. John. *Arts and Arms: Literature, Politics, and Patriotism during the Seven Years War.* Manchester: Manchester University Press, 2004.

Carter, Philip. *Men and the Emergence of Polite Society, Britain, 1660–1800.* Harlow, UK: Pearson, 2001.

Cash, Arthur H. *Laurence Sterne: The Early and Middle Years*. London: Methuen, 1975.

———. *Laurence Sterne: The Later Years*. London: Methuen, 1986.

———. *Sterne's Comedy of Moral Sentiments: The Ethical Dimension of the Journey*. Pittsburgh: Duquesne University Press, 1966.

Cash, Arthur H., and John M. Stedmond, eds. *The Winged Skull: Papers from the Laurence Sterne Bicentenary Conference*. Kent, OH: Kent State University Press, 1971.

Caudle, James C. "'Fact' or 'Invention'? James Boswell and the Legend of a Boswell-Sterne Meeting." *Shandean* 22 (2011): 30–55.

Cervantes, Miguel de. *The History and Adventures of the Renowned Don Quixote*. Translated by Tobias Smollett. Edited by Martin C. Battestin. Athens: University of Georgia Press, 2003.

Chandler, James. *An Archaeology of Sympathy: The Sentimental Mode in Literature and Cinema*. Chicago: University of Chicago Press, 2013.

———. "The Novelty of Laurence Sterne." In *The Oxford History of the Novel in English*, vol. 2, *English and British Fiction, 1750–1820*, edited by Peter Garside and Karen O'Brien, 109–128. Oxford: Oxford University Press, 2015.

Chapone, Hester. *Miscellanies in Verse and Prose*. London, 1775.

Chard, Chloe. "Crossing Boundaries and Exceeding Limits: Destabilization, Tourism, and the Sublime." In *Transports: Travel, Pleasure, and Imaginative Geography, 1600–1800*, edited by Chloe Chard and Helen Langdon, 117–149. New Haven, CT: Yale University Press, 1996.

Chico, Tita. "'The More I Write, the More I Shall Have to Write': The Many Beginnings of *Tristram Shandy*." In *Narrative Beginnings: Theories and Practices*, edited by Brian Richardson, 83–95. Lincoln: University of Nebraska Press, 2009.

Childs, John. *The Nine Years' War and the British Army, 1688–1697*. Manchester: Manchester University Press, 1991.

Cleland, John. *The Dictionary of Love*. London, 1753. A partial translation of Jean-François Dreux du Radier's *Dictionnaire d'amour*, 1741.

Cohen, Michèle. *Fashioning Masculinity: National Identity and Language in the Eighteenth Century*. London: Routledge, 1996.

———. "'Manners' Make the Man: Politeness, Chivalry and the Construction of Masculinity, 1750–1830." *Journal of British Studies* 44, no. 2 (April 2005): 312–329.

Conway, Stephen. *War, State, and Society in Mid-Eighteenth-Century Britain and Ireland*. Oxford: Oxford University Press, 2006.

Cooper, Anthony Ashley, Third Earl of Shaftesbury. *Characteristics of Men, Manners, Opinions, Times*. Edited by Laurence E. Klein. Cambridge: Cambridge University Press, 1999.

Croft, John. "Anecdotes of Sterne." *Shandean* 19 (2008): 47–55.

Cross, Wilbur L. Introduction to *The Journal to Eliza and Various Letters by Laurence Sterne and Elizabeth Draper*, by Laurence Sterne, ii–li. New York: J. F. Taylor, 1904.

———. *The Life and Times of Laurence Sterne*. New York: Macmillan, 1909.

Dames, Nicholas. "Trollope's Chapters." *Literature Compass* 7, no. 9 (2010): 855–860.

Davidson, Elizabeth. "*A Sentimental Journey*, Volume I: Yorick's Apprenticeship of Manners." *College Language Association Journal* 37, no. 4 (June 1994): 453–466.

Davidson, Jenny. *Hypocrisy and the Politics of Politeness: Manners and Morals from Locke to Austen*. Cambridge: Cambridge University Press, 2004.

Davis, Diane. "Creaturely Rhetorics." *Philosophy and Rhetoric* 44, no. 1 (2011): 88–94.

Day, W. G. "Charles Robert Leslie's 'My Uncle Toby and the Widow Wadman': The Nineteenth-Century Icon of Sterne's Work." *Shandean* 9 (1997): 83–108.

———. *Laurence Sterne: "A Sentimental Journey": A Bibliographical Catalogue of Editions Spanning Nearly Two and a Half Centuries*. York, UK: Spelman, 2005.

———. "Sternean Material Culture: Lorenzo's Snuff-Box and His Graves." In *The Reception of Laurence Sterne in Europe*, edited by Peter de Voogd and John Neubauer, 247–258. London: Thoemmes Continuum, 2004.

DeGooyer, Stephanie. "'The Eyes of Other People': Adam Smith's Triangular Sympathy and the Sentimental Novel." *ELH* 85, no. 3 (2018): 669–690.

———. "The Poetics of the Passport in *A Sentimental Journey*." In *Sterne, Tristram, Yorick: Tercentenary Essays on Laurence Sterne*, edited by Melvyn New, Peter de Voogd, and Judith Hawley, 201–218. Newark: University of Delaware Press, 2016.

Derrida, Jacques. *Limited Inc.* Translated by Jeffrey Mehlman and Samuel Weber. Evanston, IL: Northwestern University Press, 1988.

Derry, Stephen. "*Mansfield Park*, Sterne's Starling, and Bunyan's Man of Despair." *Notes and Queries* 44, no. 3 (1997): 322–323.

Descargues, Madeleine. "Fonctions d'un lettre d'amour, de la correspondance de Sterne à *A Sentimental Journey*." *XVII–XVIII: Revue de la Société d'études anglo-américaines des XVIIe et XVIIIe siècles* 31, no. 1 (1990): 143–157.

———. "*Tristram Shandy* and the Appositeness of War." In *Laurence Sterne's "Tristram Shandy": A Casebook*, edited by Thomas Keymer, 240–258. Oxford: Oxford University Press, 2006.

Dilworth, Ernest. *The Unsentimental Journey of Laurence Sterne*. New York: King's Crown, 1948.

Djordjevic, Igor. "The (In)Complete Quest of Sir Yorick, the Knight of Charity: *A Sentimental Journey* as a 'Cervantic' Romance." *Shandean* 14 (2003): 79–97.

Dussinger, John A. "Yorick and the 'Eternal Fountain of Our Feelings.'" In *Psychology and Literature in the Eighteenth Century*, edited by Christopher Fox, 259–276. New York: AMS, 1987.

Eagles, Robin. *Francophilia in English Society, 1748–1815*. Basingstoke, UK: Macmillan, 2000.

Easton, Fraser. "Christopher Smart's Elocution." In *Reading Christopher Smart in the Twenty-First Century*, edited by Min Wild and Noel Chevalier, 63–84. Lewisburg, PA: Bucknell University Press, 2013.

———. "Smart's Professors: Birdsong and Rhetorical Agency in *Jubilate Agno*." In *Mocking Bird Technologies: The Poetics of Parroting, Mimicry, and Other Starling Tropes*, edited by Christopher GoGwilt and Melanie D. Holm, 68–96. New York: Fordham University Press, 2018.

Eccles, Anastasia. "Formalism and Sentimentalism: Viktor Shklovsky and Laurence Sterne." *New Literary History* 47, no. 4 (2016): 525–545.

Ellis, Markman. *The History of Gothic Fiction*. Edinburgh: Edinburgh University Press, 2000.

———. *The Politics of Sensibility*. Cambridge: Cambridge University Press, 1996.

Ellmann, Richard. *James Joyce*. 2nd ed. Oxford: Oxford University Press, 1982.

Emmott, Catherine, and Marc Alexander. "Foregrounding, Burying and Plot Construction." In *The Cambridge Handbook of Stylistics*, edited by Peter Stockwell and Sara Whiteley, 329–343. Cambridge: Cambridge University Press, 2014.

Engberg-Pedersen, Anders. "The Refraction of Geometry: *Tristram Shandy* and the Poetics of War, 1700–1800." *Representations* 123, no. 1 (2013): 23–52.

Erasmus, Desiderius. *The Praise of Folly*. Translated by Hoyt Hopewell Hudson. Princeton, NJ: Princeton University Press, 1941.

———. *Praise of Folly and Other Writings*. Translated by Robert M. Adams. New York: Norton, 1989.

Fairer, David. "Sentimental Translation in Mackenzie and Sterne." *Essays in Criticism* 49, no. 2 (April 1999): 132–151.

Fanning, Christopher. "On Sterne's Page: Spatial Layout, Spatial Form, and Social Spaces in *Tristram Shandy*." *Eighteenth-Century Fiction* 10 (1997–1998): 429–450.

Ferguson, Adam. *An Essay on the History of Civil Society*. Edinburgh, 1767.

Ferriar, John. *Illustrations of Sterne: With Other Essays and Verse*. London: Cadell and Davies, 1798.

Festa, Lynn. *Sentimental Figures of Empire in Eighteenth-Century Britain and France*. Baltimore: Johns Hopkins University Press, 2006.

Fielding, Henry. *Joseph Andrews*. Edited by Martin C. Battestin. Oxford: Clarendon, 1967.

———. *Tom Jones*. Edited by John Bender and Simon Stern. Oxford: Oxford University Press, 1998.

Finer, Emily. *Turning into Sterne: Viktor Shklovskii and Literary Reception*. Leeds, UK: Legenda, 2010.

Finn, Margot. *The Character of Credit: Personal Debt in English Culture, 1740–1914*. Cambridge: Cambridge University Press, 2003.

Fitzgerald, Percy. *The Life of Laurence Sterne*. 2 vols. London: Chapman and Hall, 1864.

Fletcher, Anthony. *Gender, Sex and Subordination in England, 1500–1800*. New Haven, CT: Yale University Press, 1995.

Fluchère, Henri. *Laurence Sterne: From Tristram to Yorick: An Interpretation of "Tristram Shandy."* Translated by Barbara Bray. London: Oxford University Press, 1965.

Frank, Judith. *Common Ground: Eighteenth-Century English Satiric Fiction and the Poor*. Stanford, CA: Stanford University Press, 2002.

Franssen, Paul. "'Great Lessons of Political Instruction': The Earl of Clonmell Reads Sterne." *Shandean* 2 (1990): 152–201.

Fussell, Paul. *Abroad: British Literary Traveling between the Wars*. Oxford: Oxford University Press, 1980.

Genette, Gérard. *Paratexts: Thresholds of Interpretation*. Translated by Jane E. Lewin. Cambridge: Cambridge University Press, 1997.

Gentner, Timothy Q., Kimberly M. Fenn, Daniel Margoliash, and Howard C. Nusbaum. "Recursive Syntactic Pattern Learning by Songbirds." *Nature* 440, no. 7088 (2006): 1204–1207.

Gerard, W. B. "'All that the heart wishes': Changing Views toward Sentimentality Reflected in Visualizations of Sterne's Maria, 1773–1888." *Studies in Eighteenth-Century Culture* 34 (2004): 197–269.

———. "'Betwixt One Passion and Another': Continuations of Laurence Sterne's *A Sentimental Journey*, 1769–1820." In *On Second Thought: Updating the Eighteenth-Century Text*, edited by Debra Taylor Bourdeau and Elizabeth Kraft, 123–138. Newark: University of Delaware Press, 2007.

———, ed., *Divine Rhetoric: Essays on the Sermons of Laurence Sterne*. Newark: University of Delaware Press, 2010.

———. "The First 'Temptation' of Yorick, or, a Pirate Tale." *Shandean* 15 (2004): 107–116.

———. *Laurence Sterne and the Visual Imagination*. Aldershot, UK: Ashgate, 2006.

———. "Poor Maria as Model of Empathic Response." In *The Palgrave Handbook of Affect Studies and Textual Criticism*, edited by Donald W. Wehrs and Thomas Blake, 481–512. London: Palgrave Macmillan, 2017.

———. "Sterne in Wedgwood: 'Poor Maria' and the 'Bourbonnais Shepherd.'" *Shandean* 12 (2001): 78–88.

Gladfelder, Hal. *Fanny Hill in Bombay: The Making and Unmaking of John Cleland*. Baltimore: Johns Hopkins University Press, 2012.

Goodhue, Elizabeth K. "When Yorick Takes His Tea: Or, the Commerce of Consumptive Passions in the Case of Laurence Sterne." *Journal for Early Modern Cultural Studies* 6, no. 1 (2006): 51–83.

Gordon, Catherine. *British Paintings of Subjects from the English Novel, 1740–1870*. New York: Garland, 1988.

———. "'More than one handle': The Development of Sterne Illustration 1760–1820." *Words: Wai-te-Ata Studies in Literature* 4 (1974): 47–58.

Gordon, Robert C. *Arms and the Imagination: Essays on War, Politics, and Anglophone Culture*. Lanham, MD: Rowman and Littlefield, 2009.

Goring, Paul. "'Into What a Delicious Riot of Things am I Rushing?': Material Things and Humour in *Tristram Shandy*." In *Hilarion's Asse: Laurence Sterne and Humour*, edited by Anne Bandry-Scubbi and Peter de Voogd, 81–91. Newcastle, UK: Cambridge Scholars, 2013.

———. Introduction to *A Sentimental Journey through France and Italy*, by Laurence Sterne, xi–xxxii. London: Penguin, 2001.

———. *The Rhetoric of Sensibility in Eighteenth-Century Culture*. Cambridge: Cambridge University Press, 2005.

Gray, John. *Liberalism*. Edited by Frank Parkin. 2nd ed. Minneapolis: University of Minnesota Press, 1995.

Green, Robert A. *The Hurdy-Gurdy in Eighteenth-Century France*. Bloomington: Indiana University Press, 1995.

Greene, Donald. "The World's Worst Biography." *American Scholar* 62, no. 3 (1993): 365–382.

Griffith, Richard. *A Series of Genuine Letters between Henry and Frances*. Vol. 5. London, 1770.

Guest, Harriet. "Sterne, Elizabeth Draper, and Drapery." *Shandean* 9 (1997): 8–33.

Gulddal, Jesper. "Porous Borders: The Passport as an Access Metaphor in Laurence Sterne's *A Sentimental Journey*." *symploke* 25, nos. 1–2 (2017): 43–59.

Harley, J. B. "Deconstructing the Map." *Cartographica* 26, no. 2 (Spring 1989): 1–20.

Harris, Elizabeth W. "Words, Sex and Gender in Sterne's Novels." In *The Cambridge Companion to Laurence Sterne*, edited by Thomas Keymer, 111–125. Cambridge: Cambridge University Press, 2009.

Harvey, Karen. *The Little Republic: Masculinity and Domestic Authority in Eighteenth-Century Britain*. Oxford: Oxford University Press, 2012.

Haupt, Lyanda Lynn. *Mozart's Starling*. London: Little, Brown, 2017.

Hauser, Marc D., Noam Chomsky, and W. Tecumseh Fitch, "The Faculty of Language: What Is It, Who Has It, and How Did It Evolve?" *Science* 298, no. 5598 (2002): 1569–1579.

Hawhee, Debra. *Rhetoric in Tooth and Claw: Animals, Language, Sensation*. Chicago: University of Chicago Press, 2017.

Hawley, Judith. "Digressive and Progressive Movements: Sympathy and Sexuality in *Tristram Shandy*; or, Plain Stories." In *Digressions in European Literature: From Cervantes to Sebald*, edited by Alexis Grohmann and Caragh Wells, 21–35. Basingstoke, UK: Palgrave Macmillan, 2011.

Hegel, G.W.F. *Hegel's Logic: Being Part One of The Encyclopaedia of the Philosophical Sciences (1830)*. Translated by William Wallace. Oxford: Clarendon Press, 1975.

Hewins, W.A.S., ed. *The Whitefoord Papers*. Oxford: Clarendon, 1898.

Holtz, William V. *Image and Immortality: A Study of "Tristram Shandy."* Providence, RI: Brown University Press, 1970.

Hoppit, Julian. "Attitudes to Credit in Britain, 1680–1790." *Historical Journal* 33 (1990): 305–322.

Howes, Alan B. *Laurence Sterne: The Critical Heritage*. London: Routledge, 1974.

Hume, David. "Of the Rise and Progress of the Arts and Sciences." In *Essays Moral, Political and Literary*, edited by Eugene F. Miller, 111–137. Indianapolis: Liberty Classics, 1987.

Hunter, J. Paul. "From Typology to Type: Agents of Change in Eighteenth-Century English Texts." In *Cultural Artifacts and the Production of Meaning: The Page, the Image, and the Body*, edited by Margaret J. M. Ezell and Katherine O'Brien O'Keeffe, 41–69. Ann Arbor: University of Michigan Press, 1994.

Hurd, Richard. *Letters on Chivalry and Romance*. London, 1762.

Johnson, Claudia L. *Equivocal Beings: Politics, Gender and Sentimentality in the 1790s: Wollstonecraft, Radcliffe, Burney, Austen*. Chicago: University of Chicago Press, 1995.

Johnson, Samuel. *A Dictionary of the English Language in which the Words Are Deduced from Their Originals and Illustrated in Their Different Significations by Examples from the Best Writers*. 2 vols. London, 1755.

———. *A Journey to the Western Islands of Scotland*. Edited by Peter Levi. Harmondsworth, UK: Penguin, 1984.

———. *The Sermons of Samuel Johnson*. Edited by Jean Hagstrum and James Gray. New Haven, CT: Yale University Press, 1978.

Jones, Robert W. *Literature, Gender and Politics in Britain during the War for America, 1770–1785*. Cambridge: Cambridge University Press, 2011.

Jonson, Ben. *The Works of Ben Jonson, Volume the Sixth*. London, 1756.

Kay, Carol. *Political Constructions: Defoe, Richardson, and Sterne in Relation to Hobbes, Hume, and Burke*. Ithaca, NY: Cornell University Press, 1988.

Keenleyside, Heather. *Animals and Other People: Literary Forms and Living Beings in the Eighteenth Century*. Philadelphia: University of Pennsylvania Press, 2016.

———. "The First-Person Form of Life: Locke, Sterne, and the Autobiographical Animal." *Critical Inquiry* 39 (Autumn 2012): 116–141.

Kelly, Ann Cline. "Talking Animals in the Bible: Paratexts as Symptoms of Cultural Anxiety in Restoration and Early Eighteenth-Century England." *Journal for Eighteenth-Century Studies* 33, no. 4 (2010): 437–451.

Kennedy, George A. "A Hoot in the Dark: The Evolution of General Rhetoric." *Philosophy and Rhetoric* 25, no. 1 (1992): 1–21.

Keymer, Thomas. "Marvell, Thomas Hollis, and Sterne's Maria: Parody in *A Sentimental Journey*." *Shandean* 5 (1993): 9–31.

———. "Paper Wars: Literature and/as Conflict during the Seven Years' War." In *The Culture of the Seven Years' War: Empire, Identity, and the Arts in the Eighteenth-Century Atlantic World*, edited by Frans De Bruyn and Shaun Regan, 119–146. Toronto: Toronto University Press, 2014.

———. "*A Sentimental Journey* and the Failure of Feeling." In *The Cambridge Companion to Laurence Sterne*, edited by Thomas Keymer, 79–94. Cambridge: Cambridge University Press, 2009.

———. *Sterne, the Moderns, and the Novel*. Oxford: Oxford University Press, 2002.

Klein, Lawrence E. *Shaftesbury and the Culture of Politeness: Moral Discourse and Cultural Politics in Early Eighteenth-Century England*. Cambridge: Cambridge University Press, 1994.

Kraft, Elizabeth. "Laurence Sterne and the Ethics of Sexual Difference: Chiasmic Narration and Double Desire." *Christianity and Literature* 51, no. 3 (2002): 363–385.

———. *Laurence Sterne Revisited*. New York: Twayne, 1996.

Kundera, Milan. *The Book of Laughter and Forgetting*. Translated by Michael Henry Haim. Harmondsworth, UK: Penguin, 1984.

Lacey, Karen. *A Class Apart: The Military Man in French and British Fiction, 1740–1789*. Bern: Peter Lang, 2016.

Lamb, Jonathan. "Language and Hartleian Associationism in *A Sentimental Journey*." *Eighteenth-Century Studies* 13, no. 3 (Spring 1980): 285–312.

———. "Sterne, Sebald and Siege Architecture." *Eighteenth-Century Fiction* 19, no. 1 (2006): 21–41.

———. *Sterne's Fiction and the Double Principle.* Cambridge: Cambridge University Press, 1989.

Lamb, Susan. *Bringing Travel Home to England: Tourism, Gender and Imaginative Literature.* Cranbury, NJ: Associated University Presses, 2009.

Landow, George P. "*Tristram Shandy* and the Comedy of Context," *BYU Studies Quarterly* 7, no. 3 (1966): 208–224.

Langford, Paul. *A Polite and Commercial People: England, 1727–1783.* Oxford: Clarendon, 1989.

Lanham, Richard A. *"Tristram Shandy": The Games of Pleasure.* Berkeley: University of California Press, 1973.

Large, Duncan. "'The Freest Writer': Nietzsche on Sterne." *Shandean* 7 (1995): 9–29.

Leavis, F. R. *The Great Tradition.* New York: Doubleday, 1954.

Leewen, Eva C. van. *Sterne's "Journal to Eliza": A Semiological and Linguistic Approach to the Text.* Tübingen: G. Narr, 1981.

Le Neindre, Pierre, Emilie Bernard, Alain Boissy, et al. "Animal Consciousness." European Food Safety Authority, April 24, 2017. doi: 10.2903/sp.efsa.2017.EN-1196.

Lipski, Jakub. "The Masquerade Metaphor and the Paradoxes of Sentiment in *A Sentimental Journey.*" In *Sterne, Tristram, Yorick: Tercentenary Essays on Laurence Sterne*, edited by Melvyn New, Peter de Voogd, and Judith Hawley, 187–199. Newark: University of Delaware Press, 2016.

———. "'Too much for Nature': Laurence Sterne's *Continuation of the Bramine's Journal* and the Language of Theatre." *New Review: An International Journal of British Studies* 5 (2015): 53–62.

Low, Philip. The Cambridge Declaration on Consciousness. Edited by Jaak Panksepp, Diana Reiss, David Edelman, Bruno Van Swinderen, Philip Low, and Christof Koch. Presented at the Francis Crick Memorial Conference on Consciousness in Human and Non-Human Animals at Churchill College, University of Cambridge, UK, July 7, 2012.

Lupton, Christina. *Reading and the Making of Time in the Eighteenth Century.* Baltimore: Johns Hopkins University Press, 2018.

Lynch, Deidre. "Personal Effects and Sentimental Fictions." In *The Secret Life of Things: Animals, Objects, and It-Narratives in Eighteenth-Century England*, edited by Mark Blackwell, 63–91. Lewisburg, PA: Bucknell University Press, 2007.

Mahon, M. Wade. "Making the Green One Red: Elocution, Emotion, and the Impact of Print Literacy." *Eighteenth Century* 58 (2017): 321–335.

Markley, Robert. "Sentiment as Performance: Shaftesbury, Sterne, and the Theatrics of Virtue." In *The New Eighteenth-Century*, edited by Felicity Nussbaum and Laura Brown, 210–230. New York: Methuen, 1987. Also in *Critical Essays on Laurence Sterne*, edited by Melvyn New, 270–91. New York: G. K. Hall, 1998.

Martinez, Marc. "Asses, Artichokes and Macaroons: The Joco-Serious Humour of *Tristram Shandy.*" In *Hilarion's Asse: Laurence Sterne and Humour*, edited by Anne Bandry-Scubbi and Peter de Voogd, 53–65. Newcastle, UK: Cambridge Scholars, 2013.

Mason, John. *An Essay on Elocution, or, Pronunciation.* London, 1748.

Massumi, Brian. "The Autonomy of Affect." *Cultural Critique* 31 (Fall 1995): 83–109.

Mathee, Rudi. "Exotic Substances: The Introduction and Global Spread of Tobacco, Coffee, Cocoa, Tea, and Distilled Liquor, Sixteenth to Eighteenth Centuries." In *Drugs and Narcotics in History*, edited by Roy Porter and Mikuláš Teich, 24–51. Cambridge: Cambridge University Press, 1997.

McCormack, Matthew. "Citizenship, Nationhood and Masculinity in the Affair of the Hanoverian Soldier." *Historical Journal* 49, no. 4 (2006): 971–993.

———. *Embodying the Militia in Georgian England*. Oxford: Oxford University Press, 2015.

———. *The Independent Man: Citizenship and Gender Politics in Georgian England*. Manchester: Manchester University Press, 2005.

McDermott, Ray. "Yorick's Ethnographic Journey." In *Sterne, Tristram, Yorick: Tercentenary Essays on Laurence Sterne*, edited by Melvyn New, Peter de Voogd, and Judith Hawley, 169–186. Newark: University of Delaware Press, 2016.

McDowell, Paula. *The Invention of the Oral: Print Commerce and Fugitive Voices in Eighteenth-Century Britain*. Chicago: University of Chicago Press, 2017.

McGlynn, Frank. *Crime and Punishment in Eighteenth-Century England*. Oxford: Oxford University Press, 1991.

McGuirk, Carol. "Sentimental Encounter in Sterne, Mackenzie, and Burns." *Studies in English Literature, 1500–1900* 20, no. 3 (1980): 505–515.

McMaster, Juliet. "Walter Shandy, Sterne and Gender: A Feminist Foray." In *Critical Essays on Laurence Sterne*, edited by Melvyn New, 198–214. New York: G. K. Hall, 1998.

McMurran, Mary Helen. "The New Cosmopolitanism and the Eighteenth Century." *Eighteenth-Century Studies* 47, no. 1 (Fall 2013): 19–38.

Menely, Tobias. *The Animal Claim: Sensibility and the Creaturely Voice*. Chicago: University of Chicago Press, 2015.

———. "Zoöphilpsychosis: Why Animals Are What's Wrong with Sentimentality." *symploke* 15, nos. 1–2 (2007): 244–267.

Millar, John. *Observations Concerning the Distinction of Ranks in Society*. London, 1771.

Moglen, Helene. *The Philosophical Irony of Laurence Sterne*. Gainesville: University Press of Florida, 1975.

Moores, John Richard. *Representations of France in English Satirical Prints, 1740–1832*. Basingstoke, UK: Palgrave Macmillan, 2015.

Moretti, Franco. *Atlas of the European Novel, 1800–1900*. London: Verso, 1999.

Mullan, John. *Sentiment and Sociability: The Language of Feeling in the Eighteenth Century*. Oxford: Clarendon, 1988.

———. "Sentimental Novels." In *The Cambridge Companion to the Eighteenth-Century Novel*, edited by John Richetti, 236–254. Cambridge: Cambridge University Press, 1996.

Murphy, Anne L. "Making the Market: Trading Debt at the Eighteenth-Century Bank of England." EABH Papers 14-05, European Association for Banking and Financial History, 2014. https://ideas.repec.org/p/zbw/eabhps/1405.html.

New, Melvyn, ed. *Approaches to Teaching Sterne's "Tristram Shandy."* New York: Modern Language Association of America, 1989.

———, ed. *Critical Essays on Laurence Sterne*. New York: Prentice Hall, 1998.

———. "A Genius of the Cast: Celebrating Sterne." *Shandean* 26 (2015): 9–26.

———. Introduction to *Theology and Literature in the Age of Johnson: Resisting Secularism*, edited by Melvyn New and Gerard Reedy S.J., ix–xxi. Newark: University of Delaware Press, 2012.

———. "Job's Wife and Sterne's Other Women." In *Out of Bounds: Male Writers and Gender(ed) Criticism*, edited by Laura Claridge and Elizabeth Langland, 55–74. Amherst: University of Massachusetts Press, 1990. Also in *Laurence Sterne*, edited by Marcus Walsh, 69–90. London: Routledge, 2002.

———. *Laurence Sterne as Satirist: A Reading of "Tristram Shandy."* Gainesville: University Press of Florida, 1969.

———. "A Manuscript of the Le Fever Episode in *Tristram Shandy*." *Scriblerian* 23, no. 2 (1991): 165–174.

———. "Proust's Influence on Sterne: Remembrance of Things to Come." *Modern Language Notes* 103, no. 5 (1988): 1031–1055.

———. "Reading Sterne through Proust and Levinas." In *In Proximity: Emmanuel Levinas and the Eighteenth Century*, edited by Melvyn New with Robert Bernasconi and Richard A. Cohen, 111–140. Lubbock: Texas Tech University Press, 2001.

———. "*Sir Charles Grandison* and Laurence Sterne: A Study in Influence." *Modern Philology* 115, no. 2 (2017): 213–243.

———. "Sterne and the Narrative of Determinateness." *Eighteenth-Century Fiction* 4 (1992): 315–329.

———. "Three Sentimental Journeys: Sterne, Shklovsky, Svevo." *Shandean* 11 (1999–2000): 125–134.

———. *"Tristram Shandy": A Book for Free Spirits.* New York: Twayne, 1994.

New, Melvyn, Peter de Voogd, and Judith Hawley, eds. *Sterne, Tristram, Yorick: Tercentenary Essays on Laurence Sterne.* Newark: University of Delaware Press, 2016.

Newbould, M-C. *Adaptations of Laurence Sterne's Fiction: Sterneana, 1760–1840.* Farnham, UK: Ashgate, 2013.

———. "'Illustrating' *A Sentimental Journey*: The 'First Annotated Edition' of 1803?" *Shandean* 24 (2013): 103–124.

———. "Sex, Death and the Aposiopesis: Two Early Attempts to Fill the Gaps of Laurence Sterne's *A Sentimental Journey*." *Postgraduate English* 17 (March 2008): 1–27.

Newman, Gerald. *The Rise of English Nationalism: A Cultural History, 1740–1830.* London: Weidenfeld and Nicolson, 1987.

Newton, Geoff. "Divine and Human Love: Letters between John Norris and Mary Astell, Laurence Sterne and Eliza Draper." In *Theology and Literature in the Age of Johnson*, edited by Melvyn New and Gerard Reedy S.J., 183–201. Newark: University of Delaware Press, 2012.

Norris, John. *A Collection of Miscellanies.* 2nd ed. London, 1692.

Oakley, Warren L. *A Culture of Mimicry: Laurence Sterne, His Readers and the Art of Bodysnatching.* London: Maney, 2010.

———. "Physical Encounters as a Point of Contact between Sterne's *Journey* and De Quincey's *Confessions*." *Romanticism* 18, no. 2 (2012): 182–190.

O'Brien, Karen. *Women and Enlightenment in Eighteenth-Century Britain.* Cambridge: Cambridge University Press, 2009.

Ogée, Frédéric. "The Erratic and the Erotic: The Aesthetics of *A Sentimental Journey*." *Shandean* 24 (2013): 104–116.

Orr, Leah. *Novel Ventures: Fiction and Print Culture, 1690–1730.* Charlottesville: University of Virginia Press, 2017.

Owen, Jim. "Laurence Sterne and the Caged Starling of *A Sentimental Journey*." *CEA Critic* 64, nos. 2–3 (Winter–Spring/Summer 2002): 22–34.

Parkes, Simon. "Wooden Legs and Tales of Sorrow Done: The Literary Broken Soldier of the Late Eighteenth Century." *Journal for Eighteenth-Century Studies* 36, no. 2 (June 2013): 190–207.

Parnell, Tim. "A Story Painted to the Heart? *Tristram Shandy* and Sentimentalism Reconsidered." *Shandean* 9 (1997): 122–135.

Peace, Mary. "'On the soft beds of luxury most kingdoms have expired': 1759 and the Lives of Prostitutes." In *Reading 1759: Literary Culture in Mid-Eighteenth-Century Britain and France*, edited by Shaun Regan, 75–91. Lewisburg, PA: Bucknell University Press, 2013.

Pearl, Jason H. "Woodes Rogers and the Boundary of Travel Facts." *Eighteenth-Century Life* 30, no. 3 (Fall 2007): 60–75.

Peltonen, Markku. *The Duel in Early Modern England: Civility, Politeness and Honour.* Cambridge: Cambridge University Press, 2003.

Pennant, Thomas. *A Tour in Scotland, and Voyage to the Hebrides: Part 1.* 2nd ed. London, 1776.

Pickford, Susan. "Les notes éditoriales comme élément constitutif du statut d'un ouvrage classique: L'exemple de *A Sentimental Journey* de Laurence Sterne." In *L'espace de la note*, edited by Jacques Dürrenmatt and Andréas Pfersmann, 213–225. Rennes: La Licorne, 2004.

Pierce, David, and Peter de Voogd, eds. *Laurence Sterne in Modernism and Postmodernism.* Amsterdam: Rodopi, 1996.

Plotz, John. "Can the Sofa Speak? A Look at Thing Theory." *Criticism* 47, no. 1 (Winter 2005): 109–118.

———. *Portable Property: Victorian Culture on the Move.* Princeton, NJ: Princeton University Press, 2008.

Plumb, Christopher. "'The Queen's Ass': The Cultural Life of Queen Charlotte's Zebra in Georgian Britain." In *The Afterlives of Animals*, edited by Samuel J.M.M. Alberti, 17–36. Charlottesville: University of Virginia Press, 2011.

Pope, Alexander. *Memoirs of the Extraordinary Life, Works, and Discoveries of Martinus Scriblerus.* Edited by Charles Kerby-Miller. Oxford: Oxford University Press, 1988.

Pottle, Frederick A. Introduction to *London Journal*, by James Boswell, 1–37. London: William Heinemann, 1951.

Pratt, Mary Louise. "Arts of the Contact Zone." *Profession* 91 (1991): 33–40.

Putney, Rufus. "The Evolution of *A Sentimental Journey*." *Philological Quarterly* 19 (1940): 349–369.

Quintilian. *The Orator's Education.* Vol. 5. Edited and translated by Donald A. Russell. Cambridge, MA: Harvard University Press, 2001.

Rabb, Melinda Alliker. "Engendering Accounts in Sterne's *A Sentimental Journey*." In *Johnson and His Age*, edited by James Engell, 531–558. Cambridge, MA: Harvard University Press, 1984.

———. *Miniature and the English Imagination: Literature, Cognition, and Small-Scale Culture, 1650–1765.* Cambridge: Cambridge University Press, 2019.

Rasula, Jed. "Understanding the Sound of Not Understanding." In *Close Listening: Poetry and the Performed Word*, edited by Charles Bernstein, 247–251. New York: Oxford University Press, 1998.

Read, Herbert. Introduction to *A Sentimental Journey through France and Italy*, by Laurence Sterne, ix–xlii. London: Scholartis, 1929.

Reeve, Clara. *The Progress of Romance, through Times, Countries and Manners.* 2 vols. Colchester, UK: W. Keymer; London: G.G.J. and J. Robinson, 1785.

Regan, Shaun. "Peripatetic Philosophy: Sterne and Cosmopolitanism." *Textual Practice* 31, no. 2 (2017): 265–282.

———. "Print Culture in Transition: *Tristram Shandy*, the Reviewers, and the Consumable Text." *Eighteenth-Century Fiction* 14, nos. 3–4 (2002): 289–309.

———, ed. *Reading 1759: Literary Culture in Mid-Eighteenth-Century Britain and France.* Lewisburg, PA: Bucknell University Press, 2013.

Rivers, Isabel. *Reason, Grace, and Sentiment: A Study of the Language of Religion and Ethics in England, 1660–1780.* Vol. 1, *Whichcote to Wesley.* Cambridge: Cambridge University Press, 1991.

Rose, Margaret A. *Parody: Ancient, Modern, and Post-Modern.* Cambridge: Cambridge University Press, 1993.

Ross, Ian Campbell. *Laurence Sterne: A Life.* Oxford: Oxford University Press, 2001.

Rousseau, Jean-Jacques. *Emilius and Sophia; or, A New System of Education.* Vol. 4. London: T. Becket and P. A. de Hondt, 1763.

———. *Jean-Jacques Rousseau: Fundamental Political Writings.* Edited by Matthew W. Maguire and David Lay Williams. Translated by Ian Johnston. Peterborough, ON: Broadview, 2018.

Rowe, Nicolas. *The Fair Penitent*. Edited by Malcolm Goldstein. Lincoln: University of Nebraska Press, 1969.

Saintsbury, George. Introduction to *A Sentimental Journey through France and Italy* and *The Journal to Eliza*, by Laurence Sterne, vii–xv, vol. 4 of *The Works of Laurence Sterne*, edited by George Saintsbury. London: Dent, 1894.

Salter, David. "Remembering the Catholic Middle Ages: The Franciscans, English National Identity, and William Hogarth's *The Roast Beef of Old England*." *Logos: A Journal of Catholic Thought and Culture* 16, no. 4 (2013): 99–123.

Santovetti, Olivia. "The Adventurous Journey of Lorenzo Sterne in Italy." *Shandean* 8 (1996): 79–97.

Schaefer, Donovan. *Religious Affects: Animality, Evolution, and Power*. Durham, NC: Duke University Press, 2015.

Scott, James C. *The Art of Not Being Governed: An Anarchist History of Upland Southeast Asia*. New Haven, CT: Yale University Press, 2009.

Sedgwick, Eve Kosofsky. *Between Men: English Literature and Male Homosocial Desire*. New York: Columbia University Press, 1985.

Seidel, Michael. "Narrative Crossings: Sterne's *A Sentimental Journey*." *Genre* 18 (1985): 1–22.

Shakespeare, William. *Hamlet: The Texts of 1603 and 1623*. Edited by Ann Thompson and Neil Taylor. London: Arden Shakespeare, 2006.

———. *The Sonnets*. Edited by G. Blakemore Evans. Introduction by Stephen Orgel. 2nd ed. Cambridge: Cambridge University Press, 2006.

Shell, Marc. *The Economy of Literature*. Baltimore: Johns Hopkins University Press, 1978.

Sheridan, Thomas. *A Course of Lectures on Elocution*. London, 1762.

Shevelow, Kathryn. *For the Love of Animals: The Rise of the Animal Protection Movement*. New York: Henry Holt, 2008.

Shklovsky, Viktor. "A Parodying Novel: Sterne's *Tristram Shandy*." Translated by W. George Isaak. In *Laurence Sterne: A Collection of Critical Essays*, edited by John Traugott, 66–89. Englewood Cliffs, NJ: Prentice Hall, 1968.

Siskin, Clifford. *System: The Shaping of Modern Knowledge*. Cambridge, MA: MIT Press, 2013.

Smith, Adam. *Inquiry into the Nature and Causes of the Wealth of Nations*. Edited by R. H. Campbell and A. S. Skinner. 2 vols. Oxford: Oxford University Press, 1976.

———. *Lectures on Rhetoric and Belles Lettres*. Edited by John M. Lothian. London: Nelson, 1963.

Smith, Jeffrey. "Natural Desire and Natural Morality in *A Sentimental Journey* (1)." *Shandean* 22 (2011): 64–86.

———. "Natural Desire and Natural Morality in *A Sentimental Journey* (2)." *Shandean* 23 (2012): 9–36.

Smitten, Jeffrey R. "Gesture and Expression in Eighteenth-Century Fiction: *A Sentimental Journey*." *Modern Language Studies* 9 (1979): 85–97.

Smollett, Tobias. *A Complete History of England*. 3rd ed. 9 vols. London: James Rivington and James Fletcher, 1759.

———. *Travels through France and Italy*. Edited by Frank Felsenstein. Oxford: Oxford University Press, 1979.

Soud, Stephen. "'Weavers, Gardeners, and Gladiators': Labyrinths in *Tristram Shandy*." *Eighteenth-Century Studies* 28, no. 4 (1995): 397–411.

Soupel, Serge. "*The Journal to Eliza* (13 Avril–1er Novembre 1767) de Sterne: Mémoire et imagination." *XVII–XVIII: Revue de la Société d'études anglo-américaines des XVIIe et XVIIIe siècles* 26, no. 1 (1988): 25–35.

———. "Lavieille, Hédouin, Leloir and the *Voyage Sentimental*." *Shandean* 2 (1990): 202–213.

South, Robert. *Twelve Sermons Preached upon Several Occasions*. 2 vols. London, 1692.

Spacks, Patricia Meyer. *Privacy: Concealing the Eighteenth-Century Self.* Chicago: Chicago University Press, 2003.

Speltz, Andrea. "War and Sentimentalism: Irony in Voltaire's *Candide*, Sterne's *Tristram Shandy*, and Lessing's *Minna von Barhelm.*" *Canadian Review of Comparative Literature* 44, no. 2 (2017): 282–297.

Spencer, Jane. "Creating Animal Experience in Late Eighteenth-Century Narrative." *Journal for Eighteenth-Century Studies* 33, no. 4 (2010): 469–486.

Staves, Susan. "Toby Shandy: Sentiment and the Soldier." In *Approaches to Teaching Sterne's "Tristram Shandy,"* edited by Melvyn New, 80–86. New York: Modern Language Association of America, 1989.

Stedmond, John M. *The Comic Art of Laurence Sterne: Convention and Innovation in "Tristram Shandy" and "A Sentimental Journey."* Toronto: University of Toronto Press, 1967.

Steele, Joshua. *An Essay towards Establishing the Melody and Measure of Speech to be Expressed and Perpetuated by Peculiar Symbols.* London, 1775.

Stephen, Leslie. "Sterne." In *Hours in a Library*, vol. 3, 130–163. London: Smith, Elder, 1909.

Sterne, Laurence. *The Journal to Eliza and Various Letters by Laurence Sterne and Elizabeth Draper.* Edited by W. L. Cross. New York: J. F. Taylor, 1904.

———. *The Letters.* 2 parts. Edited by Melvyn New and Peter de Voogd. Florida Edition of the Works of Laurence Sterne 7–8. Gainesville: University Press of Florida, 2009.

———. *The Life and Opinions of Tristram Shandy, Gentleman: The Notes.* Edited by Melvyn New, Richard A. Davies, and W. G. Day. Florida Edition of the Works of Laurence Sterne 3. Gainesville: University Presses of Florida, 1984.

———. *The Life and Opinions of Tristram Shandy, Gentleman: The Text.* Edited by Melvyn New and Joan New. Florida Edition of the Works of Laurence Sterne 1–2. Gainesville: University Presses of Florida, 1978.

———. *The Miscellaneous Writings and Sterne's Subscribers, an Identification List.* Edited by Melvyn New and W. B. Gerard. Florida Edition of the Works of Laurence Sterne 9. Gainesville: University Press of Florida, 2014.

———. *The Novels of Sterne, Goldsmith, Dr. Johnson [and others] . . . To which are prefixed memoirs of the lives of the authors [by Sir Walter Scott].* Ballantyne's Novelist's Library 5. London, 1823.

———. *Original Letters of the Late Reverend Mr. Laurence Sterne; Never Before Published.* London, 1788.

———. *A Sentimental Journey.* Edited by Gardner D. Stout. Berkeley: University of California Press, 1967.

———. *A Sentimental Journey through France and Italy.* Edited by Herbert Read. London: Scholartis, 1929.

———. *A Sentimental Journey through France and Italy.* Edited by Katherine Turner. Peterborough, Ont.: Broadview, 2010.

———. *A Sentimental Journey through France and Italy.* Introduction by Virginia Woolf. Oxford: Oxford World's Classics, 1928.

———. *"A Sentimental Journey through France and Italy" and "Continuation of the Bramine's Journal."* Edited by Melvyn New and W. G. Day. Florida Edition of the Works of Laurence Sterne 6. Gainesville: University Press of Florida, 2002.

———. *"A Sentimental Journey" and "Continuation of the Bramine's Journal," with Related Texts.* Edited by Melvyn New and W. G. Day. Indianapolis: Hackett, 2006.

———. *A Sentimental Journey through France and Italy by Mr. Yorick.* Edited by Paul Goring. London: Penguin, 2001.

———. *The Sermons of Laurence Sterne: The Notes.* Edited by Melvyn New. Florida Edition of the Works of Laurence Sterne 5. Gainesville: University Press of Florida, 1996.

———. *The Sermons of Laurence Sterne: The Text.* Edited by Melvyn New. Florida Edition of the Works of Laurence Sterne 4. Gainesville: University Press of Florida, 1996.

Stout, Gardner D. Introduction to *A Sentimental Journey through France and Italy*, by Laurence Sterne, 1–52. Berkeley: University of California Press, 1967.

———. "Yorick's *Sentimental Journey*: A Comic 'Pilgrim's Progress' for the Man of Feeling." *ELH* 30, no. 4 (December 1963): 395–412.

Straus, Ralph. *Carriages and Coaches: Their History and Their Evolution*. London: Martin Secker, 1912.

Street, Miss. *The Letters of Maria; To which is Added, An Account of her Death*. London, 1790.

Susato, Ryu. "The Idea of Chivalry in the Scottish Enlightenment: The Case of David Hume." *Hume Studies* 33, no. 1 (April 2007): 155–178.

Szabo, Frank A. J. *The Seven Years War in Europe, 1756–1763*. Harrow, UK: Pearson Longman, 2008.

Tadié, Alexis. *Sterne's Whimsical Theatres of Language: Orality, Gesture, Literacy*. Aldershot, UK: Ashgate, 2003.

Takanashi, Kyoko. "Mediation, Reading, and Yorick's Sentimental Vehicle." *Novel: A Forum on Fiction* 49, no. 3 (2016): 486–503.

Taylor, Barbara. "Feminists versus Gallants: Manners and Morals in Enlightenment Britain." *Representations* 87 (Summer 2004): 125–148.

Taylor, Charles. *Modern Social Imaginaries*. Durham, NC: Duke University Press, 2004.

Terry, Richard. *The Plagiarism Allegation in English Literature from Butler to Sterne*. London: Palgrave, 2000.

Thackeray, W[illiam] M[akepeace]. "Sterne and Goldsmith." In *The English Humorists of the Eighteenth Century: A Series of Lectures*, 177–208. London: Grey Walls, 1949.

Thell, Anne. *Minds in Motion: Imagining Empiricism in Eighteenth-Century Travel Writing*. Lewisburg, PA: Bucknell University Press, 2017.

Thomas, Keith. *In Pursuit of Civility: Manners and Civilization in Early Modern England*. New Haven, CT: Yale University Press, 2018.

Tindal, Nicholas. *The History of England*. 3 vols. London: John and Paul Knapton, 1744.

Tomalin, Marcus. "Coquettes and Gallants: (Re-)Assessing Eighteenth-Century English Translations of French Memoirs." *Journal for Eighteenth-Century Studies* 36, no. 1 (March 2013): 85–101.

Tosh, John. "The Old Adam and the New Man: Emerging Themes in the History of English Masculinities, 1750–1850." In *English Masculinities, 1660–1800*, edited by Tim Hitchcock and Michèle Cohen, 217–238. London: Longman, 1999.

Urquhart, Robert. "Accumulation as Eternal Recurrence: Theology of the Bad Infinity," *International Review of Economics* 63, no. 1 (2016): 7–30.

Vande Berg, Michael. "'Pictures of Pronunciation': Typographical Travels through *Tristram Shandy* and *Jacques le fataliste*." *Eighteenth-Century Studies* 21 (1987–1988): 21–47.

Van Sant, Ann Jessie. *Eighteenth-Century Sensibility and the Novel: The Senses in Social Context*. Cambridge: Cambridge University Press, 1993.

Viola, Bill. *I Do Not Know What It Is I Am Like*. ARD/ZDF, AFI, Bill Viola Studio, Institute of Contemporary Art, Boston, New Television Workshop, WGBH Boston, The Contemporary Art Television Fund, 1986. Video. 89 min. https://www.youtube.com/watch?v=hgW8WbnNqqg.

Voogd, Peter de. "*Tristram Shandy* as Aesthetic Object." *Word & Image* 4, no. 1 (1988): 383–392.

Voogd, Peter de, and John Neubauer. "Introduction: Sterne Crosses the Channel." In *The Reception of Laurence Sterne in Europe*, edited by Peter de Voogd and John Neubauer, 1–9. London: Thoemmes Continuum, 2004.

Wakelam, Alexander. *Credit and Debt in Eighteenth-Century England: An Economic History of Debtors' Prisons*. London: Routledge, 2020.

Walker, John. *Elements of Elocution*. London, 1781.

Wall, Cynthia. *The Prose of Things: Transformations of Description in the Eighteenth Century*. Chicago: University of Chicago Press, 2006.

Walsh, Marcus, ed. *Laurence Sterne*. Harlow, UK: Longman, 2002.

Warner, James H. "*Émile* in Eighteenth-Century England." *PMLA* 59, no. 3 (1944): 773–791.

Watkins, W.B.C. *Perilous Balance: The Tragic Genius of Swift, Johnson and Sterne*. Princeton, NJ: Princeton University Press, 1939.

Watts, Carol. *The Cultural Work of Empire: The Seven Years' War and the Imagining of the Shandean State*. Edinburgh: Edinburgh University Press, 2007.

Wehrs, Donald R. "Anarchic Signification and Motions of Grace in Sterne's Novelistic Satire." In *Sterne, Tristram, Yorick: Tercentenary Essays on Laurence Sterne*, edited by Melvyn New, Peter de Voogd, and Judith Hawley, 77–99. Newark: University of Delaware Press, 2016.

———. "Levinas and Sterne: From the Ethics of the Face to the Aesthetics of Unrepresentability." In *In Proximity: Emmanuel Levinas and the Eighteenth Century*, edited by Melvyn New with Robert Bernasconi and Richard A. Cohen, 141–65. Lubbock: Texas Tech University Press, 2001. Also in *Critical Essays on Laurence Sterne*, edited by Melvyn New, 311–329. New York: G. K. Hall, 1998.

———. Review of *Metaphors of Mind: An Eighteenth-Century Dictionary*, by Brad Pasenek. *Scriblerian* 50, no. 1 (2017): 78–81.

West, Meredith J., and Andrew P. King. "Mozart's Starling." *American Scientist* 78 (1990): 106–114.

West, Meredith J., Neil Stroud, and Andrew P. King. "Mimicry of the Human Voice by European Starlings: The Role of Social Interaction." *Wilson Bulletin* 95, no. 4 (1983): 635–640.

Western, John R. *The English Militia in the Eighteenth Century: The Story of a Political Issue, 1660–1802*. London: Routledge, 1965.

Wetmore, Alex. "Sympathy Machines: Men of Feeling and the Automaton." *Eighteenth-Century Studies* 43, no. 1 (Fall 2009): 37–54.

Willett, Cynthia. *Interspecies Ethics*. New York: Columbia University Press, 2014.

Wilson, Kathleen. *The Sense of the People: Politics, Culture and Imperialism in England, 1715–1785*. Cambridge: Cambridge University Press, 1995.

Wollstonecraft, Mary. *"A Vindication of the Rights of Men" and "A Vindication of the Rights of Woman."* Edited by Sylvana Tomaselli. Cambridge: Cambridge University Press, 1995.

Wood, Nigel. "Adam Smith's *The Theory of Moral Sentiments* in 1759: Spectatorship, Duty, and Social Improvement." In *Reading 1759: Literary Culture in Mid-Eighteenth-Century Britain and France*, edited by Shaun Regan, 57–74. Lewisburg, PA: Bucknell University Press, 2013.

Woolf, Virginia. "Eliza and Sterne." *Times Literary Supplement*, December 14, 1922.

———. Introduction to *A Sentimental Journey through France and Italy*, by Laurence Sterne, v–xvii. Oxford: Oxford World's Classics, 1928.

———. "The 'Sentimental Journey.'" In *Collected Essays by Virginia Woolf*, edited by Stuart N. Clarke, vol. 5, 401–410. London: Hogarth, 2009.

Wright, Arnold, and William Lutley Sclater. *Sterne's Eliza: Some Account of Her Life in India: With Her Letters Written between 1757 and 1774*. London: W. Heinemann, 1922.

Wright, Auberon. "Two Readers of *A Sentimental Journey*." *Shandean* 28 (2017): 155–160.

Yahav, Amit. "The Sense of Rhythm: Nationalism, Sympathy, and the English Elocutionists." *Eighteenth Century* 52 (2011): 173–192.

Zionkowski, Linda, and Cynthia Klekar. Introduction to *The Culture of the Gift in Eighteenth-Century England*, edited by Linda Zionkowski and Cynthia Klekar, 1–12. New York: Palgrave Macmillan, 2009.

NOTES ON CONTRIBUTORS

JULIA BANISTER is a senior lecturer in English literature at Leeds Beckett University. She works on the literature of the long eighteenth century and is the author of *Masculinity, Militarism and Eighteenth-Century Culture, 1689–1815* (2018).

PETER BUDRIN is a Clarendon Scholar at Lady Margaret Hall, University of Oxford. He has taught on the theory of the novel, the Enlightenment, and the history of Russian literature and film. His doctor of philosophy thesis explored the reception of Sterne's works in Soviet Russia. He has published several essays on Sterne.

FRASER EASTON is an associate professor of English at the University of Waterloo. His articles on political economy and the novel, historical records of cross-dressing women, and elocution and eighteenth-century literature have appeared in *Genre, Past and Present, Studies in Eighteenth-Century Culture, Studies in Romanticism, Textual Practice*, and *Eighteenth-Century Fiction*.

CHRIS EWERS is a lecturer in eighteenth-century literature at the University of Exeter. He has published articles on Sir Walter Scott, Robert Bage, Sir John Hill, Thomas Love Peacock, and Agatha Christie, and his monograph *Mobility in the English Novel from Defoe to Austen* (2018) includes chapters on the invention of speed in *Tristram Shandy* and the connection between *A Sentimental Journey* and the new world of hurry and timetables introduced by the transport revolution.

W. B. GERARD taught literature and creative writing at Auburn University at Montgomery. He authored *Laurence Sterne and the Visual Imagination* (2006) and was the editor of *Divine Rhetoric: Essays on the Sermons of Laurence Sterne* (2010) and coeditor of volume 9 of the Florida Edition of the Works of Laurence Sterne, *The Miscellaneous Writings* (2014). He was the coeditor of the semiannual journal *The Scriblerian and the Kit-Cats* and general editor of *THAT Literary Review*. Sadly, Blake Gerard passed away during the final stages of this book's production.

PAUL GORING is a professor of British literature and culture at the Norwegian University of Science and Technology in Trondheim. He works primarily on eighteenth-century theater and prose fiction, with particular interests in news transmission, elocution, the visual arts, and the law. He has published several essays on Laurence Sterne and his fiction and has edited *A Sentimental Journey* for Penguin Classics (2001). His interest in debt—developed in his chapter in this volume—has grown alongside his mortgage.

ALEXANDER HARDIE-FORSYTH is a Wolfson Scholar in the Humanities at Wolfson College, Oxford, where he recently completed a thesis titled "Laurence Sterne's Textual Commerce." He has taught on Sterne, fictions and criticism of the late eighteenth century, and, separately, the works of J. M. Coetzee.

MELVYN NEW, professor emeritus at the University of Florida, has been publishing on eighteenth-century literature for fifty years. He served as general editor of the Florida Edition of the Works of Laurence Sterne, the ninth and final volume of which was published in 2014. Recent essays include "Richardson's Sir Charles Grandison and Sterne: A Study in Influence" (*Modern Philology*, 2017); and "Laurence Sterne and William Falconer: Soldiers and Sailors," *Philological Quarterly* 99.2 (2020), 229–244. He has been the book review editor for the *Scriblerian* for the past fifteen years.

M-C. NEWBOULD has taught English for many years at the University of Cambridge, where she is a bye-fellow of Pembroke College. Her *Adaptations of Laurence Sterne's Fiction: Sterneana, 1760–1840* (2013) addresses the numerous creative responses Sterne's work inspired; she has co-designed "Sterne Digital Library," an open-access resource digitizing this material hosted by Cambridge University Library. She is an editor of Sterne journal *The Shandean*.

SHAUN REGAN is a lecturer in eighteenth-century and Romantic literature at Queen's University Belfast. His publications include *Making the Novel* (2006, with Brean Hammond), *Reading 1759* (2013), and *The Culture of the Seven Years' War* (2014, with Frans De Bruyn). He has previously published articles on Sterne in relation to politeness, print culture, satire, the novel, and (most recently) cosmopolitanism.

GLYNIS RIDLEY is a graduate of the Universities of Edinburgh and Oxford, specializing in the literature of the long eighteenth century. She is currently a professor and chair of the Department of English at the University of Louisville, where she teaches both eighteenth-century and animal-studies courses across undergraduate and graduate programs.

PAT ROGERS, Distinguished University Professor Emeritus at the University of South Florida, is a fellow of the British Academy, fellow of the Royal Historical Society, and fellow of the Society of Antiquaries, as well as a former president of the British Society for Eighteenth-Century Studies and the Johnson Society of Lichfield.

JENNIFER PRESTON WILSON, an associate professor of English at Appalachian State University, is coeditor, with Elizabeth Kraft, of *Approaches to Teaching the Novels of Henry Fielding* (2015). Her recent essays appear in *The Cinematic Eighteenth Century* (2017) and *Rewriting Crusoe: The Robinsonade across Languages, Cultures, and Media* (2020).

INDEX

Abolition of slavery, 74n38. *See also* slavery
adaptations, of Sterne, 3–4, 6, 7, 14–15, 232n22
Addison, Joseph, 176, 186; *Cato*, 176, 186
Aesop, 59
affect theory, 13–14, 58, 59
agape, 163
Alps (mountain range), 92, 94
America, and the British Empire, 44
Amiens (French city), in Sterne, 64, 72, 204, 223
Andrews, John, 28, 35; *An Account of the Character and Manners of the French*, 35
animal affect, theory of, 59
animal behavior, study of, 58, 65
animals, talking, 59–60. *See also* fables; fairy tales
animal studies, 13, 58–59, 62, 148–149n55
aposiopesis: in Sterne, 121, 126, 141–142; rhetorical figure, 142. *See also* rhetoric
Aristotle, and oratory, 131. *See also* elocution; rhetoric
Arminianism, 153. *See also* free will
Arras (French city), 87
ass (animal): Biblical, 59–60; in Sterne, 58, 59, 60. *See also* Balaam's ass
Atwood, Margaret, 215
Auchinleck (Scottish village), 172. *See also* Boswell, James
Augustine, Saint, 179; *Confessions*, 179
Austen, Jane, 7, 129, 147n39, 236
Austin, Gilbert, 123, 133, 149n63. *See also* elocution
Austria, 44, 50
automata, eighteenth-century, 66, 72. *See also* materialist philosophy
Auxerre (French city), in Sterne, 87
Avignon (French city), in Sterne, 87
Babel, and language, 133
Bagehot, Walter, 7
Balaam (biblical figure), 59–60. *See also* Old Testament
Balaam's ass, Biblical animal story, 59–63, 64–65
Bank of England, the, 214
Bastille, the, 66, 84, 88, 90–91, 139, 162
Becket, Thomas (bookseller), 226, 241
Beckford, William, 236; *Vathek*, 236
begging, 28–29, 108. *See also* urbanity
Bell, Alexander Melville, 123, 145n11
Bentham, Jeremy, 72
Berkeley, George (bishop), 182, 192n41
Betjeman, John, 235
Blair, Hugh, 146n28
Bloom, Harold, 215. *See also* debt: literary
blushing, in Sterne, 49, 92, 122–126, 134–135. *See also* body language; sensibility
body language, 14, 66. *See also* communication: social; elocution; gesture
Bombay, 200, 239. See also Sterne, Laurence, works of: *Bramine's Journal*; Draper, Elizabeth
Bond Street (London), Sterne's residence there, 232
borders, concept of, 79–94
borrowing: Sterne's literary, 4, 51, 193n63, 216, 227; of money, 215, 216, 217, 219. *See also* debt: literary inheritance and
Boulogne (French city), 222
Bourbonnais (French region), in Sterne, 37, 85, 86
Boswell, James, 122, 171–188; *An Account of Corsica*, 172, 183, 185, 192n51, 192n56, 193n60; Belle du Zuylen (Zélide), 178; Germany and Switzerland, tour of, 174, 190n21; "Harvest Jaunt," 172; "in search of a wife," 174, 189n13; Italy and

Boswell, James (cont.)
France, tour of, 174; *London Journal*, 172; London, time spent in, 172–173, 185. *See also* Johnson, Samuel
British Museum, The, 7. See also Sterne, Laurence, works of: *Bramine's Journal*
Brittany, 29, 109, 161. *See also* Rennes
Brooke, Frances, 237; *The History of Lady Julia Mandeville*, 237
Brown, Robert (church minister), 174, 189n10
Brussels: Bombardment of, 50, 57n36; in Sterne, 32, 158, 204, 207, 223
Bulwer, John, 145n21, 147n46; *Chironomia*, 145n21. *See also* elocution
Bunyan, John, 67; *The Pilgrim's Progress*, 67. *See also* starlings: in Sterne
Burgundy (French wine-producing region), 137, 140
Burney, Frances, 172, 236
Burns, Robert, 3
Burton, Robert, 216; *The Anatomy of Melancholy*, 216
Byland Abbey (Yorkshire), 240
Byron, Lord, 5, 193n60

Calais (French city), in Sterne, 47–49, 52–54, 79–87, 161–165, 199–209
Cambridge (British city), 236
Cambridge Declaration on Consciousness, the (2012), 58, 62, 66
Cambridge Platonists, the, 178
captivity, motif in Sterne, 66, 70, 221
Carey, Matthew (publisher), 5
Carter, Elizabeth, 4
Cartesian dualism, 72, 151. *See also* Descartes, René
Cash, Arthur H. (critic and biographer of Sterne), 11–13, 153, 195–198, 205, 210n4, 211n6, 211n9, 234–235, 239, 241
Catholicism, eighteenth-century British attitudes toward, 49, 124, 175
Central Park, New York (city), 68
Cervantes, Miguel de, 40n28, 101, 173, 182–183, 188, 193n57, 216, 229; Don Quixote (character), 31, 182–183, 185; *Don Quixote de la Mancha*, 31, 101, 182–183; Sancho Panza (character), 34, 40n39. *See also* borrowing, Sterne's literary; Sterne, Laurence: fictional characters, La Fleur
Chapone, Hester, 24, 38n2
chapter, of a book, etymology of, 100
chaptering: concept of, 99–102, 106, 111, 117; eighteenth-century practices of, 100–103; Sterne's use of, 81–86, 91–94, 98–118, 131–135, 148n49, 150, 199–200, 214, 223–224
charity: acts of, 124, 157; and religion, 124, 181, 222; and sentimentalism, 14, 160; in Sterne, 14, 28, 124, 157, 159, 181, 206; problematic nature of, 14, 28, 124, 159
Chatham, Earl of. *See* Pitt, William (the elder)
Chatham administration, 238
Chentoff, Polia (artist), 8. *See also* illustrations, of Sterne's work
Chesterfield, Lord, 38. *Letters to His Son*, 38
chivalry: eighteenth-century concepts of, 24–25, 31–34, 40n28, 40nn31–33, 40n35, 41n47; in Sterne, 24–25, 31, 33, 34–35
Chomsky, Noam, 70
Chrysostom (fictional shepherd), 183
Cibber, Colley, 101; *An Apology for the Life of Colley Cibber*, 101
Cicero, and rhetoric, 123. *See also* rhetoric
Citizen of the World, eighteenth-century concepts of, 80, 92, 96n20
citizenship, changing concepts of, 44
civility: eighteenth-century concepts of, 24–26, 29, 39n19; in Sterne, 23, 26, 27. *See also* courtesy; gallantry; honor; politeness; *politesse*
Cleland, John, 33, 40n38, 214, 217; *The Dictionary of Love*, 33, 40n38; *Memoirs of a Woman of Pleasure*, 214
Clonmel, Earl of (John Scott), 41n50, 148n49
coats of arms, in Sterne, 71–72, 141. *See also* College of Arms; illegitimacy
Coleman, George, 172
Coleridge, Samuel Taylor, 5, 6
College of Arms, 71–72, 74n34. *See also* coats of arms; illegitimacy
Combe, William, 64–65, 73n15; *Original Letters of the Late Reverend Mr. Laurence Sterne*, 64

commercialism: in the eighteenth century, 23, 27, 29, 40n33, 54–55; of eighteenth-century books, 100, 103, 118n12, 224
Commons, the House of (British parliament), 44, 238
communication: nonverbal, 133–134, 148–149n59; sentimental, 89, 122–126, 135–136, 140–143, 144n2, 146n32, 149n63; sexual, 125, 134, 135, 137, 146n32, 149n63; social, including problems of, 27, 79, 121–122, 127–131, 134–137, 143, 165; and speech technologies, 122. *See also* body language; elocution; gesture
composition: musical, 68 (*see also* Mozart); Sterne's authorial method of, 8, 100–102, 107, 165, 196–197, 216, 235
conquest, sexual, 35–36, 54, 195
contact zone, concept of the, 80
Continent, the (European), 9, 44, 237
Continental travel, in eighteenth-century Europe, 4, 26, 28, 37–38, 174, 236, 239
Corsica, 175, 185–186, 188, 192n56, 193n60, 193n65. *See also* Boswell, James
cosmopolitanism: eighteenth-century concepts of, 79, 88, 92, 94, 110; in Sterne, 25, 39n9, 49, 80, 84, 148n54, 160
Courbet, Gustave, 231
courtesy: eighteenth-century concepts of, 24–25, 29–35; in Sterne, 25–30, 37, 49, 180. *See also* civility; gallantry; honor; politeness; *politesse*
Coxwold (Yorkshire village), 12, 196, 234, 236, 239, 240, 241; St. Michael's Church, 12. *See also* Shandy Hall
Crazy Castle, 236, 240. *See also* Hall-Stevenson, John
Critical Review, 4
Croft, Stephen, 44, 190n13. *See also* Stillington
Cross, Wilbur L. (biographer and critic of Sterne), 7–8, 10–12, 234, 240
Cumberland, Richard, 172
Curtis, Lewis Perry (biographer and critic of Sterne), 10–11, 13, 210n4. *See also* Sterne, Laurence: letters of

Dante Alighieri, 182; *The Divine Comedy*, 182
dashes (punctuation symbol), in Sterne, 93, 124, 147n38, 200. *See also* typography
Deal (British sea port), 240. *See also* Draper, Elizabeth
debt: British national, 213; concepts of, 215; eighteenth-century concepts of, 213, 217–218; eighteenth-century history of, 213–214; etymology of, 215; financial aspects of, 213–214; literary inheritance and, 227–228; mortality and, 222–223, 229–231; religious attitudes toward, 215, 221–223; in Sterne, 214–215, 218–223, 230. *See also* Sterne, Laurence: personal debts of
debtors' prisons (British), 214
Defoe, Daniel, 100, 214, 217, 236, 237; *The Complete English Tradesman*, 214; *Robinson Crusoe*, 237; *Roxana*, 214
Derrida, Jacques, 72, 149n60
Descartes, René, 182. *See also* Cartesian dualism
desobligeant (carriage), in Sterne, 23, 88, 93, 104–107, 136, 138, 151–156, 159, 165, 203–204. See also *remise* (carriage); *vis-à-vis*
Dickens, Charles, 214, 237; *Little Dorrit*, 214
Dictionary of National Biography, 7. *See also* Lee, Sidney
Dictionnaire philosophique, 175. *See also* Voltaire
Diderot, Denis, 91, 178
digression, in Sterne, 54, 67, 80–81, 85–87, 93, 150
Donne, John, 222
Dover (British sea port), 79, 130, 199, 200
Draper, Daniel, 195, 197. *See also* Draper, Elizabeth; East India Company
Draper, Elizabeth (Eliza): and *Bramine's Journal*, 7–8, 183, 186–188, 211n8, 235, 240; as Sterne's inamorata, 2, 174, 186–188, 211n9, 236, 239–240; biography of, 195, 210n4, 234; marital relationship of, 195, 197, 232n14; portrait of, 167n23, 211n14; presence in *A Sentimental Journey*, 32, 37, 130, 159, 187, 195–210. *See also* Bombay; Draper, Daniel; East India Company; India; Sterne, Laurence, works of: *Bramine's Journal*
dueling, eighteenth-century practice of, 30–31, 40n23, 47
Dutens, Louis, 181–182, 191n37

East India Company, 195, 239. *See also* Draper, Daniel; Draper, Elizabeth
economy: household, 98–99, 109–110; market, 98–99, 103, 109–110, 213, 217; narrative, 98–100, 103, 107, 110; of sentimental commerce, 157, 160
Edgeworth, Maria, 236
Edinburgh (Scottish city), 172, 185
elocution: and acoustics, 124–129, 140, 144n2, 147n38; and articulation, in Sterne, 126–128, 143; eighteenth-century concepts of, 121–124, 133, 135–136, 144n2, 145n22, 146nn27–28, 148n47, 148–149n55; elements of, 121, 123–124, 126–127, 135–136, 138, 144n2, 144n9; and eloquence in, 129; gesture in, in Sterne 126–128, 130–131, 133, 135, 143, 145n14, 148n51; manuals of, 122; memorialization in, 138, 140, 141–142, 145n21, 149n63; and sentiment, 125, 133, 134–136, 140–141; and sexuality, 125, 134, 136, 146–147n32; tone in, 125. *See also* communication; gesture; rhetoric; Sheridan, Thomas
embodied sensibility, concept of, 151
empiricism, 93
Enlightenment: French, 178; ideas of the, 80, 87, 93, 178, 183–185, 188, 191n22, 192n52; Scottish, 34
epistolary fiction, 100–101
Erasmus, Desiderius, 173, 183–184, 192n52; *Praise of Folly*, 183–184
Eugenius (pseudonymous imitator of Sterne), 4, 226, 233n23

fables, 59, 237. *See also* animals, talking
fairy tales, 59. *See also* animals, talking; Perrault, Charles
Fawkes, Francis, 172; *Poems of Theocritus*, 172
Fénelon, François, 101; *Telemachus*, 101
Ferguson, Adam, 31, 32
Ferriar, John, 4, 5, 216; *Illustrations of Sterne*, 4, 216
Fielding, Henry, 93, 101–102, 103, 236; *An Apology for the Life of Mrs. Shamela Andrews*, 101, 102; *Joseph Andrews*, 101; *Tom Jones*, 93
Fielding, Sarah, 237; *The History of Ophelia*, 237
Fitzgerald, Percy (critic and biographer of Sterne), 6–7, 8, 11, 234
Fleet Prison, 214. *See also* debtors' prisons
Florida edition, of Sterne's works, 16, 216, 235. *See also* New, Melvyn
folk tales, 59. *See also* fables; fairy tales
Fordyce, David, 36; *Dialogues Concerning Education*, 36
fragments, formal quality in Sterne, 124. See also *il non finito*; typography
France: as depicted by Sterne, 25–28, 33, 46–47, 79–80, 87, 134, 161, 199–201, 218; eighteenth-century British attitudes toward, 25, 27–28, 35, 39n9, 46; in the eighteenth century, 25, 39n15, 61, 91, 110, 130, 199, 201
Franciscan monks, 28, 29, 203. *See also* Sterne, Laurence: fictional characters, Father Lorenzo; Order of St. Francis
Frankenstein's monster (fictional character), 59
Frederick, of Prussia (king), 44
free will, 151–153, 174–175, 177, 180–181. *See also* sin

gallantry: eighteenth-century concepts of, 24–25, 29, 33–37, 40n31, 41n47, 148n49; French, 25, 35–36, 41n50; Italian, 36–37. *See also* chivalry; courtesy; honor
Garrick, David, 145n20, 172, 217; Shakespeare festival, 186. *See also* Boswell, James; Shakespeare, William: *Hamlet*; Sterne, Laurence: personal debts of
Garonne, the (French river), 87
gender: eighteenth-century concepts of, 26, 36, 43–44, 48, 94; eighteenth-century masculinity and, 25, 36, 43; eighteenth-century travel and, 25, 26; in Sterne, 25–26, 43, 48, 55, 221; study of, 15
Genesis, book of, 59–60. *See also* Old Testament
Gentner, Timothy (neurophysiologist), 70
Germany: and eighteenth-century travel, 174; and Seven Years' War, 44. *See also* Boswell, James
gesture: and civility, 26, 37, 53, 124, 130; and communication, 131–140, 142, 146n24, 153, 158, 165–166, 209; and elocution, 121–123, 126–128, 129–135, 140–143, 144nn2–3, 144n7, 144n9, 145n16,

145nn21–22, 146n24, 146n28, 147–148n46, 148n47, 149n63; and sentimentalism, 52, 122, 139. *See also* body language; elocution
Gibbon, Edward, 172
gift exchange, 61, 71, 103, 158, 159, 215, 219. *See also* debt; Sterne, Laurence: fictional characters, Father Lorenzo; snuffboxes
gifts: divine, 11, 62, 64; of nature, 34
Godwin, William, 236; *Caleb Williams*, 236
Goethe, Johann Wolfgang von, 4, 237; *The Sorrows of Young Werther*, 4, 237
Golden Rule, the, 179
Goldsmith, Oliver, 172; *The Vicar of Wakefield*, 236
Gothic mode, the, 36, 40n31, 185, 237
Gothic novel, the, 4, 32, 236
Grand Tour, the, 39n10, 81, 174, 184, 186; in Sterne, 81, 83, 88, 220. *See also* Boswell, James
graphic elements: in elocutionary manuals, 123–124, 141; in Sterne, 141–142. *See also* typography: in Sterne
Graves, Richard, 237; *The Spiritual Quixote*, 237
gravesides, in Sterne, 29, 158
Great North Road, the, 238
Griffith, Richard (contemporary of Sterne), 2, 119n27, 189n12
Griffiths, Ralph (reviewer), 2, 3
Grimm, the brothers, 59. *See also* fairy tales
Guido (Reni), 49

Hall-Stevenson, John, 240, 241. *See also* Crazy Castle
Hamburgischer Correspondent, 156. *See also* Lorenzo Cult, the
Harrogate (Yorkshire), 240
Harting, James Edward, 68; *Ornithology of Shakespeare*, 68. *See also* Shakespeare, William; starlings: in Sterne
Hartley, David, philosopher, 95n10
Harwich (British sea port), 182
Haupt, Lyanda Lynn (journalist), 67–69
Hegel, G.W.F., 209
heterosociality, 48
History of Charlotte Summers, The, 102
Hogarth, William, 49, 60, 145n14, 214; *The Four Stages of Cruelty*, 60; *Oh the Roast Beef of Old England (The Gate of Calais)*, 49; *Rake's Progress, The*, 214. *See also* France: eighteenth-century British attitudes toward; illustrations, of Sterne's work
Holbach, Baron d', 91, 151, 178; *Système de la nature*, 151. *See also* materialist philosophy
Holland (the Netherlands), 178–179. *See also* Boswell, James
Homer, 101
honor, eighteenth-century concepts of, 24, 26, 29–31, 33–37, 40n23, 109, 160–161. *See also* civility; courtesy; dueling; gallantry; masculinity
Hume, David, 34–36, 40n33, 190n20. *See also* gallantry
Hurd, Richard, 31–32, 40n31; *Letters on Chivalry and Romance*, 31. *See also* Gothic mode, the
hurdy-gurdy, 164. *See also* vielle
Hyde Park (London), 27

illegitimacy, 71–72; *See also* coats of arms
illustrations, of Sterne's work, 8, 11, 15, 145n14. *See also* Chentoff, Polia; Hogarth, William; Laboureur, J. E.
il non finito, formal quality in Sterne, 242. *See also* fragments
India, 8, 44, 195, 198, 206. *See also* Draper, Daniel; Draper, Elizabeth; East India Company
internet, the, and scholarly research, 172
intersubjectivity, and travel in Sterne, 81, 129
Italy, as depicted by Sterne, 84, 87, 139, 226, 231. *See also* Boswell, James
it-narratives, 71, 160

Jacobi, Johann Georg, 156. *See also* Lorenzo Cult, the; snuffboxes
James, Anne (correspondent of Sterne), 2, 206, 241
Jesus College (Cambridge), 236
Johnson, Samuel, 25, 33, 89, 100, 103, 122, 171, 175, 177, 182, 185, 190n21, 193n64; *Dictionary*, 25, 33, 89, 100, 103; *A Journey to the Western Islands of Scotland*, 89; *Rasselas*, 171. *See also* chaptering; Boswell, James
Jonson, Ben, 222, 238
Joyce, James, 229; *Ulysses*, 229

Kames, Lord, 172–173. *See also* Boswell, James
Kant, Immanuel, 190n20
Kauffman, Angelica, 72. *See also* Sterne, Laurence: fictional characters, Maria
Kelly, Hugh, 172
Kendall, Edward Augustus, 72; *Keeper's Travels in Search of his Master*, 72
Kenrick, William, 98
Kierkegaard, Søren, 191n22

Laboureur, J. E. (artist), 8. *See also* illustrations, of Sterne's work
Lamb, Charles, 85. *See also* Wordsworth, William
Last Supper, the, 162
Latitudinarianism, 92. *See also* materialist philosophy
Laurence Sterne Trust, The, 12. *See also* Coxwold; Monkman, Kenneth; Shandy Hall
Lee, Sidney, 7. See also *Dictionary of National Biography*
Leibnitz, 182
Lennox, Charlotte, 237; *Sophia*, 237
Leslie, C. R. (artist), 6; *See also* Sterne, Laurence: fictional characters in the works of, Uncle Toby; widow Wadman
Life and Memoirs of Mr. Ephraim Tristram Bates, The, 102, 119n25
Locke, John, 10, 143, 145n16, 146n27, 179, 182; *Essay Concerning Human Understanding*, 179
London: bookselling practices in, 12; civil unrest in, 238; as depicted by Sterne, 47, 131, 133, 200; editions of Sterne's books published in, 3, 42, 113. *See also* Sterne, Laurence
Lorenzo Cult, the, 156
Lorenzodosen, 156. *See also* Sterne, Laurence: fictional characters, Father Lorenzo; snuffboxes
Louis XV (king of France), 79, 84
Lyon (French city), in Sterne, 62–63, 65, 83, 87, 92, 202

Mackenzie, Henry, 66, 172, 236; *The Man of Feeling*, 172, 236
Maria Theresa (empress), 242n2
Martinique, 29, 161
Martin's Act (1822), 72, 74–75n38
Marvell, Andrew, 14
masculinity: concept of, 23; eighteenth-century concepts of, 23–24, 30–33, 37–38, 39n9, 40n28, 40n32, 44, 46; in Sterne, 23, 25, 29, 38, 46, 48. *See also* chivalry; gallantry
Mason, John (elocutionist), 146n28. *See also* elocution; pronunciation
massacre of St. George's Fields, 238. *See also* London; Wilkes, John
materialist philosophy, 92, 151, 154, 176. *See also* Holbach, Baron d'; Mettrie, Julien Offray de la
Medalle, Lydia (daughter of Sterne), 3, 10, 205, 240, 241
"Melville, Lewis," 234
Memoirs of the Celebrated Miss Fanny Murray, 171
memorialization, 124, 133, 135, 141, 142, 145n21, 149n63. *See also* elocution
Mettrie, Julien Offray de la, 151; *L'homme machine*, 151. *See also* materialist philosophy
Midas (king), 223–224
Milan (Italian city), as depicted by Sterne, 86, 131, 134, 182
military men, 29–30, 32–34, 40n32, 43–46, 47, 49–55, 132, 218. *See also* chivalry; gallantry; Seven Years' War
Millar, John, 32
Monkman, Kenneth, 12. *See also* Coxwold; Laurence Sterne Trust, The; Shandy Hall
Montagu, Elizabeth, 216
Montgomerie, Margaret, 16, 189–190n13. *See also* Boswell, James
Monthly Review, The, 2, 98, 226
Montpellier (French city), 218. *See also* Sterne, Laurence
Montreuil (French city), in Sterne, 28, 29, 39n18, 52
morality, in Sterne, 7
Moulins (French city), in Sterne, 72, 83, 208. *See also* Sterne, Laurence: fictional characters, Maria
Mount Taurira (Mont Tarare, France), 92, 94, 165
Mozart, Wolfgang Amadeus, 67. *See also* Haupt, Lyanda Lynn; starlings: bird
music: and animal sounds, 138–140; in the eighteenth century, 164; instruments to

play, 72; notation and, 140; performance and, 140, 164. *See also* elocution

nationalism, eighteenth-century British, 43, 46, 55. *See also* patriotism, eighteenth-century British
New, Melvyn (editor of Sterne's works), 13, 16, 61, 74n23, 113, 120n57, 120n60, 210n4, 216, 235. *See also* Florida edition, of Sterne's works
New York (city), 18n33, 240
Nietzsche, Friedrich, 8, 189n6
Nine Years' War, 43, 50
Norris, John, of Bemerton, 187, 193n63
Numbers, book of, 59. *See also* Old Testament

Old Testament, 59. *See also* Balaam; Genesis; Numbers
ontology, in Sterne, 154, 165
opera comique (Paris), in Sterne, 29, 84, 86, 126, 131, 156
orality, in Sterne, 121–122, 127
Order of St. Francis, 105. *See also* Franciscan monks; Sterne, Laurence: fictional characters, Father Lorenzo
Order of St. Louis, 29, 54, 108, 160
ornithology, 68. *See also* Shakespeare, William
Orrery, 5th Earl of (John Boyle), 172. *See also* Swift, Jonathan
Oswald, George (eighteenth-century tourist), 218, 220. *See also* debt; Sterne, Laurence
Ovid, 59; *Metamorphoses*, 59
Oxford (British city), 185

Paoli, Pasquale (Corsican statesman and military leader), 184, 186, 192n51
paratexts, 100, 107, 113, 118n12, 142. *See also* chaptering
Paris, 3, 191n37; as depicted by Sterne, 31, 37, 47–48, 53, 83–84, 92, 131–132, 139, 147n32, 147n41, 156–157, 160–162, 206–209
passports, eighteenth-century, in Sterne, 33, 47–48, 51, 66, 80–84, 91–92, 128–129, 147n41, 199, 207
patriotism, eighteenth-century British, 43–45, 55, 56n9. *See also* Pitt, William (the elder)
Pelagianism, 167n27
Perrault, Charles, 59. *See also* animals, talking; fairy tales
philanthropy, in Sterne, 28, 53, 221; *See also* sentimentalism
Pitt, William (the elder), 42, 43–44, 48, 55, 56n9, 238. *See also* patriotism, eighteenth-century British
politeness, in the eighteenth-century, 24–26, 28–29, 32, 35, 37, 39n9, 39n12, 39n14, 127. *See also* chivalry; civility; courtesy; gallantry; masculinity; *politesse*
politesse, 26–27, 88. *See also* chivalry; civility; courtesy; gallantry; masculinity; politeness
politics: eighteenth-century British, 44, 122, 238; of gender, 36, 43–44; of travel, 15. *See also* nationalism, eighteenth-century British; patriotism, eighteenth-century British
Pope, Alexander, 101, 172, 186, 216; *The Art of Sinking in Poetry*, 172; *Memoirs of Martinus Scriblerus*, 101; *Miscellanies*, 172. *See also* Swift, Jonathan
Prattware, 6. *See also* adaptations, of Sterne; Sterne, Laurence: fictional characters in the works of, Uncle Toby
predeterminism, 155
pronunciation, 146n28. *See also* elocution; Mason, John
Proust, Marcel, 10, 18n44
providentialism, 165, 178, 179, 181, 188, 191n24
Prussia, 44, 56n15. *See also*, Frederick, of Prussia (king)
Pyrenees (mountain range), 61

Quintilian, 147–148n46. *See also* rhetoric

Rabelais, François, 31, 40n25, 173, 216, 229. *See also* borrowing, Sterne's literary
Radcliffe, Ann, 237
Ray, Alexander, banker, 218; *See also* debt; Sterne, Laurence, personal finances of
Read, Herbert (editor of Sterne), 9–10, 11, 12
Reeve, Clara, 3, 237; *The Progress of Romance*, 3
remise (carriage), in Sterne, 86–88, 105, 107, 160, 181. See also *desobligeant; vis-à-vis*

Rennes (French city), 54–55, 100, 108–111. *See also* Brittany; swords, in Sterne
Reynolds, Sir Joshua, 1, 241. *See also* Sterne, Laurence, portraits of
rhetoric: art of, 121; canons of, 129, 143, 144n2; and communication, 135, 144n2, 146n27; devices of, 65, 89, 159; differing approaches to, 123–125, 148n47; and memory, 140; and non-human animals, 128, 139, 148n50, 148n55, 149n57; physical aspects of, 126–127, 134, 142, 144n7, 147n46; and sentiment, 146n27, 147n37. *See also* aposiopesis, in Sterne; Cicero, and rhetoric; elocution; Sheridan, Thomas
Richardson, Samuel, 101, 236; *Clarissa*, 150
Rockingham faction, 238. *See also* Chatham administration
Rosinante (horse), 64. *See also* Cervantes, Miguel de, *Don Quixote*
Rousseau, Jean-Jacques: and Corsican struggle for freedom, 186; and gender, 43, 46, 48, 53, 55; *Émile*, 56n7, 178, 237; meetings with, 175, 177, 178, 192n51; *On the Origin and the Foundations of Inequality among Men*, 71; and sensibility, 178; views on sentience in non-human animals, 71. *See also* Boswell, James; Sterne, Laurence, travel abroad
Rowe, Elizabeth Singer, 100; *Friendship in Death*, 100
Rowe, Nicolas, 177; *The Fair Penitent*, 177
Ruffhead, Owen (reviewer), 98

Saintsbury, George, 7, 9
Sandford and Merton, 237
Santiago de Compostela, 61
Savoy (French region), in Sterne, 106, 209
Scarborough (Yorkshire town), 240
Schieffelin, Eugene, 68. *See also* starlings
Scott, Sarah, 237; *A Description of Millennium Hall and the Country Adjacent*, 237
Scott, Walter, 5, 6, 84, 236
Scriblerians (eighteenth-century satirical group), 12, 172–173, 214, 230. *See also* Pope, Alexander; Swift, Jonathan
self-fashioning, of Sterne's Yorick, 23–24, 28, 31, 33–35, 159
sensibility: ambiguity of, in Sterne, 12, 57n31, 164; as admired in Sterne's work, 1, 2; as criticized in Sterne's work, 2, 5, 6, 14, 50; contemporary criticism on, 13–14, 24, 57n31, 146n27, 151, 159, 193n59; eighteenth-century concepts of, 11, 24, 37, 178, 188, 190–191n22, 236; and gender, in Sterne, 24, 48, 39n19; negative appraisals of, 4–5, 50, 63; and sexuality, 184–185, 192n51. *See also* Boswell, James; masculinity; sentimentalism; sentimentality; sympathy
sentimentalism: contemporary criticism on, 13, 14, 15, 109, 144n2; eighteenth-century concepts of, 6, 8, 11, 12; in Sterne, 2, 7, 14, 111. *See also* sensibility; sentimentality; sympathy
sentimentality, in Sterne, 43, 45–47, 49–53, 54–55, 58, 65, 160. *See also* sensibility; sentimentalism; sympathy
Seven Years' War (1756–1763), 30, 42–45, 46, 55, 108–109, 213
Shaftesbury, third Earl of (Antony Ashley Cooper), 41n51, 100, 103, 160
Shakespeare, William: Hamlet (character), 145, 227–228, 230; *Hamlet*, 91, 216, 228; *1 Henry IV*, 68; Hotspur, Sir Henry Percy, 68, 70; Mortimer, Edmund, 68, 70; and ornithology, 68; Shakespeare festival, 186; *Sonnets*, 222, 227; in Sterne, 47, 216, 217, 228–230. *See also* borrowing, Sterne's literary; Garrick, David; starlings: bird
shame, spiritual feeling of, 151, 153, 224
Shandean, The (scholarly journal), 15, 232–233n22, 235
Shandy Hall, 12, 43, 200. *See also* Coxwold; Laurence Sterne Trust, The; Monkman, Kenneth
Shelburne, Lord, 238–239. *See also* Chatham administration
Sheridan, Frances, 237; *Memoirs of Miss Sidney Biddulph*, 237
Sheridan, Thomas, 121–143, 144nn2–3, 144n9, 144–145n10, 145n11, 145n13, 145n16, 145n22, 146n25, 146nn27–28, 147n32, 147n36, 148n55, 149n58; *Course of Lectures on Elocution, A*, 122. *See also* elocution; rhetoric

Shklovsky, Viktor, 8, 18n35, 234
Sichel, Walter (biographer), 234
Siege of Namur (1695), 43, 50
sin, religious concept of, 90, 153, 157, 164–165, 174, 180, 184–185, 222. *See also* free will
skepticism, philosophy of, 160
slavery, eighteenth-century, 141, 185, 193n59. *See also* Abolition of slavery
Smith, Adam: and economy, 99, 118n7; and rhetoric, 148n47; and sympathy, 149n62; *Theory of Moral Sentiments*, 171, 190n22; *Wealth of Nations*, 118n7. *See also* economy: market; sensibility; sentimentalism; sympathy
Smith, Charlotte, 237; *The Old Manor House*, 237
Smollett, Tobias, 33, 35, 36–37, 66, 236, 237, 238; *The Expedition of Humphry Clinker*, 238; *Travels through France and Italy*, 25, 239
snuff, 28, 49, 156; *See also* Sterne, Laurence: fictional characters, Father Lorenzo
snuffboxes, 30, 104, 107, 109–110, 150–151, 155–159, 167n23, 205. *See also* gift exchange; Sterne, Laurence: fictional characters, Father Lorenzo; *Lorenzodosen*
sociability: eighteenth-century concepts of, 24, 34, 36, 38; in Sterne, 9, 27, 83, 208. *See also* masculinity; politeness; sentimentalism; sociality
sociality, 122, 125, 133, 141, 148n55, 152. *See also* communication; elocution; sentimentalism; Sheridan, Thomas; sociability
solipsism, in Sterne, 70
South, Robert (churchman), 154
Spanish flu pandemic, 234
spatial layout, in Sterne, 105, 147n38
Spencer, Lady, 103. *See also* gift exchange
Staffordshire ceramics, 6. *See also* adaptations, of Sterne; Sterne, Laurence: fictional characters, Maria
starlings: bird, 67–70, 74n28, 148–149n55; in Sterne, 58–59, 65–72, 83, 91, 121–126, 130, 135–144, 147n41, 148n54, 149n56, 149n58, 149n61, 221. *See also* gift exchange
Steele, Joshua (elocutionist), 145n20
Stephen, Leslie, 7
Sterne, Elizabeth (wife of Laurence Sterne), 186, 195, 197, 205, 206, 217, 236, 239, 240, 241
Sterne, Laurence: "Advertisement" to *A Sentimental Journey*, 225–226, 232n19; and bawdry, 1, 3, 5–6, 8–9, 106, 136, 142, 180–181, 203, 210n5, 224; bicentenary of the death of, 12, 234; biography of, 6, 7, 8, 10, 12–13, 195, 201, 211n6; burial place in London, 12; celebrity in London, 42, 173, 208; as clergyman, 6, 42, 44, 224, 235; Continental reception of, 15, 17n18; death of, 12, 172–175, 177, 188, 195, 210, 222–223, 226, 229, 231, 235, 236, 238, 239, 242; illness of, 10, 177, 181, 186, 195, 218, 236, 239, 241; and literary inheritance, 102, 213, 215, 216–217, 228; London, travel to and residence in, 113, 195, 196, 236, 238, 239, 241; personal debts of, 217–218, 225–226, 232n14; portraits of, 1; as preacher, 14, 187, 198, 215; religious belief of, 10, 11, 177–178, 179–183, 185, 187–188, 189n3; reputation of, 5–6, 12, 15, 65; travel abroad, 174, 180, 195, 206, 217, 218, 239, 240, 241
Sterne, Laurence, fictional characters in the works of: Count de B****, 26–27, 33, 47, 83–84, 221, 228 (*see also* passports; Shakespeare, William); Corporal Trim, 34, 45, 51–52, 123, 145n14, 148n51, 154; Dr. Slop, 123; Eugenius, 207–208, 230–231 (*see also* Hall-Stevenson, John); Father Lorenzo, 30, 49, 110, 124, 132, 135, 151, 155–159, 203; La Fleur, 24, 33–37, 40n39, 51–53, 55, 60–61, 64, 71–72, 97, 108, 126–127, 161–162, 204–206, 209, 221–222 (see also Cervantes, Miguel de: Sancho Panza [character]; gallantry; masculinity; military men; starlings: bird); Madame de L***, 32, 34–36, 86, 90, 124–127, 134–135, 137, 158–159, 205–207, 223–224; Maria, 4, 6, 14–15, 72, 74n35, 83, 85, 126, 146–147n32, 147n41, 164, 176–177, 183, 208, 239 (*see also* adaptations, of Sterne; illustrations, of Sterne's work; Moulins;

Sterne, Laurence (cont.)
Staffordshire ceramics); Marquesina di F***, 36–37, 53–54, 86–87, 131–136, 138, 140, 143, 182; Marquis d'E****, 29–31, 54–55, 83, 109–111, 161, 168n41 (*see also* Brittany; Rennes; swords); Tristram Shandy, 31, 43, 51, 62–65, 72, 83, 87–89, 98–99, 102–104, 150, 154, 199–201, 203, 213, 216, 218–219, 221–226; Uncle Toby, 6, 29–30, 39n21, 44–46, 49–53, 56n8, 56n18, 87, 123, 132, 148n51, 218–222 (*see also* Leslie, C. R.; military men; Prattware); Walter Shandy, 103, 123, 148n51, 167n22, 218–219, 222; widow Wadman, 6, 45–46, 50–51

Sterne, Laurence, works of: "Abuses of Conscience" sermon, 153, 181, 192n55; *Bramine's Journal*, 7–8, 10, 13, 16, 18n32, 175, 187, 195–197, 202–210, 210n4, 235, 240, 242; compared with *A Sentimental Journey*, 1–5, 12–13, 15–16, 46–48, 99, 104–107, 123, 154, 194, 199–202, 208–209, 214–215, 220, 225–226, 229–230, 235; compositional method of, 100, 102–104, 145n15, 194, 211n12, 223, 242; critical study of, 8–12, 15, 234–235; dedication of, 42, 238 (*see also* Pitt, William [the elder]); graphic features of, 147n38 (*see also* dashes (punctuation symbol), in Sterne; typography, in Sterne); imitations of, 3–4, 232n20; initial success of, 1–2, 12, 174, 190n13, 193n60, 233n28; *Journal to Eliza*, 7, 183, 186, 198, 235, 240 (see also *Bramine's Journal*); letters of, 3, 10, 13, 44, 64, 100, 173–174, 183–188, 195–198, 201–210, 210n4, 211n8, 211n14, 216–218, 232n14, 238–241; *The Life and Opinions of Tristram Shandy, Gentleman*—animals in, 62–64; military men in, 44–46, 51, 56n18; motif of death in, 1, 53, 102, 154, 174, 214–215, 230–231; motif of warfare in, 30, 39n21, 42–43, 46, 53, 56n8, 218–219; narrative organization of, 98–99 (*see also* chaptering); negative responses to, 1, 4, 5, 98, 119n27; oratory in, 123, 148n51 (*see also* elocution); publication history of, 6, 171, 174, 225, 235, 239, 241; quixotism in, 31, 185; sensibility in, 48; sermons, 1, 5, 11–12, 103, 123, 146n24, 150, 153–158, 163, 168n42, 181, 187–188, 191nn36–37, 192nn55–56, 198, 201, 222, 235, 241; theology in, 187, 191n36; "things" in, 151–152, 154; travel narrative in, 25, 81, 87, 174, 199, 209

Stillington, 44. *See also* Croft, Stephen

Stout, Gardner D. (editor of Sterne), 11, 13, 111–112, 117–118, 120n59, 168n42, 182

subjectivity: eighteenth-century concepts of, 81; in Sterne, 67, 94

Swieten, Gerard van (physician), 242n2. *See also* Maria Theresa (empress)

Swift, Jonathan, 172, 173, 216, 237; *Miscellanies*, 172; *Tale of a Tub*, 100. *See also* Pope, Alexander; Scriblerians

Switzerland, tours of, 174–175. *See also* Boswell, James

swords, in Sterne, 27, 29–30, 39n21, 54–55, 109–111, 160–162, 165, 168n41. *See also* Rennes (French city)

sympathy: eighteenth-century concepts of, 3, 13, 122, 125, 133, 149n62; in Sterne, 29, 46, 72, 102, 106, 133, 139, 141, 155, 160, 176, 177–178, 220. *See also* sensibility; sentimentalism; Sheridan, Thomas; Smith, Adam

tears, of sensibility, 52–54, 124, 126, 146–147n32, 148n51, 158, 184, 204. *See also* sensibility; sentimentalism; sympathy

Temple, William Johnson (correspondent of Boswell), 179, 183, 189n13, 192n51. *See also* Boswell, James

Thackeray, William Makepeace, 6, 7–8, 18n32, 240; *The English Humourists of the Eighteenth Century*, 6, 18n32, 240

Thames (river), 238

"thing" theory, 151–152

time, subjective experience of in Sterne, 83, 85

tone (acoustic), 122–126, 128–130, 134–135, 138–139, 144n2, 145n16, 145n22, 146nn24–25, 146n28, 148n55. *See also* communication; elocution; Sheridan, Thomas

Torgau, Battle of (1760), 44, 56n15

Toulouse (French city), 218

Townshend, Charles (British politician), 238

transcription, of *A Sentimental Journey*, 100, 111–112
translation: of body language, 66, 131–132, 134–136, 140, 146n27; of Sterne's works, 3, 8
travel: in the eighteenth century, 4, 15, 27, 28, 47, 81, 83–84, 91, 182, 192n38 and gender, 23; and nationality, 23; in Sterne, 2, 9, 13, 23, 27–28, 32, 37–38, 46, 53, 64, 80, 83–88, 93–94, 99, 104, 107–108, 135–138, 146n27, 152–153, 155, 163, 203–204, 217, 220, 221
travel literature, scholarship of, 13
travel writing, eighteenth-century, 2, 25, 36, 47, 81, 83, 94, 97n42, 104, 194, 237, 239
Turin (Italian city), 93, 173, 184
turnpike roads, 238
typography, in Sterne, 88, 129, 214. *See also* dashes; graphic elements

urbanity, 28, 104, 108. *See also* begging
Utrecht (city in the Netherlands), 173–174, 179. *See also* Boswell, James

Versailles (French town), in Sterne, 108, 110, 128, 207, 221, 228
Versailles Peace Conference (1910–1920), 234
Vesey, Elizabeth, 4
veterans, eighteenth-century military, 29–30, 51, 53–54, 55
vielle (musical instrument), 164–165. *See also* hurdy-gurdy
vis-à-vis (carriage), 155, 191n35, 204. See also *desobligeant; remise* (carriage)
Voltaire, 171, 175–178, 180, 190n21, 192n51; *Candide*, 171, 238. *See also* Boswell, James

Walker, John (elocutionist), 123, 133, 145n19. *See also* elocution; Sheridan, Thomas
Walpole, Horace, 1, 2, 237
War of the Austrian Succession (1740–1748), 30, 50
War of the Spanish Succession (1701–1714), 43
Watkins, W.B.C. 10, 11
Wedgwood (British stoneware), 6. *See also* adaptations, of Sterne; Sterne, Laurence: fictional characters, Maria
Wilkes, John (British politician), 238
Winged Skull, The (essay collection), 12, 234–235, 242
Wollstonecraft, Mary, 36, 41n47, 236; *Mary*, 236. *See also* chivalry; Godwin, William; masculinity
Woolf, Virginia, 9, 11, 18n36, 198
Wordsworth, William, 85, 186
Wright, Joseph (of Derby), 72. *See also* Sterne, Laurence: fictional characters, Maria

York (British city), 12, 185, 192n56, 217, 234, 236, 240, 241
York Minster (cathedral), 185
Young, Edward, 168n42

Zarephath, Widow of, 155. *See also* Sterne, Laurence: sermons